Lecture Notes in Computer Sc

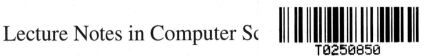

T0250850

Commenced Publication in 1973
Founding and Former Series Editors:
Gerhard Goos, Juris Hartmanis, and Jan van Leeuwen

Koen De Bosschere   David Kaeli
Per Stenström   David Whalley
Theo Ungerer (Eds.)

High Performance Embedded Architectures and Compilers

Second International Conference, HiPEAC 2007
Ghent, Belgium, January 28-30, 2007
Proceedings

 Springer

Volume Editors

Koen De Bosschere
Ghent University, Department ELIS
Sint-Pietersnieuwstraat 41, 9000 Ghent, Belgium
E-mail: koen.DeBosschere@elis.ugent.be

David Kaeli
Dana Research Center
Northeastern University
Boston, MA 02115, USA
E-mail: kaeli@ece.neu.edu

Per Stenström
Chalmers University of Technology
Department of Computer Science and Engineering
412 96 Gothenburg, Sweden
E-mail: pers@ce.chalmers.se

David Whalley
Florida State University
Computer Science Department
Tallahassee, FL 32306-4530, USA
E-mail: whalley@cs.fsu.edu

Theo Ungerer
Universität Augsburg
Institut für Informatik
Lehrstuhl für Systemnahe Informatik und Kommunikationssysteme
86135 Augsburg, Germany
E-mail: ungerer@informatik.uni-augsburg.de

Library of Congress Control Number: 2006939061

CR Subject Classification (1998): B.2, C.1, D.3.4, B.5, C.2, D.4
LNCS Sublibrary: SL 1 – Theoretical Computer Science and General Issues

ISSN   0302-9743
ISBN-10   3-540-69337-8 Springer Berlin Heidelberg New York
ISBN-13   978-3-540-69337-6 Springer Berlin Heidelberg New York

Springer is a part of Springer Science+Business Media

springer.com

© Springer-Verlag Berlin Heidelberg 2007
Printed in Germany

Typesetting: Camera-ready by author, data conversion by Scientific Publishing Services, Chennai, India
Printed on acid-free paper   SPIN: 11966753   06/3142   5 4 3 2 1 0

Preface

It is a pleasure for us to introduce the proceedings of the second edition of the International Conference on High-Performance Embedded Architectures and Compilers (HiPEAC 2007). This conference fills a gap in that it focuses on how to meet the challenging performance requirements of future embedded systems through a concerted effort at both sides of the hardware/software interface. As a result, this year's edition covered topic areas spanning from low-power, secure, and adaptive architectures via evaluation tools/methods to compiler optimization techniques. The program also featured a keynote presentation by Tom Conte of North Carolina State University.

This year we received 65 submissions of which 9 papers were committee papers. Papers were submitted from 15 different nations (about 40 % from Europe, 30% from Asia, and 30% from North America), which is a token of the global visibility of the conference.

We had the luxury of having a strong Program Committee consisting of 34 experts in all areas within the scope of the conference and we kept all reviewing within the Program Committee. Thus, each paper was typically reviewed by four Program Committee members. We collected 258 reviews and we were happy to note that each paper was rigorously reviewed before any decisions were made, despite the fact that we shortened the review phase and that reviewing took place during most reviewers' precious vacation time.

The Program Committee meeting was held in the center of Rome, the ancient capital of Italy. Despite a long trip for many members of the Program Committee, 21 members attended the meeting. For virtually all papers, more than one reviewer was present. The papers were discussed in the order of average score including Program Committee papers too. When a paper was discussed where a participating Program Committee member was either a co-author or had conflicts with that paper, that person left the room. At the end, we accepted 19 papers of which two are Program Committee papers, yielding an acceptance rate of 29%.

The strong program of this edition was due to the hard work of many people. First of all, we would like to thank all contributing authors for the fine work they submitted to this conference. The timely delivery of reviews and the thoughtful analysis of these papers at the Program Committee meeting confirmed that we really recruited a top-class Program Committee for this year's conference. Thanks to all of you for your hard work!

Michiel Ronsse, the conference software mastermind, made the review process run very smoothly. In addition, he added important functionality to the software to make the Program Committee meeting as efficient as possible.

We would also like to thank Nacho Navarro (Publicity Chair), Thomas Van Parys (Web Chair), and Wouter De Raeve (Financial Chair) for their efforts in promoting the conference and for taking care of the administration.

Many thanks also go to Theo Ungerer (Publication Chair), his scientific assistants Faruk Bagci and Jörg Mische for volume preparation, and Springer for publishing the proceedings in the *Lecture Notes in Computer Science* series.

We would also like to thank Lieven Eeckhout for organizing an extra day of high-quality workshops and tutorials. We are convinced that these extra activities made the conference even more attractive, hence strongly contributing to the success of HiPEAC 2007.

Finally, we would also like to mention the support from the Sixth Framework Programme of the European Union, represented by project officer Mercè Griera i Fisa, for sponsoring the event and for the travel grants.

We hope that you learn and get much inspiration from the high-quality contributions in this volume.

October 2006   Koen De Bosschere and David Kaeli
                                                                              General Chairs
                                                      Per Stenstrom and David Whalley
                                                                              Program Chairs

Organization

Executive Committee

General Chairs	Koen De Bosschere (Ghent University, Belgium)
	David Kaeli (Northeastern University, USA)
Program Committee Chairs	Per Stenstrom (Chalmers University, Sweden)
	David Whalley (Florida State University, USA)
Publicity Chair	Nacho Navarro (UPC, Spain)
Publication Chair	Theo Ungerer (University of Augsburg, Germany)
Financial Chair	Wouter De Raeve (Ghent University, Belgium)
Workshop Chair	Lieven Eeckhout (Ghent University, Belgium)
Web Chair	Thomas Van Parys (Ghent University, Belgium)

Program Committee

David August	Princeton University, USA
Rajeev Barua	University of Maryland, USA
Mats Brorsson	KTH, Sweden
Bruce Childers	University of Pittsburgh, USA
Fredrik Dahlgren	Ericsson, Sweden
Jack Davidson	University of Virginia, USA
Bjorn De Sutter	IMEC, Belgium
Marc Duranton	Philips, Netherlands
Nikil Dutt	U.C. Irvine, USA
Kristian Flautner	ARM Ltd., Cambridge, UK
Roberto Giorgi	University of Siena, Italy
Rajiv Gupta	University of Arizona, USA
Mark Hill	University of Wisconsin, USA
Mahmut Kandemir	Pennsylvania State University, USA
Manolis Katevenis	ICS, FORTH, Greece
Stefanos Kaxiras	University of Patras, Greece
Chandra Krintz	U.C. Santa Barbara, USA
Scott Mahlke	University of Michigan, USA
Avi Mendelson	Intel, Israel
Frank Mueller	North Carolina State University, USA
Michael O'Boyle	University of Edinburgh, UK
Yunheung Paek	Seoul National University, Korea

Steering Committee

Table of Contents

IV   Architecture Evaluation Techniques

V   Generation of Efficient Embedded Applications

VI   Optimizations and Architectural Tradeoffs for Embedded Systems

Invited Program

Keynote: Insight, Not (Random) Numbers: An Embedded Perspective

Thomas M. Conte

Center for Embedded Systems Resesrch
Department of Electrical and Computer Engineering
North Carolina State University

Abstract. Hamming said that the purpose of computing was "insight, not numbers." Yet benchmarking embedded systems is today a numbers game. In this talk, I will dissect Hamming's famous quote and provide some reasons to hope we can making benchmarking of embedded systems into a science. In particular, I will discuss how to model and measure quantities so that one can gain confidence in the results. I will use the industry standard EEMBC benchmark set as an example. Along the way, I will (I hope) give some insight into what the EEMBC benchmarks are trying to test.

K. De Bosschere et al. (Eds.): HiPEAC 2007, LNCS 4367, p. 3, 2007.

I Secure and Low-Power Embedded Memory Systems

Compiler-Assisted Memory Encryption for Embedded Processors

Vijay Nagarajan, Rajiv Gupta, and Arvind Krishnaswamy

University of Arizona, Dept. of Computer Science, Tucson, AZ 85721
{vijay,gupta,arvind}@cs.arizona.edu

Abstract. A critical component in the design of secure processors is memory encryption which provides protection for the privacy of code and data stored in off-chip memory. The overhead of the decryption operation that must precede a load requiring an off-chip memory access, decryption being on the critical path, can significantly degrade performance. Recently hardware counter-based one-time pad encryption techniques [11,13,9] have been proposed to reduce this overhead. For high-end processors the performance impact of decryption has been successfully limited due to: presence of fairly large on-chip L1 and L2 caches that reduce off-chip accesses; and additional hardware support proposed in [13,9] to reduce decryption latency. However, for low- to medium-end embedded processors the performance degradation is high because first they only support small (if any) on-chip L1 caches thus leading to significant off-chip accesses and second the hardware cost of decryption latency reduction solutions in [13,9] is too high making them unattractive for embedded processors. In this paper we present a compiler-assisted strategy that uses minimal hardware support to reduce the overhead of memory encryption in low- to medium-end embedded processors. Our experiments show that the proposed technique reduces average execution time overhead of memory encryption for low-end (medium-end) embedded processor with 0 KB (32 KB) L1 cache from 60% (13.1%), with single counter, to 12.5% (2.1%) by additionally using only 8 hardware counter-registers.

1 Introduction

There is significant interest in the development of secure execution environments which guard against software piracy, violation of data privacy, code injection attacks etc. [7,13,11,5,14,15,12]. Memory encryption is a critical component of such secure systems. While the code and data residing on-chip are considered to be safe, code and data residing off-chip can be subject to attacks. Thus, for example, to provide defense against software piracy and to protect the privacy of data, memory encryption is employed. Data leaving the chip must be encrypted before being sent off-chip for storing and when this data is referenced again by the processor, and brought on-chip, it must be decrypted.

The overhead of decryption operations that precede loads requiring access to off-chip memory can be very high and hence can lead to significant performance degradation. Techniques based on one-time-pad encryption or counter

K. De Bosschere et al. (Eds.): HiPEAC 2007, LNCS 4367, pp. 7–22, 2007.

mode block ciphers [13,11,9] have been proposed that encrypt/decrypt data using a *one-time-pad* derived from a *key* and a mutating *counter* value. This enables the computation of the one-time-pad to be decoupled from the reading of encrypted data from off-chip memory. For high-end processors the performance impact of decryption has been successfully limited due to two reasons. First, the presence of fairly large on-chip L1 and L2 caches reduce the frequency of off-chip accesses. Second in [13,9] additional hardware support has been proposed to reduce decryption latency. The techniques in [13] and [9] enable the *one-time-pad* to be precomputed while data is being fetched from off-chip memory by caching counter values and predicting them respectively. While the combination of above techniques is quite effective in limiting performance degradation in high-end processors, they rely on significant on-chip hardware resources. An additional cache is used [13] for caching the counter values. It is well known that caches occupy most of the on-chip space (about 50%) in embedded processors [18]. For this reason, several embedded processors are built without a cache as shown in Table 1. To obviate a large counter cache, the prediction technique [9] uses multiple predictions to predict the value of the counter and speculatively perform the multiple decryptions. As it performs multiple decryptions, 5 decryptions are performed in parallel, this technique requires multiple decryption units. In the prototype implementation of the AEGIS single-chip secure embedded processor [10], each encryption unit causes significant increase in the gate count (3 AES units and an integrity verification unit caused a 6 fold increase in the logic count). Thus, the hardware cost of decryption latency reduction solutions in [13,9] is too high making them unattractive for low- to medium-end embedded processors. For such processors the performance degradation is high because first they do not support on-chip L2 data caches and they only support small (if any) on-chip L1 data caches thus leading to significant off-chip accesses. Table 1 presents a list of commercial embedded processors which have no on-chip L2 cache, many of them have no on-chip L1 data cache while others have L1 data caches varying from 2 KB to 32 KB.

Table 1. Data Cache Sizes of Embedded Processors

D-Cache	Embedded Processor – 20 MHz to 700 MHz
0 KB	[18] ARM7EJ-S, ARM Cortex-M3, ARM966E-S
	[19] SecureCore SC100/110/200/210
2 KB	[20] STMicro ST20C2 50
4 KB	[16] NEC V832-143, Infineon TC1130
	[16] NEC VR4181, Intel 960IT
8 KB	[20] NEC V850E-50, Infineon TC11B-96
	[16] Xilinx Virtex IIPro
16 KB	[16] Motorola MPC8240, Alchemy AU 1000
32 KB	[20] MIPS 20Kc, AMD K6-2E, AMCC 440GX
	[20] AMCC PPC440EP, Intel XSscale Core

In this paper we develop a compiler-assisted strategy where the expensive task of finding the counter value needed for decrypting data at a load is performed under compiler guidance using minimal hardware support. Thus, the need to either cache or predict counter values using substantial on-chip hardware resources is eliminated. In addition to the global counter, our technique uses multiple compiler allocated counters for each application. The additional counters are implemented as special registers which reside on chip. The compiler allocates these counters for store instructions. Instructions that compute the one-time-pad (using the allocated counter value) are introduced preceding the stores and loads by the compiler. For a store, the counter used is the one that is allocated to it. For a load, the counter used is the one belonging to its matching store – this is the store that frequently writes the values that are later read by the load. Through its allocation policy, the compiler tries to ensure that when a load is executed, the value of the counter allocated to its matching store has not changed since the execution of the store. Thus, the pad needed for decryption can usually be determined correctly preceding the load using the counter associated with the matching store. In other words, a prediction for the counter that is to be used for a load is being made at compile-time and hard coded into the generated code. Our experiments show that for vast majority of frequently executed loads and stores, matches can be found that produce highly accurate compile-time predictions. When a prediction fails, the value of the pad is computed using the information fetched from off-chip memory (the counter value used in encryption). The global counter is used to handle all loads and stores that cannot be effectively matched by the compiler. Our experiments show that this compiler-assisted strategy supports memory encryption at a reasonable cost: minimal on-chip resources; and acceptable code size and execution time increases.

The remainder of this paper is organized as follows. In section 2 we review how encryption/decryption is performed and motivate this work by showing the high overhead of memory encryption for low- and medium-end embedded processors. In section 3 we present our compiler-assisted strategy in detail. Experimental results are presented in section 4. Additional related work is discussed in section 5 and we conclude in section 6.

2   Background and Motivation

Let us begin by reviewing the encryption/decryption scheme used in [11] – the organization of secure processor is shown in Fig. 1. When a plaintext data value

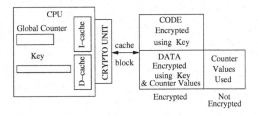

Fig. 1. Secure Processor

p is to be written to off-chip memory, the corresponding ciphertext c that is actually written is computed as follows:

$$c = p \oplus Encrypt(K, Addr + Counter)$$

where '+' is the concatenation operator, K is the *key* that is kept secure inside the processor chip, *Addr* is the (block) address to which p is to be written, and *Counter* is a value that is used once to produce the one-time-pad and hence is incremented after being used. A mutating counter is needed because in its absence the same pad, i.e. $Encrypt_K(Addr)$, will be repeatedly used during sequence of writes to the same memory location. Thus, a skilled attacker will be able to easily crack the ciphertexts stored in memory [13]. It should be noted that counter is needed only in case of data but not for code since code is read-only and thus never written back to off-chip memory.

Ciphertext read from the off-chip memory is decrypted by the following operation performed on-chip:

$$p = c \oplus Encrypt(K, Addr + Counter).$$

The off-chip memory is augmented with additional memory locations where the actual counter value used during encryption of data is stored. Thus, the counter value can be fetched along with the data so that decryption can be performed. However, doing so causes load latency to increase because computation of one-time-pad cannot be performed till the Counter value has been fetched. In the presence of an on-chip data cache, blocks of data are transferred across the chip boundary. All data items in a given block share the same counter value. Therefore, as described in [11], when a cache block is fetched from off-chip memory, the counter value which is one word can be fetched much faster than the larger cache block and therefore the computation of one-time-pad can be partly performed while the cache block is being fetched. This optimization takes advantage of the difference in sizes of a cache block and the counter and hence is more effective for high performance processors which have bigger cache blocks. It should be noted that the counter values are not stored in encrypted form because from these values an attacker cannot decrypt the data values stored in memory [1].

Table 2. Processor Configurations

Low-end parameters	Medium end parameters
Processor speed : 100 MHz	Processor speed: 600 MHz
Issue: inorder	Issue: inorder
L2 cache: none	L2 cache: None
Data cache: 0, 2, 4 KB, 16B line	Data cache: 8, 16, 32 KB, 32B line
Instruction cache: 8 KB	Instruction cache: 32 KB
Memory latency (1st chunk): 12 cycles	Memory latency (1st chunk): 31 cycles
Memory bus: 100 MHz 4-B wide	Memory bus : 600 MHz 8-B wide
Load/store queue size: 4	Load/store queue size : 8
Decryption latency : 14 cycles	Decryption latency: 31 cycles
Source: [6] [20]	Source : [22]

We measured the execution time overhead of supporting memory encryption according to [11] as described above for two processor configurations: a low-end processor configuration is based upon parameters provided in [20,6]; and a medium-end processor configuration uses parameters consistent with Intel Xscale. The decryption latency was computed based upon two real implementations of encryption and decryption hardware units described in [21] – the high performance implementation is used for medium-end processor configuration and lower performance implementation is assumed for low-end processor configuration. For low-end configuration we considered data cache sizes of 0, 2, and 4 KB while for medium-end configuration we considered data cache sizes of 8, 16, and 32 KB. The proccesor configurations are shown in Table. 2. For low-end configuration the average overhead is 60% in absence of on-chip L1 data cache while it is 12.3% and 9.9% for 2 KB amd 4 KB L1 data caches. For medium-end configuration the average overhead is 20.2%, 14.3%, and 13.1% for 8 KB, 16 KB, and 32 KB L1 data caches respectively.

3   Compiler-Assisted Encryption

In this section we show that determining the appropriate counter value can be transformed into a software (compiler) intensive task with minimal hardware support beyond the single global counter used in [11]. This transformation requires that we provide *a small number of additional on-chip counters*. These additional counters are *allocated* by the compiler to *stores* to ensure that *matching loads* (loads that read values written by the stores) can at compile-time determine which counter is expected to provide the correct counter value.

function f() {
 	
 ....
 $Store_f\ A_f$
 g();
 $Load_f\ A_f$
 ....
 }
 	
 function g() {
   while (..) {
 	
     $Store_g\ A_g$
   ....
 }}
	function f() {
	 ....
	 $Encrypt(K, A_f +^{++} C_0)$
	 $Store_f\ A_f$
	 g();
	 $Encrypt(K, A_f + C_{find})$
	 $Load_f\ A_f$
	 ....
	 }
	
	 function g() {
	   while (..) {
	
	     ....
	     $Encrypt(K, A_g +^{++} C_0)$
	     $Store_g\ A_g$
	     ....
	 }}
		function f() {
		 ....
		 $Encrypt(K, A_f + Cid_1 +^{++} C_1)$
		 $Store_f\ A_f$
		 g();
		 $Encrypt(K, A_f + Cid_1 + C_1)$
		 $Load_f\ A_f$
		 ....
		 }
		
		 function g() {
		   while (..) {
		
		     ....
		     $Encrypt(K, A_g + Cid_0 +^{++} C_0)$
		     $Store_g\ A_g$
		     ....
		 }}

(a) Original Code.	(b) Single Counter.	(c) Multiple Counters.

Fig. 2. Making Counter Predictable by Compile-time Allocation of Counters

We illustrate the basic principle of the above approach using the example in Fig. 2. Let us assume that function f in Fig. 2 contains a store $Store_f$ and its matching load $Load_f$ as they both reference the same address A_f. Following

$Store_f$ and preceding $Load_f$ the call to function g results in execution of $Store_g$ zero or more times. For the time being let us assume that A_g can never be the same as A_f. Fig. 2b shows how the key K and counter C_0 are used preceding the stores to generate the one-time-pad by the technique in [11]. However, when we reach $Load_f$ the generation of the one-time-pad requires the counter value C_{find} – this value is fetched from off-chip memory in [11], found using caching in [13] and using prediction in [9]. Instead let us assume we are provided with additional on-chip counter-register C_1. We can use C_1 to generate one-time-pad for $Store_f$ and then regenerate this pad at $Load_f$ again by using C_1 as shown in Fig. 2c. C_1 is guaranteed to contain the correct counter value for $Load_f$ because $Store_g$ does not modify C_1 as it still relies on counter C_0. Thus by using a separate counter-register for $Store_f$ and its matching load $Load_f$, we are able to avoid the interference created by $Store_g$. Under the assumption that A_f and A_g are never the same, the one-time-pad produced in the above manner for $Load_f$ is always correct.

From the above discussion it is clear that we need to use a separate counter-register for $Store_f$. However, as we can see, we have also introduced a prefix to the counters, *counter-id* (*Cid*). Next we explain the reason for adding the counter-ids. Recall that in the above discussion we assumed that A_f and A_g are never the same. Now we remove this assumption and consider the situation in which $Store_f$ A_f and $Store_g$ A_g can write to the same address. Since these stores use different counter-registers, the values of these counter-registers can be the same. When this is the case, the pads they use to write to the same address will also be the same. Obviously this situation cannot be allowed as the purpose of using counters to begin with was to ensure that pads are used only once. Hence by using a unique prefix (counter-id) for each counter, we ensure that the one-time-pads used by $Store_f$ and $Store_g$ are different even if their counter-register values match ($C_1 = C_0$) and they write to the same addresses. In other words, the counter, in our scheme is composed of the counter-id and the contents of the counter-register. Since the counter-registers are allocated at compile time, the counter-id of each allocated counter-register is known at compile time. Hence the counter-ids are hard coded into the instructions that are introduced (before stores and loads) to compute the pads.

Finally, we would like to point out that in the above example when A_f and A_g happen to be the same, it has another consequence. The pad computed at $Load_f$ in Fig. 2c will be incorrect. One way to view our technique is that it relies on the compiler to specify the identity of the counter that is *likely* to contain the needed counter value at a load but not guaranteed to contain it. When the counter value is incorrect, first we must detect that this is the case. As is the case in [11], when off-chip memory is written to, in associated storage the counter value that was used to produce the value is also stored. In our case, since each counter is prefixed by a counter-id, in addition to the counter value, the counter-id is also written. When data is fetched from memory, the counter-id and counter value are also fetched and compared with the counter-id and and counter value used to precompute the pad. If the match fails, we must recompute the pad before performing decryption; otherwise decryption can proceed right away and latency of computing the pad is hidden. Thus, incorrect precomputation of a pad does not impact the correctness of decryption but rather it affects the performance as pad computation time cannot be hidden.

The task of the compiler is to identify matching (store,load) pairs and allocate counter-registers (and counter-ids) accordingly. Finally, the counter register and counter-id assignments made to the stores and loads are communicated to the hardware through special instructions which are introduced preceding the appropriate stores and loads. For this purpose, the ISA is extended with instructions that manipulate the counter registers. We introduce two new instructions: the incctr instruction is used to increment a specified counter-register (C_k); and the Counter instruction that specifies the counter-register (C_k) and counter-id (Cid), to use for encryption/decryption. These instructions are implemented using an unimplemented opcode in the ARM processor. Stores and loads that cannot be effectively matched are simply handled using the global counter – in other words no instructions are introduced to handle them.

Fig. 3 summarizes the modified secure processor model needed by our technique. The global counter (C_0) is used in the encryption of all data written by stores that do not have any matching counterparts. Counter-registers ($C_1, C_2, ...C_n$) are the counters that are allocated by the compiler to stores. Data memory contents are now encrypted and for each block of memory in it, a word of memory containing additional information is present which includes the counter-register value and the counter-id that was used to encrypt the data.

Security of the scheme. Note that the use of multiple counters does not adversely affect the security of the encryption scheme. The concatenation of the (counter-id, counter value) pair in our scheme can be considered as the unique counter and hence our compiler-assisted encryption scheme is a direct implementation of the counter-mode encryption scheme, which is proved to be a secure symmetric encryption scheme [1]. Further it is shown that the the counters may be safely leaked without compromising the security [1]. Hence the counter values and counter-ids are not stored in encrypted form.

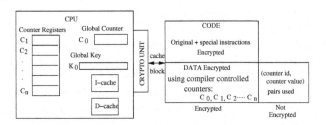

Fig. 3. Secure Processor

We have explained the basic principles of our technique. Obviously, the number of counter-registers needed for a program to carry out the above task is an important issue, since counter-registers require additional on chip hardware. The size of the counter-id field is directly dependant on the number of counters allocated. Although counter-ids do not take up on-chip resource, it is still desirable to keep the size of this field minimal, since counter ids are to be stored along with each memory block. As our experiments show, with careful allocation of counters, it is sufficient to support 8 counter-registers and generate up to 32 counter ids (5 bits of counter-id).

In our implementation we use 32 bits to store the combined counter-id and counter value. When data value stored is encrypted using the Global Counter, we indicate the use of Global counter by having the most significant bit as 1 and remaining 31 bits represent the Global Counter Value. When data stored is encrypted using an allocated counter-register, the most significant bit is always 0, next 7 bits represent the counter-id (this restricts the maximum number of counter-ids to 128, which is more than sufficient), and the remaining 3 bytes are used to store the counter-register Value. Using 3 byte counter-register is sufficient in our design because multiple counter- registers are used and each such register is shared by a smaller number of stores. The Global Counter, on the other hand, is shared by a larger number of stores and therefore we maintain a 31 bit Global Counter. Our experiments confirm that smaller size counters are adequate.

Next we describe the compiler algorithm used to assign counter-ids and counter-registers to selected stores and the generation of code based upon counter-registers used for matching loads. Before we present this algorithm we first discuss how opportunities for sharing counter-registers across multiple stores arise and can be exploited.

Sharing Counter-Registers. We assign different generated counter-ids to different static stores. Therefore, two stores being handled using two different counter-ids need not always use different counter values and hence different counter-registers. Two different counter-registers are necessary only if these two static stores interfere with each other as was illustrated by our example in Fig. 2. Next we show that the above observation can be exploited to enable counter-register sharing in certain cases. We describe two general categories of sharing opportunities: *intraprocedural sharing* and *across procedure sharing*. We describe these opportunities using examples given in Fig. 4.

In the first example in Fig. 4, function f contains three stores which have all been assigned different generated counter-ids (Cid_1, Cid_2, and Cid_3). Let us assume that we have a counter-register C_f which is incremented each time the function f is entered. The counter C_f's value can be used without any restriction by $Store_1$ and $Store_3$ since they are executed at most once in the function. While $Store_2$ is executed multiple times, if the compiler can determine that during each iteration of while loop address A_2 changes, then $Store_2$ can also use C_f's value that is computed upon entry to f for deriving its pad. In other words, during a single invocation of f, it is safe for all three stores to use the same value of C_f to derive their pads, as they use different counter-ids. The load at the end of the function now knows to refer to counter-register C_f irrespective of which

function f() {
$C_f^{++};$
....
$Encrypt(K, A_1 + Cid_1 + C_f)$
$Store_1\ A_1$
while (..) {
....
$Encrypt(K, A_2 + Cid_2 + C_f)$
$Store_2\ A_2$
....
}
$Encrypt(K, A_3 + Cid_3 + C_f)$
$Store_3\ A_3$
....
$Encrypt(K, A_l + Cid_l + C_f)$
$Load\ A_l$
....
}
	function f() {
	$C_{fg}^{++};$
	....
	$Encrypt(K, A_f + Cid_f + C_{fg})$
	$Store_f\ A_f$
	.... no (in)direct calls to f/g()
	$Encrypt(K, A_f + Cid_f + C_{fg})$
	$Load_f\ A_f$
	....
	}
	
	function g() {
	$C_{fg}^{++};$
	....
	$Encrypt(K, A_g + Cid_g + C_{fg})$
	$Store_g\ A_g$
	.... no (in)direct calls to f/g()
	$Encrypt(K, A_g + Cid_g + C_{fg})$
	$Load_g\ A_g$
	....
	}

(a) Intraprocedural Sharing.	(b) Across Procedure Sharing.

Fig. 4. Sharing Counters Across Multiple Stores

of the three stores it is matched to and the counter-id Cid_l is one of the three depending upon which store the load is matched to based upon the profile data.

The above example showed how three different stores shared the same counter registers. But note that the three stores used unique counter-ids. The second example in Fig. 4 illustrates *across procedure sharing* of both counter-ids and counter-registers. In this example two functions are shown such that each of these functions contains a counter-register to handle its local pairs of matching stores and loads: $(Store_f, Load_f)$ in function f and $(Store_g, Load_g)$ in function g. Moreover these functions are such that in between the matching pair in one function, no function call exists that can lead to the execution of either function. In other words, execution of matching store load pair in one function cannot be *interleaved* by execution of the matching pair in the other function. Thus, when we reach a store $(Store_f$ or $Store_g)$, counter C_{fg} is incremented and used and when we reach a load $(Load_f$ or $Load_g)$ C_{fg}'s value can be used as it has not changed since the execution of the corresponding store. Since the execution of these functions can never be interleaved, sharing the same counter-register by the two functions does not lead to any interference. It should be noted that due to sharing of the counter-register, the two store load pairs in this example are guaranteed never to use the same counter value and thus they can safely share the same counter-ids. Thus *across procedural sharing* can lead to reduction of counter-ids as well as counter-registers.

In conclusion, first code can be analyzed intraprocedurally to allow sharing of counters among multiple stores in a function. Then, by analyzing the call graph and hence the lifetimes of pairs of functions, we can determine if two functions in a pair can use the same counter. Based upon the examples already presented, the conditions under which we allow sharing are as follows:

- **Intraprocedural sharing.** *Given a function, a subset of stores in the function share the same counter register, if each of the stores in the subset writes to a unique address during a single invocation of the function.* To simplify counter-register allocation, we assign at most one counter to each function and this counter is used to cover a subset of stores that satisfy the above condition. The remaining stores make use of the default global counter.
- **Across-procedure sharing.** *Given two functions, they can be assigned the same counter (counter-id, counter-register) if there does not exist a pair of store live ranges, one from each function, such that the execution of these live ranges interfere (i.e., can be interleaved with each other). Here a store live range is the program region that starts from the store instruction and extends up to and including all of its matching loads. If a function call is present within a store live range of one function that can lead to the execution of another function and hence its store live range, then the execution of two store ranges interfere with each other.* To simplify the analysis for computing interferences, we apply this optimization only to those functions whose store live ranges are local to the function (i.e., the store and all its matching loads appear within the function).

Counter-id and Counter-register Allocation Algorithm. Now we are ready to describe the steps of the complete compiler algorithm required by our technique. This algorithm operates under the constraint that we are given a certain maximum number of counter-ids (N_K) and counter-registers (N_C).

1. *Match Stores and Loads.* The first step of our algorithm is to carry out profiling and identify matching static store and load pairs. If a load matches multiple stores (as at different times during execution it receives values from different static stores) only the most beneficial matching pair is considered because in our technique a load is matched to a single store. Note that a store may match multiple loads during the above process, this is allowed by our technique.

2. *Find Counter-register Sharing Opportunities.* We look at one function at a time and identify the subset of stores in the function that satisfy the *intraprocedural counter sharing* condition given earlier. Given a function f_i, $f_i.Stores$ denotes the subset of stores identified in this step. During counter allocation in the next step, if a function f_i is allocated a counter-register, then the stores in $f_i.Stores$ will make use of that counter. For every pair of functions f_i and f_j we determine whether these functions can share the same counter according the *across procedure counter sharing* condition presented earlier. In particular, we examine the interferences among live ranges of stores in $f_i.Stores$ and $f_j.Stores$. If sharing is possible, we set $Share(f_i, f_j)$ to true; otherwise it is set to false.

3. *Allocate Counter-registers.* For each function f_i we compute a *priority* which is simply the expected benefit resulting from allocating a counter-register to function f_i. This benefit, which is computed from profile data, is the total number of times values are passed from stores in $f_i.Stores$ to their matching loads. In order of function priority, we allocate one counter per function.

Before allocating a new counter-register to a function f_i, we first check if a previously allocated counter-register can be reused. A previously allocated counter-register C can be reused if $Share(f_i, f_j)$ is true for all f_j's that have been assigned counter-register C. If a previously allocated counter-register cannot be reused, a new one is allocated if one is available. After going through all the functions in the order of priority this step terminates.

4. *Assign Counter-ids.* For each counter-register C, we examine the set of functions F that have been assigned this counter-register. Each function $f \in F$ will use as many counter-ids as the number of stores in the $f.Stores$ set. However, the same counter-ids can be shared across the functions in F. Therefore the number of generated counter-ids that are needed to handle the functions in F is the maximum size of the $f.Stores$ set among all $f \in F$. The above process is repeated for all counter-registers. It should be noted that in this process we may exceed the number of counter-ids available N_K. However, this situation is extremely rare. Therefore we use a simple method to handle this situation. We prioritize the counter-ids based upon the benefits of the stores with which the counter-ids are associated. The stores corresponding to the low priority counters are then handled using the global counter such that the number of generated counter-ids does not exceed N_K.

5. *Generate Code.* All static stores that have been assigned a generated counter-id and allocated a counter register, and their matching loads, are now known. Thus we can generate the appropriate instructions for computing the pad preceding each of these instructions. All stores and loads that have not been assigned a generated counter-id and a counter register during the above process will simply make use of the global counter and thus no code is generated to handle them.

4   Experimental Evaluation

We conducted experiments with several goals in mind. First and foremost we study the effectiveness of our approach in reducing execution time overhead of memory encryption over the scenario where memory encryption is implemented using simply the global counter-register. This study is based on the low- and medium-end processor configurations with varying L1 cache sizes as described in Table. 2. We also evaluate the effectiveness of our compiler techniques in detecting opportunities for counter sharing. Since code size is an important concern in embedded systems, we measure the static code size increase due to our technique.

Our implementation was carried out using the following infrastructure. The `Diablo` post link time optimizer [17,4] was used to implement the compiler techniques described in the paper.

The `Simplescalar/ARM simulator` [2] was used to collect profiles and simulate the execution of modified binaries. As we mentioned earlier, the processor configurations (low and medium) from Table. 2 are used. We use the 128 bit AES algorithm to compute the one-time-pad using a crypto unit in hardware as mentioned before.

Experiments were performed on the `MiBench` benchmark suite [6]. The small datasets from `MiBench` were used to collect profiles and the large datasets were used in the experimental evaluations. Not all the benchmarks could be used in the experiments because at this point some of them do not go through the `Diablo` infrastructure being used.

4.1 Evaluation of Sharing Optimizations

We studied the effectiveness of our counter sharing strategy by conducting the following experiment. For each program we examined the profile data and identified all of the matching store load pairs, i.e. pairs that can benefit by our technique. The number of statically distinct stores covered by these pairs represents the number of counter-ids, and hence the number of counters, that will be needed if no counter sharing is performed. Application of sharing techniques reduces this number greatly. While the intraprocedural sharing reduces the number of counter-registers, the across-procedural sharing reduces both the number of counter-ids and counter-registers. Next we present results that show the reductions in number of counter-registers and counter-ids that is achieved by our optimizations. These results are given for different thresholds, where the threshold represents the percentage of dynamic loads covered during counter allocation. Here the percentage is with respect to all dynamic loads that can derive some benefit from our technique if enough counter-registers were available.

In Table 3 we present the number of counter-registers that are needed for each program in following cases: (APS+IS) with both Across-Procedure and Intraprocedural Sharing, (IS) only intraprocedural sharing, and (Unopt) without sharing. In addition, the number of counter-registers used with full sharing as a percentage of counter-registers needed without any sharing is also given. As we can see, this number is computed by threshold settings of 100%, 99% and 98%. From the data in Table 3 we draw three conclusions. First the counter sharing strategy is highly effective. For example, for threshold of 100%, the number of counter-registers used after sharing ranges from 4% to 23% of the number used without sharing (on an average we have a 5 fold reduction). Second we

Table 3. Number of Counter-registers Used: APS+IS:IS:Unopt

Benchmark	Threshold of Dynamic Loads Covered		
	100%	99%	98%
bitcount	19:46:106 (20%)	3:8:40 (8%)	2:5:16 (1%)
sha	24:55:161 (15%)	2:3:25 (8%)	1:2:24 (4%)
adpcm	12:29:58 (21%)	7:19:46 (15%)	7:18:44 (16%)
fft	23:59:191 (12%)	8:20:108 (7%)	8:19:102 (8%)
stringsearch	16:34:69 (23%)	8:18:48 (17%)	8:17:45 (18%)
crc	23:52:137 (17%)	15:35:88 (17%)	12:28:54 (22%)
dijkstra	25:60:174 (14%)	6:14:76 (8%)	5:13:67 (7%)
rijndael	21:47:226 (9%)	8:17:140 (6%)	7:15:130 (5%)
jpeg	40:138:560 (7%)	10:24:217 (5%)	6:19:178 (3%)
lame	49:144:1344 (4%)	9:30:811 (1%)	7:23:660 (1%)
qsort	25:57:164 (15%)	7:15:52 (13%)	5:11:45 (11%)

observe that even if we set the threshold to 99%, in all cases 16 counter-registers are sufficient. Third we observe that both intraprocedural and across-procedure sharing optimizations contribute significantly although intraprocedural sharing contributes more than across-procedure sharing.

We also measured the number of counter-ids used with and without sharing (detailed results not presented due to lack of space). We found that across-procedure sharing resulted in use of only 55% of number of counter-ids needed without sharing. Although the counter-ids do not represent a hardware resource, reducing the number of counter-ids(counters) is beneficial as the size of counter-id allocated can be reduced.

4.2   Execution Time Overhead

Next we conducted experiments to study the effectiveness of our strategy in *reducing* execution time overhead. We present the overheads of the two techniques: (Encrypted Optimized) which is our compiler-assisted strategy; and (Encrypted Unoptimized) which is the version in which memory encryption was performed using simply the global counter (i.e., this corresponds to [11]). Execution times were normalized with respect to the execution time of the (Unencrypted) configuration, i.e. the configuration that does not perform memory encryption. The results of this experiment are given in Fig. 5 for low-end and medium-end processor configurations respectively. For each benchmark the three bars correspond to the three cache sizes. Each bar is stacked to allow comparison of the overheads of the (Encrypted Optimized) and (Encrypted Unoptimized). As we can see,

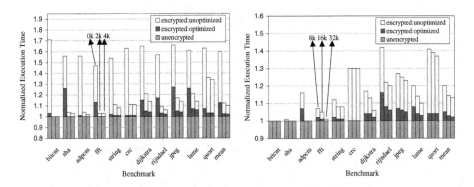

Fig. 5. Overhead of Memory Encryption - Low and Medium

for a low-end processor configuration, while the average overhead of (Encrypted Unoptimized) method is 60% (0 KB), 12.4% (2 KB), and 9.9% (4 KB), the overhead of our (Encrypted Optimized) method is 12.5% (0 KB), 2.3% (2 KB), and 1.9% (4 KB). Thus, the benefits of using our technique are substantial for the low-end processor configuration. As expected, we observe that the benefit of our technique is greatest for processors that support no on-chip L1 cache. Moreover, our technique is beneficial for all benchmarks in this case. However, when an on-chip L1 data cache is provided, due to very low data cache miss rates, some of the benchmarks (bitcount, sha, adpcm, and fft) do not benefit from our technique. In case of the medium-end configuration the savings are substantial again (excluding the first four benchmarks that have very low miss rates). While the average overhead of (Encrypted Unoptimized) method is 20.1% (8 KB), 14.3% (16 KB), and 12.3% (32 KB), the overhead of our (Encrypted Optimized) approach is 5.0% (8 KB) 2.8% (16 KB), and 2.1% (32 KB). In the above experiment we always used 8 counter-registers and up to 32 generated counter-ids. We conducted a sensitivity study (not shown in the paper) that basically showed that the above parameters yielded the highest benefit.

Static Code Size Increase. We measured the increase in static code size due to the introduction of additional instructions. We found that the increase in the static code size was less than 1% on an average and was 3% at the maximum.

5   Related Work

We have already shown the benefits of using a small number of additional compiler controlled counter-registers over the basic technique of [11] which only uses a single global counter. As mentioned earlier, hardware enhancements to [11] have been proposed in [13] and [9]. However, significant on-chip resources are devoted for caching [13] or prediction [9] which makes these solutions unattractive for embedded processors. Memory predecryption [8] is also a technique used to hide the latency of the decryption. The basic idea here is to prefetch the L2 cache line. Prefetch can increase workload on the front side bus and the memory controller. Moreover in the absence of on-chip L1 cache prefetch would be needed for every load making this approach too expensive.

Our paper deals essentially with support for memory encryption in embedded processors which is useful for among other things for protecting the privacy of code and data in off-chip memory. Other types of attacks have also been considered by researchers which we briefly discuss next. Work has been carried out to detect tampering of information stored in off-chip memory [7,5]. The hardware cost of detecting tampering is very high. In context of embedded processors where on-chip resources are limited, it is more appropriate to follow the solution proposed by the commercial DS5002FP processor [23]. Tamper-detection circuitry is provided that prevents writes to be performed to off-chip memory. However, off-chip memory can be read; hence techniques are still needed to protect privacy of code and data in off-chip memory. Address leakage problem has been studied and techniques have been proposed for its prevention in [14,15]. However, this is orthogonal to the problem we have studied. The solutions proposed in [14,15] are still applicable. Defense against code injection attacks is also an important problem which is being extensively studied (e,g., see [3,12]). Memory encryption techniques, such as what we have described in this paper, are also a critical component in building a defense against remote code injection attacks [3].

6   Conclusions

In this paper we argued that existing techniques for caching [13] and predicting [9] counter values for reducing memory encryption overhead, although suitable for high-performance processors, are not suitable for low- and medium-end embedded processors for which on-chip hardware resources are not plentiful. Therefore we developed a strategy in which a small number of additional counter-registers are allocated in a manner that enables that the counter-register to be used at each load is determined at compile-time. The specified counter-register is expected to contain the correct counter value needed for decryption. The only hardware cost is due to small number of counter-registers that must be supported on-chip. Our experiments show that the proposed technique reduces average execution time overhead of memory encryption for low-end (medium-end) embedded processor with 0 KB (32 KB) L1 cache from 60% (13.1%), with single counter, to 12.5% (2.1%) by additionally using only 8 compiler controlled counter-registers that accommodate 32 different counters.

Acknowledgments

We would like to thank the anonymous reviewers for providing useful comments on this paper. This work is supported by a grant from Intel and NSF grants CNS-0614707, CCF-0541382, and CCF-0324969 to the University of Arizona.

References

1. M. Bellare, A. Desai, E. Jokipii, and P. Rogaway, "A Concrete Security Treatment of Symmetric Encryption: Analysis of the DES Modes of Operation," *38th Symposium on Foundations of Computer Science*, IEEE, 1997.
2. D. Burger and T.M. Austin, "The Simplescalar Tool Set, Version 2.0," *Computer Architecture News*, pages 13–25, June 1997.
3. C. Cowan, S. Beattie, J. Johansen, and P. Wagle, "Pointguard: Protecting Pointers from Buffer Overflow Vulnerabilities," *12th USENIX Security Symposium*, August 2003.
4. De Bus, B. De Sutter, B. Van Put, L. Chanet, D. and De Bosschere, K, "Link-Time Optimization of ARM Binaries," *ACM SIGPLAN/SIGBED Conference on Languages, Compilers, and Tools for Embedded Systems* (LCTES'04).
5. B. Gassend, G. Edward Suh, D.E. Clarke, M. van Dijk, and S. Devadas, "Caches and Hash Trees for Efficient Memory Integrity," *Ninth International Symposium on High-Performance Computer Architecture* (HPCA), pages 295-306, 2003.
6. M.R. Guthaus, J.S. Ringenberg, D. Ernst, T.M. Austin, T. Mudge, and R.B. Brown, "MiBench: A Free, Commercially Representative Embedded Benchmark Suite," *IEEE 4th Annual Workshop on Workload Characterization*, December 2001.
7. D. Lie, C. Thekkath, M. Mitchell, P. Lincoln, D. Boneh, J. Mitchell, and M. Horowitz, "Architectural Support for Copy and Tamper Resistant Software," *Ninth International Conference on Architectural Support for Programming Languages and Operating Systems* (ASPLOS), pages 168-177, November 2000.

8. B. Rogers, Y. Solihin, and M.Prvulovic, "Memory Predecryption: Hiding the Latency Overhead of Memory Encryption," *Workshop on Architectural Support for Security and Anti-Virus,* 2004.

9. W. Shi, H.-H.S.Lee, M.Ghosh, C.Lu and A.Boldyreva, "High Efficiency Counter Mode Security Architecture via Prediction and Precomputation," *32nd Annual International Symposium on Computer Architecture* (ISCA), June 2005.

10. G.E. Suh, C.W.O'Donell, I.Sachdev, and S. Devadas "Design and Implementation of the AEGIS Single-Chip Secure Processor using Physical Random Functions" *32nd Annual International Symposium on Computer Architecture* (ISCA), June 2005.

11. G.E. Suh, D. Clarke, B. Gassend, M. van Dijk, and S. Devadas, "Efficient Memory Integrity Verification and Encryption for Secure Processors," *36th Annual IEEE/ACM International Symposium on Microarchitecture* (MICRO), pages 339-350, December 2003.

12. N. Tuck, B. Calder, G. Varghese, "Hardware and Binary Modification Support for Code Pointer Protection From Buffer Overflow," *37th Annual International Symposium on Microarchitecture* (MICRO), pages 209-220, 2004.

13. J. Yang, Y. Zhang, L. Gao, "Fast Secure Processor for Inhibiting Software Piracy and Tampering," *36th Annual IEEE/ACM International Symposium on Microarchitecture* (MICRO), pages 351-360, December 2003.

14. X. Zhuang, T. Zhang, and S. Pande, "HIDE: An Infrastructure for Efficiently Protecting Information Leakage on the Address Bus," *11th International Conference on Architectural Support for Programming Languages and Operating Systems* (ASPLOS), pages 72-84, October 2004.

15. X. Zhuang, T. Zhang, H-H. S. Lee, and S. Pande, "Hardware Assisted Control Flow Obfuscation for Embedded Processors," *International Conference on Compilers, Architecture, and Synthesis for Embedded Systems* (CASES), September 2004.

16. C. Zhang, F. Vahid, and W. Najjar, "A Highly Configurable Cache Architecture for Embedded Systems," *30th Annual International Symposium on Computer Architecture* (ISCA), pages 136-, 2003.

17. DIABLO, *http://www.elis.ugent.be/diablo/.*

18. http://www.arm.com/products/CPUs/embedded.html

19. http://www.arm.com/products/CPUs/securcore.html

20. Benchmark reports from http://www.eembc.org/

21. http://www.opencores.org/projects.cgi/web/ aes_core/overview/

22. Intel XScale *http://www.intel.com/design/intelxscale/*

23. DS5002FP Secure Microprocessor Chip, Dallas Semiconductor, MAXIM, *http://www.maxim-ic.com/.*

Leveraging High Performance Data Cache Techniques to Save Power in Embedded Systems

Major Bhadauria[1], Sally A. McKee[1], Karan Singh[1], and Gary S. Tyson[2]

[1] Computer Systems Lab
School of Electrical and Computer Engineering
Cornell University
{major,sam,karan}@csl.cornell.edu
[2] Department of Computer Science
Florida State University
tyson@cs.fsu.edu

Abstract. Voltage scaling reduces leakage power for cache lines unlikely to be referenced soon. Partitioning reduces dynamic power via smaller, specialized structures. We combine approaches, adding a voltage scaling design providing finer control of power budgets. This delivers good performance and low power, consuming 34% of the power of previous designs.

1 Introduction

Power consumption is a first order design criteria for most embedded systems. This is particularly true for newer high-end embedded systems designed for handheld devices such as PDAs, GPS navigators, media players, and portable gaming consoles. These systems not only have faster processor frequencies, but they also place a greater burden on the memory system. This in turn requires large caches both to reduce access latency, and (just as importantly) to avoid large energy costs of off-chip memory accesses when a miss occurs. These larger caches consume a greater portion of the die area and account for a larger percentage of total system power.

Previous research has targeted both static (leakage) power and dynamic switching power. Leakage power can be reduced by reducing the cache size, either by making a cache smaller, or by shutting off portions of it. As an alternative to shutting off parts of the cache, it is possible to reduce the operating voltage for those parts, which reduces the leakage current but increases access latency. Such drowsy caches [6] usually reduce voltage on all cache lines periodically, "waking up" (bringing back to normal voltage) lines as they are accessed. Infrequently accessed lines remain in drowsy mode for long periods.

Switching power can also be minimized by reducing the size of the cache. Unlike leakage power, which is determined by the total area of all powered portions of the cache, switching power is only consumed by the portion of the cache being accessed. This enables a partitioning strategy to be used to reduce switching power. For instance, a single cache can be partitioned into multiple sub-cache

K. De Bosschere et al. (Eds.): HiPEAC 2007, LNCS 4367, pp. 23–37, 2007.

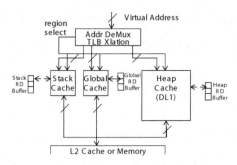

Fig. 1. Organization of Region-Based L1 Caches

structures that are accessed independently. When a reference is made, only one of the cache partitions is accessed; the selection of which cache to access depends on the partitioning strategy. Region caches [20,18,19,7] partition the data cache into separate stack, global and heap caches (as in Figure 1) that retain data from the corresponding memory regions. The heap cache serves as a general L1 Dcache for data not falling in other regions. This partitioning strategy uses a simple address decoder (using only a few address bits) to identify the region and route the reference to the appropriate cache. Switching power goes down, since the region caches are smaller (particularly the stack and global regions).

Our research builds on both the drowsy cache and the region caching work. We develop a new region cache model that maintains original hit rates while reducing leakage via smaller multi-access column associative [1] (CA) and MRU [12] caches. These structures exhibit excellent implementation cost, performance, and energy tradeoffs for the target applications. We also employ a drowsy policy that is simple to implement, scales better than previous policies, and allows finer control over cache power management. This *Reuse Distance* (RD) policy tracks lines being accessed, keeping a limited (potentially configurable) number of lines awake. Figure 1 illustrates our organization (RD buffers are much smaller than depicted). The RD buffer records IDs corresponding to cache lines being kept awake. When the buffer is full and a new cache line is accessed, the LRU line is made drowsy and its ID is overwritten by the new line's. A buffer of N entries only needs N counters of log_2N bits, since they are incremented every memory access (and not every cycle, as in some previous drowsy policies).

By adapting techniques originally proposed to improve cache *performance*, we develop robust cache organizations to conserve energy in high performance embedded systems. On the MiBench suite, our multiple-access associative RD drowsy policy delivers IPCs of more complicated drowsy designs while using 16% less total power via our multiple-access associative RD policy. Compared to non-drowsy designs, we reduce power by 65% on average, while remaining within 1.2% of the original mean IPC.

2   Related Work

Inoue et al. [13] survey techniques for reducing memory access energy while maintaining high performance. We discuss those techniques most related to our investigations: partitioned, drowsy, and multi-access cache organizations.

2.1   Partitioned Hierarchies

Breaking monolithic memories into separate components enables optimizing those components to achieve better performance or conserve energy. Early "horizontal" partitioning broke L1 caches into separate instruction (Icache) and data (Dcache) designs, and "vertical" partitioning added multiple levels to the hierarchy. Modern vertical partitionings may create an L0 memory level between the processor and L1, as in line buffers [14,9,27] and filter caches [17]. These small structures reduce average access energy for hits (i.e., accesses with high temporal locality) at the expense of increased access latency for misses (which increases average L1 latency). Horizontal partitioning reduces dynamic power by a different means: directing accesses at the same hierarchy level to different structures or substructures, as in cache subbanking [9,27], allows smaller structures. Specialized loop caches [10] and scratchpad memories [29,21] can improve performance for scientific or embedded applications, for instance. Since different data references exhibit different locality characteristics, breaking the L1 data cache into separate, smaller horizontal structures for stack, global, and heap accesses [20,18,19,7] better exploits temporal and spatial locality behavior of the different data *regions*. This can improve hit rates and cut dynamic and static energy consumption. The Bell Labs C Machine [5] has a separate stack hardware structure, and thus constitutes an early example of a region-based cache.

2.2   Drowsy and Decay Caches

Turning off dead portions of cache after writing dirty lines back to the next level of memory helps control leakage energy. Such *decay caches* [23,15] often trade performance for reduced power consumption. By predicting dead lines, Kaxiras et al. [15] reduce L1 leakage energy by up to a factor of five with little performance impact. A two-bit counter per line tracks the current working set, and at each adaptive decay interval they set line states based on counter values.

Even when cache lines are still live, they may be read infrequently. Placing idle cache lines in a dormant state-preserving (*drowsy*) condition reduces static power consumption by decreasing supply voltage of the wordlines via dynamic voltage scaling. Drowsy lines must be brought back to normal voltage before being loaded in the sense-amplifiers, thus access latency to these lines is increased. Repeatedly changing state causes high performance and power overheads. Drowsy wordlines consist of a drowsy bit, voltage control mechanism, and wordline gating circuit [16]. The drowsy bit controls switching between high and low voltages, and the wordline gate protects data from being accessed in drowsy mode. Flautner et al. [6] investigate *simple* and *noaccess* strategies to keep most lines drowsy and avoid frequent state changes. The simple policy sets all cache lines to drowsy after a preset number of clock cycles, waking up individual lines as they are accessed; the noaccess policy sets all lines not accessed within the interval to drowsy. The simple policy offers aggressive leakage reduction, whereas the noaccess policy is intended to yield better performance by keeping actively used lines awake. In practice, the policies exhibit minor performance differences, and thus most drowsy structures use the simple policy for its ease of implementation [6]. Geiger et al. add drowsiness to their heap cache [8] and explore a separate, smaller, non-drowsy *hot heap cache* to hold lines with highest temporal locality [7]. Since the stack and global caches service most references, an aggressive drowsy policy in the heap cache has negligible effects on performance. Petit et al. [22] propose a *Reuse Most Recently used On* (RMRO) drowsy cache that behaves much like a noaccess policy adapted for set associativity, using update intervals to calculate how often a set is accessed. The MRU way remains awake during the interval, but other ways of infrequently used sets are turned off. RMRO is more sophisticated than the simple policy, but requires additional hardware per set and uses dynamic power every cycle. None of these policies can place a hard limit on total cache leakage.

2.3   Multiple-Access Caches

A two-way associative cache delivers similar performance to a direct mapped cache twice the size, but even on accesses that hit, the associative cache wastes power on the way that misses: two banks of sense-amplifiers are always charged simultaneously. *Multiple-access* or *Hybrid Access* caches address the area and power issues of larger direct mapped or conventional two-way associative caches by providing the benefits of associativity—allowing data to reside at more places in the cache, but requiring subsequent lookups at *rehashed* address locations on misses—to trade a slight increase in complexity and in average access time for lower energy costs. Smaller structures save leakage power, and charging shorter bitlines or fewer sets saves dynamic power. Examples include the hash-rehash (HR), column associative (CA) [1], MRU [12], Half-and-Half [28], skew associative [25], and predictive sequential associative [4] caches. Hash-rehash caches swap lines on rehash hits to move the most recently accessed line to the original lookup location. CA caches avoid thrashing lines between the original and rehash locations by adding a bit per tag to indicate whether a given line's tag represents a rehashed address. Adding an MRU bit to predict the way to access first in a two-way associative cache reduces power consumption with minimal performance effects. Their ease of implementation and good performance characteristics make CA and MRU way-predictive associative structures attractive choices for low power hierarchies; other multiple-access designs focus on performance over energy savings.

Table 1. Baseline Processor Configuration

Process	70nm
Operating Voltage	1.0V
Operating Temperature	65° C
Frequency	1.7 GHz
Fetch Rate	1 per cycle
Decode Rate	1 per cycle
Issue Rate	1 per cycle
Commit Rate	1 per cycle
Functional Units	2 Integer, 2 FP
Load/Store Queue	4 entries
Branch Prediction	not taken
Base Memory Hierarchy Parameters	32B line size
L1 (Data) Size	32KB, direct mapped
L1 (Data) Latency	2 cycles
L1 (Instruction) Size	16KB 32-way set associative
L1 (Instruction) Latency	1 cycle (pipelined)
Main Memory	88 cycles

Table 2. Region Drowsy Cache Configuration Parameters

L1 (Data) Size	16KB, CA or 2-Way Set Associative
L1 (Data) Latency	1 cycle
L1 (Stack)Size	4KB, direct-mapped
L1 (Stack) Latency	1 cycle
L1 (Global) Size	4KB, direct-mapped
L1 (Global) Latency	1 cycle
Drowsy Access	1 cycle

3 Experimental Setup

We use SimpleScalar [3] with HotLeakage [30] (which models drowsy caching) for the ARM [24] ISA to model the 32 benchmarks from the MiBench suite [11]. This suite represents a range of commercial embedded applications from the automotive, industrial, consumer, office, network, security, and telecom sectors. Our simulator has been adapted for region caching [7], and we incorporate column associativity and MRU way prediction, along with our RD drowsy policy. The processor is single-issue and in-order with a typical five-stage pipeline, as in Table 1. We calculate static power consumption via HotLeakage, and use both CACTI 3.2 [26] and Wattch [2] to calculate dynamic power consumption. We calculate memory latency for single accesses via CACTI. To establish a valid baseline comparison with Geiger et al.'s previous region caching work [8] we use their cache configuration parameters: separate, single-ported 32KB L1 instruction and data caches with 32B lines. Table 2 gives full details of our region based caching configurations.

The main forms of power dissipation are static current leakage and dynamic switching of transistors transitioning among different operating modes. HotLeakage calculates static cache leakage as a function of the process technology and operating temperature (since leakage doubles with every 10° C increase). Operating temperature is 65° C, which is suitable for embedded systems for personal electronics. Dynamic power consumption for typical logic circuits is $\frac{1}{2}CV^2f$, a

	Cache Accesses Check These Bits	Drowsy Misses Increment These Bits
0	124	3
1	11	4
2	325	7
3	804	0
4	806	2
5	125	6
6	803	5
7	805	1

Fig. 2. Organization of Drowsy LRU Structure for an RD of Eight

function of the frequency, capacitance and operating voltage. We choose CACTI over Wattch [2] to model dynamic power for all our caches since the former more accurately calculates the number of sense amplifiers in associative caches. We convert CACTI energy numbers to power values based on architecture parameters in Table 2. We use CACTI values to accurately model dynamic power and combine these with HotLeakage's leakage numbers to compute total power. Since CACTI reports energy and uses 0.9V for 70nm while Wattch and HotLeakage use power and 1.0V for that process technology, we convert our numbers using the appropriate frequency (1.7GHz) scaling $P=E/t$ where $E=\frac{1}{2}C \times V^2$ for V=0.9 to V=1. These conversions ensure accuracy of numbers being added from different modeling tools.

Figure 2 illustrates the organization of a Reuse Distance drowsy mechanism. The RD policy tracks lines being accessed, keeping a limited number of lines awake. The RD buffer stores IDs corresponding to awake cache lines. When the buffer is full and a new cache line is accessed, the LRU line is made drowsy and its ID is overwritten by the new line's. Counters track which buffer entry is the LRU. The RD circuitry never dictates what lines to awaken, but only which lines to make drowsy, which keeps it off the critical path (making RD timing irrelevant). Power consumption and silicon area are accounted for (but negligible). An RD buffer of N entries only needs N counters of log_2N bits that are updated every memory access (and not every cycle). Assuming a reuse distance size of eight and 1024 cache lines (as for a 32KB 32-Byte line baseline cache), storing the awake cacheline IDs and current LRU counts requires 104 bits ($[log_21024 + log_28$ bits] * 8), of which only a single buffer's count value (three bits) would be reset every cache access. Power consumption for this extra circuitry is akin to the simple policy's single counter's dynamic power, since more bits are used but are accessed less frequently.

4   Evaluation

We compare our baseline region caches to organizations in which the heap cache is replaced with a multiple-access cache (CA or MRU) of half the size. Access patterns for the stack and global cache make their direct mapped organizations work well, thus they need no associativity. We study drowsy and non-drowsy region caches, comparing simple, noaccess, and RD drowsy policies. Keeping all lines drowsy incurs an extra cycle access penalty that lowers IPC by up to 10% for some applications. If performance is not crucial, using always drowsy caches is an attractive design point. We find that the noaccess drowsy policy always uses slightly more power than the simple policy, although it yields slightly higher average IPC by about 0.6%. Given the complexity of implementation, the low payoff in terms of performance, and the lack of energy savings, we use the simple policy in our remaining comparisons.

We find that keeping only three to five lines awake at a time yields good results. Many applications reuse few lines with high temporal locality, while others have such low temporal locality that no drowsy policy permits line reuse: our policy works well in both cases. The RD drowsy policy is implemented with a buffer (per region cache) that maintains an N-entry LRU "cache" of the most recently accessed set IDs. The RD buffer LRU information is updated on each cache access, and when a line not recorded in the buffer is accessed and awakened, the LRU entry is evicted and put to sleep. Unlike the simple and noaccess policies, RD requires no counter updates or switching every clock cycle, and thus consumes no dynamic power between memory accesses. We approximate RD's dynamic power consumption as the number of memory accesses multiplied by the switching power of a number of registers equal to the buffer size. Static power overhead is negligible relative to cache sizes. RD is essentially a simplified implementation of the noaccess policy, but is based on the last unique N lines, not lines accessed during an arbitrary update interval. We experiment with buffers of three, five, 10, and 20 entries, finding that buffers of only three entries reduce power significantly over those with five, while only negligibly decreasing IPC. Larger buffers suffer larger cache leakage penalties because more lines are kept awake, in return for reducing the number of drowsy accesses. Figure 3 illustrates the percentage of total accesses that are accessed within the last N or fewer memory references. On average, the last three and four memory accesses capture 43.5% and 44% of the total accesses to the heap cache. The increase is not linear, as the last 15 unique memory line accesses only capture 45.5% of all heap accesses.

Update window size for the other drowsy policies is 512 cycles for the heap and stack cache, and 256 cycles for the global cache[1]. We find RD's power and performance to be highly competitive with the simple policy for the caches we study. Note that our small update windows are aggressive in their leakage energy savings: windows of 4K cycles, as in Flautner et al. [6] and Petit et al. [22], suffer 20% more leakage energy. Thus the simple drowsy policy is dependent on update window size, whereas the RD policy is independent of any update interval (and CPU frequency). This means it scales well with number and sizes of caches: hardware overhead is minimal and fixed.

To provide intuition into simple drowsy policy performance and motivation for our RD configuration, we track the number of awake lines during update

---

[1] These values were found to be optimal for simple drowsy policies and region caches [8].

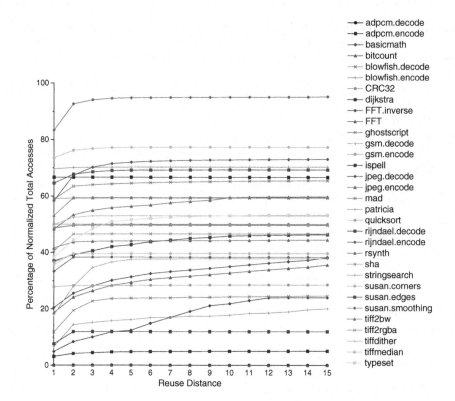

Fig. 3. Reuse Distances for Last 15 Cache Lines

intervals. Figure 4 shows that for all benchmarks, on average, 66% of the intervals access fewer than four lines. These data are normalized to the total number of intervals per benchmark so that detail for shorter-running benchmarks is preserved. Benchmarks such as jpeg.decode use eight or more lines during 42% of their intervals, but larger active working sets mean increased leakage. RD's performance on jpeg.decode is within 2% of simple's, and RD saves 5% more leakage energy by limiting the number of lines awake at a time. These examples indicate that a configurable RD buffer size would allow software to trade off performance and energy savings: systems or applications would have fine-grain control in enforcing strict performance criteria or power budgets.

Although CA organizations potentially consume higher dynamic power on a single access compared to a direct mapped cache, this slight cost is offset by significant leakage savings since the CA cache is half the capacity. The CA strategy consumes less dynamic power than a conventional two-way set associative cache that charges two wordlines simultaneously (which means that the two-way consumes the same power on hits and misses). In contrast, a CA cache only charges a second line on a rehash access. The second lookup requires an extra cycle, but rehash accesses represent an extremely small percentage of total accesses.

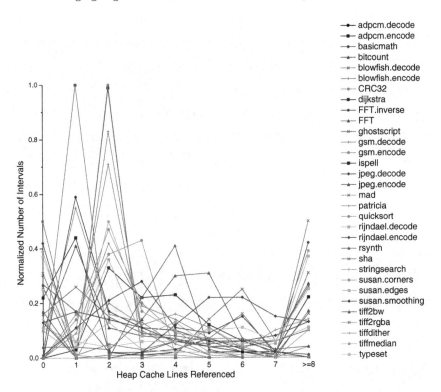

Fig. 4. Number of Heap Cache Lines Accessed During *simple* Intervals (512 Cycles)

Figure 5 shows percentages of accesses that hit on first lookup, hit on rehash lookup, or miss the cache: on average, 99.5% of all hits occur on the first access.

MRU associative caches use a one-bit predictor per set to choose which way to charge and access first. This performs well because most hits occur to the way last accessed. On a miss of both ways, the prediction bit is set to the way holding the LRU line to be evicted. On an incorrect guess or miss, MRU caches suffer an extra cycle of latency over a normal two-way associative cache. This is offset by significant power savings on correct predictions: since the MRU cache is physically partitioned into two sequential sets, it only charges half the bitline length (capacitance) of a same size direct mapped or CA cache. Figure 5 shows percentages of hits in the predicted way, hits in the second way, and misses. On average, 98.5% of all hits are correctly predicted, resulting in a 50% reduction in dynamic power. The remaining accesses (the other 1.5% that hit plus the misses) consume the same dynamic power as a two-way associative cache.

4.1 Sustaining Performance

Figure 6 graphs IPCs relative to direct mapped caches with the best update windows from Geiger et al. [8]. In the majority of benchmarks, two-way set associative, CA, and MRU caches match or exceed the performance of their direct

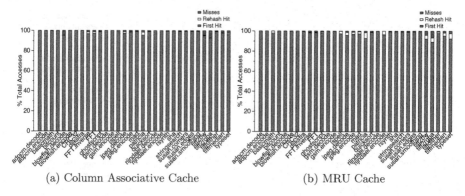

(a) Column Associative Cache   (b) MRU Cache

Fig. 5. Heap Accesses Broken Down by Category

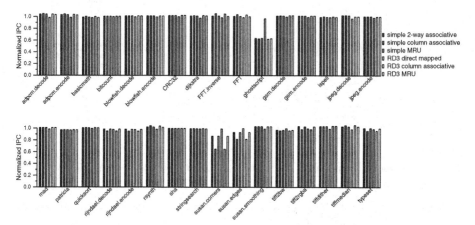

Fig. 6. IPCs Normalized to *simple* Drowsy Direct Mapped Region Caches

mapped counterparts, but they do so at half the size. Hit rates are competitive, and MRU caches afford smaller access latencies from correct way predictions. Exceptions are ghostscript and the susan image processing benchmarks, which have a higher hit rate with the associative configuration, but a lower IPC than the direct-mapped cache configuration.[2] Overall, IPCs are within 1% of the best baseline case, as with the simple and noaccess results of Flautner et al. [6]. These differences are small enough to be attributed to modeling error.

4.2   Reducing Dynamic Power

Figure 7 shows heap cache dynamic power normalized to a direct mapped baseline (note that dynamic power is independent of drowsy policy). CACTI indicates that

---

[2] We find these results to be anomalous: porting to the Alpha ISA and running on a single-issue, in-order, architecturally similar Alpha simulator results in the way-associative caches having higher IPCs for these benchmarks.

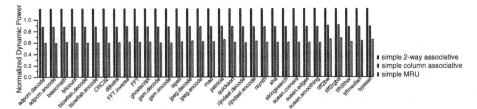

Fig. 7. Dynamic Power Consumption of Associative Heap Caches Normalized to a Direct Mapped Heap Cache

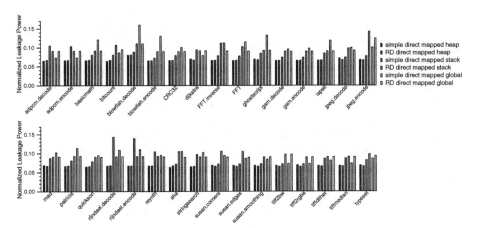

Fig. 8. Static Power Consumption of Different Drowsy Policies with Direct Mapped Region Caches Normalized to Non-Drowsy Direct Mapped Region Caches

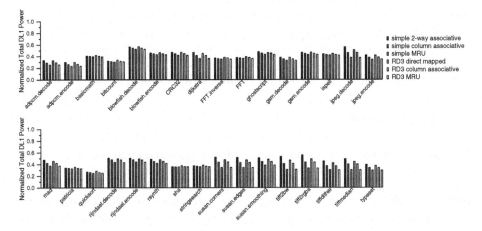

Fig. 9. Total Power of Drowsy Policies (for All Region Caches) and Heap Cache Organizations Normalized to Direct Mapped Region Caches

the two-way associative cache uses 19% more power, the CA cache uses 7.3% less power, and the MRU cache uses 50% less power on a single lookup. Figure 7 illustrates this for CA and MRU organizations: rehash checks and way mispredictions increase power consumption for some scenarios.

4.3 Reducing Leakage Current

Access pattern has little effect on static leakage. However, static power consumption is higher for benchmarks for which associative organizations yield lower IPCs than the direct mapped baseline. Reducing sizes of associative caches reduces leakage on average by 64% over the baseline direct mapped caches. Although IPC degrades by 1% between non-drowsy and drowsy caches, the leakage reduction in drowsy organizations is substantial, as shown in Figure 8. Performance for the RD policy is slightly worse, but differences are sufficiently small as to be statistically insignificant. The noaccess policy has highest IPCs, but suffers greatest leakage, dynamic power, and hardware overheads; we exclude it in from our graphs to make room for comparison of the more interesting design points. The simple and RD policies exhibit similar savings, but the RD mechanism is easier to implement and tune, without requiring window size calibration for each workload. Ideally, update window size for simple drowsy policies and RD buffer sizes would be software-configurable for optimal power-performance tradeoffs among different workloads. No single setting will always yield best results.

The effects of heap cache dynamic energy savings shown in Figure 7 represent a small contribution to the total L1 Dcache power consumption shown in Figure 9. Implementing drowsy policies across all memory regions plays a significant role in the power reductions we observe, with RD again having lowest power consumption of the different policies. MRU caches implementing RD drowsiness yield the lowest power consumption of the organizations and policies studied. This combination delivers a net power savings of 16% compared to the best baseline region organization implementing simple drowsiness, and 65% compared to a typical non-drowsy, partitioned L1 structure. These significant power savings come at a neglible performance reduction of less than 1.2%.

5   Conclusions

We adapt techniques developed to improve cache performance, using them to address both dynamic and leakage power. We revisit multiple-access caches within the arena of high-performance embedded systems, finding that they generally achieve equal hit rates to larger direct mapped caches while a) reducing static power consumption compared to direct mapped caches, and b) reducing dynamic power consumption compared to normal associative caches. We employ multiple-access region caches with drowsy wordlines to realize further reductions in both dynamic and static power. With respect to drowsy caching, a simple three- or five-entry Reuse Distance (RD) buffer that maintains a small number of awake (recently accessed) cache lines performs as well as the more complex policies used in most studies in the literature. Our RD drowsy mechanism is easy to implement, scales well with different cache sizes, scales well with number of caches, and offers finer control of power management and performance tradeoffs than other published drowsy policies.

Results for most competing drowsy caching solutions are highly dependent on update window sizes. These execution-window based solutions generally employ different intervals for different types of caches. Performance and power properties of all such policies are intimately tied to CPU speed, which means that intervals must be tuned for every microarchitectural configuration (and could be tuned for expected workloads on these different configurations). In contrast, behavioral properties of the RD drowsy mechanism depend only on workload access patterns. Combining multiple-access "pseudo-associativity" with region caching and our RD drowsy policy reduces total power consumption by 16% on average compared to a baseline direct mapped cache with a simple drowsy policy. This savings comes with less than 1% change in IPC. Compared to a direct mapped, non-drowsy region caching scheme, we remain within 1.2% of IPC while realizing power reductions of 65%.

Future research will investigate combining an L2 decay cache with drowsy L1 data caches. Well managed drowsy caches will be important to a range of CMP systems, and thus we are beginning to study combinations of energy saving approaches to memory design within that arena. For shared cache resources within a CMP, drowsy policies relying on specified windows of instruction execution become more difficult to apply, making the CPU-agnostic RD mechanism more attractive. In addition, we believe our RD drowsy mechanism to be particularly well suited to asynchronous systems.

References

1. A. Agarwal and S. Pudar. Column-associative caches: A technique for reducing the miss rate of direct-mapped caches. In *Proc. 20th IEEE/ACM International Symposium on Computer Architecture*, pages 169–178, May 1993.
2. D. Brooks, V. Tiwari, and M. Martonosi. Wattch: A framework for architectural-level power analysis and optimizations. In *Proc. 27th IEEE/ACM International Symposium on Computer Architecture*, pages 83–94, 2000.
3. D. Burger and T. Austin. The simplescalar toolset, version 2.0. Technical Report 1342, University of Wisconsin, June 1997.
4. B. Calder, D. Grunwald, and J. Emer. Predictive sequential associative cache. In *Proc. 2nd IEEE Symposium on High Performance Computer Architecture*, pages 244–253, Feb. 1996.
5. D. Ditzel and H. McLellan. Register allocation for free: The c machine stack cache. In *Proc. Symposium on Architectural Support for Programming Languages and Operating Systems*, pages 48–56, Mar. 1982.
6. K. Flautner, N. Kim, S. Martin, D. Blaauw, and T. Mudge. Drowsy caches: Simple techniques for reducing leakage power. In *Proc. 29th IEEE/ACM International Symposium on Computer Architecture*, pages 147–157, May 2002.

7. M. Geiger, S. McKee, and G. Tyson. Beyond basic region caching: Specializing cache structures for high performance and energy conservation. In *Proc. 1st International Conference on High Performance Embedded Architectures and Compilers*, Nov. 2005.

8. M. Geiger, S. McKee, and G. Tyson. Drowsy region-based caches: Minimizing both dynamic and static power dissipation. In *Proc. ACM Computing Frontiers Conference*, pages 378–384, May 2005.

9. K. Ghose and M. Kamble. Reducing power in superscalar processor caches using subbanking, multiple line buffers and bit-line segmentation. In *Proc. IEEE/ACM International Symposium on Low Power Electronics and Design*, pages 70–75, Aug. 1999.

10. A. Gordon-Ross and F. Vahid. Frequent loop detection using efficient nonintrusive on-chip hardware. *IEEE Transactions on Computers*, 54(10):1203–1215, Oct. 2005.

11. M. Guthaus, J. Ringenberg, D. Ernst, T. Austin, T. Mudge, and R. Brown. MiBench: A free, commercially representative embedded benchmark suite. In *Proc. IEEE 4th Workshop on Workload Characterization*, pages 3–14, Dec. 2001.

12. K. Inoue, T. Ishihara, and K. Murakami. Way-predicting set-associative cache for high performance and low energy consumption. In *Proc. IEEE/ACM International Symposium on Low Power Electronics and Design*, pages 273–275, Aug. 1999.

13. K. Inoue, V. Moshnyaga, and K. Murakami. Trends in high-performance, low-power cache memory architectures. *IEICE Transactions on Electronics*, E85-C(2):303–314, Feb. 2002.

14. M. Kamble and K. Ghose. Analytical energy dissipation models for low power caches. In *Proc. IEEE/ACM International Symposium on Low Power Electronics and Design*, pages 143–148, Aug. 97.

15. S. Kaxiras, Z. Hu, and M. Martonosi. Cache decay: Exploiting generational behavior to reduce cache leakage power. In *Proc. 28th IEEE/ACM International Symposium on Computer Architecture*, pages 240–251, June 2001.

16. N. Kim, K. Flautner, D. Blaauw, and T. Mudge. Circuit and microarchitectural techniques for reducing cache leakage power. *IEEE Transactions on VLSI*, 12(2):167–184, Feb. 2004.

17. J. Kin, M. Gupta, and W. Mangione-Smith. Filtering memory references to increase energy efficiency. *IEEE Transactions on Computers*, 49(1):1–15, Jan. 2000.

18. H. Lee. *Improving Energy and Performance of Data Cache Architectures by Exploiting Memory Reference Characteristics*. PhD thesis, University of Michigan, 2001.

19. H. Lee, M. Smelyanski, C. Newburn, and G. Tyson. Stack value file: Custom microarchitecture for the stack. In *Proc. 7th IEEE Symposium on High Performance Computer Architecture*, pages 5–14, Jan. 2001.

20. H. Lee and G. Tyson. Region-based caching: An energy-delay efficient memory architecture for embedded processors. In *Proc. 4th ACM International Conference on Compilers, Architectures and Synthesis for Embedded Systems*, pages 120–127, Nov. 2000.

21. M. Ohmacht, R. A. Bergamaschi, S. Bhattacharya, A. Gara, M. E. Giampapa, B. Gopalsamy, R. A. Haring, D. Hoenicke, D. J. Krolak, J. A. Marcella, B. J. Nathanson, V. Salapura, and M. E. Wazlowski. Blue Gene/L compute chip: Memory and ethernet subsystem. *IBM Journal of Research and Development*, 49(2-3):255–264, 2005.

22. S. Petit, J. Sahuquillo, J. Such, and D. Kaeli. Exploiting temporal locality in drowsy cache policies. In *Proc. ACM Computing Frontiers Conference*, pages 371–377, May 2005.

23. M. Powell, S.-H. Yang, B. Falsafi, K. Roy, and T. Vijaykumar. Gated-vdd: A circuit technique to reduce leakage in deep-submicron cache memories. In *Proc. IEEE/ACM International Symposium on Low Power Electronics and Design*, pages 90–95, July 2000.

24. S. Santhanam. StrongARM SA110: A 160MHz 32b 0.5W CMOS ARM processor. In *Proc. 8th HotChips Symposium on High Performance Chips*, pages 119–130, Aug. 1996.

25. A. Seznec. A case for two-way skewed-associative cache. In *Proc. 20th IEEE/ACM International Symposium on Computer Architecture*, May 1993.

26. P. Shivakumar and N. Jouppi. CACTI 3.0: An integrated cache timing, power, and area model. Technical Report WRL-2001-2, Compaq Western Research Lab, Aug. 2001.

27. Su and A. Despain. Cache designs for energy efficiency. In *Proc. 28th Annual Hawaii International Conference on System Sciences*, pages 306–315, Jan. 1995.

28. K. Theobald, H. Hum, and G. Gao. A design framework for hybrid-access caches. In *Proc. 1st IEEE Symposium on High Performance Computer Architecture*, pages 144–153, Jan. 1995.

29. M. Verma, L. Wehmeyer, and P. Marwedel. Cache-aware scratchpad allocation algorithm. In *Proc. ACM/IEEE Design, Automation and Test in Europe Conference and Exposition*, pages 21264–21270, Feb. 2004.

30. Y. Zhang, D. Parikh, K. Sankaranarayanan, K. Skadron, and M. Stan. Hotleakage: A temperature-aware model of subthreshold and gate leakage for architects. Technical Report CS-2003-05, University of Virginia Department of Computer Science, Mar. 2003.

Applying Decay to Reduce Dynamic Power in Set-Associative Caches

Georgios Keramidas[1], Polychronis Xekalakis[2,*], and Stefanos Kaxiras[1]

[1] Department of Electrical and Computer Engineering, University of Patras, Greece
[2] Department of Informatics, University of Edinburgh, United Kingdom
{keramidas,kaxiras}@ee.upatras.gr, p.xekalakis@ed.ac.uk

Abstract. In this paper, we propose a novel approach to reduce dynamic power in set-associative caches that leverages on a leakage-saving proposal, namely Cache Decay. We thus open the possibility to unify dynamic and leakage management in the same framework. The main intuition is that in a decaying cache, dead lines in a set need not be searched. Thus, rather than trying to predict which cache way holds a specific line, we predict, for each way, whether the line could be live in it. We access all the ways that possibly contain the live line and we call this way-selection. In contrast to way-prediction, way-selection cannot be wrong: the line is either in the selected ways or not in the cache. The important implication is that we have a fixed hit time — indispensable for both performance and ease-of-implementation reasons. In order to achieve high accuracy, in terms of total ways accessed, we use Decaying Bloom filters to track only the live lines in ways — dead lines are automatically purged. We offer efficient implementations of such autonomously Decaying Bloom filters, using novel quasi-static cells. Our prediction approach grants us high-accuracy in narrowing the choice of ways for hits as well as the ability to predict misses — a known weakness of way-prediction.

1   Introduction

Power consumption is a prime concern for the design of caches and numerous techniques have been proposed to reduce either leakage [9,14,19] or dynamic power [11,12,25,26] but without a clear understanding of how to integrate them in a single implementation. We propose a new approach for reducing dynamic power in set-associative caches by exploiting a previous leakage-saving proposal. Specifically, we use Cache Decay [14] to identify dead cachelines, which we then exclude from the associative search.

Our proposal is different from way-prediction proposals that precede it. We do not try to predict a single way for an access but we base our approach on information about what is live and what is dead in the cache. In effect, instead of

---

* This work has been conducted while Polychronis Xekalakis was studying at the University of Patras, Greece.

K. De Bosschere et al. (Eds.): HiPEAC 2007, LNCS 4367, pp. 38–53, 2007.

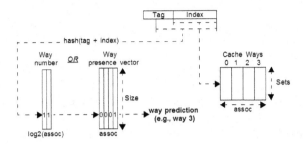

Fig. 1. Way-Prediction implemented as an array of way-number predictions or as way-presence vectors with at most one bit set per vector

predicting a way number, we predict whether an access refers to a live line. We make this prediction for each cache way and we access only the ways that can possibly hold the line in a *live state* — we call this *way-selection*. Way-selection cannot be wrong: the accessed line is either among the selected lines or it is a miss. As a result, we have a *fixed hit time* as opposed to way-prediction. This is a significant advantage in terms of implementation complexity (with respect to cache pipelining) but more importantly, interms of performance [8]. Variable hit latency in L1 not only slows down the cache, but creates many difficulties in efficiently scheduling depended instructions in the core.

To achieve high-prediction accuracy, we use a special form of membership-testing hash tables called Bloom filters [3] to track liveliness information for individual lines, per cache way. A normal Bloom filter (per way) would tell us whether a line possibly appeared before in a specific way, but without accounting for the possibility of the line being already dead. By decaying Bloom filter entries in concert with corresponding lines, a Decaying Bloom filter reflects the presence of the live lines only.

A significant benefit of decaying Bloom filter entries is the early prediction of cache misses. This is due to the Bloom filters reflecting the presence of live data in the cache and responding negatively to accesses that are going to miss. Early miss prediction is a boost to both performance and power savings since the cache can be bypassed completely on misses [8].

For simple and efficient implementations we propose and study various forms of Decaying Bloom filters, including Self-Decaying Bloom filters which decay their entries autonomously and require no decay feedback from the cache. To support power-efficient implementations of self-decaying Bloom filters we propose novel quasi-static cells designed to offer the necessary decay functionality for Bloom filters

Structure of the Paper: Section 2 motivates the need for a new approach and presents our proposal. Section 3 discusses details for efficient implementations. Section 4 presents our methodology and Section 5 our results. Section 6 reviews previous work and Section 7 concludes with a summary.

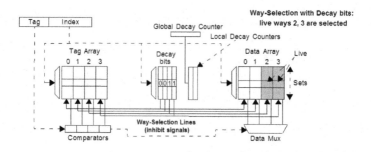

Fig. 2. Decay and Way-Selection using Decay bits

2   Way-Selection and Decaying Bloom Filters

2.1   What Is Wrong with Way-Prediction?

Way-prediction was initially proposed to address latency in set-associative caches [2,4,5]. These techniques also lead to power savings since they circumvent the associative search [10,11,13,25,26]. Way-prediction techniques aim to predict a single way where a reference might hit. Figure 1 shows the general view of way-prediction for a 4-way set-associative cache. For an n-way cache, the way-predictor can be viewed either as an array of log2(n)-bit binary numbers or a n-bit presence vector.

A correct prediction results in a *fast* hit and yields power benefits roughly proportional to the associativity (a single way out of n is accessed). On the other hand, a way misprediction, results in no power savings, and a slow hit, not only because the rest of the ways need to be searched with a subsequent cache access but also because the instructions that depend on the accessed value need to be flushed and re-issued in the core [8,22]. A variable hit latency also complicates cache pipelining adding to its overall complexity with special cases such as a slow-hit (a replay of a mispredicted hit).

For fast scheduling of dependent instructions it is very important not only to have a fixed hit time (as we propose) but also to be able to predict misses early. Way-prediction techniques cannot predict misses — predictions are produced even on misses. Additional mechanisms to handle misses are required, e.g., predicting misses with an instruction-based predictor [26], or using Bloom filters to detect some of the misses [8]. Our approach eliminates the need to handle misses separately, encompassing the work of [8].

Some of the most sophisticated way-prediction techniques are those based on a combination of *selective direct-mapping* (DM) and way-prediction [11,26]. In this paper we compare against one such scheme called MMRU [26]. We will describe this scheme further in Section 2.

2.2   Way-Selection

Cache decay was initially proposed to reduce leakage power in caches [14]. It is based on the generational behavior of cachelines, whereupon a cacheline initially

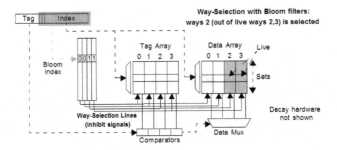

Fig. 3. Bloom Filters (one per way) sized to disambiguate 2 tag bits (Bloom filters not drawn to scale)

goes through a "live time", where it is accessed frequently, followed by a "dead time", where it simply awaits eviction. Cache decay shuts-off unneeded cachelines after some period of inactivity — called decay interval — assuming the lines have entered their dead time. The decay interval is measured with coarse 2-bit counters, local to each line, that are advanced by a global cycle counter (local counters are reset with accesses to the lines). A decay (valid) bit in the tag shows whether the line can be accessed or is dead (Fig. 2).

The simplest scheme to take advantage of cache decay for dynamic power reduction is to consult the decay status bits of the lines to enable accesses only to the live ways, and obtain dynamic power savings. We call this technique *way-selection* to distinguish it from way-prediction. The difference is that way-selection selects *zero* or more ways (up to *all* the ways) for each access whereas way-prediction strictly chooses a single way to access at all times. Because of this difference way-prediction can mispredict and require a second access, while way-selection cannot. In the case where all the lines in a set are dead, our technique predicts the miss simply by looking at the decay bits.

Decay bits, however, do not offer very high accuracy: many times more than one line in a set is live and it is rare to find a completely dead set (in order to predict a miss). In other words, decay bits do not disambiguate beyond the cache index. Ideally, we want to disambiguate addresses at a chosen depth. Thus, we can predict with high probability whether a *specific* line is live rather than obtain a blanket prediction of which ways are live in the line's set. The benefits are two-fold: high probability of identifying a *single* way for a line for possible hits and high probability of *identifying misses early*.

Furthermore, decay bits are typically embedded in the tag array, while we would like to have a separate array that we can access prior to the cache, similarly to other way-prediction structures [4,11,26]. We accomplish our goals using appropriately sized Bloom filters [3] instead of decay bits as our predictors.

2.3   Decaying Bloom filters

Bloom filters [3] are hash tables that implement a non-membership function. Each Bloom filter entry is a single bit: 1 denotes presence of an object hashed on

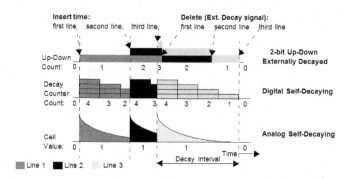

Fig. 4. Behavior equivalence for 3 different implementations of a single Decaying Bloom filter entry which accomodates 3 distinct cachelines overlapping in time

this entry; *0 denotes absence of any object* that can hash on this entry. A Bloom filter tells us with certainty when something is *not present*, but it cannot tell us what exactly is present because of possible conflicts in its entries. Way-selection with Bloom filters is shown in Fig. 3 where the role of the decay bits now is performed by Bloom filters sized to disambiguate two additionaltag bits.

The main weakness of Bloom filters is that it is difficult to update them as there is no way to tell what is in them. In order to solve this problem, Peir et al. use helper structures called *Collision Detectors* [8] while Sethumadhavan et al. propose using small n-bit up-down saturating counters as Bloom filter entries [17]. In this case, a Bloom filter entry stores the number of objects that hash on it. As long as the total number of inserted objects does not exceed the maximum count, the Bloom filter works as expected. In contrast, we use *decay* to update our Bloom filters: deletion of a dead line from the Bloom filters is equivalent to the decay of the corresponding Bloom entry. Note that, a Bloom entry stays live until the last of the lines that hash on it decays.

Decaying Bloom filters track only live data and thus are more accurate. Their entries can decay using feedback from a decaying cache, or *autonomously*. The latter variety, which we call *Self-Decaying Bloom filters (SDBF)* is very appealing in terms of implementation simplicity since it *does not require a feedback* connection to the cache.

While feedback or externally decayed Bloom filters are implemented with 2-bit counters [17], SDBFs can be digital or analog implementations. Digital implementations use 2-bit counters corresponding to the local decay counters of the cache, so they can be quite expensive. Thus, for SDBFs, the analog design offers the least expensive implementation. We propose using decaying 4-Transistor quasi-static RAM cells [23] as Bloom filter entries. Once written, these cells lose their charge because of leakage after some preset **decay interval** unless they are accessed and, consequently, recharged.

Functionally, all the decaying Bloom filter implementations are equivalent. Figure 4 shows the behavior of a single Bloom entry on which three distinct lines are hashed. The top diagram depicts the behavior of a 2-bit saturating counter

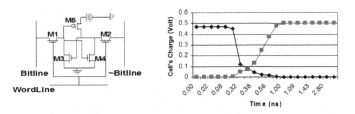

Fig. 5. 5-T Asymmetrically Decaying Bit

which is externally decayed. As live lines are hashed on the entry its counter is increased to three; it is decremented upon decay of the lines. The middle diagram shows the behavior of a digitally implemented SDBF. The decay counter is reset to its maximum count whenever a line is accessed and progressively decreases. Only when all lines decay the entry's counter can fall to zero. Finally, the bottom diagram shows an analog SDBF where the behavior of the decay counter is replaced by the discharge behavior of a quasi-static memory cell.

3   Efficient Analog Implementations

Analog implementations of SDBFs being inexpensive and power-efficient, are appealing. We need, however, to carefully design them for the required functionality. This section discusses analog implementations issues and our solutions.

A decayed 4T cell yields a random value. Regardless of the value written in the 4T cell, decay means that its high node drops to the level of its low node (which floats slightly above ground at the decayed state). Thus, a decayed 4T cell is not capable in producing a significant voltage differential on its bit lines, causing the sense-amps to assume a random state at the end of their sense time. Furthermore, the cell itself might flip to a random state when connected to the bit lines. This is not a concern if the 4T stores non-architectural state [23]. But in our case, we wish to have a specific decay behavior: ones decay to zeros to signify absence of the corresponding line but zeros should remain intact since the benefit in Bloom filters comes from the certainty they provide.

Figure 5 shows our solution. We simply re-instate one of the pMOS transistors connected to Vdd of the 6T design in the 4T design. By doing so we create an asymmetric cell, that stores logical zeroes in a static fashion and flips decayed logical ones to zeros. In Fig. 5 we can see a SPICE simulation of a typical flipping procedure. While the cell is in the flipping phase, reading its value is unpredictable. Fortunately, the window that this can happen is very small (Table 1). We handle such transient states as a soft error. Even though these reading errors might not be as infrequent as soft errors, they are still quite rare and this is why they are not a significant source of performance degradation [20].

For our 5T cells it is important to control the retention and flip times. These times greatly depend on technology: as we move to nano-scale technologies, retention times and flip times become smaller. Frequencies scale too, but in a more

Table 1. Retention and Flip Times for Various RAM Cells

Type of Cell	Retention Time	Flip Time (cycles)
6T (cycle=0.2ns)	- (cycles)	-
5T (cycle=0.2ns)	1500 (cycles)	75
5T+1 (cycle=0.2ns)	1500000 (cycles)	590000
4T (cycle=0.2ns)	700 (cycles)	-
4T+1 (cycle=0.2ns)	4500 (cycles)	-

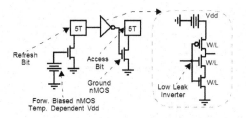

Fig. 6. Decoupled access-refresh decay cells

conservative way. We need retention times in the range of a few thousand cycles but a 5T cell cannot achieve such long retention times by itself. To adjust its retention time we introduce an extra nMOS in series to ground. Forward-biasing such ground nMOS allows us to precisely control leakage currents, practically placing a resistor in the 5T cell's path to ground. Table 1 shows a typical set of retention and flip times for 4T, 5T, and 6T cells, for 70nm technology, and a 5GHz clock, with and without ground transistors. Our aim here is not to give absolute numbers but to show that we have the capability to design retention times that suit our architectural needs.

Our design also solves another problem with 4T decay, namely its dependence to temperature (leakage is exponential to temperature). An inexpensive 4T Decay Temperature sensor [15,16] monitors temperature and biases the ground transistor appropriately to yield desired decay times.

A live cell is recharged when read. This is an inherent property of the quasi-static cells and the basis of keeping accessed entries alive. However, the problem is that we inadvertently keep other Bloom-filter entries alive (which should have decayed) just by reading them. The correct refresh behavior is to refresh only the entry corresponding to a hit and nothing else. Our solution is to decouple an entry's access from its refresh. Each entry is composed of two bits: an access bit (just for reading) and a refresh bit (for updating). The refresh bit is charged only in the case of a hit in the corresponding way while the access bit is redundantly refreshed with every access. The novelty of our design is that these two bits are coupled in such a way that when the refresh bit decays, it forces the access bit to promptly follow. This is accomplished simply by connecting the high node of the refresh bit to the leakage-control ground transistor of the access bit via a low-leak inverter. When the refresh bit decays, leakage in the access bit is increased by two orders of magnitude. The detailed design is shown in Fig. 6.

Soft errors and short decay intervals. Soft-errors, 5T transient states, or thermal variations, can lead to Bloom decay errors which appear as artificially shortened decay intervals. In this case, a Bloom filter entry decays before its corresponding cacheline. The Bloom filter reports misleadingly that the line is not in the cache. Since the benefit comes from trusting the Bloom filter and not to search the cache, in case of an error we experience a *Bloom-Induced Miss* — the line is still in the cache.

The solution to the Bloom-induced misses is readily provided in cache hierarchies that support coherency — such as those in the majority of high-performance processors today. Coherent cache hierarchies typically adhere to the inclusion property [1], e.g., L1's contents are strictly a subset of L2's. To support inclusion, snooping caches implement an inclusion bit alongside their other coherence bits (MESI). The inclusion bit is set if the line exists at a higher level and cleared in the opposite case. Under this scenario *the L2 does not expect a miss from the L1 for a line whose inclusion bit is set* — a sign of a Bloom-induced miss. Thus, the L2 acts as a safety net for L1 Bloom-misses. Bloom-induced misses are detected in L2 and L1 is advised of its mistake. The penalty for a Bloom-induced miss is an access of the L2's tags. There is no other associated overhead, such as data transfer. It is evident that this safety-net protection is not offered for the L2 (the level before main memory) where the cost of a Bloom-induced miss — a main memory access — is also very high. In this case we use digital SDBFs or digital externally-decayed Bloom filters.

4   Methodology

Here, we discuss our simulation setup, details of the MMRU scheme we compare against and latency and power issues affecting the comparisons.

Simulation Setup. For our simulations we use Wattch [6] and Cacti [24]. We simulate a 4-issue processor with 32K, 32-byte block, 3-cycle L1 cache and a 1M, 64-byte block, 8-way, 15-cycle L2 cache. For the L1 we assume, optimistically, a 3-cycle pipelined design [22]. Although we do not penalize competing approaches with mis-scheduling overhead we refer the reader to [8] for its performance quantification. Our performance results do reflect, however, the negative impact of slow hit times (3+3 cycles) for way-prediction as well as the latency benefits of predicting misses (1 cycle). We run all SPEC2000 benchmarks with the reference inputs, skipping the first billion instructions and collecting statistics for the second half billion. In all graphs the benchmarks are sorted by the base case miss-rate (lowest to highest).

MMRU and Bloom filter sizing. Multi-MRU or MMRU [26] is a virtual "selective-DM" extension of the Most Recently Used (MRU) way-prediction [4]. MRU returns the most recently accessed way of a set as its prediction but MMRU

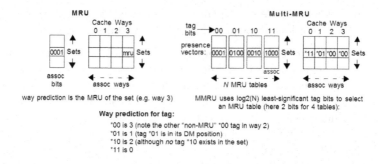

Fig. 7. Multi-MRU employes N MRU predictors (N = assoc) to disambiguate among different tags

Fig. 8. 4 partitions of 4 BFs (one per way) sized to disambiguate 2 tag bits. Total size is equal to MMRU and differences (with Fig. 7) are shown for tags *00 and *10.

allows multiple MRU predictors to disambiguiate among different tags (Fig. 7). All tags in a set ending with the same bits are tracked by the same MRU table.

While we can use Bloom filters of any size — trading their accuracy — we size the Bloom filters to equal aggregate size to MMRU way-predictors. This configuration is shown in Fig. 8 for 4-way caches. The Bloom filters are shown partitioned according to the two lower tag bits for direct comparisons with the MMRU. Note the important differences from Fig. 7: the four Bloom filters per way collectively allow more than one bit in the presence vector for the *00 tag; the presence vector for a decayed tag (e.g., tag *10) is 0 — it is the decay of the Bloom entries that give us the ability to predict misses.

Latency issues. Early way-prediction papers focused on reducing the latency of L1 set-associative caches [2,4,5,10]. For such schemes to work well, way-prediction must be performed prior to cache access. Approximate-address indexing schemes [4] or instruction-PC indexing [2,5] were proposed for this reason. PC-based schemes suffer from low prediction accuracy and implementation complexity [11]. Consistently, using the effective address yields the highest prediction accuracy [2,4,5,11].

Our view is that it is not as critical any longer to use approximate indexing schemes, given that L1 caches are not single-cycle. L1 caches are by necessity pipelined [22]. In this environment, predictor access can take place in the first pipeline stage or even occupy its own stage. Predictor access proceeds in parallel with decode and halts further operations in subsequent cycles once the predictor outcome is known. Our Cacti simulations show that accessing a small predictor

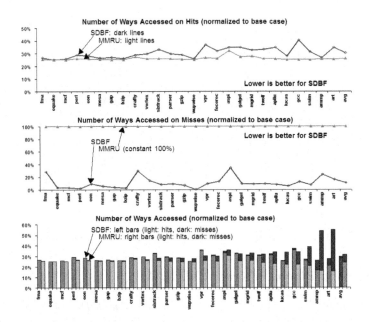

Fig. 9. 4-way SDBF vs. MMRU: ways accessed on hits, on misses and in total

structure of few kilobits is comparable in latency to L1 decode, in accordance to previous work. Power expended in cache decode, in parallel with predictor access, is fully accounted in our methodology.

Power issues. Our approach introduces two sources of additional power: i) Bloom filters arrays, and ii) decay-induced misses. Our Cacti estimates showed that energy for accessing the largest predictor (Bloom or MMRU) is less than 1% of a full L1 access (in accordance to prior work [11,26]).

We consider the extra dynamic power of decay-induced misses (extra accesses to lower level caches due to incorrect decay of cachelines) to be part of the leakage savings [14]. Having a decaying cache to reduce leakage, one would have to pay for this dynamic-power penalty regardless of any additional mechanism for dynamic power reduction. Of course, *we do not count leakage savings* as part of our benefits. However, we do take into account the performance penalty due to decay. As we will show, we turn this performance penalty into a performance benefit with way-selection and SDBF.

5   Results

We show simulation results for two cases: first we show how decaying Bloom filters compare against MMRU for 4-way caches. We then show the scalability of our approach to higher associativity (8-way and 16-way).

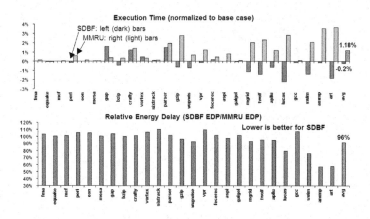

Fig. 10. 4-way SDBF vs. MMRU: execution time, relative EDP

5.1 Decaying Bloom Filters vs. MMRU

The main result of this section is that *way-selection with Decaying Bloom filters* is more power-efficient than the highly accurate MMRU. As we show, this is mainly because our approach predicts misses.

SDBFs use a decay interval of 8Kcycles. They are coupled to a decaying cache (32KB) with the same decay interval. We use a fixed decay interval without adaptive decay [7,14]. However, 8Kcycles is not the ideal decay interval for many of the benchmarks [21]. With SDBFs, one can adjust only a global decay interval, thus Adaptive Mode Control [7] or the Control-theoretic approach of [18] are appropriate adaptive schemes for our case but not the per-line adaptive decay [14]. We expect that adaptive decay is largely orthogonal to our work and it will further improve our proposal. The most interesting results in this section, however, are about SDBF vs. MMRU. Both are equal in cost and disambiguate 2 tag bits beyond the cache index.

The top graph in Fig. 9 shows the number of ways accessed on hits for SDBF and MMRU. The numbers are normalized to the number of ways accessed by the base case without any prediction. SDBF lags behind MMRU — this is the result of selecting more than one way to access in our predictions. In contrast, SDBF does very well in reducing the number of ways accessed on misses (Figure 9, middle), predicting zero ways for most misses for an average of 10% of the total ways of the base case for misses. In fact, the greater the miss rate of the benchmark, the better SDBF does compared to MMRU which always accesses 100% of the ways of the base case on misses. On average SDBF accesses 29% of the total ways of the base case, while MMRU accesses 31% (Fig. 9, bottom).

In terms of execution time, SDBF speeds up many benchmarks, MMRU slows down most benchmarks (by about 1% on average, but more than 3% for the high-miss-rate ammp and art as shown in Fig. 10, top graph). The very small slowdown of MMRU attests to the fact that we do not simulate in enough detail the negative effects of variable hit latency on the cache pipeline or on the

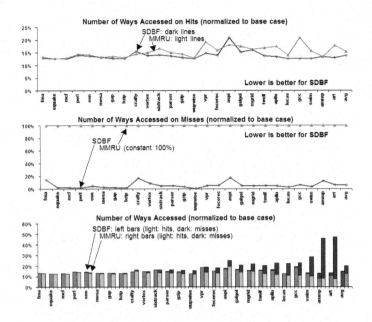

Fig. 11. 8-way SDBF vs. MMRU: ways accessed on hits, on misses and in total

scheduling of dependent instructions [8]. On the other hand, it should be noted that SDBF speeds-up a decaying cache which is inherently at a performance disadvantage (compared to a normal non-decaying cache) because of decay-induced misses. Under these conditions the relative energy-delay product (EDP) of the SDBF is 9% better than MMRU's (Fig. 10, bottom graph).

5.2   Scaling with Associativity

In this section we discuss how associativity affects SDBF and MMRU. Fig. 11 and Fig. 12 show the results for an 8-way 32KB L1 cache. SDBF improves dramatically in 8-way caches for both hits and misses. Its improvement in hits (Fig. 11, top graph) allows it to easily approach MMRU while further increasing its distance for the misses (Fig. 11, middle graph). Note also the improvement in the two high-miss-rate benchmarks ammp and art because of the improved prediction of misses.

With respect to execution time (Fig. 12, top graph) for SDBF, overhead due to decay-induced misses tends to be more pronounced since the base 8-way cache has an improved miss rate. However, this is balanced by the improved prediction of misses and the resulting "fast" misses. Overall, we have no significant change for SDBF speed-up. For MMRU, we have a small increase in its slow-down (across most benchmarks) as a combined effect of decreased accuracy and improved miss-rate of the base case. In 8 ways, energy-delay is improved for MMRU but not as much as for SDBF which doubles its distance from MMRU to 21%.

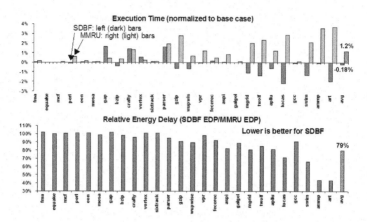

Fig. 12. 8-way SDBF vs. MMRU: execution time and relative EDP

Table 2. Comparison of SDBF and MMRU for various cache associativities

	4-ways		8-ways		16-ways	
	MMRU	SDBF	MMRU	SDBF	MMRU	SDBF
ways accessed on hits	26%	30%	14%	15%	7%	7%
ways accessed on hits	100%	10%	100%	5%	100%	2%
total ways accessed	31%	29%	20%	15%	14%	7%
power savings	59%	61%	69%	74%	75%	81%
relative EDP	91%		79%		69%	

Finally, Table 2 compares the averages (over all benchmarks) for the various metrics for up to 16-ways. Ways accessed are reported as a percentage of the base case without prediction. As we can see SDBF matches the performance of MMRU on hits in 16-ways while at the same time increases its distance significantly for the misses. The result is that SDBF halves its percentage of total ways accessed (29% for 4-ways, 15% for 8-ways, 7% for 16-ways) with each doubling in associativity while MMRU improves much slower (31%, 20%, 14% respectively). Power savings follow the trend of the total ways accessed and relative EDP improves with each doubling of the associativity: SDBF is 9%, 21% and 31% better than MMRU in EDP for 4-, 8- and 16-way caches.

6   Related Work

Techniques for dynamic-power reduction in caches can be divided into two categories: cache resizing and way-prediction. Cache resizing (e.g., DRI cache [19], CAM-tag resizing [12]) is a straightforward technique to reduce dynamic, static, and precharge power in caches. However, our approach can be contrasted more directly to way-prediction.

The most sophisticated way-prediction techniques are a combination of selective direct-mapping (DM) and way-prediction [11,26]. The idea of selective direct-mapping is to assign each line to a specific way based on its lower log2 (associativity) tag bits. Either the line truly occupies its assigned way or this assignment is virtual and used simply to obtain predictions for this line [26]. There are two separate proposals for the combined selective-DM/way-prediction technique: by Zhu and Zhang [5,26] and by Powell et al. [11] based on an earlier (latency-focused) paper by Batson and Vijaykumar [2].

We have already described the Zhu and Zhang proposal [26] (MMRU), a virtual "selective-DM" extension of the MRU way-prediction [4]. Zhu et al. also examine schemes where the DM assignment is actual rather than virtual but such schemes require line swapping and complex replacement policies.

The selective DM approach of Powell et al. [11] is an actual DM assignment where the lines are placed in their DM position unless they generate conflicts. In terms of prediction power this scheme aims to place as many lines as it can in their DM positions and handle the rest with a way-predictor. MMRU tracks all such lines, both those in their DM position and those in other positions, thus yielding approximately the same prediction accuracy — for both schemes, on average 92% of the predictions result in first hits for 4-way caches [11,26]. Because of this prediction equivalence we compare our approach to MMRU noting that our conclusions would be similar with respect to the Powell approach.

Finally, way-selection is similar to the way-halting cache proposed by Zhang et al. [25] where accesses to ways that cannot possibly contain the desired line are "halted". Way-halting is limited by the use of expensive CAMs for the lower four bits of the tags to determine tag mismatch per way and thus difficult to scale to a large number of sets. In contrast, we use Bloom filters instead of CAM-based halt tags, thus providing better scalability. Our decay techniques, however, can benefit way-halting too, clearing the halt tags from useless entries and increasing their effectiveness in predicting misses.

7   Conclusions

In this paper, we propose a dynamic power application for a leakage-power mechanism, allowing the seamless integration of the two. To achieve dynamic power reduction with decay we propose way-selection (similar to way-halting) and Decaying Bloom filters. Way-selection offers a significant advantage over way-prediction: that of a fixed hit time. We also propose several variations of Decaying Bloom filters, most notably the analog Self-Decaying Bloom filters, that decouple decay in our predictors from decay in the cache. This gives us the flexibility to use Decaying Bloom filters with non-decaying caches (or for instance state-preserving Drowsy caches). Decay, however, is necessary for the Bloom filters to be efficient. Another advantage of our approach is that it integrates prediction of misses. We have shown that our approaches can outperform some of the most sophisticated way-prediction proposals. And this, without taking into account leakage savings of the integrated dynamic/leakage power mechanism.

Acknowledgments

This work is supported by the HiPEAC Network of Excellence, the European SARC project No.027648 and by Intel Research Equipment Grant #15842.

References

1. J.-L. Baer and W. Wang. On the inclusion properties for multi-level cache hierarchies. In *Proc. of the Int. Symp. of Computer Architecture*, 1988.
2. B. Batson and T. N. Vijaykumar. Reactive-associative caches. In *Proc. of PACT*, 2001.
3. B. Bloom. Space/time trade-offs in hash coding with allowable errors. *Commun. ACM*, 13(7), 1970.
4. B. Calder et al. Predictive sequential associative cache. In *Proc. of the Symp. on High-Performance Computer Architecture*, 1996.
5. C. Zhang et al. Two fast and high-associativity cache schemes. *IEEE Micro*, 17(5), 1997.
6. D. Brooks et al. Wattch: a framework for architectural-level power analysis and optimizations. In *Proc. of the Int. Symp. of Computer Architecture*, 2000.
7. H. Zhou et al. Adaptive mode control: A static-power-efficient cache design. *Trans. on Embedded Computing Sys.*, 2(3), 2003.
8. J.-K. Peir et al. Bloom filtering cache misses for accurate data speculation and prefetching. In *Proc. of the Int. Conference on Supercomputing*, 2002.
9. K. Flautner et al. Drowsy caches: Simple techniques for reducing leakage power. In *Proc. of the Int. Symp. of Computer Architecture*, 2002.
10. K. Inoue et al. Way-predicting set-associative cache for high performance and low energy consumption. In *Proc. of ISLPED*, 1999.
11. M. Powell et al. Reducing set-associative cache energy via way-prediction and selective direct-mapping. In *Proc. of the Int. Symp. on Microarchitecture*, 2001.
12. M. Zhang et al. Fine-grain cam-tag cache resizing using miss tags. In *Proc. of ISLPED*, 2002.
13. R. Min et al. Location cache: a low-power l2 cache system. In *Proc. of ISLPED*, 2004.
14. S. Kaxiras et al. Cache decay: exploiting generational behavior to reduce cache leakage power. In *Proc. of the Int. Symp. of Computer Architecture*, 2001.
15. S. Kaxiras et al. 4t-decay sensors: a new class of small, fast, robust, and low-power, temperature/leakage sensors. In *Proc. of ISLPED*, 2004.
16. S. Kaxiras et al. A simple mechanism to adapt leakage-control policies to temperature. In *Proc. of ISLPED*, 2005.
17. S. Sethumadhavan et al. Scalable hardware memory disambiguation for high-ilp processors. *IEEE Micro*, 24(6), 2004.
18. S. Velusamy et al. Adaptive cache decay using formal feedback control. In *Proc. of the Workshop on Memory Performance Issues.*, 2002.
19. S. Yang et al. An integrated circuit/architecture approach to reducing leakage in deep-submicron high-performance i-caches. In *Proc. of the Int. Symp. on High-Performance Computer Architecture*, 2001.
20. V. Degalahal et al. Analyzing soft errors in leakage optimized sram design. In *Proc. of the Int. Conference on VLSI Design*, 2003.

21. Y. Li et al. State-preserving vs. non-state-preserving leakage control in caches. In *Proc. of the Conference on Design, Automation and Test in Europe*, 2004.
22. Z. Chishti et al. Wire delay is not a problem for smt (in the near future). In *Proc. of the Int. Symp. of Computer Architecture*, 2004.
23. Z. Hu et al. Managing leakage for transient data: decay and quasi-static 4t memory cells. In *Proc. of ISLPED*, 2002.
24. S. Wilton and N. Jouppi. Cacti: An enhanced cache access and cycle time model. In *IEEE Journal of Solid-State Circuits, Vol. 31(5):677-688*, 1996.
25. C. Zhang and K. Asanovic. A way-halting cache for low-energy high-performance systems. *ACM Trans. Archit. Code Optim.*, 2(1), 2005.
26. Z. Zhu and X. Zhang. Access-mode predictions for low-power cache design. *IEEE Micro*, 22(2), 2002.

II Architecture/Compiler Optimizations for Efficient Embedded Processing

Virtual Registers: Reducing Register Pressure Without Enlarging the Register File

Jun Yan and Wei Zhang

Dept. of ECE, Southern Illinois University, Carbondale, IL 62901
{jun,zhang}@engr.siu.edu

Abstract. This paper proposes a novel scheme to mitigate the register pressure for statically scheduled high-performance embedded processors without physically enlarging the register file. Our scheme exploits the fact that a large fraction of variables are short-lived, which do not need to be written to or read from real registers. Instead, the compiler can allocate these short-lived variables to the virtual registers, which are simply place holders (instead of physical storage locations in the register file) to identify dependences among instructions. Our experimental results demonstrate that virtual registers are very effective at reducing the number of register spills; which, in many cases, can achieve the performance close to the processor with twice number of real registers. Also, our results indicate that for some multimedia and communication applications, using a large number of virtual registers with a small number of real registers can even achieve higher performance than that of a mid-sized register file without any virtual registers.

1 Introduction

The register file is critical to the performance of microprocessors. Recent advancements in architectural design and compiler optimizations demand large multi-ported register files for exploiting high instruction-level parallelism (ILP) to achieve better performance. However, large multi-ported register files are not only expensive and power hungry, but also can compromise the clock cycle time of microprocessors [14]; potentially degrading performance. In this paper, we propose a novel and cost-effective approach to exploiting virtual registers to reduce the real register pressure for VLIW-based embedded processors. The idea is to exploit the short-lived variables and the data forwarding network to minimize the demand on real registers. Previous work has found that a large fraction of variables are short-lived in the sense that their live ranges span only a few instructions [1,6], the similar trend is also observed in this paper for multimedia and communication applications (see Figure 4 for details). In a pipelined processor, data can be forwarded from the output of a functional unit to the inputs of the same or other functional units in the subsequent clock cycles; which has been widely used in instruction pipelines to minimize the data hazards [16]. Therefore, if the live range of a variable is within the maximum length of the data forwarding path (i.e., a short-lived variable), it does not need to be written back to the architectural registers. Moreover, *this variable does not even need to be allocated to an architectural register*, since a place holder is enough to identify the data dependence relations for forwarding the data to the right instructions. In this paper, *the place holders (i.e., tags) extended in*

K. De Bosschere et al. (Eds.): HiPEAC 2007, LNCS 4367, pp. 57–70, 2007.

the operand fields of the ISA are called virtual registers. In contrast, the architectural registers that have physical storage places in the register file are called real registers (also called register for simplicity) in this paper. Since a large fraction of variables are shorted-lived (see Figure 4 for details), this paper proposes to allocate virtual registers (instead of real registers) to the short-variables whose live ranges are less than or equal to the maximum length of the data forwarding path. As a result, the real registers can be used for other variables more efficiently to reduce the number of register spills. Another possible benefit is the reduction of the register file power dissipation, since less number of real registers are needed by exploiting virtual registers. However, the energy evaluation of our approach is out of the scope of this paper. Our experimental results indicate that virtual registers are very successful in reducing the register spills, leading to higher performance without enlarging the register file physically.

The rest of the paper is organized as follows. We discuss related work in Section 2 and introduce the basics of data forwarding network in Section 3. We elaborate our approaches to exploiting virtual registers for reducing the real register pressure in Section 4. The experimental results are given in Section 5. Finally, we conclude this paper in Section 6.

2   Related Work

A number of research efforts have focused on exploiting the short-lived variables for performance [1] and energy optimizations [6,7,8]. While the research efforts in [6,7,8] focused on reducing the register file energy dissipation, the work in [1] is closest to this study in that both explore the short-lived variables in order to improve the register allocation for better performance; however, there are some important distinctions. In [1], Lozano et al. proposed an architecture extension to avoid the useless commits of the values produced by short-lived variables and a compiler-based approach to avoiding assigning the short-lived variables to the real registers. In their work [1], the reorder buffer entries (ROB) are treated as the extension of real registers, which are still physically existed. In contrast, this paper uses virtual registers that do not physically exist to help enhance the allocation of real registers to long-lived variables. Second, the work in [1] concentrated on studying the short-lived variables for general-purpose and scientific benchmarks (i.e., SPEC 92 and Livermoore loops); while this paper is geared towards the short-lived variables for multimedia and communication applications (i.e., Mediabench [22]). Third, in [1], the short-lived variables are defined as those whose live ranges are smaller than or equal to the size of the reorder buffer (which is typically much larger than the length of the data forwarding path, i.e., 3). By comparison, the short-lived variables in this paper refer to those whose live ranges are smaller than or equal to the length of the data forwarding path (i.e., 3 in our simulated processor, see Section 3 for details). Finally, the approach studied in this paper can potentially complement Lozano's scheme [1] to further enhance performance for superscalar processors; since certain short-live variables (i.e., whose live ranges are within the length of the data forwarding path) do not even need to be allocated to reorder buffer entries by exploiting virtual registers, leading to less register spills and ROB saturation.

There have been several research efforts [13,15,9,10,11,12,2,4] to provide a large number of registers without significantly increasing the register file complexity or compromising the clock cycle time. In contrast to these hardware-centric techniques, our approach is based on compilers, which can allocate the limited number of real registers more efficiently by exploiting virtual registers for short-lived variables. Also, many of these hardware-centric techniques target the physical registers used in the dynamic renaming logic for dynamically-scheduled processors. By comparison, our approach targets architectural registers visible in the ISA; which can be used to statically scheduled architectures without the dynamic register renaming support. In the field of embedded computing, researchers have also proposed compiler-controlled scratch-pad memories (SPM) [29,30,31,32]; however, this paper studies compiler management of register values by exploiting both virtual and real registers.

Recently, Gonzalez et al. introduced the concept of virtual-physical registers, which are the names used to keep track of dependences [3]. The virtual-physical registers [3] and virtual registers proposed in this paper are similar in the sense that both do not use any physical storage locations; however, there are some significant differences. First, virtual-physical registers [3] are used to delay the allocation of physical registers (not architectural registers) in dynamically scheduled processors; while virtual registers proposed in this paper can be exploited to mitigate the pressure on architectural registers for any processors, regardless of the dynamic register renaming. Second, virtual-physical registers [3] are invisible to the compiler; while virtual registers proposed in this paper can be explicitly managed by the compiler to reduce the register spills physically.

3   Background on Data Forwarding Network

Data forwarding (also called bypass) network is a widely-used mechanism to reduce the data hazards of pipelined processors [16], which is critical to achieve high performance for pipelined processors. Data forwarding network is also used in VLIW processors, such as Philips LIFE processor [17]. It should be noted that a full bypass network is costly in terms of area and wire delay for multi-issue processors [26]; however, there are some proposes to reduce the complexity of bypass network without significantly compromising performance [27,28]. In this paper, however, we assume a VLIW processor with 5-stage pipelines provided with full data forwarding logic, and our goal is to exploit the bypass network to significantly reduce the register pressure. The 5-stage pipeline is depicted in Figure 1 [1], which include the following stages:

- IF: Instruction Fetch from the I-cache.
- ID: Instruction Decode and operand fetch from the Register File (RF).
- EX: Execution.
- MEM: Memory access for load/store operations.
- WB: Write-Back results into the RF.

As can be seen from Figure 1, three forwarding paths (i.e., EX-EX, MEM-EX and MEM-ID) provide direct links between pairs of stages through the pipeline registers

---

[1] For simplicity, we just illustrate the data forwarding path for a scalar pipeline.

(i.e., EX/MEM and MEM/WB inter-stage pipeline registers). Therefore, given a sequence of VLIW instructions $I_1...I_k...I_n$, the instruction I_k can read its operands from the following instructions:

- I_{k-1}: through the EX-EX forwarding path (when I_k is in the EX stage).
- I_{k-2}: through the MEM-EX forwarding path (when I_k is in the EX stage).
- I_{k-3}: through the MEM-ID forwarding path (when I_k is in the ID stage).
- I_{k-j}: through the RF where j > 3.

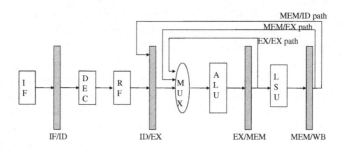

Fig. 1. The 5-stage pipelined VLIW forwarding architecture, where DEC stands for decoder and LSU represents Ld/St Unit

3.1   Problem Formulation

Given an instruction pipeline with data forwarding network F, we define the length of the data forwarding path $L(F)$ to be the maximum number of clock cycles between the producer instruction that forwards the value and the consumer instruction that takes this value. Given a variable v, we define its live range $LR(v)$ to be the number of machine instructions (including nops) in the longest path between its definition points and last-use points, including the instruction at the definition point. We say a variable v is a short-lived variable if its live range is smaller than or equal to the length of the data forwarding path, i.e., $LR(v) \leq L(F)$.

Given these definitions, the problem to be studied in this paper can be described as follow:

Problem - Reducing Pressure on Real Registers: Given a pipelined machine M with the length of data forwarding path $L(F)$ and a program P, we want to develop compiler techniques and architectural support to ensure that the short-lived variables in P will use as less number of real registers in M as possible to minimize the number of register spills without violating the program semantics.

4   Our Solution

To solve the aforementioned problem, we propose to create virtual registers for short-lived variables. A virtual register is simply a tag to identify the data dependences among instructions, which is not corresponding to a physical storage location in the register file.

```
for (k = 0 ; k <in; k++) {
    t = b0[k] + b1[k];
    b1[k] = b0[k] – b1[k];
    b0[k] = t;
}
```

(a)

```
Loop:
(1)  add $r0 #b0 $r5;       add $r6 $r6 1;
(2)  lw $r2 $r0;            add $r1 #b1$r5;
(3)  lw $r3 $r1;            la $br1 <Loop>;
(4)  add $t $r2 $r3;        sub $r4 $r2 $r3;   cmp $br0 $r6 #in;
(5)  sw $r4 $r1;            add $r5 $r5 4;
(6)  sw $t $r0;
(7)  brct $br1 $br0;
```

(b)

Fig. 2. The code segment: (a) the source code, (b) the assembly code for the target VLIW processor

Since the virtual registers can keep track of the data dependence relations, the values of short-lived variables can be forwarded to the dependent instructions on the pipelines without accessing the register file. Therefore, with appropriate architectural support, the compiler can modify the register allocation algorithm to allocate virtual registers to as many short-lived variables as possible while maintaining the program semantics. Consequently, real registers can be kept for long-lived variables in order to minimize the number of register spills, leading to high performance even without physically enlarging the register file.

The idea of exploiting virtual registers can be explained by the example code shown in Figure 2, which is extracted from rasta. Figure 2 (a) gives the source code, and Figure 2 (b) gives the corresponding assembly code for the HPL-PD architecture [21]. Note that in Figure 2 (b), multiple operations can be scheduled by the VLIW compiler to take advantage of the parallel VLIW functional units for higher ILP; however, due to the page limitation, we do not exactly follow the HPL-PD [21] VLIW instruction format and we omit the Nop operations. The live range of each variable used in Figure 2 is depicted in Figure 3. As can be seen, this code segment includes five short-lived variables, i.e., $r1, $r2, $r3, $r4 and $t, whose live ranges are less than or equal to 3, as well as three long-lived variables, including $r0, $r5 and $r6. As we can see, the live ranges of the short-lived variables and the long-lived variables are overlapped, necessitating at least six real registers in order to not spill values to memory if there is no virtual register. Nevertheless, by exploiting virtual registers for the short-lived variables, only 3 real registers (in addition to 3 virtual register) are sufficient. Therefore, in case there are only three real registers available for this code segment, exploiting the virtual registers can reduce the number of register spills, potentially leading to higher performance.

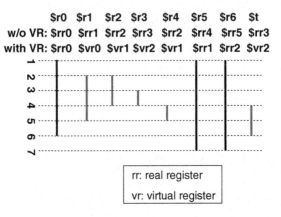

Fig. 3. Live ranges and the register allocation of the code segment without and with virtual registers

Clearly, the success of our approach depends heavily on how many variables are actually short-lived. If only a small fraction of variables are short-lived, its impact on the real register allocation and the reduction of register spills will be insignificant. Since in our 5-stage pipelined forwarding architecture depicted in Figure 1, the length of the forwarding path is 3; only the variables whose live ranges are equal to or less than 3 will be identified as short-lived, according to our definition of short-lived variables in subsection 3.1. Figure 4 shows the percentage of short-lived variables for the selected benchmarks from Mediabench [22] (more details of our evaluation methodology can be found in Section 5). As we can see, all the benchmarks have 50% of short-lived variables, implying that multimedia and communication applications also contain abundant short-lived variables. On average, 70.3% of variables of all the benchmarks are short-lived, indicating plenty of opportunities to exploit virtual registers for mitigating real register pressure.

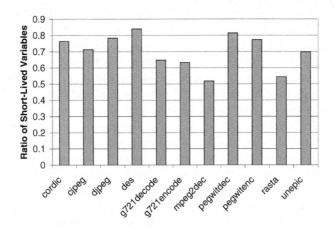

Fig. 4. Percentage of short-lived variables

4.1   Architectural Support

To support the use of virtual registers, we need to make slight extensions of the underlying architecture. The assumed architectural support is depicted in Figure 5 (b) [2]. Compared with original ISA shown in Figure 5 (a), 1 bit (called the virtual bit) needs to be added into the ISA for each destination and source operand field. By default, the leftmost virtual bit is set to 0, and the remaining 5 bits of the operand field are used to specify a real register. When the virtual bit is set to 1, a virtual register (i.e., the tag consisting of all the 6 bits in the operand field) will be used to identify the data dependences associated with short-lived variables. Moreover, the decoder must be extended to recognize the additional virtual bits. In addition, we add a Rs Inhibit bit and a Rt Inhibit bit to the register file; which when enabled (i.e., 1), will inhibit the reading of the Rs or Rt register respectively, as shown in Figure 5 (b). Likewise, the virtual bit of the Rd field is connected with a NOT gate, whose output is then passed to the RegWrite Enable signal that is typically already existed in the register file to enable (1) or disable (0) the register write operations.

Clearly, adding 1 virtual bit to each of the three operand fields of a 32-bit instruction format will increase the instruction width by 9.3%, which also requires the corresponding increase of the instruction memory size. This overhead can be partly mitigated by exploiting unused instruction encoding bits; however, this will restrict the proposed approach only to the subset of ISA operations with unused encoding bits in the instruction format. Also, differential encoding proposed by Zhuang et al. [18] can be used to address a large number of registers (virtual or real) without increasing the length of ISA.

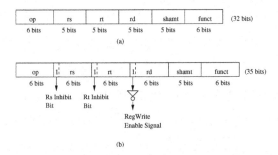

Fig. 5. The architecture support for virtual registers: (a) the original instruction format, (b) the extended instruction format by adding 1 virtual bit to each operand field

4.2   Compiler Support

With the architectural support for virtual registers, the compiler's job is to modify the register allocation to exploit these virtual registers for short-lived variables while freeing as many real registers as possible for long-variables. Conceptually, the compiler first performs analysis to identify short-lived variables (called the short-liveness

---

[2] Here we just illustrate the modification of a single operation. A VLIW instruction consisting of multiple operations needs to extend the operand fields of each operation.

analysis in this paper), which are dependent on the length of the data forwarding path of the processor. Then the compiler attempts to allocate virtual registers to short-lived variables, and to allocate real registers to long-lived variables (called virtual/real register allocation in this paper).

This short-liveness analysis is implemented by using the Rebel intermediate representation of the Elcor compiler [19], which is composed of three steps: 1) perform standard dataflow analysis to identify def-use chains [5]; 2) for each variable v, calculate its live range $LR(v)$ based on our definition in Subsection 3.1; 3) identify v as a short-lived variable if $LR(v) \leq 3$; otherwise, v is treated as a long-lived variable.

The virtual/real register allocation algorithm built upon the region-based register allocation [25] of the Elcor compiler [19], which itself is based on Chow and Hennessy's priority-based coloring algorithm [23]. The pseudo code of our algorithm is provided in Figure 6. In this algorithm, for each variable of a region, if it is a short-lived variable, the compiler first attempts to allocate a virtual register to it. Otherwise, a real register or spilling has to be used for this variable. The long-lived variables will follow the existing register allocation process without touching virtual registers. In case there is no real register available, a variable still needs to be either spilled or splitted, which is controlled by the parameter in the configuration file of our experimental framework [19]. After register spilling or splitting, this allocation algorithm will be repeated, until all the variables have been binded to virtual or real registers, or spilled to memory.

```
Algorithm Virtual_Real_Register Allocation (var, Region)
vr // vertual register bank
pr // physical register bank
{
For each var do
   if (short_liveness_analysis(var) == True) then
      if Try(vr, var) = unBlocked then
         Binding(vr, var, status)
      else if Try(pr, var) = unBlocked then
         Binding(pr, var, status)
      else
         Spilling(var, status)
      end if
   end if
}
```

Fig. 6. The algorithm of the virtual/real register allocation

4.3 Precise Interrupt

Exploiting virtual registers in the pipelines can cause problems to the precise interrupt (or exception) [24]. Since virtual registers do not have corresponding physical storages, the values that are associated with virtual registers will be lost after interrupts. Therefore, if an instruction needs to use a virtual register as a source operand, while thevalue associated with this virtual register is produced by an instruction before the faulting instruction or by the faulting instruction itself; the dependent instruction will not be able to fetch the data correctly. To solve this problem, we propose to store the values in the pipeline registers as part of the processor state when dealing with interrupts or exceptions. Precisely, only the content of the EXE/MEM and MEM/WB pipeline registers needs to be saved before interrupts handling and restored after interrupt handling, so that instructions that use virtual registers as source operands can still get the right values from the pipeline registers through the data forwarding network. Since interrupts are not frequent events, the performance overhead to restore the EXE/MEM and MEM/WB pipeline registers before restarting the instructions after the faulting instruction will not be significant.

5   Evaluation

5.1   Experimental Setup

We used simulation to evaluate the proposed virtual/real register allocation algorithm on a VLIW processor based on HPL-PD architecture [21]. The Trimaran v3.7 [19] was used for the compiler implementation and architecture simulation. Trimaran is comprised of a front-end compiler IMPACT, a back-end compiler Elcor, an extensible intermediate representation (IR) Rebel, and a cycle-level VLIW/EPIC simulator that is configurable by modifying the machine description file [19]. The virtual/real register allocation algorithm was implemented as the last optimization phase in Elcor. The machine description file of Trimaran was configured to simulate VLIW processors with various number of real and virtual registers. By default, the simulated VLIW processor consists of two IALUs (integer ALUs), two FPALUs (floating-point ALUs), one LD/ST (load/store) unit and one branch unit. Other system parameters used for our default setting are provided in Table 1. The benchmark set is drawn from Mediabench [22].

Table 1. Default parameters used in our simulations

Parameter	Value
Register File	16 registers, 4 read ports and 4 write ports
L1 instruction cache	16KB direct-mapped with 8 sub-banks, 1 cycle latency
L1 data cache	32KB 2-way, 2 cycle
L1 cache line size	32 bytes
Unified L2 cache	512KB 4-way cache, 10 cycles
L2 cache line size	64 bytes
Memory latency	100 cycles

5.2   The Effect of Different Number of Real Registers

To understand the impact of the number of registers on the performance of VLIW processors, Figure 7 depicts the number of execution cycles of processors with the number of real registers varying from from 8 to 16, 32, 64 and 128, which are normalized with the execution cycles of 8 real registers, assuming the clock cycle time is fixed. As we can see, all the benchmarks have better or at least the same performance with a larger number of registers. In particular, we observe significant performance improvement (i.e., reduced number of the execution cycles) as the size of the register file increases from 8 to 16, from 16 to 32, and from 32 to 64. Except for a few benchmarks, such as djpeg and des, increasing the number of registers from 64 to 128 leads to diminishing returns. Overall, we find that with the same frequency, larger register files result in better performance; because more data can be placed in the registers and the number of register spills can be reduced. Therefore, it is desirable to provide a virtually large register file without physically expanding the number of real registers.

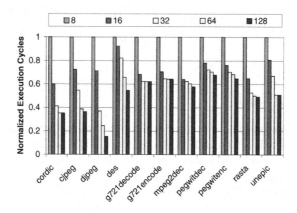

Fig. 7. Normalized execution cycles by increasing the number of real registers from 8 to 16, 32, 64 and 128, which are normalized with the execution cycles of 8 real registers

5.3   The Effect of Exploiting Virtual Registers

In this section, we study the impact of the proposed virtual/real register allocation algorithm on the performance of VLIW processors of 16 real registers and of 16 or 48 additional virtual registers (note that in order to exploit the additional 16 or 48 virtual registers, each operand field of the ISA needs to be lengthened by 1 or 2 bits respectively). Figure 8 illustrates the performance of 16 real registers, 16 real registers and 16 virtual registers (i.e., 16/16), 32 real registers, 16 real registers and 48 virtual registers (i.e., 16/48), and 64 real registers; which are normalized with respect to the execution cycles of 16 real registers. As can be seen, the exploitation of 16 virtual registers leads to better performance than that of 16 real registers only; which is even close to that of 32 real registers. Also, using 48 virtual registers in addition to 16 real registers can achieve performance close to that of 64 real registers. On average, the 16/16, 32, 16/48 and 64 schemes reduce the number of execution cycles of 16 real registers by 13.5%, 16.9%, 22.4% and 25.9% respectively. Interestingly, we discover that exploiting 48 virtual registers in addition to 16 real registers can achieve even superior performance to that of 32 real registers for many benchmarks, indicating the great potential of the proposed virtual/real register allocation scheme.

Moreover, as can be seen from Figure 8, there are noticeable performance differences between the 16/16 scheme and the 32 scheme for cordic, cjpeg, djpeg, des, rasta and unepic; while for the rest of the benchmarks, the 16/16 scheme can achieve the performance similar to that of the 32 scheme. To investigate the reason for these different impacts on performance, we also study the effects of using different number of real and virtual registers on the number of dynamic register spills. Table 2 gives both the number and ratio (relative to that of 16 real registers) of the dynamic register spills for 16/16, 32, 16/48 and 64 schemes. As we expect, the number of dynamic register spills is reduced dramatically by exploiting additional virtual or real registers. As can be seen from Table 2, compared with the 16/16 scheme, the 32 scheme can reduce the number of register spills more significantly than the 16/16 scheme for g721decode, g721encode, mpeg2dec, pegwitdec, pegwitenc and rasta, which explains the noticeable performance differences between the 16/16 scheme and the 32 scheme in Figure 8. Also, for these 6 benchmarks, the 32 scheme can reduce the number of dynamic register spills more than that of the 16/48 scheme, which elucidates why the 32 scheme has better performance than the 16/48 scheme for those benchmarks in Figure 8. In contrast, for the rest of the benchmarks, the 16/16 scheme is very effective at reducing the number of dynamic register spills, leading to performance increase similar to that of 32 real registers. Also, the 16/48 scheme can reduce more number of register spills than that of 32 real registers, leading to superior performance for those benchmarks.

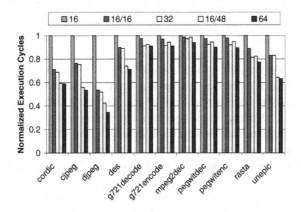

Fig. 8. Normalized execution cycles of 16 real registers (16), 16 real registers and 16 virtual registers (16/16), 32 real registers (32), 16 real registers and 48 virtual registers (16/48), and 64 real registers (64), which are normalized with the execution cycles of 16 real registers

In addition, as we can observe from Figure 8, exploiting 16 virtual registers in addition to 16 real registers have various impacts on the performance for different applications. More specifically, six benchmarks, including cordic, cjpeg, djpeg, des, rasta and unepic, result in significant performance increases by exploiting 16 additional virtual registers, which vary from 10.1% for des up to 46.1% for djpeg. On the other hand, the rest of the benchmarks only have relatively small performance improvement; although all the benchmarks have significant reduction on the number of dynamic register spills, as depicted in Table 2. In order to estimate the impact of register spills on the overall performance, we use a new metric called the *ratio of spill cycles*, which is defined as the ratio of the reduced number of register spills (as compared to the base

Table 2. Number and ratio of dynamic register spills with 16 real registers (16), 16 real registers and 16 virtual registers (16/16), 32 real registers (32), 16 real registers and 48 virtual registers (16/48), and 64 real registers (64); the ratios are normalized with the number of dynamic register spills of 16 real registers

Benchmarks	16	16/16		32		16/48		64	
	Number	Number	Ratio	Number	Ratio	Number	Ratio	Number	Ratio
cordic	2060120	740184	0.359	740152	0.359	160240	0.078	160160	0.078
cjpeg	12426664	7616152	0.613	7231164	0.582	2432488	0.196	1683046	0.135
djpeg	7987102	3778270	0.473	3543668	0.444	2832862	0.355	1613830	0.202
des	2934580	2642866	0.901	2606502	0.888	2196222	0.748	2094574	0.714
g721decode	61274096	47722110	0.779	28907704	0.472	29784938	0.486	27727544	0.453
g721encode	69240144	55021838	0.795	36873756	0.533	37176556	0.537	35693596	0.516
mpeg2dec	557771189	469923711	0.843	306527313	0.550	431973499	0.774	266834891	0.478
pegwitdec	27694866	26500576	0.957	23727580	0.857	25624742	0.925	22757364	0.822
pegwitenc	41998820	40741966	0.970	35394588	0.843	39647678	0.944	34050564	0.811
rasta	1909207	1230353	0.644	641475	0.336	1037769	0.544	338381	0.177
unepic	4423038	2415730	0.546	2399608	0.543	470480	0.106	32922	0.007

scheme, i.e., with 16 registers) to the overall number of execution cycles, as shown in Equation 1. In this equation, $Spills_{original}$ represents the original number of dynamic register spills without using virtual registers, $Spills_{virtual}$ represents the number of dynamic register spills after exploiting virtual registers, and $Cycles$ stands for the number of execution cycle of the baseline (without using virtual registers). The intuition behind this metric is that we assume each register spill reduction will lead to 1 clock cycle saving in performance, as it takes at least 1 cycle to access data from the memory hierarchy. However, it should be noted that the *ratio of spill cycles* is just an estimate (not an exact metric) of the potential performance improvement due to reduced register spills; since the reduced registers spills may not be on the critical path, and the load/store operations may not hit in the L1 data cache, and also the memory access latency may be overlapped by the other instructions, etc. However, the *ratio of spill cycles* is more accurate than the estimation based purely on the number of register spills reduction, which does not take into account the execution cycle of the program. Table 3 gives the *ratio of spill cycles* for the 16/16, 32, 16/48, and 64 schemes. As can be seen, five benchmarks, i.e., g721decode, g721encode, mpeg2dec, pegwitdec and pegwitenc have very low *ratio of spill cycles* by using 16 additional virtual registers (i.e., the 16/16 scheme);

Table 3. The *ratio of spill cycles* of 16 real registers and 16 virtual registers (16/16), 32 real registers (32), 16 real registers and 48 virtual registers (16/48), and 64 real registers (64)

Benchmarks	16/16	32	16/48	64
cordic	0.303	0.303	0.436	0.436
cjpeg	0.183	0.197	0.379	0.408
djpeg	0.378	0.399	0.462	0.572
des	0.073	0.083	0.186	0.212
g721decode	0.047	0.112	0.109	0.116
g721encode	0.044	0.100	0.099	0.104
mpeg2dec	0.010	0.028	0.014	0.032
pegwitdec	0.023	0.078	0.041	0.097
pegwitenc	0.015	0.078	0.028	0.094
rasta	0.111	0.207	0.143	0.257
unepic	0.158	0.160	0.312	0.346

although the number of register spills is reduced substantially as presented in Table 2. Therefore, these benchmarks only have limited performance increase by exploiting additional virtual registers. By comparison, the rest of the benchmarks have relatively larger *ratio of spill cycles*, varying from 7.3% for des to 30.3% for cordic, leading to higher performance improvement after performing the virtual/real register allocation.

$$Ratio\_of\_spill\_cycles = \frac{(Spills_{original} - Spills_{virtual})}{Cycles} \tag{1}$$

6   Concluding Remarks

This paper proposes a cost-effective scheme for high-performance embedded processors based on VLIW architectures to reduce the register pressure substantially. We propose to add virtual bits to the operand fields of the ISA to create virtual registers that do not have physical storage locations in the register file. These virtual registers can be used to keep track of the data dependence relations among instructions, making them suitable to be associated with short-lived variables of programs running on pipelined processors with data forwarding support. With the simple architectural extension to support virtual registers, we modify the region-based register allocation algorithm [25] to exploit the additional virtual registers for the short-lived variables. Our experimental results indicate that virtual registers are very effective at reducing the number of register spills; which, in many cases, can achieve the performance close to the processor with twice number of real registers. Also, our results demonstrate that for some applications, exploiting a large number of virtual registers with a small number of real registers can even attain higher performance than that of a mid-sized register file without any virtual register.

Acknowledgement

This work was funded in part by NSF grant 0613244. We would like to thank the anonymous referees for the detailed comments that helped us improve the paper.

References

1. L. A. Lozano et al. Exploiting short-lived variables in superscalar processors. In Proc. of MICRO, 1995.
2. R. Yung et al. Caching processor general registers. In Proc. of ICCD, 1995.
3. A. Gonzalez et al. Virtual-physical registers. In Proc. of HPCA, 1998.
4. D. W. Oehmke et al. How to fake 1000 registers. In Proc. of MICRO, 2005.
5. S. S. Muchnick. Advanced compiler design and implementation. Morgan Kaufmann Publishers, 1997.
6. Z. Hu et al. Reducing register file power consumption by exploiting value lifetime characteristics. WCED, 2000.
7. M. Sami et al. Exploiting data forwarding to reduce the power budget of VLIW embedded processors. In Proc. of DATE, 2001.
8. S. Park et al. Bypass aware instruction scheduling for register file power reduction. In Proc. of LCTES, 2006.

9. R. Balasubramonian et al. Reducing the complexity of the register file in dynamic superscalar processors. In Proc. of MICRO, 2001.
10. M. Postiff et al. Integrating superscalar processor components to implement register caching. In Proc. of ICS, 2001.
11. J.L. Cruz et al. Multiple-banked register file architectures. In Proc. of ISCA 2000.
12. J.H. Tseng et al. Banked multiported register files for high-frequency superscalar micro-processors. In Proc. of ISCA 2003.
13. K.I. Farkas et al. The multicluster architecture: reducing cycle time through partitioning. In MICRO-30, 1997.
14. K. I. Farkas et al. Register file design considerations in dynamically scheduled processors. In Proc. of HPCA, 1998.
15. V.V. Zyuban et al. Inherently low-power high-performance superscalar architectures. IEEE Trans. on Computers, March, 2001.
16. D. A. Patterson et al. Computer organization and design, third edition. Morgan Kaufmann Publishers, 2004.
17. N. Kannan et al. Compiler assisted data forwarding in VLIW/EPIC architectures. In Proc. of the HiPC, 2002.
18. X. Zhuang et al. Differential register allocation. In Proc. of PLDI, 2005.
19. Trimaran homepage, http://www.trimaran.org.
20. SPEC homepage, http://www.spec.org.
21. V. Kathail et al. HPL-PD architecture specification: version 1.1. HPL Technical Report, 2000.
22. C. Lee et al. MediaBench: a tool for evaluating and synthesizing multimedia and communications systems. In Proc. of MICRO, 1997.
23. F. C. Chow et al. Register allocation by priority-based coloring. In Proc. of CC, 1984.
24. J. E. Smith et al. Implementing precise interrupts in pipelined processors. IEEE Transactions on Computers, 37(5), May 1988.
25. H. Kim. Region-based register allocation for EPIC architecture. Ph.D. Thesis, NYU, 2001.
26. S. Palacharla. Complexity-effective superscalar processors. Ph.d. Thesis, Wisconsin, Madison, 1998.
27. P. Ahuja, et al. The performance impact of incomplete bypassing in processor pipelines. In Proc. of MICRO, 1995.
28. K. Fan, et al. Systematic register bypass customization for application-specific processors. In Proc. of ASSAP, 2003.
29. P. R. Panda et al. Efficient utilization of scratch-pad memory in embedded processor applications. In Proc. of ECDT, 1997.
30. R. Banakar, et al. Scratchpad memory: a design alternative for cache on-chip memory in embedded systems. In Proc. of CODES, 2002.
31. M. kandemir, et al. Dynamic management of scratch-pad memory space. DAC, 2001.
32. S. Udayakumaran, et al. Compiler-decided dynamic memory allocation for scratch-pad based embedded systems. In Proc. of CASES, 2003.

Bounds Checking with Taint-Based Analysis

Weihaw Chuang[1], Satish Narayanasamy[1], Brad Calder[1,2], and Ranjit Jhala[1]

[1] CSE Department, University of California, San Diego
[2] Microsoft
{wchuang,satish,calder,jhala}@cs.ucsd.edu

Abstract. We analyze the performance of different bounds checking implementations. Specifically, we examine using the x86 **bound** instruction to reduce the run-time overhead. We also propose a compiler optimization that prunes the bounds checks that are not necessary to guarantee security. The optimization is based on the observation that buffer overflow attacks are launched through external inputs. Therefore, it is sufficient to bounds check only the accesses to those data structures that can possibly hold the external inputs. Also, it is sufficient to bounds check only the memory writes. The proposed optimizations reduce the number of required bounds checks as well as the amount of meta-data that need to be maintained to perform those checks.

1 Introduction

Bounds checking is the process of keeping track of the address boundaries for objects, buffers, and arrays, and checking the loads and stores that access those structures to make sure that they do not stray outside of the bounds. The bounds are typically represented by a lower and upper address, in between which the loads and stores can validly access. The bounds check consists of checking a memory access to make sure the address is within these bounds. If a violation occurs, the check may issue an exception [1,2,3], or circumvent the error [4] in a safe fashion.

Buffer overflow attacks can be prevented using bounds checking. Consider a fixed size buffer allocated on a stack. A buffer overflow can occur when the application copies external data into the buffer but does not check for the size of the input data, especially while copying strings (e.g. using strcpy). An adversary can exploit this by copying malicious data or even a program into the buffer. When the buffer is located on the stack, the adversary can overwrite the return address as illustrated in Figure 1, and the control will jump to execute the malicious code upon return from the function. This form of buffer overflow attack is called "Stack Smashing" [5]. Stack smashing has been used in Code Red, Nimda and Slammer, just to name a few Internet worms.

The main goal of our research is to provide efficient bounds checking for pointer based applications such as C and C++, as programs written in these languages are error prone and are easily exploited by adversaries. If the bounds checking overhead is reasonable, then it can be used in the production software to make it secure.

K. De Bosschere et al. (Eds.): HiPEAC 2007, LNCS 4367, pp. 71–86, 2007.
© Springer-Verlag Berlin Heidelberg 2007

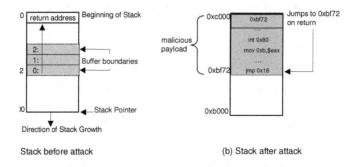

Fig. 1. Stack Smashing example

We first examine the efficiency of various possible bounds checking implementations for C programs. Specifically, we examine the advantages of using the x86 **bound** instruction, which has largely been ignored in the previous studies, and compare its performance with a two-branch [2] and a single-branch [6] bounds check implementations. The bounds instruction reduces the bounds check performance overhead. Also, as it reduces the dynamic instruction count we can obtain significant energy savings.

We focus on static compiler optimizations to provide efficient bounds checking for improving security. The proposed algorithms are based on recent works on preventing buffer overflow attacks. Suh et al. [7], and Crandall and Chong [8] examined using hardware support to tag each memory word with a *taint* bit indicating if the data put into memory was stored there from untrusted sources like the network. Then if any memory address is executed with this taint bit set, a buffer overflow attack is flagged. Assuming this hardware support, they were able to provide this protection with only a few percent slowdown. More recently Newsome and Song [9] implemented this approach using dynamic binary emulation to track data from external sources. They were able to do this without any hardware support, but with a slowdown of 5 times over native execution. Our goal is to achieve the same level of security using bounds checking, but with minimal additional hardware support and performance overhead.

We discuss static compiler algorithms to reduce the number of bounds checks required to guard against buffer overflow attacks. To protect against buffer overflow attacks, not all the memory accesses need to be bounds checked. If we know the memory locations that are prone to buffer overflow attacks, then only the accesses to those locations have to be bounds checked and the rest can be safely pruned away. An adversary can launch a buffer overflow attack only by providing malicious data to the program. Hence, in our analysis, we assume that any memory location that can potentially hold data received from sources external to the program to be vulnerable to buffer overflow attacks. Statically, we can determine such locations by looking for places where the program *interfaces* with the external world through external library calls such as system calls. Any memory location that can receive external data directly from the external sources is considered to be *tainted*. Also, those memory locations that get values from a tainted location is considered to be tainted as well (which can be determined through a simple data-flow analysis). Only the pointer de-references to tainted locations are bounds checked. We call this optimization as the *interface* optimization.

We improve the interface optimization by further limiting the bounds checks to only memory writes, because a worm has to write the malicious data to memory to launch an attack. Also, we can limit the bounds checks to only those memory locations that can hold the data received from the network. All these reductions in the number of bounds checks will also results in reductions in the amount of meta-data that needs to be maintained to perform those checks.

2 Methodology

In this section we summarize our compiler that was derived from McGary's GCC patch [2]. We also describe our experimental methodology and the benchmarks used.

2.1 Compiler

Our compiler is based on Greg McGary's bounds checker [2]. His project contains a patch to the 2.96 GCC sources where the patched compiler generates fat-pointers and compare-branch bounds checks discussed in Section 3. We made several general modifications, as we wanted to experiment with different bounds check implementations, described in Figure 2. To interface with non-bounds checked code, we wrote bounds checking wrappers for many library functions. To eliminate simple bounds check redundancy we modified the GCC value numbering optimization to recognize the bounds instruction and eliminated useless checks. We also implemented simple loop hoisting of bounds checks. Both correspond to an acyclic and cyclic bounds optimization mentioned in Markstein et.al. [10]. Lastly, we modified the compiler to let us do inter-procedural analysis of type information as described in Section 4.

2.2 Benchmarks

Our goal is to reduce the overhead of bounds checking while maintaining the security coverage that bounds checking provides. To measure the performance overhead, we used the SPEC 2000 Integer benchmarks. We provide results for all seven of the C SPEC 2000 Integer programs that compile and run correctly with our baseline McGary gcc compiler. These are compiled on GCC with the -O3 option. The remaining four (gcc, perl, gap and vortex) failed to compile on the baseline McGary compiler.

2.3 Measurements

Our performance measurements are based on using the hardware counters on commercially available processors. For each result, we executed the program three times to factor out random effects while executing on a real processor. Our results are based on the AMD Athlon 2400+ XP (K7), including all of our hardware performance counter numbers.

We did a micro-architectural analysis of the overhead to get a deeper understanding of bounds checking, using Petterson's hardware performance Linux kernel patch [11]. These results include branch misprediction, L1 data cache miss, memory instruction count, and total instruction count. Pettersson's tool provides application level access to these low level hardware performance counters and handles operating system details such as saving and restoring state during context switch.

3   Efficient Bounds Checking for C

In this section we describe three standard representations for the bounds meta-data and the baseline implementations we consider for bounds checking.

3.1   Representing Bounds Information

A bounds checker needs bounds information to perform its verification. We will now describe how this bounds meta-data information is organized and used when a pointer is dereferenced.

Bounds information for static objects is determined completely by the compiler, while bounds information for dynamic objects is determined at run-time. The bounds for an object are created using its size (which can be deduced from the object's type), and the memory location of the object. The bounds are typically represented using a *low bound* and a *high bound*. Alternatively, they may contain the low bound and the object's size.

There are three ways of storing the bounds meta-data to perform bounds checking. They are (a) fat-pointers, (b) a meta-data table, and (c) adjacent to the object (referenced by pointer). A fat-pointer [2,12,3,6] contains the object's low and high bounds adjacent to the pointer. Thus, it changes the pointer's format. This form of bounds representation requires no additional code to locate the meta-data (bounds information), and so it is fast. A second representation of the bounds information is the table lookup approach [13,1]. The bounds meta-data table is indexed using the pointer value to retrieve its bounds. This representation does not require changes to the memory layout of the data objects but lookup incurs significant run-time overhead. Another method for tracking bounds meta-data is to store them with the object. The meta-data for a pointer can be located by adding a fixed offset to the base address of the pointer and so the look-up is efficient. However, this representation may not be reliable with C pointers which can potentially get modified. Also, it doesn't work when the base address for the pointer is not available. Hence, in this paper we use fat-pointers as our baseline, and in some experiments use object meta-data to improve array bounds checking code (where we do not have the issues that we mentioned).

```
start:                      start:                          start:
   flag=(ptr >= low)           tmp=(unsigned)(ptr-low)         bound ptr, b_ptr
   if(flag) then low_pass      flag=(tmp < size)
   trap                        if(flag) then ok
low_pass:                      trap
   flag=(ptr < high)        ok:
   if(flag) then high_pass
   trap
high_pass:
(a) Two Branch              (b) Single branch               (c) x86 bounds
```

Fig. 2. Pseudo-Code for three possible implementations of Bounds Check. (a) Two Branch (b) Single Branch (c) Bound Instruction.

3.2   Check Implementation

We now describe the three main implementations for doing a bounds check. The bounds checks are annotated into the program at the pointer dereference operator and at the array subscript operator.

A bounds check can be done by keeping track of lower and upper bounds for the object and comparing them against the effective address used while dereferencing a pointer as shown in Figure 2(a). McGary's compiler, which we build on, uses this method [2]. This implementation requires the execution of at least four CISC instructions including two branches. There is an alternative implementation [6] that requires the execution of just a single branch as shown in Figure 2(b), using low bound and size, resulting in at least three instructions. A third possible implementation for bounds checking is to use a dedicated **bound** check instruction that exists in the x86 instruction set as shown in Figure 2(c). The **bound** instruction is functionally identical to implementation (a) but eliminates the two additional branches, the extra compares and other arithmetic instructions in the binary.

Prior work on bounds checking has not performed a direct comparison of the different bounds checking implementations. In addition, the prior techniques have not explored the use of the x86 **bound** instruction for their implementations. In this section we provide performance results comparing the three implementations of bounds checking. Before that, we first present a code generation optimization for using **bound** instruction for checking array references.

3.3   Code-Generation of x86 Bound Instruction for Arrays

The x86 bounds instruction has only two operands as shown in Figure 2(c). The first input (**ptr**) specifies a general purpose register containing the effective address that needs to be bounds checked, and the second input (**b_ptr**) is a memory operand that refers to a location in memory containing the low and high bounds. Limiting this second operand to be a memory location requires that the bounds check needs to be located in memory and cannot be specified as a constant or a register value. On execution, the bounds instruction checks if the address specified by the first operand is between the low and high bounds. If the bounds are exceeded, a bounds-checking exception is issued.

For the approach we focus on, we assume the use of fat pointers. Since we use fat pointers, the bounds information for pointers will be stored in memory adjacent to the actual pointer. We would like to use the bound instruction for all bounds checks, but an issue arises when we try to do bounds checking for global and stack arrays, as they are referenced in C and C++ without pointers. To allow the **bound** instruction to be used for these references, we allocate memory adjacent to statically declared arrays to hold the meta-data bounds information, which will be created and initialized when the arrays are created. Since the bounds information for the global and local arrays are now located adjacent to the object data memory, the **bound** instruction can take in the corresponding memory location as its second operand to do bounds checking for these arrays. This memory location is located at a fixed offset from the base of the array. Out of the techniques we examined, we found this method to provide the best performance for bounds checking array references, and we call this configuration *bnd-array*.

3.4   Analysis

We now examine the performance of the three implementations of bounds checking. The two-branch bounds check (*GM*) implementation is used by the baseline McGary compiler [2]. It has a compare-branch-compare-branch sequence. The single branch (*1BR*) uses one (unsigned) subtract-compare-branch-trap sequence [6]. We compare these checks to our *bnd-array* results that uses *bounds* instruction bounds check with the array meta-data. Reported numbers are overheads in comparison to the baseline without any bounds checking. All three code combinations are shown in Figure 2. We would also like to understand to what extent one can reduce the bounds checking overhead, if one implements the **bound** instruction as efficiently as possible in a processor. To do this, we generated a binary similar to *bnd-array* but removed all the **bound** instructions, only leaving behind the bounds meta-data in the program and the instructions to maintain them. We call this configuration as *bnd-ideal*.

Figure 3 shows the percent slowdown for running the programs with the different bounds implementations on an AMD Athlon, when compared to an execution without any bounds checking. The first result of our comparison is that bounds checking using McGary's (GM) compiler results in overheads of 71% on average. The second result is that using the single branch compare implementation *1BR* reduces the average performance overhead from 72% down to 48% on the Athlon. The third result is that the x86 bound instruction overhead (*bnd-array*) provides the lowest bounds checking overhead when compared to these two techniques with an average slowdown of 40% on Athlon. Finally, performance overhead for *bnd-ideal* is 30% which is only 10% less than the *bnd-array* configuration. In other words, 30% slowdown is due to just maintaining the meta-data.

One important component of overhead is due to increased dynamic instruction count as seen in Figure 4. As expected there is significant instruction count

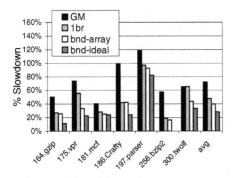

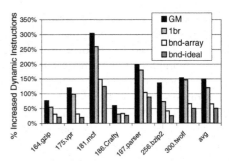

Fig. 3. Run-time overhead of bounds checking (AMD Athlon)

Fig. 4. Increased dynamic instructions due to bounds checking

overhead for *GM* (149%), which is reduced to 121% for *1BR*, and roughly half of that (65% overhead) for *bnd-array*. Of the 65% instruction count overhead in *bnd-array*, only 14% are due to *bounds* instructions and the rest 51% are due to support instructions required to maintain the bounds meta-data (this result is deduced from *bnd-ideal* result which shows just the overhead of maintaining the bounds meta-data).

We also examine the branch misprediction and data cache hardware counters to determine the reasons for the *bounds* performance improvements (graphs not shown due to space limitations). The two-branch *GM* (256%) has much higher branch misprediction rate than the *bnd-array* (11.5%) and the one branch version *1BR* (105%), explaining some of the performance advantages of using *bound* instructions over branched versions. Data cache misses increase in the bounds checking implementations as the bounds information required to perform the checks increases the memory footprint. This overhead is fairly constant across all the implementations as they all keep track of same amount of meta-data.

3.5   Issues to Address for Bounds Checking in C

Because bounds checking requires bounds meta-data to be maintained and associated with pointers, there are a few issues to address. Many of these problems are well known and have solutions, which we cite and use in our implementations.

The type-cast operator in C, might cast a pointer to integer and back to a pointer against, which could strip the bounds meta-data when represented as the integer. One proposed solution, which we use in this paper, is to wrap the integer with bounds meta-data just like how a regular pointer is wrapped [14]. For the programs we compiled for, we found that we had to do this form of type cast infrequently, affecting few variables, and resulting virtually no code bloat. In terms of pointer-to-pointer casts, these are already handled by default because the bounds are transferred to the destination. Even if the pointers have different type representation, the bounds remain valid as the allocated low and high bounds are unchanged.

Linking libraries with application code containing fat-pointers needs to be addressed. The conservative solution is to mandate that library interfaces are fat-pointers in the case where library calls need bounds information. This means that libraries also need to perform bounds checking. McGary's distribution provided a fully bounds checked with fat-pointers patch of libc. Another approach is to use wrappers to interface with non-bounds checked library code, that converts the pointers and performs any safety checks on passed data, as was done by CCured [14]. We use this approach in our simulations, where we wrap each library call by copying the pointer value of a fat-pointer to a normal (skinny) pointer and pass that to the system call. Then on return from the system call, we copy the value of the normal pointer back to the fat-pointer, with the appropriate meta-data, and return. We verified there was no loss in performance or security (for the user code). These interface wrappers can be generated automatically [14].

Buffer overflow can cause denial-of-service when the victim program crashes. Recent work using CRED demonstrates that bounds checkers can continue running even after bounds violations are detected, without any loss of protection [4]. These failure tolerant CRED programs have the same overhead as the original bounds checked versions.

4   Taint-Based Bounds Checking

Bounds checking verifies all pointer and array accesses. While this provides complete protection against all kinds of buffer overflow attacks, it has significant performance overhead. In this section, we present a technique to limit the scope of bounds checking to only those objects that are vulnerable to a buffer overflow attack. The goal of this optimization is to filter away those bounds checks that are not necessary to guarantee security against buffer overflow attacks. The proposed optimization is based on the observation that only the accesses to objects that can hold data received from external interfaces need to be bounds checked.

4.1   Interface Analysis Algorithm

Buffer overflow attacks are launched by an adversary by providing malicious input through the external interfaces to the application. External sources of malicious inputs to the program include, the return values from the library calls such as *gets*, and the command line argument *argv*. In order to protect against buffer overflow attacks, it should be sufficient to bounds check accesses to only those objects that get their values from the external input. We call such objects (and their pointer aliases) as TAINTED and all the other objects as SAFE. A TAINTED object can get assigned to external input either directly from the external interfaces or indirectly from another TAINTED object. Figure 5 shows a simple code example to illustrate what would be labeled as TAINTED when performing our analysis, which we will go through in this section.

Limiting bounds checking to only TAINTED objects can decrease bounds checking overhead but at the same time provide a high level of security against

```
1.  char* gets(char* s);
2.  int main(int argc, char** argv)
3.  {
4.    char tainted_args[128], tainted_gets[128], indirect[64];
5.    char *tainted_alias = tainted_gets; // Pointer alias to object
6.    strcpy(tainted_args, argv[1]);  // source of malicious input: argv
7.    gets(tainted_alias); // source of malicious input: gets()
8.    for(i=0; (tainted_alias[i] != '\0') ; i++)
      { // indirect is TAINTED because it 'uses' tainted_alias
9          indirect[i] = tainted_alias[i];
      }
10.   char safe_array[128] = "I am not tainted"; // SAFE and THIN
      // foobar never passes safe_array to external
      // interfaces nor assigns it tainted data
11.   foobar(safe_array);
      ...
}
```

Fig. 5. Accesses through the pointers and arrays named `tainted_args`, `tainted_gets`, `tainted_alias` and `indirect` need to be bounds checked. The array and pointer `tainted_args` and `tainted_alias` get their values directly from the external interfaces - `argv` and the library call `gets` respectively. Hence, they are of type TAINTED. The object `indirect`'s value is defined by a use of `tainted_alias` pointer and hence it is also of type TAINTED. All pointer aliases to TAINTED objects are fat pointers. Also, the fat pointer `tainted_alias` will propagate TAINTED to the array `tainted_gets` on line 5. Finally, `safe_array` is determined to be SAFE because it is passed to a function `foobar`, which does not pass `safe_array` to external interfaces and does not assign `safe_array` data from an external interface.

buffer overflow attacks. Reduction in the performance overhead can result from the following two factors. First, we can eliminate the bounds checks for accesses to SAFE objects. Hence, we will be able to reduce the number of instructions executed to perform bounds checking. Second, we do not have to maintain bounds information for all the pointers. This is because the pointers to the SAFE objects need to be only normal pointers instead of being fat pointers. We call the type of normal pointers as THIN and the type of fat pointers as FAT. Reducing the number of FAT pointers also reduces the overhead in initializing them and also copying them while passing those pointers as parameters to functions. More importantly, our optimization can reduce the memory footprint of the application and hence we can improve the cache performance.

Figure 6 shows the steps used for the Interface Analysis algorithm. The goal of the Interface Analysis is to find all the objects and their aliases that should be classified as TAINTED in order to perform bounds checking on their dereferences. As described earlier, a TAINTED object is one that gets assigned with external data either directly from an external interface or from another TAINTED object.

1. Construct the inter-procedural data-flow graph, and initial pointer
   aliasing information for points-to.
2. We forward propagate the points-to alias relationships though the
   data-flow pointer assignment network, generating additional aliases.
3. All objects (including pointers) are initialized to type SAFE. All
   pointers are also initialized to type THIN.
4. Apply the TAINTED type qualifier to the pointers and objects that
   are either assigned to the return values of the external interface
   functions, are passed as reference to external interface functions, or
   get assigned to the command line parameter ARGV.
5. Using the data-flow graph propagate TAINTED forward along scalar
   dependencies and mark them as TAINTED.
6. Add bounds checking to all pointers and array dereferences that are
   marked as TAINTED.
7. All pointers that are bounds checked are assigned to be type FAT.
8. Backwards propagate FATNESS through the pointer assignment network.

Fig. 6. Algorithm for interface optimization

Our algorithm represents information using inter-procedural data-flow, and
points-to graphs. The data-flow graph directly represents the explicit assignments
of scalar and pointer values. The points-to graph represents the relationship
between the pointer and its referenced object. These graphs operate on arrays,
scalars and pointers objects with other types reduced to these basic types. The
TAINTED and SAFE properties apply to all object, while FAT and THIN apply
only to pointers.

The first step of the Interface Analysis is to construct the assignment data-
flow graph, and to discover the initial points-to information from the pointer
initialization. Address operators and dynamic memory allocator functions perform this initialization, returning the reference of an object to a pointer. Next
we propagate the pointer alias relationship, building up our points-to database.
We describe properties of the points-to maintained at this step in the following
section 4.2. Third, we initialize all the pointer and object types to SAFE. The
fourth step in our algorithm is to classify those pointers and objects that are assigned to the command line parameter argv and the return value of library calls
as TAINTED. If this is a pointer, then the object referenced is TAINTED. Also,
those objects whose value can be modified by library calls (pass by reference) are
classified as TAINTED. In our example, in Figure 5, the objects tainted_args
and tainted_gets will be classified as TAINTED after this step. In step five, we
propagate the TAINTED type information forward along the scalar data-flow
graph dependencies, including values from array references. We assume that operations other than copy (e.g. arithmetic) will destroy the taintedness of the
scalar assignment. In addition, we use the points-to analysis to mark any pointers that reference a TAINTED object as TAINTED. This step iterates until the
TAINTED set no longer changes. In doing this propagation, additional objects
may be marked as TAINTED. After this propagation, the array indirect will
get classified as TAINTED in our example code through forward propagation,

```
char x[100]; int c, i=0;
char *y=x,*z;
while ((c = getchar()) != EOF){
  x[i++]=c;
}
z=y;
```

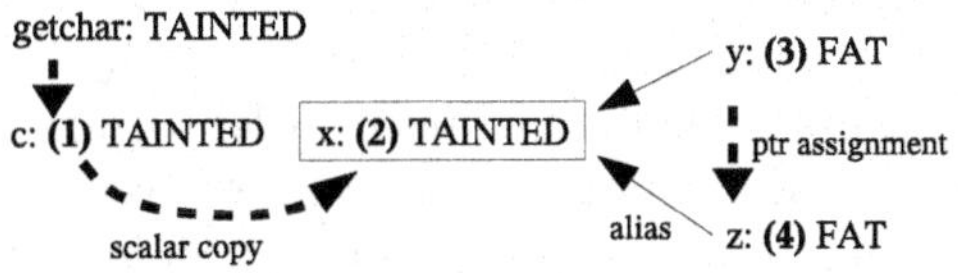

Fig. 7. TAINTED flow via scalar assignment and aliasing

and the array `tainted_gets` will be classified as TAINTED through points-to analysis. In step six, we add bounds checks to all dereferences of pointers and arrays that are marked as TAINTED. In seven, all pointers that are bounds checked will be marked as FAT, and the rest will be marked as THIN. In step eight we backwards propagate FAT through the pointer assignment network to initialization, ensuring bounds information can reach the check.

4.2   Aliasing Properties

We use points-to analysis to determine the objects that pointers alias [15,16,17] for two different purposes. Our first use is to allow pointers to determine if they reference a TAINTED object for which we use Andersen [16] to represent multiple alias relationships. From object aliasing we determine if the pointer references a TAINTED or SAFE object, consequently whether the pointer must be designated FAT or THIN. The second use is to fuse the multiple pointer-to-pointer aliases into a single class, as fusing simplifies how we use the alias information. This version of points-to helps us recognize nested pointers, and prevent conflicting pointer representations. Steensgaard [15] analysis does this fused points-to analysis for us. Consider as an example the type `char **`, which is a pointer to a char pointer `char *`. Variables that assign to or are assigned from the `char *` must have all of the same label, which is either THIN or FAT. TAINTED is similarly made consistent. Both points-to analysis use the pointer propagation data-flow to discover additional aliases.

Consider the following example of data-flow and alias analysis in figure 7. We propagate TAINTED forward through scalars to correctly mark the array `x`, where getchar() is an external interface that may attempt to inject insecure code. Dataflow discovers pointer assignment `z=y`; meaning `z` shares `y` aliases, and points-to analysis would discover that pointers `y` and `z` aliases `x`. The pointer `y` and `z` become FAT, and remain FAT even if they later in the control flow point to a SAFE object.

4.3   Memory Writer Algorithm

In addition to the above *interface* optimization, we also perform another optimization which we call the *memory-writer* optimization. Buffer overflow attacks for remote execution of malicious code are launched by writing beyond the boundaries of a buffer, which implies that we have to do bounds checking only for memory accesses that are writes in order to guard against write attacks. Write attacks are the most common form of buffer overflow attack, and probably the most serious due to the possibility of its use in injecting malicious code. We now describe the memory writer algorithm that can be used by itself, and then explain how it can be used with the interface optimization.

Mem-Write Only - The first step is to mark all writes to array and pointer dereferences as being bounds checked. These are left hand side of assignments through array and pointer dereferences. All of these pointers are marked as FAT. The next step is to find any pointer that will directly or indirectly (through data-flow) define these writes, so that they will also be marked as FAT. They need to be FAT, since they need to also maintain bounds meta-data information for the bounds check. For this we start from the FAT writes and propagate the type FAT backwards, along the edges of the data-flow graph through pointer assignments, to find all pointers that *define* the value of any FAT pointer.

Mem-Write with Interface Optimization - For this approach, we first perform the interface algorithm in Figure 6. The only modification is step 6, where we only add bounds checking for arrays or pointers to buffers that are written as described above and marked as TAINTED.

4.4   Implementation Details

We build a data-flow framework to prune the unnecessary bounds checks. Our variable naming scheme is similar to the one used by Austin et.al. [6] capable of differentiating scalars, references, arrays and fields in structures. Next, we build a graph representing assignments of data-flow information, derived from program assignment statements, address operators, function parameters and return values. After building our data-flow graph on a per function level, we merge the graphs to create a global inter-procedural graph. Our type-based data-flow analysis is path-insensitive; a qualifier that is computed for a variable holds throughout the entire program. Changes to the representation are seen by the entire program, not just the path whose assignment caused it. Similarly, type information passed through procedure calls to other functions must be consistent across all the call sites as we permit only one representation (no function specialization) of that parameter inside of the function. For example, if a pointer parameter becomes FAT at one call site, then that same parameter will be labeled as FAT for all other call sites to that function. In other words, our inter-procedural analysis is context insensitive. Both path and context insensitivity greatly simplify the analysis. In addition, indirect function calls are also treated conservatively, where all possible function definitions that might match an indirect call site will have their parameters assigned with the same FAT or THIN label.

4.5   Network External Interface Results

Our analysis and the pruning of bounds checking can be applied to all external interfaces to an application, which would include disk, keyboard, mouse, cross-process communication, network traffic, etc. Or it could be applied to just a subset of these interfaces.

The current systems based upon dynamic taint analysis only focus on bounds checking accesses to tainted data received from the network [7,8,9], since this is the channel through which a worm attack can occur. Hence, we can limit bounds check to buffers that are passed to the network system calls, and any of the data in the program that is tainted by it.

To analyze this optimization, we performed our bounds checking analysis on the benchmark ATPhttpd-0.4b, which is a small web server, with a buffer overflow vulnerability [9]. In applying our external interface only guarding against write attacks as described above, we experience only a 6% slowdown over no bounds checking. We also verified that the vulnerability was caught using our taint-based bounds checking approach.

4.6   All External Interface Results

Since the SPEC integer benchmark suite does not have any network traffic, the amount of bounds checking is zero, which is not that interesting of a result to analyze. Therefore, we also examined applying our interface optimization for all system call interfaces to the program. For this set of benchmarks this means that we are bounds checking accesses to data that the application receives from the operating system interface, and anything tainted by it.

In this section we will analyze the advantages of our two optimizations, *interface* and *memory-writer*. The binaries that we used for this analysis are generated using the bounds check implementation that uses the x86 **bound** instruction. The code generator that we used is the same as the one used for generating the *bnd-array* binaries that we discussed in Section 3.3. We conducted this experiment on a AMD Athlon processor.

Figure 8 shows the performance advantage of our optimizations. The result labeled as *bnd-interface-only* corresponds to implementing only the interface optimization. The result corresponding to the label *bnd-mem-write* refers to our memory-writer only optimization, and *bnd-interface+mem-write* stands for the implementation where we applied both.

When each of the two optimizations are applied individually, the interface optimization reduces the overhead to 29%, whereas the memory-writer optimization reduces the overhead down to 28%. When both of the optimizations are applied together we find that the average overhead is reduced to 24%, which is a significant reduction when compared to our previous best result of 40% that we achieved using the *bnd_array* implementation.

The *bnd-interface-only* represents performing bounds checks and maintaining fat pointers for all tainted data coming from external interfaces. This provides protection against both write and read buffer overflow attacks. Since write buffer

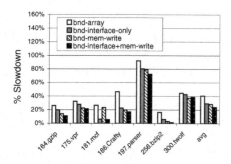
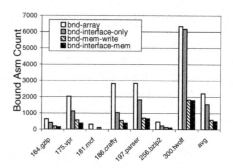

Fig. 8. Performance advantage of interface and memory-writer optimizations

Fig. 9. Reduction in the number of static bounds instruction in the binary

overflow attacks are the most harmful, *bnd-interface+mem-write* provides protection for all writes that write data from external interfaces.

To analyze the main source of reduction in the performance overhead, in Figure 9 we show the number of *static* bounds check instructions that remain in the binary after applying our optimizations. We can see that the *bnd-array* implementation, where we bounds check all of the memory accesses through pointers, contains 2203 x86 bounds instructions on average. Our interface optimization which eliminates the bounds checks to the SAFE objects is able to remove 660 bounds checks from the binary to 1573 on average. The memory-writer optimization eliminates the bounds check to all the load memory operations. Hence, it significantly reduces the number of checks to 581 on average. When both the optimizations are combined together there are about 495 bounds checks left in the binary on average.

The performance savings shown in Figure 8 are proportional to the number of bounds checks that we managed to eliminate. We would like to highlight the result for our pointer intensive application mcf. For mcf, we see significant performance reduction for interface only optimization. The reason for this is that the there was a decent size reduction in the heap memory used as a result of our interface optimization as it managed to classify 50% of the pointers as THIN pointers.

4.7 Verification

We used Wilander security benchmarks [18] and the Accmon [19] programs with buffer overflow vulnerabilities to verify that our interface optimization and memory-writer optimization do not compromise security. For this analysis, we applied our taint-based bounds checking to all the system calls. Wilander provides a set of kernel tests that behave as if it is an adversary trying a buffer overflow exploit [18]. It checks for overwriting of the return address, base pointer, function pointers, and long jump buffer. This is done for the stack and heap over twenty tests. All the exploits in the Wilander and Accmon benchmarks were caught by our bounds checking mechanism that is optimized using the *interface* and *memory-writer* optimization techniques.

5   Conclusion

Bounds checking can prevent buffer overflow attacks. The key limitation in using bounds checking in the production software is its performance overhead, reducing this was the focus of our work. We first examined how to efficiently provide complete bounds checking for all pointer dereferences using the x86 **bound** instruction, which resulted in 40% overhead. We then examined performing bounds checks for only tainted data received from the external interfaces. This provides protection against both write and read buffer overflow attacks, and resulted in an average overhead of 29%. If we only care about write buffer overflow attacks, then we need to bounds check only the writes, which incurred 24% overhead. Finally, if we are only interested in bounds checking data from the network, we showed that overhead can be reduced to just 6%. Bounds checking provides greater protection than the hardware and dynamic taint based approaches [7,8,9] as it protects not only against control but also data buffer overflow attacks. In addition, it does not require any additional hardware [7,8]. When compared to using dynamic emulation system [9] it incurs less performance overhead.

Acknowledgments

We would like to thank the anonymous reviewers for providing helpful comments on this paper. This work was funded in part by NSF grant CNS-0509546 and grants from Microsoft and Intel.

References

1. Ruwase, O., Lam, M.: A practical dyanmic buffer overflow detector. In: 11th Annual Network and Distributed Security Symposium (NDSS 2004), San Diego, California (2004) 159–169
2. G. McGary: Bounds Checking in C and C++ using Bounded Pointers (2000) http://gnu.open-mirror.com/software/gcc/projects/bp/main.html.
3. Necula, G.C., McPeak, S., Weimer, W.: CCured: Type-safe retrofitting of legacy code. In: Symposium on Principles of Programming Languages. (2002) 128–139
4. Rinard, M., Cadar, C., Dumitran, D., Roy, D., Leu, T., Jr., W.S.B.: Enhancing server availability and security through failure-oblivious computing. In: 6th Symposium on Operating System Design and Implementation(OSDI). (2004)
5. Levy, E.: Smashing the stack for fun and profit. Phrack **7**(49) (1996)
6. Austin, T.M., Breach, S.E., Sohi, G.S.: Efficient detection of all pointer and array access errors. In: Symposium on Programming Language Design and Implementation. (1994) 290–301
7. Suh, G., Lee, J., Zhang, D., Devadas, S.: Secure program execution via dynamic information flow tracking. In: Eleventh International Conference on Architectural Support for Programming Languages and Operating Systems. (2004)
8. Crandall, J., Chong, F.: Minos: Control data attack prevention orthogonal to memory model. In: 37th International Symposium on Microarchitecture. (2004)

9. Newsome, J., Song, D.: Dynamic taint analysis for automatic detection, analysis, and signature generation of exploits on commodity software. In: 12th Annual Network and Distributed System Security Symposium. (2005)
10. Markstein, V., Cocke, J., Markstein, P.: Optimization of range checking. In: Symposium on Compiler Construction. (1982) 114–119
11. Pettersson, M.: Hardware performance counter (2004) http://user.it.uu.se/ mikpe/linux/perfctr/.
12. Jim, T., Morrisett, G., Grossman, D., Hicks, M., Cheney, J., Wang, Y.: Cyclone: A safe dialect of c. In: USENIX Annual Technical Conference. (2002) 275–288
13. Jones, R., Kelly, P.: Backwards-compatible bounds checking for arrays and pointers in c programs. In: Automated and Algorithmic Debugging. (1997) 13–26
14. Harren, M., Necula, G.C.: Lightweight wrappers for interfacing with binary code in ccured. In: Software Security Symposium (ISSS'03). (2003)
15. Steensgaard, B.: Points-to analysis in almost linear time. In: Symposium on Principles of Programming Languages. (1996) 32–41
16. Andersen, L.: Program Analysis and Specialization for the C Programming Language. PhD thesis, DIKU, University of Copenhagen (1994) (DIKU report 94/19).
17. II, M.S., Horwitz, S.: Fast and accurate flow-insensitive points-to analysis. In: Symposium on Principles of Programming Languages. (1997) 1–14
18. Wilander, J., Kamkar, M.: A comparison of publicly available tools for dynamic buffer overflow prevention. In: Proceedings of the 10th Network and Distributed System Security Symposium. (2003) 149–162
19. Zhou, P., Liu, W., Fei, L., Lu, S., Qin, F., Midkiff, Y.Z.S., Torrellas, J.: Accmon: Automatically detecting memory-related bugs via program counter-based invariants. In: 37st International Symposium on Microarchitecture. (2004)

Reducing Exit Stub Memory Consumption in Code Caches

Apala Guha, Kim Hazelwood, and Mary Lou Soffa

Department of Computer Science
University of Virginia

Abstract. The interest in translation-based virtual execution environments (VEEs) is growing with the recognition of their importance in a variety of applications. However, due to constrained memory and energy resources, developing a VEE for an embedded system presents a number of challenges. In this paper we focus on the VEE's memory overhead, and in particular, the code cache. Both code traces and exit stubs are stored in a code cache. Exit stubs keep track of the branches off a trace, and we show they consume up to 66.7% of the code cache. We present four techniques for reducing the space occupied by exit stubs, two of which assume unbounded code caches and the absence of code cache invalidations, and two without these restrictions. These techniques reduce space by 43.5% and also improve performance by 1.5%. After applying our techniques, the percentage of space consumed by exit stubs in the resulting code cache was reduced to 41.4%.

1 Introduction

Translation-based VEEs are increasingly being used to host application software because of their power and flexibility. The uses of VEEs include binary retranslation [1,2], program shepherding [3,4], power management [5] and many others. Although VEEs have been used in PC environments, they have not been thoroughly explored in the embedded world.

Embedded systems are widely used today. Personal mobile devices, sensor networks, and consumer electronics are fields that make extensive use of embedded technology. VEEs can have the same benefits in the embedded world as they do in the general-purpose world. For example, there are many different embedded instruction-set architectures, and as a result, little reuse of embedded software. Binary retranslation VEEs can address this issue. Security is important on embedded devices such as PDAs which often download third-party software, and program shepherding VEEs are important in this respect. In some situations, VEEs may be more important for embedded devices than general-purpose devices. For example, power management VEEs are arguably more important to battery-powered embedded devices than general-purpose machines.

VEEs introduce an extra software layer between the application and the hardware and use machine resources in addition to the guest application. For instance,

K. De Bosschere et al. (Eds.): HiPEAC 2007, LNCS 4367, pp. 87–101, 2007.

Strata [3,6] has an average slowdown of 16% for the x86 architecture. Meanwhile, DynamoRIO has been shown to have a 500% memory overhead [7].

A code cache is used in most VEEs to store both application code and exit stubs. If the next instruction to be executed is not in the code cache, exit stubs (or trampolines) are used to return control to the VEE to fetch the next instruction stream. It is beneficial to reduce the space demands of a code cache. First, a small code cache reduces the pressure on the memory subsystem. Second, it improves instruction cache locality because the code is confined to a smaller area within memory, and is therefore more likely to fit within a hardware cache. Third, it reduces the number of cache allocations and evictions. Solutions for managing the size of code caches (using eviction techniques) have been proposed elsewhere [7], yet those studies focused on code traces. To our knowledge, this is the first body of work that focuses specifically on the memory demands of exit stubs. Furthermore, this is the first code cache investigation that focuses on an embedded implementation.

Exit stubs typically have a fairly standard functionality. They are duplicated many times in the code cache and are often not used after the target code region is inserted into the code cache, providing ample opportunity for optimization.

In this paper, we explore the memory overhead of stubs in a translation-based VEE and examine techniques for minimizing that space. We present four techniques that work for both single-threaded and multi-threaded programs. The first two techniques delete stubs that are no longer needed but assume unlimited code caches and the absence of flushing. They remove stubs in their entirety when these stubs are guaranteed not to be needed anymore. Although there are many such applications which do not violate these assumptions and still have a reasonable code cache size, it is also important to be able to handle situations where flushing occurs. The last two techniques, therefore, lift these restrictions and identify stub characteristics that can reduce space requirements.

The specific contributions of this paper are:

- A demonstration of the overhead of exit stubs in a code cache.
- The presentation of two schemes that use a deletion approach to reduce the space occupied by stubs in an application independent and partially VEE-independent manner.
- The presentation of two schemes which identify characteristics of stubs which can be further optimized to minimize their space requirements.
- Experimental results that demonstrate these schemes not only save space but also improve performance.

In Sect. 2, we provide an overview of the internal workings of a VEE, including the translation engine, the code cache, and an overview of exit stubs. In Sect. 3, we describe the four techniques developed for reducing the size of the code cache by optimizing the exit stubs. The experimental evaluation of our techniques is presented in Sect. 4. We describe related work in Sect. 5 and conclude in Sect. 6.

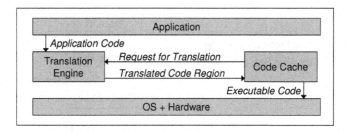

Fig. 1. Block diagram of a typical translation-based VEE

2   Background

A VEE hosts and controls the execution of a given application. It can dynamically modify the application code to achieve functionality that is not present in the original application. Fig. 1 is a simplified diagram of a translation-based VEE. The VEE is shown to consist of two components – a translation engine and a software code cache. The software code cache is a memory area managed by the translator, which contains code from the guest application. The translation engine is responsible for generating code and inserting it into the code cache dynamically. This code executes natively on the underlying layers. While the VEE may appear below the OS layer or may be co-designed with the hardware, the software architecture still corresponds to Fig. 1.

2.1   Translation Engine

The translation engine dynamically translates and inserts code into the code cache. As the cached code executes, it may be necessary to insert new code into the code cache. Requests to execute target code are generated on the fly and sent to the translation engine. After generating and inserting the desired code, the translation engine may patch the requesting branch to point to the newly inserted code. If the requesting branch is a direct branch or call, patching is always done to link the branch to its target. However, in the case of indirect branches, linking does not occur because the branch target may change.

2.2   Code Cache

The code cache is a memory area allocated to store the guest application code. It may be allocated as a single contiguous area of memory or in regions (called *cache blocks*), which may appear at arbitrary memory locations. If composed of several blocks, these blocks may be allocated at one time or on demand.

The code cache consists of application code and exit stubs. Application code is fetched from the guest application (and may or may not appear in the same physical order as in the original application). Some extra code may be interleaved with the original code to achieve the VEE's goal. For example, Pin [8] interleaves instrumentation code with the guest application code. The application code can

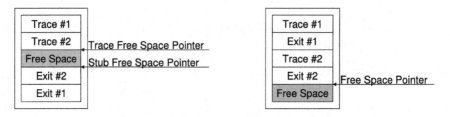

(a) Traces and stubs filled from opposite ends of code cache

(b) Traces and stubs contiguous in code cache

Fig. 2. Two typical arrangements of traces and exit stubs in code cache

be cached at several different granularities, e.g., traces (single-entry, multiple-exit code units), basic blocks (single-entry, single-exit code units), or pages. For every branch instruction in the application code, there exists an exit stub in the code cache.

Fig. 2 shows two typical arrangements of application code and exit stubs in the code cache. In Fig. 2, the code is inserted into the code cache as traces (which is common). A trace has several trace exits. There is a stub for each trace exit, and the stubs for a particular trace form a chain. Each block marked *Exit* in Fig. 2 symbolizes a chain of stubs for a given trace. As shown in Fig. 2(a), a code cache may be filled by inserting traces and stubs in different portions (opposite ends, for example) of the code cache, or a trace and its corresponding stubs can be contiguous in the code cache as shown in Fig. 2(b).

If a point is reached when there is not enough free space for insertion of a code unit into the code cache, new cache blocks are allocated. If the code cache is limited and the limit is reached, or allocation is not allowed, then some cached code must be deleted to make room for the new code. Deletions may occur at several granularities: (1) the entire code cache may be flushed, (2) selected cache blocks may be flushed, (3) selected traces may be flushed. Whenever a code unit is marked for flushing, all branch instructions that point to it must be redirected to their stubs, so that control may return to the translator in a timely manner. When all the incoming links for the code unit are removed, it can be flushed. Flushing may occur all at once, or in a phased manner. For example, for multithreaded host applications, code caches are not flushed until all threads have exited the corresponding code cache area.

2.3   Exit Stubs

An exit stub is used to return control to the translator and communicate the next instruction to translate, if it is not available in the code cache. Some code and data are needed to transfer control to the translator. The code will typically consist of saving the guest application's context, constructing arguments to be passed or loading the address of previously stored arguments and branching into

```
1  sub sp, sp, 80h              1  mov eax, [predef memory location]
2  stm sp, [mask = 0xff]        2  mov [addr of stub data], eax
3  ld r0, [addr of args]        3  jmp [addr of translator handler]
4  ld pc, [addr of handler]
```

(a) Pin's exit stub code for ARM   (b) DynamoRIO's exit stub code for x86

```
1  pusha
2  pushf
3  push [target PC]
4  push [fragment addr]
5  push reenter code cache
6  jmp [addr of fragment builder]
```

(c) Strata's exit stub code for x86

Fig. 3. Examples of exit stub code from different VEEs

the translator handler. The data typically consists of arguments to be passed, such as the target address for translation.

Fig. 3 shows the exit stub code for three different VEEs – Pin, DynamoRIO, and Strata. In line 1 of Fig. 3(a), the application stack pointer is shifted to make space for saving the context. In line 2, the application context is saved using the store multiple register (stm) command. The mask 0xff specifies that all 16 registers have to be saved. In line 3, register r0 is loaded with the address of translator arguments. In line 4, the program counter is loaded with the translator handler's address, which is essentially a branch instruction.

Fig. 3(b) shows DynamoRIO's exit stub code. The eax register is saved in a pre-defined memory location in line 1. In line 2, eax is loaded with the address of exit stub data and line 3 transfers control to the translator handler.

Fig. 3(c) shows a Strata exit stub. The context is saved and arguments are passed to the translator. The address for reentering the code cache is saved for tail call optimization. The last instruction transfers control to the translator.

Exit stubs have associated data blocks that are arguments passed to the translator. The exact arguments depends on the particular VEE. In Pin, the target address for the branch instruction corresponding to the stub is stored. The exit stub can correspond to direct or indirect branches or calls to emulate code and each branch is serviced differently. So, the exit stub stores the type of branch it services, and other data, such as a hash code corresponding to the region of code requested.

Fig. 4 shows two possible layouts of stubs for a given trace. In Fig. 4, stubs 1 and 2 are constituents of the *Exit* block in Fig. 2. The code and data for each stub may appear together as shown in Fig. 4(a), or they may be arranged so that all the code in the chain of stubs appear separately from all the data in the chain of stubs, as shown in Fig. 4(b). As we show in Sect. 3.3, the first layout conserves more space.

| Stub #1 Code |
| Stub #1 Data |
| Stub #2 Code |
| Stub #2 Data |

| Stub #1 Code |
| Stub #2 Code |
| Stub #1 Data |
| Stub #2 Data |

(a) Intermixed stub code and data   (b) Separated stub code and data

Fig. 4. Two arrangements of stubs for a given trace in the code cache

Initially, all branches are linked to their corresponding exit stubs. However, when a branch gets linked to its target, these exit stubs become unreachable.

Table 1. Percentage of code cache consisting of exit stubs

VEE	Exit Stub Percentage
Pin	66.67%
Strata	62.59%
DynamoRIO	62.78%

Table 1 shows the space occupied by exit stubs in Pin, Strata and Dy-namoRIO [9]. As the numbers demonstrate, the large amount of space occupied by stubs show that a lot of memory is being used by code that does not correspond to the hosted application. The data for Pin and Strata were obtained using log files generated by the two VEEs. The data for DynamoRIO[9] was calculated from space savings achieved when exit stubs are moved to a separate area of memory.

3   Methodology

In this section, we describe our approaches for improving the memory efficiency of VEEs by reducing the space occupied by stubs. We describe four techniques, all of which are applicable to both single-threaded and multi-threaded applications. The first set of solutions eliminate stubs, while the latter set reduces the space occupied by stubs. However, the first two approaches are restricted to the case of unbounded code caches where no invalidations of cached code occur. The last two approaches are free of these restrictions.

3.1   Deletion of Stubs (D)

In the deletion of stubs (D) scheme, we consider deleting those stubs that become unreachable when their corresponding branch instructions are linked to their targets. We delete only those exit stubs that border on free space within the code cache. For example, assume the code cache is filled as in Fig. 2(a) and the stubs are laid out as in Fig. 4(a). If the branch corresponding to stub 1 is linked

```
1  if (branch corresponding to an exit stub is linked to a trace)
2      if (end of exit stub coincides with free space pointer)
3          move free space pointer to start of exit stub
```

Fig. 5. Algorithm for deletion of stubs

and stub 1 is at the top of the stack of exit stubs, stub 1 can be deleted. We chose not to delete stubs that are in the middle of the stack of exit stubs, as this will create fragmentation which complicates the code cache management. (We would have to maintain a free space list which uses additional memory. In fact, each node on the free space list will be comparable to the size of the exit stub.) Deletions are carried out only in those areas of the code cache where insertions can still occur. For example, if the code cache is allocated as a set of memory blocks, deletions are only carried out in the last block.

Fig. 5 shows our stub deletion algorithm. A code cache has a pointer to the beginning of free space (as shown in Fig. 2) to determine where the next insertion should occur. If the condition in line 1 of Fig. 5 is found to be true, the free space pointer and the exposed end of the stub are compared in line 2. If the addresses are equal, then the stub can be deleted by moving the free space pointer to the other end of the stub and thereby adding the stub area to free space, as shown in line 3.

The limitation of this scheme is that the trace exits whose stubs have been deleted may need to be unlinked from their targets and reconnected to their stubs during evictions or invalidations. So, this scheme can work only when no invalidations occur in the code cache (because we would need to relink all incoming branches back to their exit stubs prior to invalidating the trace). It can work with a bounded code cache only if the entire code cache is flushed at once, which is only possible for single-threaded applications.

We did not explore other techniques such as compaction and regeneration of stubs for this paper. We believe that a compaction technique is complicated to apply on-the-fly and needs further investigation before its performance and space requirements can be optimized enough for it to be useful. Regeneration of stubs on the other hand, creates a sudden demand for free code cache space. This is not desirable because regeneration of stubs will be needed when cache eviction occurs and cache eviction usually means that there is a shortage of space. Creating space by removal of traces relates to the same problem of requiring the stubs for branches which link to these traces.

3.2 Avoiding Stub Compilation (ASC)

In Scheme D, many stubs whose corresponding trace exits were linked to their targets could not be deleted because the stubs were not at the edge of free space in the code cache. To alleviate this problem, we observed that among such stubs there are many that never get used. The reason is that the trace exits corresponding to them get linked before the trace is ever executed. This linking occurs if the targets are already in the code cache. In these situations, it is not

```
1   for every trace exit
2       targetaddr = address of trace exit
3       targetfound = false
4       for every entry in a code cache directory
5           if (application address of entry == targetaddr)
6               patch trace exit to point to code cache address of entry
7               targetfound = true
8           break
9       if (targetfound == false)
10          generate stub
```

Fig. 6. Algorithm for avoiding compilation of traces

necessary to compile the stub because it will never be used. This strategy saves not only space but also time.

Fig. 6 displays the algorithm for the avoiding stub compilation (ASC) scheme. For every trace exit, the target address is noted in line 2. A flag is reset in line 3 to indicate that the target of the trace exit does not exist in the code cache. Line 4 iterates over all entries in the code cache directory. The application address of each directory entry and the target address are compared in line 5. If a match is found, the trace exit is immediately patched to the target in line 6. After the code cache directory is searched, if the target has not been found, the stub for the trace exit is generated in line 10.

For this scheme, it is always possible for a translator to find target traces that exist already in the code cache and hence avoid compilation. Thus this scheme is independent of the particular VEE's architecture. However, it suffers from the same limitation as Scheme D in that individual deletions may not be allowed. The next schemes overcome these limitations and result in greater savings of time and space.

3.3   Exit Stub Size Reduction (R)

There are some circumstances when exit stubs are necessary, such as during a multi-threaded code cache flush, or a single trace invalidation. In these cases, traces must be unlinked from their target, and relinked to their exit stub. Schemes D and ASC are not adequate for applications that exhibit this behavior. We now present a scheme to minimize the size of a stub and still maintain its functionality.

In the exit stub size reduction (R) scheme, some space is saved by identifying the common code in all stubs. We use a common routine for saving the context and remove corresponding instructions from the stubs. However, the program counter has to be saved before entering the common routine in order to remember the stub location. Fig. 7 shows the code in the stub after this optimization. Saving the context may take several instructions, depending on the architecture. Here, only one register, the program counter is being saved. Factoring of common code is a simple technique that has been implemented in some form in systems (e.g., DynamoRIO), already.

Save Program Counter
Branch to translator Handler
Target Address
Translator Handler Address

Fig. 7. Structure of stub after optimization using reduction in stub size

We handle only the case of direct branches and calls as they are the only branches that are actually linked to their targets. As a result, we know the kind of service being requested and hence can avoid storing the type of service in the stub data area. A specialized translator handler handles these stubs.

We also avoid storing any derivable data within the stub. We reconstruct the derivable arguments to the translator before entering the translator handler. The code for reconstructing the derivable arguments is put in a common bridge routine between the stubs and the translator handler. Thus, we save space by avoiding the storing of all the arguments to the translator and avoid storing code to construct these arguments in the stub. This gives rise to a trade-off with performance but since stubs are not heavily accessed, such reconstruction is not a large time penalty. The stub in Fig. 7 stores only the target address which is not derivable. Storage of derivable data such as a hash of the target address which may enable a faster search of the code cache directory is avoided.

We adhere to the layout in Fig. 4(a) to avoid storing or loading the address of stub data, since the stub data appears at a fixed offset from the start of the stub. (This is not possible for the configuration in Fig. 4(b).) The stub's start address is known from the program counter saved in the context.

This scheme is applied to all exit stubs corresponding to direct branches and calls. Phased flushing and invalidations can be handled by Scheme R as we have modified only the stub structure. Our mechanism is independent of the flushing strategy and the number of threads being executed by the program.

3.4 Target Address Specific Stubs (TAS)

The main task of a stub is to provide the translator with the address of code to be translated next. Yet more than one source location often targets the same address, but uses a different exit stub. For our final scheme, target address specific stub generation (TAS), we ensure that trace exits requesting the same target address use the same exit stub.

Fig. 8 shows the algorithm used in this scheme. The target address of each trace exit is examined. The stub corresponding to the target address of each trace exit is searched in line 3. If the required exit stub exists, it is designated as the exit stub for the trace exit in line 4. Otherwise a new stub is generated and this stub's location is recorded in lines 6-7.

Reuse of exit stubs can occur at several different granularities. For example, stubs may be reused across the entire code cache. Or the code cache may be partitioned and stubs may be reused only inside these partitions. In our implementation,

```
1   for each trace exit
2       targetaddr = target address of trace exit
3       if there exists a stub for targetaddr in this block
4           designate this stub as the exit stub for this trace exit
5       else
6           generate an exit stub for this trace exit
7           store address of exit stub for targetaddr
```

Fig. 8. Algorithm for using target address specific stubs

we reused stubs only at the partition level. These partitions are the *blocks* in line 3 of Fig. 8. The granularity of reuse is important because flushing cannot be carried out at a granularity finer than that of reuse. If flushing is carried out at a finer granularity then there is the danger of not having the required stubs within the code cache portion being flushed. We used the medium granularity as that provides good performance as shown elsewhere [7].

The challenge in applying this technique is that it is not known beforehand whether the trace being compiled will fit into the current block and will be able to reuse the stubs from the current block. We optimistically assume that the trace being compiled will fit into the current block. If it does not ultimately fit, we simply copy the stubs into the new block. However, the case in which the current block gets evicted, copying cannot be carried out. To safeguard against such a situation, we stop reusing stubs when a certain percentage of the code cache size limit has been used, such that the remaining unused portion is larger than any trace size in the system.

All the techniques mentioned above are complementary and can be combined together. If all four techniques are combined, then there is the limitation of cache flushing. However if only the R and TAS techniques are combined, then this limitation does not exist. However, flushing has to be carried out at an equal or coarser granularity than that of stub reuse in TAS.

4   Experimental Results

We evaluated the memory efficiency and performance of our proposed techniques. As a baseline, we used Pin [8] running on an ARM architecture. We implemented our solutions by directly modifying the Pin source code. Before starting the evaluation, we improved indirect branch handling in Pin to predict branch targets without returning to the translator (which was not implemented in the ARM version). This makes Pin faster and the process of experimentation easier. This optimization was included in both the baseline and our modified versions of Pin.

For the experiments, we ran the SPEC2000 integer suite[1] on a iPAQ PocketPC H3835 machine running Intimate Linux kernel 2.4.19. It has a 200 MHz StrongARM-1110 processor with 64 MB RAM, 16 KB instruction cache and a 8 KB data cache. The benchmarks were run on test inputs, since there was

---

[1] We omitted SPECfp because our iPAQ does not have a floating-point unit.

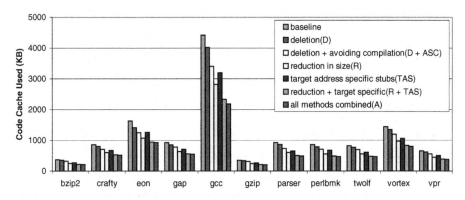

Fig. 9. Memory usage (reported in kilobytes) of Pin baseline (leftmost bar) and after incorporating our optimizations (rightmost bars)

not enough memory on the embedded device to execute larger inputs (even natively). Among the SPEC2000 benchmarks, we did not use mcf because there was not enough memory for it to execute natively, regardless of input set. We chose SPEC2000 rather than embedded applications in order to test the limits of our approach under memory pressure.

Pin allocates the code cache as 64 KB cache blocks on demand. Pin fills the code cache as shown in Fig. 2(a) and lays out stubs as shown in Fig. 4(b).

4.1   Memory Efficiency

The first set of experiments focused on the memory improvement of our approaches. Fig. 9 shows the memory used in the code cache in each version of Pin as kilobytes allocated. The category *original* is the number of KBs allocated in the baseline version.

For Scheme D, the average memory savings is 7.9%. The benefits are higher for the larger benchmarks. For example, it offers little savings in bzip2 and gzip, which have the two smallest code cache sizes. But in gcc which has the largest code cache size, it eliminates 9% of the code cache space. This shows that this scheme is more useful for applications with large code cache sizes, which is precisely what we are targeting in this research.

The next scheme combines ASC and D. Here, the average memory savings increase to 17.8%. Similar to Scheme D, it is more beneficial for applications with larger code cache sizes and less so for those with smaller code caches.

In Scheme R, the memory efficiency is considerably improved from the previous schemes. The average savings in memory in this scheme is 37.4%. The increase is due to the fact that memory is saved from all stubs corresponding to direct branches and calls, which are the dominant form of control instructions (they form 90% of the control instructions in the code cache for the SPEC benchmarks).

Scheme TAS shows a memory efficiency improvement of 24.3%. Furthermore, it is complementary to Scheme R. The combination of schemes TAS and R result in a 41.9% improvement in memory utilization.

Table 2. Percentage of code cache occupied by exit stubs after applying our techniques

Scheme	Exit Stub Percentage
Baseline	66.67%
Deletion (D)	63.92%
Avoiding compilation + Deletion (ASC + D)	59.68%
Reduction in Stub Size (R)	51.24%
Target address specific stubs (TAS)	55.76%
Reduction in size + Target specific stubs (R + TAS)	43.37%
All schemes combined (A)	41.40%

The four schemes combined together achieve memory savings of 43.6%. Therefore, we see that the bulk of the benefit comes from schemes TAS and R which do not carry flushing restrictions.

Table 2 shows the percentage of code cache occupied by stubs (with respect to the code cache size after every optimization) before and after each of our solutions. We were able to reduce stub occupancy from 66.7% to 41.4%.

4.2   Performance Evaluation

In this section, we evaluate the performance of our approaches. Fig. 10 shows the normalized performance of our schemes with respect to the baseline version. Scheme D has almost the same performance as the original version. Extra work is being done in Scheme D to delete stubs. At the same time, more traces inserted into a cache block resulted in improved instruction cache locality. Code cache management time is reduced due to less cache block allocations.

In Scheme ASC + D, some extra time is spent searching the code cache directory for each branch instruction to determine whether an exit stub needs to be compiled. At the same time, the amount of compilation is reduced. Combining these factors with Scheme D yields an improvement in performance.

Scheme R performs as well as ASC + D. Here performance suffers from the fact that derivable arguments are constructed on each entry into the translator due to a direct branch or call instruction. As before, better instruction cache locality and reduced compilation and code cache management time contribute positively to performance. Using TAS also yields about the same improvement.

Using a combination of techniques yields overall performance improvement of about 1.5%, which is especially encouraging given that our main focus was memory optimization. It is important to note here is that the techniques perform better for benchmarks with larger code cache sizes. For example gcc yields 15-20% improvement when combination techniques are applied to it. Smaller benchmarks such as bzip2 and gzip do not reap great benefits in comparison. Benchmarks that use a lot of indirect branches such as eon also do not show considerable improvement. This is due to the fact that the indirect branch handling methods in the XScale version of Pin could benefit from further refinement.

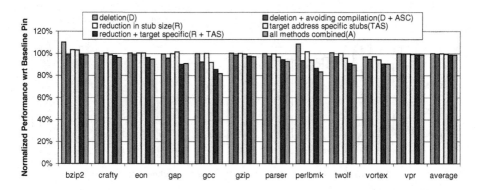

Fig. 10. Performance of proposed solutions as normalized percentages. (100%) represents the baseline version of Pin and smaller percentages indicate speedups.

4.3 Performance Under Cache Pressure

In our next set of experiments, we measure the performance of our approaches in the case of a limited code cache. We evaluated the R and TAS approaches in the presence of cache pressure. We set the cache limit at 20 cache blocks (1280 KB) as this is a reasonable code cache size on our given system. We did not include gcc because the ARM version of Pin fails with this code cache limit for gcc, even without any of our modifications.

Our approaches performed 5-6% better on average. The performance improvement is due to a smaller code cache and a reduced number of code cache flushes. In the limited cache situation, Scheme R performs better than the Scheme TAS (the case was opposite in the unlimited code caches). This is because Scheme R needs fewer cache flushes. The combined Scheme R + TAS performs best in all cases except perlbmk.

5   Related Work

Several VEEs have been developed for general-purpose machines. Among them are Dynamo [10], DynamoRIO [11] and Strata [6]. These VEEs provide features such as optimization and security. In the embedded world, there are relatively few VEEs, with most being Java virtual machines. Standards such as Java card, J2ME/CLDC and J2ME/CDC have been built for embedded JVMs. JEPES [12] and Armed E-Bunny [13] are examples of research on embedded JVMs. Pin [8] is a VEE which supports the XScale platform, but is not a JVM.

There have been many research efforts to reduce the memory footprint of embedded applications [12,14,15]. Management of code cache sizes has been explored [7]. Hiser et al. [16], explore the performance effects of putting fragments and trampolines in separate code cache areas and eliding conditional transfer instructions. However, to the best of our knowledge, reducing memory footprint of VEEs by reducing the size of exit stubs has not been explored before.

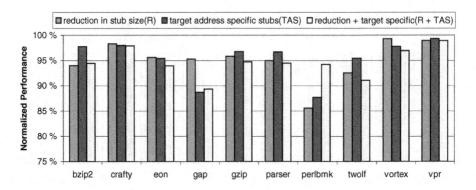

Fig. 11. Performance of `exit stub reduction` and `target address specific stub generation` with cache limit of 20 blocks (1280 KB)

6   Conclusions

Memory usage by VEEs needs to be optimized before they can be used more extensively in the embedded world. In this paper, we explore memory optimization opportunities presented by exit stubs in code caches. We identify reasons that cause stubs to occupy more space than they require and solve the challenge by developing schemes that eliminate a major portion of the space consumed by exit stubs. We show that memory consumption by the code cache can be reduced up to 43% with even some improvement in performance. We also show that performance improvement is even better for limited size code caches which are used when the constraints on memory are even more severe.

References

1. Dehnert, J., Grant, B., Banning, J., Johnson, R., Kistler, T., Klaiber, A., Mattson, J.: The transmeta code morphing software. In: 1st Int'l Symposium on Code Generation and Optimization. (2003) 15–24
2. Ebcioglu, K., Altman, E.R.: DAISY: Dynamic compilation for 100% architectural compatibility. In: 24th Int'l Symposium on Computer Architecture. (1997)
3. Hu, W., Hiser, J., Williams, D., Filipi, A., Davidson, J.W., Evans, D., Knight, J.C., Nguyen-Tuong, A., Rowanhill, J.: Secure and practical defense against code-injection attacks using software dynamic translation. In: Conference on Virtual Execution Environments, Ottawa, Canada (2006)
4. Kiriansky, V., Bruening, D., Amarasinghe, S.: Secure execution via program shepherding. In: 11th USENIX Security Symposium. (2002)
5. Wu, Q., Martonosi, M., Clark, D.W., Reddi, V.J., Connors, D., Wu, Y., Lee, J., Brooks, D.: A dynamic compilation framework for controlling microprocessor energy and performance. In: 38th Int'l Symposium on Microarchitecture. (2005)
6. Scott, K., Kumar, N., Velusamy, S., Childers, B., Davidson, J., Soffa, M.L.: Reconfigurable and retargetable software dynamic translation. In: 1st Int'l Symposium on Code Generation and Optimization. (2003) 36–47

7. Hazelwood, K., Smith, M.D.: Managing bounded code caches in dynamic binary optimization systems. Transactions on Code Generation and Optimization (TACO) **3** (2006) 263–294
8. Luk, C.K., Cohn, R., Muth, R., Patil, H., Klauser, A., Lowney, G., Wallace, S., Janapareddi, V., Hazelwood, K.: Pin: Building customized program analysis tools with dynamic instrumentation. In: Conference on Programming Language Design and Implementation, Chicago, IL (2005)
9. Bruening, D.L.: Efficient, Transparent and Comprehensive Runtime Code Manipulation. PhD thesis, Massachusetts Institute of Technology, Cambridge, MA (2004)
10. Bala, V., Duesterwald, E., Banerjia, S.: Dynamo: A transparent dynamic optimization system. In: Conference on Programming Language Design and Implementation. (2000) 1–12
11. Bruening, D., Garnett, T., Amarasinghe, S.: An infrastructure for adaptive dynamic optimization. In: 1st Int'l Symposium on Code Generation and Optimization. (2003) 265–275
12. Schultz, U.P., Burgaard, K., Christensen, F.G., Knudsen, J.L.: Compiling java for low-end embedded systems. In: Conference on Languages, Compilers, and Tools for Embedded Systems, San Diego, CA (2003)
13. Debbabi, M., Mourad, A., Tawbi, N.: Armed e-bunny: a selective dynamic compiler for embedded java virtual machine targeting arm processors. In: Symposium on Applied Computing, Santa Fe, NM (2005)
14. Bacon, D.F., Cheng, P., Grove, D.: Garbage collection for embedded systems. In: EMSOFT '04: Proceedings of the 4th ACM international conference on Embedded software, New York, NY, ACM Press (2004)
15. Zhou, S., Childers, B.R., Soffa, M.L.: Planning for code buffer management in distributed virtual execution environments. In: Conference on Virtual Execution Environments, New York, NY, ACM Press (2005)
16. Hiser, J.D., Williams, D., Filipi, A., Davidson, J.W., Childers, B.R.: Evaluating fragment construction policies for sdt systems. In: Conference on Virtual Execution Environments, New York, NY, ACM Press (2006)

III Adaptive Microarchitectures

Reducing Branch Misprediction Penalties Via Adaptive Pipeline Scaling

Chang-Ching Yeh, Kuei-Chung Chang, Tien-Fu Chen, and Chingwei Yeh

National Chung Cheng University, Chia-Yi 621, Taiwan, R.O.C.

Abstract. Pipeline scaling provides an attractive solution for increasingly serious branch misprediction penalties within deep pipeline processor. In this paper we investigate *Adaptive Pipeline Scaling (APS)* techniques that are related to reducing branch misprediction penalties. We present a dual supply-voltage architecture framework that can be efficiently exploited in an deep pipeline processor to reduce pipeline depth depending on the confidence level of branches in pipeline. We also propose two techniques, *Dual Path Index Table (DPIT)* and *Step-By-Step (STEP)* manner, that increase the efficiency for pipeline scaling . With these techniques, we then show that *APS* not only provides a fast branch misprediction recovery, but also speeds up the resolve of mispredicted branch. The evaluation of *APS* in a 13-stage superscalar processor with benchmarks from SPEC2000 applications shows a performance improvement (between 3%-12%, average 8%) over baseline processor that does not exploit *APS*.

1 Introduction

The major trend for current high performance processor relies on deeper pipeline to increase operating frequency for higher performance operation. But the increase in pipeline depth often leads to some performance loss due to increasing latency penalties within each branch misprediction. Hence, deep pipeline is generally used to allow aggressive clock rates by sacrificing some IPC. Branch misprediction is the single largest contributor to performance degradation as pipelines are stretched [1].

Since the high control penalties originated from mispredicted branch are inspired by long pipeline length. If the mispredicted branch can occur in shallow pipeline while the other instructions still execute in deep pipeline, the deep pipeline processor should be able to keep high frequency operation in addition to IPC improvement. In this paper, *pipeline scaling* [2] is used as a performance efficient scheme for deep pipeline processor to decrease the considerable misprediction penalties with low architecture overhead. It is both desirable to run as high frequency as deep pipeline and as high IPC as shallow pipeline.

For a mispredicted branch, we make the case that adjacent pair of pipeline stages can be merged to form a shallower pipeline by allowing the latches between them transparent [3] and the corresponding shift to high voltage via a dual-voltage transistor switch [4][5]. If this operation could be occurred rightly during

K. De Bosschere et al. (Eds.): HiPEAC 2007, LNCS 4367, pp. 105–119, 2007.
© Springer-Verlag Berlin Heidelberg 2007

the case of branch misprediction, the large performance penalties should be mitigated, and we could still keep the exclusive high frequency operation held in deep pipeline.

A main drawback for the employment of dual-voltage scheme applied to merge pairs of pipeline stages may incur some additional energy consumption. This makes us to minimize the energy overhead by scaling the pipeline more accurately and strictly. Consequently, the main purpose of *APS* is to improve the performance while retaining the original energy consumption. The contributions of this work are:

– *APS* makes a case for leading the trade-off between performance and energy consumption at the architectural level. It is selectively applied according to the number of low confidence branches. The benefits of this method are demonstrated using a detailed pipeline-level superscalar simulator. The results show a significant reduction in branch misprediction penalties as well as performance improvement.
– We speed up the pipeline scaling via two tricks:
    • Merging pipeline is often delayed by instruction occupancy and voltage transition. A confidence estimator appended with Dual Path Index Table (*DPIT*) is introduced to accelerate the merging period.
    • Splitting pipeline could generally be employed quickly for low power operation. On the contrary, we delay the splitting process and adopt a *Step-By-Step* way to permit a fast branch misprediction recovery.
– It finds that *APS* improves a significant amount of performance (about 8% on the average and up to 12%). In fact, *APS* is so effective that it can not only cut the recovery time of branch misprediction by half but also accelerate the resolve of mispredicted branch.

The structure of this paper is organized as follows. Related work is described in Section 2. We discuss the *APS* architecture and the related mechanism in Section 3. The overall simulation environment, branch misprediction analysis, performance results, and scaling characteristics are presented in Section 4. Section 5 concludes this paper.

2   Related Work

In addition to the improve of branch prediction accuracy, the other way to decrease branch misprediction penalty relies on fetching or executing multiple paths following a conditional branch [6][7]. Since more instructions are in flight at once, the datapath size including register file, instruction window and reorder buffer has to be increased. Moreover, additional functional units and memory ports were also required for more instructions executed. Therefore a large amount of architecture complexity is introduced into the processor design. *Dual path Instruction Processing (DPIP)* [8] is proposed as a brevity style to fetch, decode and rename, but not execute instructions from the alternative path of low confidence branch predictions.

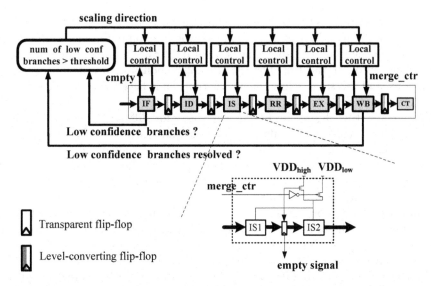

Fig. 1. Adaptive pipeline scaling architecture

For a mispredicted branch, previously proposed *Adaptive Pipeline Scaling (APS)* [2] introduce latch controllers to regulate pipeline depth for limit speculation in single-issue asynchronous pipeline. They allow fewer speculative instructions in the pipeline whereby the energy wasted in discarded instructions could be decreased. With the use of asynchronous design style, they could control each stage independently and do not need any variation on voltage or frequency.

In [9], dynamic pipeline scaling (DPS) is proposed as an alternative power reduction methodology in addition to dynamic voltage scaling *(DVS)* technique for synchronous pipeline processor. Due to the lower bound in shrinking voltage, dynamic voltage scaling *(DVS)* cannot be further exploited while the processor is on lower frequency. Therefore, instead of scaling down the supply voltage, they try to improve instructions-per-cycle (IPC) by merging adjacent pipeline stage for power reduction. To allow dependent instructions executed in consecutive cycles, half-word bypassing is applied in the issue logic.

3   Adaptive Pipeline Scaling

3.1   Architecture

We will use the schematic of the out-of-order superscalar processor shown in Figure 1 to depict *APS*. The baseline is a 13-stage deep pipeline processor. The pipeline shrinks to shorter depth only when the number of low confidence branches exceed threshold. Two operation modes are employed within each pipeline stage. In the shallow mode, the superscalar datapath is built around a seven-stages pipeline consisting of the fetch stage IF, the instruction dispatch stage ID, the issue stage IS, the register read stage RR, the execute stage EX, the write back stage WB, and the commit stage CT. Each stage can be further split into two stages for the deep mode except the commit stage. 1 and 2 are appended to the names of split stages separately. For example, the issue stage (IS) is split into IS1 and IS2. The IS1 stage is responsible to wake up ready instructions, and IS2 stage select the instructions and check the available function unit for execution.

Level-converting flip-flops ($LCFF$) are used for different voltage level conversion. The transparent flip-flop [3] provides that each pair of pipeline stages can be merged or split individually. For each pipeline stage in the processor one of two voltages is selected using large transistor switches [4]. The transparent flip-flops and large transistor switches in each pipeline stage are controlled by the corresponding local controller.

Branch prediction occurs at IF1 stage. Conditional branches are resolved in WB2 stage, and the branch prediction result is updated in CT stage. Finally, a confidence estimator is used to assess the quality of each branch prediction. A low confidence value means that there is a larger possibility of misprediction for the consulted branch. Confidence counter is incremented when a low confidence branch is fetched, and is decremented for a resolved low confidence branch. The pipeline scaling direction for selecting voltage and tuning the corresponding transparent flip-flop to the target pipeline configuration is determined according to the number of low-confidence branches located in each pipeline register.

The IPC(Instructions Per Cycle) in deep pipeline is always affected by the execution latency of critical loops [10]. For example, wakeup and selection logic together have to be accomplished in a single cycle to facilitate back-to-back execution of dependent instructions. To pipeline the scheduling logic, we employ *speculative wakeup* [11] [12] to allow dependent instructions to be scheduled in consecutive cycles.

3.2   Circuit-Level Issues

Instead of running the deep pipeline circuits at fixed low voltage, we scale the supply voltage and pipeline depth for each branch misprediction event. Merging pairs of pipeline stages requires an increase in supply voltage for longer signal propagation path. To keep circuit complexity simple, we limit APS to two supply voltages. The two voltages are referred as VDD_{high} and VDD_{low}. The values of dual supply voltages are located with 0.18um CMOS technology, *Wattch* power simulator [13] and the variable supply voltage applications in [5]. The information shows that the low voltage VDD_{low} is 1.2V and the high voltage VDD_{high} is 2.0V for double speed operation.

Because the static CMOS circuits allow continuous operation during voltage transition, processor does not need to halt for pipeline scaling. However, during the first 1ns from 1.2V to 2.0V, the circuit still operates at lower supply voltage than 2.0V due to the delay associated with the dual-voltage-supply circuit. Therefore, we assume a voltage transition delay of 1 cycle for at most 1 GHz operating frequency [4] [5].

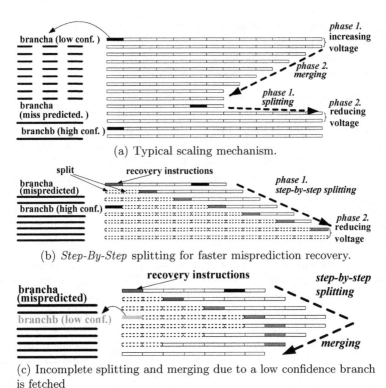

(a) Typical scaling mechanism.

(b) *Step-By-Step* splitting for faster misprediction recovery.

(c) Incomplete splitting and merging due to a low confidence branch is fetched

Fig. 2. Adaptive pipeline scaling mechanism

The additional delay penalty for level conversion could be efficiently allevi-ated by level converter combined with a flip-flop (LCFF). For example, pulsed-precharged level converter (PPR), proposed by [14], achieves a comparable delay to normal D flip-flop. The relative energy and area overhead could be very small to be negligible. Alternatively, the clock racing based differential level convert-ing flip-flop ($CRLC$), introduced in [15], also shows comparable speed compared to the non-level-converting flip-flop. Therefore the inclusion of $LCFF$ in APS could implement level conversion with negligible overhead.

We merge pairs of pipeline stages to form a shallower pipeline by allowing the flip-flops between them transparent, the glitches may also propagate down the pipeline and cause extra power consumption. However, the number of transpar-ent pipeline segment in this application is only one stage, opaque LCFFs act as barriers and prevent the glitches to propagate down the pipeline.

3.3   APS Mechanism

Since the deep pipeline is dynamically merged for misprediction penalty re-duction, there are two steady modes for whole pipeline operation: (a) In the *deep-pipeline* mode, the processor operates at VDD_{low} and deep pipeline for low power dissipation. This is the default mode of operation; (b) In the *shallow-pipeline* mode, the processor operates at VDD_{high} and shallow pipeline for high performance operation. A pipeline scaling example is shown in Figure 2, we suppose processor is initially at *deep pipeline* mode.

Deep-to-shallow pipeline mode transition. APS monitors the number of low confidence branch events. As shown in Figure 2(a), if the confidence counter exceeds threshold while brancha instruction is predicted and evaluated as low confidence, APS begins increasing V_{dd}. During V_{dd} transition, processor still work due to static CMOS design style. This needs 1 cycle for V_{dd} transition as discussed in Section 3.2. After reaching VDD_{high}, empty stages are located for pipeline merging. As there are always many instructions executed in each pipeline stage concurrently due to the high degree of Instruction Level Parallelism (ILP) for superscalar architecture, merging process for busy stages is allowed to wait certain cycles and switch to the shallow pipeline mode.

Shallow-to-deep pipeline mode transition. In the shallow pipeline mode, APS looks for the chance to guide switching back to the deep-pipeline mode for avoiding additional power dissipation by high voltage. As shown in Figure 2(a), the pipeline begins splitting once the number of low confidence branches is below the threshold due to brancha is resolved or branchb fetched in later cycles is classified as high confidence. As pipeline can operate at VDD_{high} even if the pipeline is in the deep pipeline mode, the reduction of voltage is behind the splitting of corresponding pipeline stages. Thus pipeline splitting can be employed quickly.

Since voltage transition and pipeline occupancy does not restrict the pipeline splitting operation, APS could split the overall shallow pipeline in one cycle or step-by-step. The first way is simple but does not consider the recovery process. Once the mispredicted brancha is resolved, recovery instructions just enter processor but the overall pipeline has been switched to deep depth and incurred longer recovery time. Consequently, APS is splitting the shallow pipeline too fast to speed up the recovery operation. With this problem, the second way provides a fast branch misprediction recovery, we try to split the stages in a ***step-by-step*** manner as shown in Figure 2(b). Once the stages (as indicated by the gray box) are refilled with the recovery instructions, APS can split them (as indicated by the dotted box) in next cycle. Hence, the time to recover from branch misprediction should be able to be reduced by short-lived shallow pipeline depth. A detailed analysis for the *step-by-step* splitting is demonstrated in Section 4.2.

Furthermore, if the splitting procedure is not yet complete, another low confidence branches are fetched and low confidence counter exceeds threshold. As shown in Figure 2(c), pipeline operation switches from splitting to merging. Since the initial pipeline is not deep completely, merging pipeline will be faster. Therefore ***step-by-step*** manner could also speedup the merging operation.

3.4   Confidence Estimator

The actions to gate pipeline [16] or execute multiple program paths [8] for low confidence branch predictions can often be processed quickly. But architecture

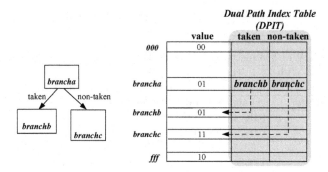

Fig. 3. The confidence estimator added with Dual Path Index Table

variation of pipeline scaling always has to spend multiple cycles to go forward due to the slow voltage transition and the busy of some pipeline registers. The pipeline latches cannot be made transparent until the downstream stage has finished processing its instruction and is ready for the next [2]. Therefore, the cycles this procedure needed is unfixed depending on the distribution of instruction occupancy in each pipeline register.

With the unfixed cycles for pipeline merging, mispredicted branch may have been resolved but APS still wait the chance to merge pipeline. In other words, the scaling direction is shallow, the branch misprediction may still be taken under deep depth due to incomplete pipeline merging. A way to improve this is to provide more cycles for merging deep pipeline before branch is resolved. The decision for scaling direction should be made as early as possible to give more spaces for locating empty stages. To allow the confidence information is captured ahead of time, we exploit a dual path index function within the confidence estimator.

For the conditional branches, there are generally only two possible execution paths. If the confidence information for the next branches in the two possible paths are both included in the confidence estimator, the confidence values for the next branch could be pre-acquired while the current branch is predicted or resolved. With these values, scaling direction can be predicted for the branches which is not yet fetched. The decision of pipeline scaling direction is critical for scaling efficiently. This is done by adding a Dual Path Index Table ($DPIT$) into original confidence estimator.

As shown in Figure 3, once brancha enters into the processor, the next branch can be presumed based on the current prediction result. With a earlier trigger by the overflow of low confidence branch number, APS has more additional time to merge, thus unify more pipeline stages and reduce more latency penalties. A pipeline merging speed simulation to demonstrate the $DPIT$ efficiency is further presented in Section 4.5.

We use a JRS confidence estimator [17]. Our simulation discussed in Section 4 obtains an average SPEC=59% and PVN=32% for all benchmarks in SPECint2000. The PVN values are relatively low compared with other confidence estimator, but the increase in PVN requires considerable extra hardware,

Table 1. The baseline configuration

Fetch Queue	8 entries
Fetch/Decode Width	8 instructions per cycle
Issue/Commit Width	8 instructions per cycle
Function Units	8 integer alu, 2 integer mult, 2 FP alu, 1 FP mult
Branch Predictor	gshare, 16K table, 14-bits history
L1 ICache	64K, 2-way, 32B
L1 DCache	64K, 2-way, 32B
L2 Cache	256KB, 4 way, 6 cycles hit latency
TLB size	ITLB: 16 set 4 way, DTLB: 32 set 4 way
	4KB page size, 30 cycles penalty
Memory	8 bytes/line, virtual memory 4 KB pages, 18 cycles latency

and it is less expensive to increase the scaling threshold [17]. The scaling threshold is used to provide a secondary filter for pipeline merging by determining the maximum number of low confidence branches allowed in the pipeline. Although the processor performance is not degraded if the confidence estimator labels a prediction as low confidence and the prediction shifts to be right, this will increase additional energy consumption for unnecessary merging operation in the transparent latch as well as the voltage transition.

4   Performance Evaluations

4.1   Experiment Model

We use the *SimpleScalar/Alpha* toolset with the *Wattch* power extensions [13]. The simulator parameters are summarized in Table 1. The simulator had been heavily modified based on the architecture described in Section 2.1. The power model in *Wattch* was also extended with the dual power evaluation for the dual supply voltage operation. We use the activity-sensitive power model with aggressive non-ideal conditional clocking (cc3 mode). All applications from SPECint2000 benchmarks are used in our experiments. We skip the first 500 million instructions and simulate the next 500 million instructions. The benchmark characteristics are listed in Table 2.

The branch predictor used in all experiments is a *gshare* with 16k-entry and the JRS confidence estimator has a 4k-entry table with 2-bit resetting counters. *DPIT* needs 8k entries with 12 bits to index the confidence table. Hence the area overhead is less than 10% of the branch predictor. And the extra logic required for index decoding could be shared with confidence estimator. The configuration for different experiments are:

1. *gshare+APS*: The deep pipeline processor improve performance with *APS* mechanism.
2. *gshare+APS(DPIT)*: To speed up the pipeline merging procedure, a *Dual Path Index Table* is appended to the *JRS* confidence estimator.

Table 2. Benchmarks

Benchmark	input set	Branch Inst	MisPred (%)
164.gzip	input.graphic 60	45M	9.69
175.vpr	net.in	48M	11.09
176.gcc	166.i	80M	7.15
181.mcf	inp.in	102M	1.8
186.crafty	crafty.in	53M	11.25
197.parser	ref.in	75M	6.48
252.eon	cook algorithm	54M	4.4
253.perlbmk	scrabbl.in	73M	2.82
254.gap	ref.in	29M	5.78
255.vortex	lendian1.raw	82M	4.86
256.bzip2	input.source 58	51M	8.09
300.twolf	ref	69M	12.41

3. *gshare+APS(DPIT+STEP)*: To slow the pipeline splitting procedure, *APS* split the pipeline stages in a *Step-By-Step* manner.
4. *gshare+APS(Perfect)*: The perfect confidence estimator labels low confidence only on mispredicted branches for pipeline scaling.
5. perfect branch predictor.

4.2   Branch Misprediction Penalty Analysis

In [8], the penalties can be further divided into three distinct subsets: *pipeline-fill penalty, window-fill penalty, and serialization penalty.* The most important components in overall branch misprediction penalty are the *pipeline-fill penalty* (54% of the total loss) and *serialization penalty* (40% of the total loss). All three penalties may be eliminated using multi-path execution, but *pipeline-fill penalty* is greatly reduced since the instructions following the recovery path could be immediately executed once a mispredicted branch is resolved. *DPIP* could only reduce the *pipeline-fill penalty* and *window-fill penalty* [8]. As discussed in previous sections, *APS* reduces the pipeline depth for each branch misprediction. The recovery path is much shorter so as to reduce some requisite cycles for misprediction recovery. Therefore the major sources of the branch misprediction penalty, *pipeline-fill penalty*, can be mitigated by *APS*.

Figure 4(a) shows the recovery instruction ratio with respect to the relative requisite cycles. According to the pipeline architecture discussed in Section 2.1, the minimum *pipeline-fill penalty* for a mispredicted branch is 6 and 12 cycles with respect to the shallow and deep pipeline depth. For each branch misprediction event, we keep track of its recovery period until the first recovery instruction reaches WB2 stage. We can see, in Figure 4(a), that over 60% instructions need 12 cycles to recover the deep pipeline processor and 70% instructions only need 6 cycles for shallow depth. The *APS* processor, as we expected, need 6 cycles to recover by 50% instructions.

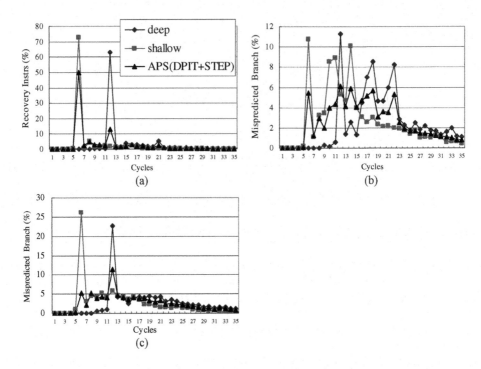

Fig. 4. The analysis of mispredicted branch, correct branch and recovery instructions

Secondly, the time to resolve mispredicted branch could be advanced because branch estimated with low confidence in fetch stage triggers the unifying of empty pipeline stages whereby shorter pipeline length permits faster mispredicted branch move and the recovery instructions could enter the pipeline more "earlier". In other words, the second sources of misprediction penalty, *serialization penalty*, could also be reduced by *APS*.

Figure 4(b) illustrates the relationship between the mispredicted branch ratio and the relative cycles spent in the pipeline. We trace the cycles of each mispredicted branch taken from IF1 stage to WB2 stage. As expected, most portions of mispredicted branches in *APS* need fewer cycles to be resolved. The shallow and deep pipeline still spend 6 and 12 clock cycles respectively. As the reduced clock cycles spent for most mispredicted branches could fetch recovery instructions ahead of time, *serialization penalty* can be reduced.

Finally, we trace the distribution ratio of correct predicted branches. As shown in Figure 4(c), although some portions of correct predicted branches for *APS* move forward to 6 cycles, most still retain 12 cycles. This indicates that large portions of mispredicted branches by using *APS* can be detected more earlier than deep pipeline, as well as the most correct prediction of branches remain at the deep pipeline for avoiding additional energy consumption. *APS* can reduce the large misprediction penalties caused by deep pipeline path, and retains original energy consumption.

Table 3. Average latency of mispredicted branch, correct-predicted branch and recovery instructions

	recovery instruction (cycles)	mispredicted branch (cycles)	correct branch (cycles)
deep	15.9	24.6	21.7
APS	13.4	22.4	20
APS (DPIT)	12.4	21.5	19.3
APS (DPIT+STEP)	10.4	20.5	18.8
APS (perfect)	9.3	20.4	19.6
shallow	8.3	17.5	14.5

Table 3 shows the average weighted latency achieved with different pipeline scaling applications. The average misprediction recovery for deep pipeline processor can be decreased by *APS* from 15.9 cycles to 13.4 cycles. Secondly, for *APS(DPIT)*, pipeline recovery could be reduced to 12.4 cycles, whereas for *APS(DPIT+STEP)* could further achieve 10.4 cycles. To show the potential effect of *APS*, we also apply perfect confidence estimator and provide an average of 9.3 cycles. This result is close to the *APS(DPIT+STEP)*. Thus, with the application of *DPIT* and *STEP* in *APS* can compensate the insufficient accuracy of imperfect confidence estimator and achieve a better improvement for branch misprediction recovery.

The latency for the detection of mispredicted branch has the same trend as previous recovery instruction. With the great improvement in branch misprediction penalty by using *APS*, the negative effect of additional energy consumption caused by high voltage transition should also be accounted. As shown in Table 3, average cycles spent for correct branches has limit decrease from 21.7 to 18.8.

In these simulations, the average cycles are larger than the pipeline length due to the out-of-order processor architecture used in the sim-outorder simulator such that the branches in pipeline must always spend an arbitrarily longer time to resolve. Consequently, the *APS* mechanism has a great reduction on the two major components of branch misprediction, serialization penalty and pipeline-fill penalty, by placing mispredicted branches in shallow pipeline but still exploiting most other instructions executed in deep pipeline for avoiding energy overhead. Figure 4 shows the potential of the *APS* techniques.

4.3   Performance Results

Figure 5 compares the performance benefits of the proposed schemes. IPC is reported as normalized metric number where the normalization is with respect to the metrics of baseline processor. Since *APS* merge the pipeline stages by switching the corresponding voltage, performance may be improved at the cost of arbitrarily increasing in energy consumption. Therefore we profile the suitable number of low confidence branches permitted in the pipeline and get a number

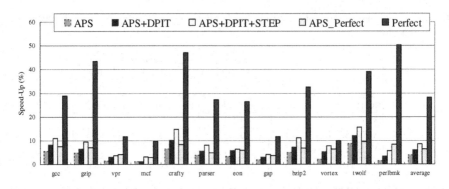

Fig. 5. Relative IPC speedup by *APS* techniques, with respect to the baseline architecture. Higher is better.

of two (as discussed in next section) for retaining a balance between performance and energy consumption.

The *APS* result shows approximately the same trend in performance improvement for all benchmarks we analyzed. The performance improvement ranges from 1.38% (in *perlbmk* benchmark) to 8.7% (in *twolf* benchmark). On average, the obtained speedup for all benchmarks is 3.8%.

To improve pipeline merging speed, the *Dual Path Index Table* is included in the confidence estimator. Since the average branch misprediction penalties for *APS(DPIT)* in Table 3 shows a slight better result over pure *APS*, the performance should be able to be improved. Therefore, as shown in Figure 5, the second experiment *APS(DPIT)* shows an average improvement with 6.5%(up to 12% for *twolf*).

Because the fast splitting in *APS* could result in more time to recover the flushed pipeline, we split in *Step-By-Step* manner and achieve more performance improvement as shown in Table 3. In Figure 5, Experiment *APS(DPIT+STEP)* further improve IPC with 8% on average.

Finally, the potential of *APS* is evaluated using a perfect confidence estimator which use the exact branch decision to determine the direction of pipeline scaling. Since the really mispredicted branch is not found until it reaches the *dispatch* stage, the performance efficiency still cannot have a overall improvement. We can observe in Figure 5 that a perfect confidence estimator yields an average speedup of 7% with relative to the baseline deep pipeline processor. Compared with the speed-up of 3.8% in *APS* configuration, this shows an opportunity for more improvement by using better confidence estimator. *DPIT* are not implemented in *APS(Perfect)* due to the perfect confidence estimation cannot be made early. In most cases the *APS(DPIT+STEP)* actually provides slightly better performance than the Perfect Confidence Configuration. We believe this unexpected result is due to the fact that *DPIT* and *STEP* can aggressively encourage more pipeline merging and reduce more pipeline recovery penalties, thus giving a better improvement in IPC.

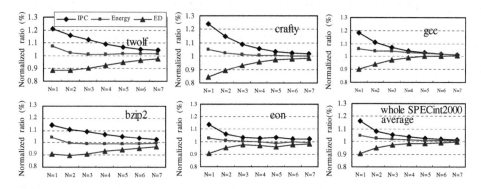

Fig. 6. Average IPC, energy and EDP evaluate as a function of different threshold values(N). The data are normalized to the baseline processor.

4.4   Varying the Scaling Threshold

In order to locate the appropriate parameters applied to pipeline scaling, we take the approach of doing a sensitivity study with the threshold number of low confidence branches. The maximum number of low confidence branches allowed in the pipeline before merging is engaged, N, is a threshold parameter. To find a suitable threshold number, a thorough analysis for every possible value of N is evaluated with $APS(DPIT+STEP)$ scheme.

As shown in Figure 6, the leftmost case shows the evaluation for a configuration with scaling threshold of $N = 1$. This can aggressively trigger pipeline merging while there is just one low confidence branch in pipeline, which provides the best performance improvement with a high energy cost. Moreover, the use of $DPIT$ also represents a relative lower accuracy of confidence prediction. Therefore the performance improvement achieves 17% at the cost of more energy consumption.

If we consider the APS application for locating the balance between performance and energy consumption. In this case, using a threshold value of $N = 2$, there is about a 8.5% improvement in performance with 1.8% energy cost. Furthermore, the configuration with $N=3$ has 5.6% improvement with less 1% energy cost. Therefore, as N increases, energy overhead could be released accompanied with lower speedup. To improve performance while retaining original energy consumption, this figure shows a good choice of scaling threshold to compensate for a low PVN value.

5   Conclusion

In this paper, *Adaptive Pipeline Scaling* (APS) is explored as an efficient way to reduce the branch misprediction penalty for deep pipeline processor. A control machine based on the number of low confidence branches is introduced to guide the scaling direction. This is an alternative heuristic selection between lower power dissipation in deep pipeline and fewer branch latency penalties in shallow

pipeline. Simulation results show that *APS* not only reduces the recovery path
of branch misprediction by half but also detects mispredicted branch more faster,
even though multi-path application [8] could reduce the recovery path completely
after a misprediction. Moreover, combining *APS*, *Dual Path Index Table (DPIT)*,
and *Step-By-Step* splitting could achieve average improvement in performance of
8% with less 2% energy overhead.

References

1. Sprangle, E., Carmean, D.: Increasing processor performance by implementing deeper pipelines. In: Proceedings of the 29th International Conference on Computer Architecture. (2002) 25–34
2. Efthymiou, A., Garside, J.D.: Adaptive pipeline depth control for processor power-management. In: Proceedings of International Conference on Computer Design. (2002) 454–457
3. Jacobson, H.M.: Improved clock-gating through transparent pipelining. In: Proceedings of the International Symposium on Low Power Electronics and Design. (2004) 26–31
4. Suzuki, H., Jeong, W., Roy, K.: Low-power carry-select adder using adaptive supply voltage based on input vector patterns. In: Proceedings of the International Symposium on Low Power Electronics and Design. (2004) 313–318
5. Li, H., Cher, C.Y., Vijaykumar, T.N., Roy, K.: VSV: L2-miss-driven variable supply-voltage scaling for low power. In: Proceedings of the International Symposium on Microarchitecture. (2003) 19–28
6. Kaluser, A., Paithanker, A., Grunwald, D.: Selective eager execution on the poly-path architecture. In: Proceedings of the International Symposium on Computer Architecture. (1998)
7. Ahuja, P.S., Skadron, K., Martonosi, M., Clark, D.W.: Multipath execution: opportunities and limits. In: Proceedings of the International Conference on Supercomputing. (1998) 101–108
8. Aragon, J.L., Gonzalez, J., Gonzalez, A., Smith, J.E.: Dual path instruction processing. In: Proceedings of the International Conference on Supercomputing. (2002) 220–229
9. Koppanalil, J., Ramrakhyani, P., Desai, S., Vaidyanathan, A., Rotenberg, E.: A case for dynamic pipeline scaling. In: Proceedings of the International Conference on Compilers, Architecture, and Synthesis for Embedded Systems. (2002) 1–8
10. Palacharla, S., Jouppi, N.P., Smith, J.E.: Complexity-effictive superscalar processors. In: Proceedings of International Symposium on Computer Architecture. (1997)
11. Stark, J., Brown, M.D., Patt, Y.N.: On pipelining dynamic instruction scheduling logic. In: Proceedings of International Symposium On Microarchitecture. (2000)
12. Brown, M.D., Stark, J., Patt, Y.N.: Select-free instruction scheduling logic. In: Proceedings of International Symposium On Microarchitecture. (2001)
13. Brooks, D., Tiwari, V., Martonosi, M.: Wattch: A framework for architectural-level power analysis and optimizations. In: Proceedings of the International Symposium on Computer Architecture. (2000) 83–94
14. Ishihara, F., Sheikh, F., Nikolic, B.: Level conversion for dual-supply systems. IEEE Transactions on VLSI (2004)

15. Bai, R., Sylvester, D.: Analysis and design of level-converting flip-flops for dual-v_{dd}/v_{th} intergrated circuits. In: Proceedings of the International Symposium on System-on-Chip. (2003) 151–154
16. Manne, S., Klauser, A., Grunwald, D.: Pipeline gating: speculation control for energy reduction. In: Proceedings of the International Symposium on Computer Architecture. (1998) 132–141
17. Jacobsen, J., Rotenberg, E., Smith, J.: Assigning confidence to conditional branch predictions. In: Proceedings of the International Symposium on Microarchitecture. (1996) 142–152

Fetch Gating Control Through
Speculative Instruction Window Weighting

Hans Vandierendonck[1] and André Seznec[2]

[1] Ghent University, Department of Electronics and Information Systems/HiPEAC,
B-9000 Gent, Belgium
hvdieren@elis.ugent.be
[2] IRISA/INRIA/HiPEAC Campus de Beaulieu, 35042 Rennes Cedex, France
seznec@irisa.fr

Abstract. In a dynamic reordering superscalar processor, the front-end
fetches instructions and places them in the issue queue. Instructions are
then issued by the back-end execution core. Till recently, the front-end
was designed to maximize performance without considering energy consumption. The front-end fetches instructions as fast as it can until it is
stalled by a filled issue queue or some other blocking structure. This approach wastes energy: (i) speculative execution causes many wrong-path
instructions to be fetched and executed, and (ii) back-end execution rate
is usually less than its peak rate, but front-end structures are dimensioned to sustained peak performance. Dynamically reducing the front-
end instruction rate and the active size of front-end structure (e.g. issue
queue) is a required performance-energy trade-off. Techniques proposed
in the literature attack only one of these effects.

In this paper, we propose Speculative Instruction Window Weighting
(SIWW), a fetch gating technique that allows to address both fetch gating
and instruction issue queue dynamic sizing. A global weight is computed
on the set of inflight instructions. This weight depends on the number and
types of inflight instructions (non-branches, high confidence or low confidence branches, ...). The front-end instruction rate can be continuously
adapted based on this weight. SIWW is shown to perform better than previously proposed fetch gating techniques. SIWW is also shown to allow to
dynamically adapt the size of the active instruction queue.

1   Introduction

Dynamic reordering superscalar architectures are organized around an instruction queue that bridges the front-end instruction delivery part to the back-end
execution core. Typical performance-driven designs maximize the throughput
of both the front-end and the back-end independently. However, it has been
noted [2,3,12] that such designs waste energy as the front-end fetches instructions as fast as it can up to the point where the back-end fills up and the front-end
necessarily stalls. All of this fast, aggressive work may be performed at a lower
and more power-efficient pace, or it may even turn out to be unnecessary due to
control-flow misspeculation.

K. De Bosschere et al. (Eds.): HiPEAC 2007, LNCS 4367, pp. 120–135, 2007.

Historically, the first step to lower the front-end instruction rate relates to fetching wrong-path instructions. By assigning confidence to branch predictions, Manne *et al* [14] gate instruction fetch when it becomes likely that fetch is proceeding along the wrong execution path. However, with the advent of highly accurate conditional [7,10,16] and indirect branch predictors [5,17], the impact of wrong-path instructions on energy decreases [15].

Besides fetching wrong-path instructions, it has been shown that the front-end flow rate may well exceed the required back-end rate [2,3]. Closely linked to this flow-rate mismatch is a mismatch between the required issue queue size and the available issue queue size. Consequently, fetch gating mechanisms are combined with dynamic issue queue adaptation techniques to increase energy savings [3].

This paper contributes to this body of work by presenting a new fetch gating algorithm built on these principles. Our fetch gating algorithm simultaneously tracks branch confidence estimation and the set of already inflight and unissued instructions. In effect, it modulates branch confidence estimation by issue queue utilization: as issue queue utilization is higher, uncertainty in the control-flow speculation weighs stronger to limit the front-end flow rate. Hereby, our technique avoids both wrong-path work and it matches the front-end flow rate to the back-end flow rate.

To illustrate the advantage of our technique, let us consider the two following situations. In example (A), 50 instructions, a low-confidence and 6 high-confidence branches have already been fetched. In example (B), 5 instructions and a single low-confidence branch have been fetched. If the next instruction is a low-confidence branch then a fetch gating control mechanism based only on branch confidence estimation and boosting [14] will take exactly the same decision for the two situations. A simple analysis shows that for (A), delaying the next instruction fetch for a few cycles (but maybe not until the low confidence branch resolves) is unlikely to degrade performance while for (B), delaying it is very likely to induce a few cycles loss if the two low-confidence branchs are correctly predicted.

The first contribution of this paper is Speculative Instruction Instruction Window Weighting (SIWW). Instead of only considering confidence on inflight branches for controlling fetch gating, we consider the overall set of already inflight and unissued instructions, i.e. the speculative instruction window. SIWW tries to evaluate whether or not the immediate fetch of the next instruction group will bring some extra performance. When the expected benefit is low, then fetch is gated until the benefit has increased or a branch misprediction has been detected. This expected performance benefit increases when (i) branch instructions are resolved or (ii) instructions execute and the number of unissued instructions in the issue queue drops. Our experiments show that fetch gating based on SIWW easily outperforms fetch gating schemes based on confidence boosting [14], fetch throttling [1] as well as issue queue dynamic sizing techniques [3].

A second contribution of this paper is to show that fetch gating control through SIWW can be efficiently implemented without any extra storage table for confidence estimation. Current state-of-the-art branch predictors such as O-GEHL [16] and piecewise linear branch prediction [10] provide a confidence estimate for free. We show that this estimate does not work very well for fetch gating control through boosting, but it works well with SIWW fetch gating and instruction queue dynamic sizing.

The remainder of the paper is organized as follows. Section 2 quickly reviews related work on fetch gating or throttling and dynamic sizing of instruction queues. Section 3 describes our proposal to use SIWW for fetch gating. Our experimental framework is presented in Section 4. Section 5 presents the performance of SIWW and compares it to confidence boosting, the previous state-of-the-art approach. Finally, Section 6 presents possible future research directions and summarizes this study.

2   Related Work

Gating the instruction fetch stage on the first encountered low-confidence branch results in significant performance loss. By delaying gating until multiple low-confidence branches are outstanding – a technique called *boosting* – it is possible to limit this performance loss while still removing extra work [14].

Fetch throttling slows down instruction fetch by activating the fetch stage only once every N cycles when a low-confidence branch is in-flight [1]. This reduces the performance penalty of pipeline gating, but sacrifices energy reduction by allowing additional extra work.

Decode/commit-rate fetch gating is an instruction flow-based mechanism that limits instruction decode bandwidth to the actual commit bandwidth [2]. This technique saves energy even for correct-path instructions, as only the required fetch bandwidth is utilized.

Buyuktosunoglu *et al* [3] combine fetch gating with dynamic issue queue adaptation in order to match front-end and back-end instruction flow rates and to match the issue queue size to its required size. They propose to gate instruction fetch based on the observed parallelism in the instruction stream. Fetch is gated during one cycle when instruction issue occurs mostly from the oldest halve of the reorder buffer and the issue queue is more than half full.

Several techniques to dynamically adapt the issue queue size have been proposed in the literature. Folegnani and Gonzalez [6] divide the reorder buffer into portions of 8 instructions. The reorder buffer grows and shrinks by units of a portion. The reorder buffer is dimensioned by monitoring the number of instructions that issue from the portion of the reorder buffer holding the youngest instructions.

Just-in-time (JIT) instruction delivery [12] applies a dynamic reconfiguration algorithm to adapt the reorder buffer size. It determines the smallest reorder buffer size that yields a performance degradation less than a preset threshold.

In [4], the issue queue is also divided into portions of 8 instructions but the queue size is determined by its average utilization over a time quantum.

3   Speculative Instruction Window Weighting

Instead of only considering confidence on inflight branches for controlling fetch gating, we consider the overall set of already inflight instructions, i.e. the speculative instruction window. Speculative Instruction Window Weighting (SIWW) tries to evaluate whether or not the **immediate** fetch of the next instruction group will bring some performance benefit. Our thesis is that this benefit decreases with the number of already inflight instructions, with the number of branches and with the quality of the branch prediction (i.e. with the confidence in the predictions). The performance benefit may also depend on the precise type of already inflight instructions and parameters such as latency (e.g. divisions, multiplications, loads that are likely to miss), etc.

For this purpose, a global Speculative Instruction Window (SIW) weight is computed on the overall set of unexecuted inflight instructions. The SIW weight is intended to "evaluate" the performance benefit that immediately fetching new instructions would deliver.

The SIW weight is constantly changing. It increases when instructions are fetched and it decreases as instructions are executed. When the SIW weight exceeds a pre-set threshold, instruction fetch is halted. As soon as the SIW weight drops below the threshold, the instruction fetch is resumed (Figure 1).

3.1   Computing the SIW Weight: Principle

The SIW weight is computed from the overall content of the instruction window. To obtain a very accurate indicator, one should take into account many factors, such as dependencies in the instruction window, instruction latency, etc. However, realistic hardware implementation must also be considered. Therefore, we propose to compute the SIW weight as the sum of individual contributions by the inflight instructions. These contributions are determined at decode time.

As an initial implementation of SIWW, we assign a SIW weight contribution to each instruction by means of its instruction class. The instruction classes and SIW weight contributions used in this paper are listed in Table 1.

The weight contributions reflect the probability of a misprediction. Thus, low-confidence branches are assigned significantly higher weight contributions than

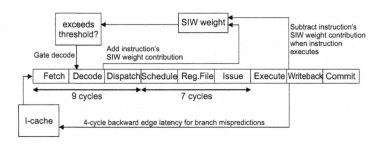

Fig. 1. Block diagram of a pipeline with speculative instruction window weighting

Table 1. SIW weight contributions

Instruction type	Contrib.
high-confidence conditional branches	8
low-confidence conditional branches	40
returns	8
high-confidence indirect branches	8
low-confidence indirect branches	40
unconditional direct branches	1
non-branch instructions	1

high-confidence branches. High-confidence branches are assigned higher weight contributions than non-branch instructions because high-confidence branches too are mispredicted from time to time. Return instructions have a small weight contribution because they are predicted very accurately.

Unconditional direct branches have the same weight contributions as non-branch instructions as their mispredict penalty is very low in the simulated architecture. Mispredicted targets for unconditional direct branches are captured in the decode stage. Fetch is immediately restarted at the correct branch target.

The weight contributions depend on the accuracy of the conditional branch predictor, branch target predictor and return address stack and may have to be tuned to these predictors. The weight contributions describe only the speculativeness of the in-flight instructions and are therefore independent of other micro-architectural properties.

3.2   A Practical Implementation of SIW Weight Computation

In principle, the SIW weight is computed from the old SIW weight by adding the contributions of all newly decoded instructions and substracting the contributions of all executed instructions. Initially, the SIW weight is zero. However, when a branch misprediction is detected, the SIW weight represents an instruction window where some instructions that have been fetched before the mispredicted branch are still to be executed. Restoring the SIW weight to its correct value while resuming instruction fetch after the mispredicted branch would require to retrieve the contributions of these instructions and perform an adder tree sum.

To sidestep a complex adder tree, we approximate the SIW weight by setting it to zero on a misprediction. The SIW weight then ignores the presence of unexecuted instructions in the pipeline. However, the SIW weight contribution of these instructions may not be substracted again when they execute. To protect against substracting a contribution twice, we keep track of the most recently recovered branch instruction. Instructions that are older (in program order) should not have their SIW weight contribution substracted when they execute.

Experimental results have shown that this practical implementation performs almost identical to the exact scheme. In most cases, when a mispredicted branch is detected, the instruction window will be largely drained, causing the exact SIW weight to drop to the range 20–50 (compare this to the SIW threshold of 160). Most of these remaining instructions are executed before the first corrected path instructions reach the execution stage. At this time, the approximate SIW weight is already very close to its maximum value, minimizing the impact of the temporary underestimation.

3.3 Dynamically Adapting the SIW Weight Contributions

The weight contributions proposed in Table 1 are based on the prediction accuracy of particular types of branches (low-confidence vs. high-confidence, conditional vs. indirect, etc.). However, the prediction accuracy varies strongly from benchmark to benchmark, so the weight contributions should reflect these differences. To improve the SIWW mechanism, we investigated ways to dynamically adapt the weight contributions based on the prediction accuracy.

We dynamically adjust the weight contribution of each instruction class in Table 1 where the baseline contribution differs from 1. Each contribution is trained using only the instructions in its class. The contribution is increased when the misprediction rate is high (high probability of being on the wrong execution path) and is decreased when the misprediction rate in its instruction class is low. To accomplish this, we use two registers: a p-bit register storing the weight contribution and a $(p + n)$-bit register storing a counter. Practical values for p and n are discussed below.

The counter tracks whether the weight contribution is proportional to the misprediction rate. For each committed instruction in its class, the counter is incremented with the weight. If the instruction was mispredicted, it is also decremented by 2^p. Thus, the counter has the value $c - f2^p$ where c is the current weight contribution and f is the misprediction rate. As long as the counter is close to zero, then the contribution is proportional to the misprediction rate. When the counter deviates strongly from zero, then the weight contribution needs adjustment. When the counter overflows, the weight contribution is decremented by 1 because it was higher than the misprediction rate. When the counter underflows, the weight contribution is incremented by 1. At this point, the counter is reset to zero to avoid constantly changing the weight contribution.

When computing the overall SIW weight, the weight contributions for branch instructions are no longer constants but are read from the appropriate register.

The values for p and n used in this paper are 7 and 8, respectively. Note that the size of the counter (n) determines the learning period. In total, we need 5 7-bit registers, 5 15-bit registers and a small number of adders and control to update these registers. This update is not time-critical because these registers track the average over a large instruction sequence and change slowly over time.

3.4   Selecting the SIW Threshold

The SIW threshold remains fixed. Selecting the SIW threshold involves a trade-off between reducing wrong-path instructions (smaller thresholds) and execution speed (larger thresholds). The SIW threshold also depends on the weight contributions: larger weight contributions lead to a larger SIW weight, so to gate fetch under the same conditions a larger SIW threshold is required too. Finally, the SIW threshold depends on branch prediction accuracy too. We analyze SIWW using multiple SIW thresholds in order to quantify this trade-off.

4   Experimental Environment

Simulation results presented in this paper are obtained using sim-flex[1] with the Alpha ISA. The simulator is modified and configured to model a future deeply pipelined processor (Table 2). The configuration is inspired by the Intel Pentium 4 [8], but at the same time care is taken to limit the extra work that the baseline model performs for wrong-path instructions. Amongst others, we use conservative fetch, decode and issue widths of 4 instructions per cycle because this is a good trade-off between power consumption and performance and it is a more realistic number if power efficiency is a major design consideration.

Gating control resides in the decode stage because the instruction type, confidence estimates and SIW contributions are known only at decode. To improve the effectiveness of the gating techniques, the fetch stage and the decode stage are simultaneously gated.

Two different branch predictors are considered in this study: gshare and O-GEHL. These predictors feature 64 Kbits of storage. For gshare, we considered 15 bits global history, a JRS confidence estimator [9] with 4K 4 bit counters and 15 as the confidence threshold. Power consumption in the JRS confidence estimator is modeled by estimating power dissipation in the JRS table. For O-GEHL, we simulated the baseline configuration presented in [16]. As in [11], we use the update threshold as the confidence estimator for O-GEHL. If the absolute value of the weight sum is above the update threshold then we classify the branch as high confidence, and low-confidence otherwise. We call this self confidence estimation as in [11]. Self confidence estimation consumes no additional power.

A cascaded branch target predictor [5] is implemented. Confidence is estimated as follows. Each entry is extended with a 2-bit resetting counter. The counter is incremented on a correct prediction and set to zero on an incorrect prediction. An indirect branch is assigned high confidence when the counter is saturated in the highest state.

We simulate SPEC CPU 2000 benchmarks executing the reference inputs.[2] Traces of 500 million instructions are obtained using SimPoint[3].

---

[1] http://www.ece.cmu.edu/~simflex

[2] Our simulation infrastructure cannot handle the perlbmk inputs, so we resort to the SPEC'95 reference scrabble input.

[3] http://www.cs.ucsd.edu/~calder/SimPoint/

Table 2. Baseline Processor Model

Processor core	
Issue width	4 instructions
ROB, issue queue	96
Load-store queue	48
Dispatch-execute delay	7 cycles
Fetch Unit	
Fetch width	4 instructions, 2 branches/cycle
Instruction fetch queue	8 instructions
Fetch-dispatch delay	9 cycles
Cond. branch predictor	gshare or O-GEHL
Return address stack	16 entries, checkpoint 2
Branch target buffer	256 sets, 4 ways
Cascaded branch target predictor	64 sets, 4 ways, 8-branch path history
Memory Hierarchy	
L1 I/D caches	64 KB, 4-way, 64B blocks
L2 unified cache	256 KB, 8-way, 64B blocks
L3 unified cache	4 MB, 8-way, 64B blocks
Cache latencies	1 (L1), 6 (L2), 20 (L3)
Memory latency	150 cycles

5   Evaluation

Table 3 displays the characteristics of our benchmark set considering gshare and OGEHL as branch predictors. Column CND and IND represents the misprediction rate in mispredicts per 1000 instructions for conditional branches and indirect branches. Notwithstanding high prediction accuracy, the extra fetch work (EFW) represents between 15.5% and 93.6% extra work on the SPECint benchmarks when using the O-GEHL predictor. The SPECfp benchmarks exhibit less than 10% extra fetch work. Using gshare instead of O-GEHL as branch predictor reduces the overall base performance by 5.65%. It also induces more work on the wrong path: the average extra instruction fetch work is increased from 39.2% to 52.4%.

In Table 3, we also illustrate performance as instruction per cycle (IPC) and power consumption as energy per instruction (EPI) using the SimFlex technological parameters. EPI is represented for the base configuration

Table 3. Characteristics of the benchmarks

	IPC	CND	IND	EFW	EPI	ORA
O-GEHL	1.77	2.76	0.33	39.2%	18.6	17.5
gshare	1.67	4.23	0.38	52.4%	18.9	17.4

and an Oracle configuration assuming that fetch is stopped as soon as a mispredicted branch is decoded. The overall objective of fetch gating in terms of power consumption can be seen as reducing as much as possible the extra EPI over the oracle configuration while inducing performance loss as small as possible compared with the base configuration.

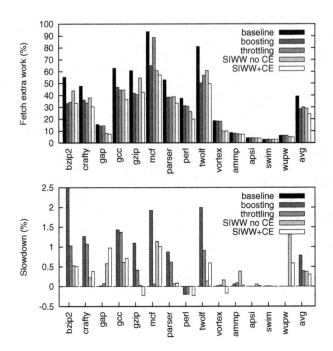

Fig. 2. Comparison between SIWW and boosting for the O-GEHL predictor. The boosting level is 2 low-confidence branches. Throttling fetches only once every two cycles when a low-confidence branch is inflight. The SIWW threshold is 224 ("SIWW no CE") or 160 ("SIWW+CE").

5.1 Analysis of SIWW

We compare SIWW with pipeline gating by boosting the confidence estimate and by throttling. We measure the benefits of pipeline gating using extra work metrics [14], i.e. the number of wrong-path instructions that pass through a pipeline stage divided by the number of correct-path instructions.

First, Figure 2 compares the three gating techniques on a per benchmark basis on configurations favoring a small performance reduction rather than a large extra fetch reduction. The O-GEHL predictor is used here. SIWW (label "SIWW+CE") incurs less performance degradation than boosting: 0.31% on average compared to 0.79% for boosting. Furthermore, extra fetch work is reduced from 39.2% to 24.2% for SIWW vs. 28.4% for boosting level 2. In total, SIWW removes 38.1% of the extra fetch work.

Throttling is known to perform better than boosting. When a low-confidence branch is inflight, fetch is activated once every two cycles. This improves performance slightly over boosting at the expense of a little extra fetch work. However, throttling may be very ineffective for particular benchmarks, e.g. mcf, where hardly any improvement over the baseline is observed.

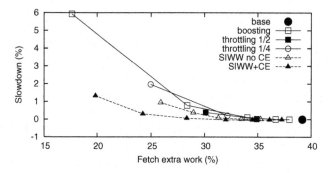

Fig. 3. Varying boosting levels (1 to 5), throttling parameters (threshold 1 and 2, frequency 1/2 and 1/4) and SIWW (thresholds "SIWW no CE" 192 to 320, "SIWW+CE" 128 to 256)

SIWW works correctly even without using any confidence estimator. We run an experiment without using any confidence estimator i.e. assigning the same weight to each indirect or conditional branch. 16 was the assigned weight. On Figure 2, the considered SIW threshold is 224. This configuration of SIWW ("SIWW no CE") achieves average extra fetch work and slowdown very similar to throttling. This is explained by the fact that there is still a correlation between the number of inflight branches and the probability to remain on the correct path. Since the weight of a branch is higher than the weight of a non-branch instruction, SIWW enables fetch gating when the number of inflight branches is high.

SIWW allows to fully exploit the self-confidence estimator. Figure 3 illustrates SIWW versus boosting when varying boosting levels and SIWW thresholds. Decreasing the boosting level to 1 significantly decreases the performance by 5.9% and reduces the extra fetch work from 39.2% to 17.7%. Therefore with fetch gating based on confidence, the designer has the choice between a limited extra work reduction, but small performance reduction with boosting level 2 or higher, or a large performance degradation, but also a larger extra work reduction with no boosting. This limited choice is associated with intrinsic properties of the self confidence estimator. Manne et al. [14] pointed out that a good trade-off for a confidence estimator for fetch gating based on boosting is high coverage (SPEC) of mispredicted branches (e.g. 80% or higher) and medium *predictive value of a negative test* (PVN)(10-20%). The self-confidence estimator for O-GEHL exhibits medium SPEC and PVN metrics. The SPECint benchmarks show SPEC values in the range of 40%–57% and PVN values above 30%, except for the highly predictable benchmarks gap and vortex.

On the other hand, this property of the self confidence estimator is not a handicap for SIWW. In addition to providing better performance-extra work trade-off than boosting or throttling, SIWW offers the possibility to choose the SIW threshold level in function of the desired performance/extra work trade-off. For instance, with SIWW theshold 128, one sacrifices 1.3% performance but reduces the extra fetch work from 39.2% to 19.9%.

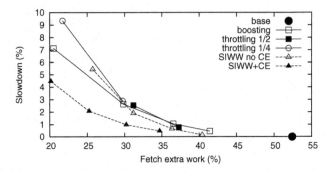

Fig. 4. Gshare branch predictor. Varying boosting levels (2 to 5), throttling parameters (threshold 1 and 2, frequency 1/2 and 1/4) and SIWW thresholds (both cases 128 to 224).

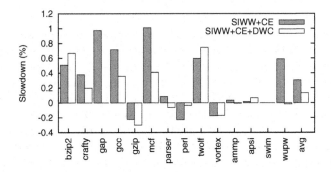

Fig. 5. Slowdown obtained with dynamic weight contributions (DWC). SIW thresholds are 160 (SIWW+CE) and 96 (SIWW+CE+DWC). Both schemes have almost equal extra work metrics. The O-GEHL predictor is used.

SIWW Works for all Branch Predictors. In order to show that fetch gating control through SIWW works for all branch predictors, we analyze SIWW assuming a gshare branch predictor.

Figure 4 shows that SIWW performs better than boosting and throttling both in terms of fetch extra work and in terms of slowdown. For instance SIWW removes more than half of the extra fetch work at a slowdown of 2.1% while boosting level 3 only removes 43% of the extra fetch work but involves a slowdown of 2.6%.

5.2   Dynamic Adaptation of SIW Weight Contributions

The SIWW mechanism is improved by dynamically adapting the SIW weight contributions depending on the predictability of branch conditions and targets in each benchmark. We find that dynamically adapting the SIW weight yields only small reductions in extra work. On the other hand, it is useful to limit slowdown because decreasing the SIW weight contribution for highly predictable instruction classes avoids unnecesary fetch gating. The lower slowdown also translates into energy savings.

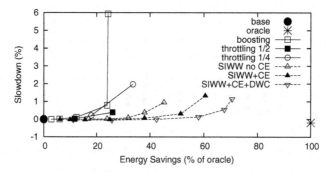

Fig. 6. Reduction of EPI relative to the oracle scheme; the O-GEHL predictor is used

Figure 5 compares SIWW with fixed weight contributions from the previous section (SIWW+CE) to SIWW with dynamically adapted weight contributions. The dynamic adaptation algorithm is effective in reducing slowdown. E.g. slowdown is reduced to almost zero for gap and wupwise. The slowdown is reduced from an average of 0.31% to 0.13%. We found that the extra work metrics change little, e.g. extra fetch work reduces slightly from 24.2% to 24.0%. However, we will see in the following section that dynamic adaptation is effective at reducing energy consumption.

Analysis of the trained weight contributions shows large variations across benchmarks. Furthermore, the difference between the weight contribution for low-confidence branches and high-confidence branches also varies strongly. This difference is small when the PVN of the confidence estimator is small. Then, low-confidence branches are still likely to be predicted correctly and are assigned a lower weight contribution.

We attempted to select fixed weight contributions based on the trained values. This, however, yields only small benefits over the fixed weight contributions used throughout this paper.

5.3   SIWW Control for Fetch Gating Is Energy-Efficient

Figure 6 illustrates the trade-off between the EPI (energy per committed instruction) reduction and the slowdown. The graph shows the baseline architecture without fetch gating and an oracle fetch gating scheme that gates fetch for all mispredicted instructions. The oracle scheme defines an upper bound on the *total* energy savings obtainable with fetch gating, which is 5.8% in our architecture. The fact that this upper bound on *total* energy savings is quite low simply means that we did a good job at selecting a baseline architecture that is already power-efficient. This is achieved by limiting fetch and issue width to four instructions, by using the highly accurate O-GEHL predictor and by adding history-based branch target prediction.

Within this envelope, SIWW is most effective in realizing an energy reduction. The three variations of SIWW reduce energy in the range of 40–70% for a limited

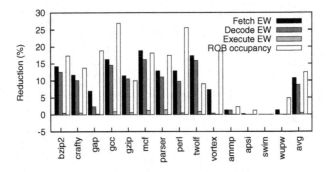

Fig. 7. Reduction of fetch, decode and execute work and reduction of reorder buffer occupancy, using the O-GEHL predictor

slowdown ($< 1\%$). Previously known techniques, such as throttling and pipeline gating realize no more than 26% of the envelope for the same slowdown.

Note that boosting with level 1 does not save more energy than boosting level 2, this is due to a particularly high loss of performance on a few benchmarks where both performance and power consumption are made worse.

5.4   SIWW and Flow Rate Matching

In the previous sections, we evaluated SIWW for the purpose of gating-off wrong-path instructions. Using the same parameters as in Figure 2, Figure 7 illustrates that SIWW reduces the activity in all pipeline stages. The reduction of activity in the execute stage is small. However, SIWW exhibits the potential to reduce power consumption in the schedule, execute and wake-up stages as the occupancy of the reorder buffer is strongly reduced compared to the baseline, up to 27% for gcc. This property can be leveraged to reduce power further by dynamically scaling the size of the reorder buffer or the issue queue [3,6].

We compare SIWW to PAUTI [3], a parallelism and utilization-based fetch gating mechanism. We assume a non-collapsing issue queue in our baseline processor because of its energy-efficiency [6]. SIWW is not dependent on the issue queue design but PAUTI is specified for a collapsing issue queue [3]. We adapted PAUTI to a non-collapsing issue queue in the following way. During each cycle, PAUTI decides on gating fetch for one cycle based on the issued instructions. If more than half of the issued instructions are issued from the oldest half of the issue queue and the number of issuable instructions in the issue queue exceeds a preset threshold, then fetch is gated during one cycle. Otherwise, fetch is active. We use an issue queue fill threshold of 48 instructions.

The energy-efficiency of a flow-rate matching technique (e.g. PAUTI or SIWW) is amplified by dynamically adapting the issue queue size [3]. The issue queue is scaled using a method we refer to as ADQ [4]. The usable issue queue size is determined at the beginning of a time quantum (e.g. 10000 cycles), depending on the average issue queue utilization during the previous quantum. If the average

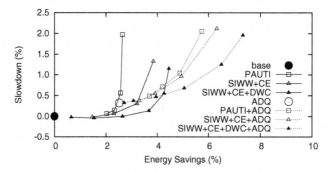

Fig. 8. Energy reduction vs. slowdown for several configurations of each scheme. The issue queue fill thresholds for PAUTI are 40, 48, 56 and 64. The SIWW thresholds are 128, 160, 192 and 224 with fixed weights and 72, 80, 96, 112, 128 and 160 with dynamically adapted weights.

occupation is less than the usable queue size minus 12, then the usable queue size is reduced by 8. If the average occupation exceeds the usable queue size during the last quantum minus 8, then the usable queue size for the next quantum is increased by 8. The thresholds are chosen such that reducing the issue queue size further would cause an unproportionally large slowdown.

A different trade-off between slowdown and energy consumption is obtained depending on the configuration of the fetch gating scheme (issue queue fill threshold for PAUTI or SIWW threshold). Figure 8 shows that, regardless of the configuration, the SIWW methods achieve higher energy savings for the same slowdown. Analysis shows that SIWW and PAUTI achieve their energy savings in different areas. SIWW removes more fetch stage energy while PAUTI removes more issue stage energy. Total energy savings however, average out to the same values for PAUTI and SIWW with fixed weight contributions when slowdown is restricted to 1% (energy savings are 4.88% and 4.94%, respectively). SIWW with dynamic weight contributions obtains a significantly higher energy reduction (6.5% of total energy) because it removes more fetch extra work than SIWW with fixed weight contributions and it allows for almost the same reduction in the issue queue size as PAUTI.

6   Conclusion

Fetch gating improves power-efficiency because of (i) eliminating energy consumption on wrong-path instructions and (ii) matching the front-end instruction rate to the back-end instruction rate.

Previous proposals for wrong-path fetch gating relied only on branch confidence estimation, i.e. counting the number of inflight low-confidence branches. These proposals were not taking into account the structure of the remainder of the speculative instruction window (number of instructions, number of inflight high-confidence branches, ...). SIWW takes this structure into account and therefore allows more accurate decisions for fetch gating. Fetch gating control through SIWW allows to reduce extra work on the wrong path in a more dramatic fashion than fetch gating through confidence boosting and throttling.

Fetch gating mechanisms have been proposed that focus on matching the front-end and back-end instruction flow-rates, neglecting to filter out wrong-path instructions. The SIWW method combines both: by weighting control transfers heavily, wrong-path instructions are gated-off and the front-end flow rate is limited during phases with many hard-to-predict control-transfers.

Future directions for research on SIWW include new usages of SIWW, e.g., optimizing thread usage in SMT processors. We have shown that SIWW limits resource usage by wrong-path instructions, which is very important for SMT processors [13]. Furthermore, by setting a different SIW threshold per thread, different priorities can be assigned to each thread.

Acknowledgements

Hans Vandierendonck is a Post-doctoral Research Fellow with the Fund for Scientific Research-Flanders (FWO-Flanders). Part of this research was performed while Hans Vandierendonck was at IRISA, funded by FWO-Flanders. André Seznec was partially supported by an Intel research grant and an Intel research equipment donation.

References

1. J. L. Aragón, J. González, and A. González. Power-aware control speculation through selective throttling. In *HPCA-9: Proceedings of the 9th international symposium on high-performance computer architecture*, pages 103–112, Feb. 2003.
2. A. Baniasadi and A. Moshovos. Instruction flow-based front-end throttling for power-aware high-performance processors. In *ISLPED '01: Proceedings of the 2001 international symposium on low power electronics and design*, pages 16–21, Aug. 2001.
3. A. Buyuktosunoglu, T. Karkhanis, D. H. Albonesi, and P. Bose. Energy efficient co-adaptive instruction fetch and issue. In *ISCA '03: Proceedings of the 30th Annual International Symposium on Computer Architecture*, pages 147–156, June 2003.
4. A. Buyuktosunoglu, S. E. Schuster, M. D. Brooks, P. Bose, P. W. Cook, and D. H. Albonesi. A circuit level implementation of an adaptive issue queue for power-aware microprocessors. In *Proceedings of the 11th Great Lakes Symposium on VLSI*, pages 73–78, Mar. 2001.
5. K. Driesen and U. Holzle. The cascaded predictor: Economical and adaptive branch target prediction. In *Proceeding of the 30th Symposium on Microarchitecture*, Dec. 1998.
6. D. Folegnani and A. González. Energy-effective issue logic. In *Proceedings of the 28th Annual International Symposium on Computer Architecture*, pages 230–239, June 2001.
7. H. Gao and H. Zhou. Adaptive information processing: An effective way to improve perceptron predictors. In *1st Journal of Instruction-Level Parallelism Championship Branch Prediction*, page 4 pages, Dec. 2004.

8. G. Hinton, D. Sager, M. Upton, D. Boggs, D. Carmean, A. Kyker, and P. Roussel. The microarchitecture of the Pentium 4 processor. *Intel Technology Journal*, 5(1), 2001.

9. E. Jacobsen, E. Rotenberg, and J. Smith. Assigning confidence to conditional branch predictions. In *MICRO 29: Proceedings of the 29th Annual ACM/IEEE International Conference on Microarchitecture*, pages 142–152, Dec. 1996.

10. D. Jiménez. Piecewise linear branch prediction. In *ISCA '05: Proceedings of the 32nd Annual International Symposium on Computer Architecture*, pages 382–393, June 2005.

11. D. A. Jiménez and C. Lin. Composite confidence estimators for enhanced speculation control. Technical Report TR-02-14, Dept. of Computer Sciences, The University of Texas at Austin, Jan. 2002.

12. T. Karkhanis, J. Smith, and P. Bose. Saving energy with just in time instruction delivery. In *Intl. Symposium on Low Power Electronics and Design*, pages 178–183, Aug. 2002.

13. K. Luo, M. Franklin, S. S. Mukherjee, and A. Seznec. Boosting SMT performance by speculation control. In *Proceedings of the 15th International Parallel & Distributed Processing Symposium (IPDPS-01)*, Apr. 2001.

14. S. Manne, A. Klauser, and D. Grunwald. Pipeline gating: speculation control for energy reduction. In *ISCA '98: Proceedings of the 25th Annual International Symposium on Computer Architecture*, pages 132–141, June 1998.

15. D. Parikh, K. Skadron, Y. Zhang, M. Barcella, and M. R. Stan. Power issues related to branch prediction. In *HPCA-8: Proceedings of the 8th iInternational Symposium on High-Performance Computer Architecture*, pages 233–246, Feb. 2002.

16. A. Seznec. Analysis of the O-GEometric History Length branch predictor. In *ISCA '05: Proceedings of the 32nd Annual International Symposium on Computer Architecture*, pages 394–405, June 2005.

17. A. Seznec and P. Michaud. A case for (partially) TAgged GEometric history length branch prediction. *Journal of Instruction-Level Parallelism*, Feb. 2006.

Dynamic Capacity-Speed Tradeoffs in SMT Processor Caches*

Sonia López[1], Steve Dropsho[2], David H. Albonesi[3],
Oscar Garnica[1], and Juan Lanchares[1]

[1] Departamento de Arquitectura de Computadores y Automatica,
U. Complutense de Madrid, Spain
[2] School of Computer and Communication Science, EPFL, Switzerland
[3] Computer Systems Laboratory, Cornell University, USA

Abstract. Caches are designed to provide the best tradeoff between access speed and capacity for a set of target applications. Unfortunately, different applications, and even different phases within the same application, may require a different capacity-speed tradeoff. This problem is exacerbated in a Simultaneous Multi-Threaded (SMT) processor where the optimal cache design may vary drastically with the number of running threads and their characteristics.

We propose to make this capacity-speed cache tradeoff dynamic within an SMT core. We extend a previously proposed globally asynchronous, locally synchronous (GALS) processor core with multi-threaded support, and implement dynamically resizable instruction and data caches. As the number of threads and their characteristics change, these adaptive caches automatically adjust from small sizes with fast access times to higher capacity configurations. While the former is more performance-optimal when the core runs a single thread, or a dual-thread workload with modest cache requirements, higher capacity caches work best with most multiple thread workloads. The use of a GALS microarchitecture permits the rest of the processor, namely the execution core, to run at full speed irrespective of the cache speeds. This approach yields an overall performance improvement of 24.7% over the best fixed-size caches for dual-thread workloads, and 19.2% for single-threaded applications.

1 Introduction

Simultaneous Multi-Threading (SMT) [18,19] is a widely used approach to increase the efficiency of the processor core. In SMT, multiple threads simultaneously share many of the major hardware resources, thereby making use of resources that may lie partially unused by a single thread. SMT processors have the significant advantage of dynamically trading off instruction-level parallelism (ILP) for thread-level parallelism (TLP). That is, hardware resources that are partially unoccupied due to insufficient single-thread ILP can be filled by instructions from a second thread. This leads to a significant boost in

* This research was supported in part by Spanish Government Grant TIN2005-05619, National Science Foundation Grant CCF-0304574, an IBM Faculty Partnership Award, a grant from the Intel Research Council, and by equipment grants from Intel and IBM.

K. De Bosschere et al. (Eds.): HiPEAC 2007, LNCS 4367, pp. 136–150, 2007.

instruction throughput over a single threaded processor with only a modest increase in hardware resources.

Despite this advantage, large variations in runtime load cause greater pipeline inefficiencies in an SMT processor. These load fluctuations arise due to increased variation in workload phase behavior, due to individual application phase differences coupled with variations in the number of actively running threads. There are several reasons why the number of running threads may differ from the maximum supported in the SMT hardware:

- A server will not always operate at 100% load, leaving some processors running with fewer than the maximum number of threads;
- Lock contention in systems such as databases can restrict the number of threads that can run simultaneously on the processor core;
- A parallel program will have parallel portions running many threads, and serial portions in which only a single thread runs.

Thus, a significant challenge for SMT processor core microarchitects is devising a single core microarchitecture that is near optimal under a variety of single and multiple thread operating conditions. Whereas a single thread, and some dual-thread workloads, benefits from a streamlined pipeline with small, fast, hardware structures, such an organization would yield sub-optimal performance for many multi-threaded workloads. Rather, larger structures would yield a better tradeoff between hardware resource complexity and operating speed.

To address this disparity, we propose a phase-adaptive cache hierarchy whose size and speed can dynamically adapt to match varying SMT workload behavior. We implement a dual-threaded core, and begin with a small, fast cache that works well for single threaded, and some dual-threaded, workloads with modest working sets. The addition of a second running thread often puts more demand on cache capacity, and this greater demand is met by dynamically *upsizing* the cache. We adopt the *Accounting Cache* design of [8] for our resizable caches.

Because the upsized cache has a higher access time, we also adopt a Globally Asynchronous, Locally Synchronous (GALS) design style, in particular, the *Multiple Clock Domain (MCD)* approach of [16] to decouple the adaptive caches from the execution core. Unlike [16], our MCD processor supports SMT and a different domain organization. Since the integer and floating point domains are at fixed frequency, and there is negligible interaction between them (and thus negligible synchronization cost), they in effect serve as a single "execution core" domain. This execution core operates at full speed while the front-end and load/store domains adapt their frequencies to the resizing of the caches.

Our results demonstrate that adaptive caches are very effective at reacting to single and dual-threaded workload phase behavior. As expected, larger cache configurations are more prominent for the dual-thread workloads due to the higher cache pressure of running two simultaneous threads. The cache control algorithm often dynamically chooses more optimal smaller, faster caches for single-threaded workloads, and in several cases different cache configurations run for non-trivial periods of execution, demonstrating the benefit of phase-adaptive multi-threaded workload adaptation. The result is an average 24.7% performance improvement over an aggressive baseline

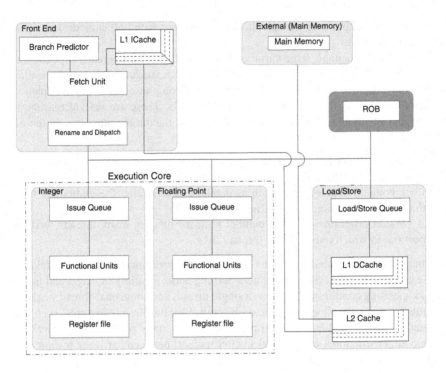

Fig. 1. Adaptive MCD microarchitecture. Boxes with multiple borders indicate resizable structures.

synchronous architecture with fixed cache designs for two-threaded workloads, and 19.2% for single-threaded applications.

The rest of this paper is organized as follows. The next section discusses the adaptive SMT MCD microarchitecture, including the adaptive cache organizations. Section 3 briefly reviews the Accounting Cache algorithm for resizing the caches and modifying their domain frequencies. Our simulation infrastructure and benchmarks are described next, followed by our results. Finally, we discuss related work in Section 6, and present our conclusions in Section 7.

2   Adaptive SMT MCD Microarchitecture

The base MCD microarchitecture highlighted in Figure 1 has five independent clock domains, comprising the front end (L1 ICache, branch prediction, rename and dispatch); integer processing core (issue queue, register file and execution units); floating-point processing core (issue queue, register file and execution units); load/store unit (load/store queue, L1 DCache and unified L2 cache); and ROB (Reorder Buffer). The integer and floating-point domains have fixed structures and run at fixed frequency at all times. Since there is little interaction between them (and thus their interface introduces negligible synchronization cost), they are effectively one fixed-frequency execution core domain.

The ROB lies in its own independent domain running at all times at full frequency. Since the speed of both dispatch and commit depends on the operating speed of the ROB, decoupling the ROB in this manner permits the front and back-end domains to be independently adapted [21]. The dynamic frequency control circuit within the two adaptive domains (front end and load / store) is a PLL clocking circuit based on indus-trial circuits [7,10]. The lock time in our experiments is normally distributed with a mean time of $15\mu s$ and a range of 10–$20\mu s$. As in the XScale processor [7], we as-sume that a domain is able to continue operating through a frequency change. Main memory operates at the same fixed base frequency as the processing core and is also non-adaptive.

Data generated in one domain and needed in another must cross a domain bound-ary, potentially incurring synchronization costs. The MCD simulator models synchro-nization circuitry based on the work of Sjogren and Myers [17]. It imposes a delay of one cycle in the consumer domain whenever the distance between the edges of the two clocks is within 30% of the period of the faster clock. Both superscalar execution (which allows instructions to cross domains in groups) and out-of-order execution (which re-duces the impact of individual instruction latencies) tend to hide synchronization costs, resulting in an average overall slowdown of less than 3% [15]. Further details on the baseline MCD model, including a description of the inter-domain synchronization cir-cuitry, can be found in prior papers [12,14,15,16] . We extend this model with SMT (dual-thread) support, the details of which are provided in Section 4.

In this paper, we focus on the varying caching needs of SMT workloads. We therefore make the L1 ICache in the front end domain adaptive, as well as the L1 DCache and L2 cache of the load / store domain. This *adaptive SMT MCD architecture* has a base con-figuration using the smallest cache sizes running at a high clock rate. For applications that perform better with larger storage, caches can be upsized with a corresponding re-duction in the clock rate of their domain. In this study, the three non-adaptive domains, integer, floating point, and main memory, run at the base frequency of 1.0 GHz. Only the front end and load / store domains make frequency adjustments. The L1 DCache and L2 cache are resized in tandem.

Having adaptable structures and a variable clock means that structures may be safely oversized [9]. The greater capacity (and lower domain frequency) is used only if a workload attains a net benefit; Section 5 demonstrates that this occurs more often under dual-thread conditions. Workloads that do not require the extra capacity, such as many single-threaded workloads, configure to a smaller size and run at a higher frequency. This approach permits the tradeoff between per-domain clock rate and complexity to be made for each workload phase.

Implementing adaptive structures incurs two static performance penalties. First, the degree of pipelining in each domain matches the high frequency that supports the small-est dynamic configuration. When the clock frequency is lowered to accommodate the additional delay of an upsized structure, the resulting stage delay imbalance results in a design that is over-pipelined with respect to the new frequency. This results in a longer branch mis-predict penalty compared with a tuned synchronous design. In our study, the adaptive SMT MCD microarchitecture incurs one additional front end cycle and two additional integer cycles for branch mispredictions. Second, we have found that the resizable structures should be optimized in terms of sub-banking for fast access at the smallest size. However, for modularity, the larger configurations consist of duplicates of this baseline structure size. These larger configurations may have a different sub-bank organization than the same size structure that has been optimized for a non-adaptive design. We model this cost as additional access latency for the larger configurations.

2.1   Resizable Caches

In the load / store domain, the adaptive L1 DCache and L2 cache are up to eight-way set associative, and resized by ways [2,8]. This provides a wide range of sizes to accommodate a wide variation in workload behavior. The base configuration (smallest size and highest clock rate) is a 32 KB direct-mapped L1 DCache and a 256 KB direct-mapped L2 cache. Both caches are upsized in tandem by increasing their associativity. We restrict the resizing to one, two, four, and eight ways to reduce the state space of possible configurations (shown in Table 1).

We use version 3.1 of the CACTI modeling tool [20] to obtain timings for all plausible cache configurations at a given size. The *Optimal* columns in Table 1 list the configurations that provide the fastest access time for the given capacity and associativity, without the ability to resize. The number of sub-banks per way in the *Adapt* columns were chosen by adopting the fastest configuration of the minimal-size structure and then replicating this configuration at higher levels of associativity to obtain the larger configurations. This strategy ensures the fastest clock frequency at the smallest configuration, but may not produce the fastest possible configuration when structures are upsized. Since CACTI configures a 32 KB direct-mapped cache as 32 sub-banks, each additional way in the adaptive L1 DCache is an identical 32 KB RAM. The reconfigurable L2, similarly, has eight sub-banks per 256 KB way. In contrast, the number of sub-banks in an optimal fixed L1 varies with total capacity, and the optimal L2 structure has four sub-banks per way for all sizes larger than the minimum.

In the front end domain, the L1 ICache is adaptive; the configurations are shown in Table 2. The cache adapts by ways as with the L1 DCache, but with associativities of one, two, three, and four.

Table 1. Adaptive L1 DCache and L2 Cache configurations. The *Size* column refers to the size of the *A* partition selected by the cache control algorithm, as discussed in Section 3. The column *Adapt* provides the number of sub-banks per way for each adaptive cache configuration, while *Optimal* gives the number that produces the fastest access time at that size and associativity.

	L1 DCache		Sub-banks		L2 Cache		Sub-banks	
Configuration	Size	Assoc	Adapt	Optimal	Size	Assoc	Adapt	Optimal
D0	32 KB	1	32	32	256 KB	1	8	8
D1	64 KB	2	32	8	512 KB	2	8	4
D2	128 KB	4	32	16	1 MB	4	8	4
D3	256 KB	8	32	4	2 MB	8	8	4

Table 2. Adaptive L1 ICache configurations

Configuration	I-cache, dynamic		
	Size	**Assoc**	**Sub-banks**
I0	16 KB	1	32
I1	32 KB	2	32
I2	48 KB	3	32
I3	64 KB	4	32

3   Phase Adaptive Cache Control Algorithm

To control the reconfigurable caches, we employ the *Accounting Cache* algorithm previously applied to improving cache energy efficiency [8]. Due to the fact that the smaller
configurations are subsets of the larger ones, the algorithm is able to collect statistics for
all possible configurations simultaneously. This permits the calculation of the number
of hits and misses that *would have* occurred over a given span of time for any of the
possible configurations.

In a four-way set associative Accounting Cache there are four possible configurations, as shown in Figure 2. In this example, the *A* partition can be one, two, three, or
four ways. The *B* partition is the remaining portion. The *A* partition is accessed first.
If the data block is found, it is returned. Otherwise a second access is made to the *B*
partition, which causes blocks to be swapped in the *A* and *B* partitions. Note that the *B*
partition is not considered a lower level of cache. In the adaptive MCD architecture, all
three caches (L1 ICache, L1 DCache, and combined L2 Cache) have their own *A* and *B*
partitions. An access to an L1 cache accesses its *A* partition first; on a miss, the access
is sent to the *B* partition and simultaneously to the L2 *A* partition. A hit in the L1 *B*
partition squashes the in-flight L2 access.

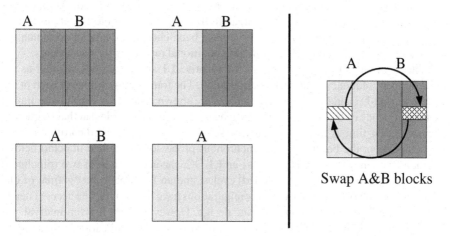

Swap A&B blocks

Fig. 2. Partitioning options for a four-way Accounting Cache

A cache with a small *A* partition runs at a higher frequency than one with a larger *A* partition. (The *B* partition access latency is an integral number of cycles at the clock rate dictated by the size of the *A* partition.) At runtime, the cache control algorithm attempts to continually maintain the best balance between the speed of an *A* access and the number of slower *B* accesses.

As described in detail in previous work [8], the Accounting Cache maintains full most-recently-used (MRU) state on cache lines. Simple counts of the number of blocks accessed in each MRU state are sufficient to reconstruct the precise number of hits and misses to the *A* and *B* partitions *for all possible cache configurations, regardless of the current configuration.* The control algorithm resets the counts at the end of every 15K instruction interval, choosing a configuration for the next interval that would have minimized total access delay cost in the interval just ended. This interval length is comparable to the PLL lock-down time. Thus, during a frequency change we always run with a permissible configuration: downsizing at the beginning of the change when speeding up the clock, upsizing at the end of the change when slowing down. The control algorithm circuitry requires 10K equivalent gates and 32 cycles per cache configuration decision [9].

4   Evaluation Methodology

The simulation environment is based on the SimpleScalar toolset [5] with MCD processor extensions [16]. The modifications include splitting the Register Update Unit (RUU) into a Reorder Buffer and separate issue queues and physical register files for both the integer and floating point domains. The time management code has also been re-written to emulate separate clocks for each domain, complete with jitter, and to account for synchronization delays on all cross-domain communication.

For this study, we extended this model to support an SMT core. The SMT processor extensions include independent program counters for each thread; thread IDs for caches and predictor history tables; and per-thread ROBs and queues. Table 3 contains a summary of the simulation parameters. These have been chosen, in general, to match the characteristics of the Alpha 21264, but with additional resources for two threads.

Table 4 provides timing parameters for adaptive L1 and L2 caches, as well as the clock domain frequencies for each configuration. The four configurations of each of the load/store (D0-D3) and fetch (I0-I3) domains are shown. Listed for each configuration are the frequency of the domain and the cache access times (in cycles) at that frequency. The first access time is for *A* partition accesses and the second is the *B* partition access. For comparison, the baseline fully synchronous processor (described in detail below) runs at a frequency of 1.0 GHz and has an L1 DCache access time of two (pipelined) cycles, L2 access time of 12 (pipelined) cycles, and an L1 ICache access time of one cycle. Note that larger adaptive cache configurations have over double the access latency (in ns) of the fully synchronous baseline design. However, if for a given interval, the larger cache could have reduced the number of misses of an application sufficiently to compensate for this extra delay on every access, then the reconfiguration algorithm will upsize the cache for the next interval.

Table 3. Architectural parameters for simulated processor

Fetch queue (per thread): 16 entries
Issue queue (per thread): 32 Int, 32 FP
Branch predictor: Combined gshare & 2-level PAg
   Level 1 1024 entries, history 10
   Level 2 4096 entries
   Bimodal predictor size 2048
   Combining predictor size 4096
   BTB 4096 sets, 2-way
Branch mispredict penalty: 10 front-end + 9 integer cycles
Decode, issue, and retire widths: 8, 11, and 24 instructions
Memory latency: 80 ns (1st access), 2 ns (subsequent)
Integer ALUs: 6 + 1 mult/div unit
FP ALUs: 4 + 1 mult/div/sqrt unit
Load/store queue (per thread): 32 entries
Reorder buffer (per thread): 256 entries

Table 4. Cache latencies (in cycles) and domain frequency for each cache configuration

Load/Store Domain				
Configuration	D0	D1	D3	D4
Frequency	1.59 GHz	1.00 GHz	0.76 GHz	0.44 GHz
L1 DCache Latency (A/B)	2/7	2/5	2/2	2/-
L2 Cache Latency (A/B)	12/42	12/27	12/12	12/-

Front End Domain				
Configuration	I0	I1	I3	I4
Frequency	1.62 GHz	1.14 GHz	1.12 GHz	1.10 GHz
L1 ICache Latency (A/B)	2/3	2/2	2/2	2/-

Table 5. SPEC2000 benchmarks, input datasets used, and simulation windows

Benchmark	Datasets	Simulation window
Integer		
bzip2	source 58	100M–200M
gzip	source 60	100M–200M
parser	ref	100M–200M
vpr	ref	190M–290M
Floating-Point		
art	ref	300M–400M
equake	ref	100M–200M
galgel	ref	100M–200M
mesa	ref	100M–200M
mgrid	ref	100M–200M

Table 6. SPEC2000 dual-thread workloads

Integer
`bzip2-vpr, parser-gzip, vpr-parser`
Floating-Point
`art-galgel, equake-galgel, mesa-mgrid`
Combined Integer and Floating-Point
`galgel-bzip2, gzip-equake, vpr-art`

Our workload consists of nine programs from the SPEC2000 suite, which we combine into nine dual-thread workloads, shown in Table 6. Table 5 specifies the individual benchmarks along with the instruction windows and input data sets.

We chose a fully synchronous baseline processor based on a prior study [9]. In that study on *single thread* performance, an exhaustive search of the design space was made to determine the best overall baseline fully synchronous design for a set of 32 applications (of which the benchmarks in this study are a subset). The study ran 1024 configuration combinations on each of the 32 applications and required 160 CPU months to simulate. The result for a single threaded processor was that best overall performance is achieved with a direct-mapped L1 ICache, L1 DCache, and L2 cache with sizes 64 KB, 32 KB, and 256 KB, respectively. To create a fully synchronous SMT competitor to the adaptive SMT MCD architecture, we made the L1 instruction cache two-way set-associative to support SMT and reduced its access time to one cycle from two cycles (we determined a faster L1 ICache access is more important than additional cache capacity), and doubled the L1 DCache and L2 cache (to 64 KB and 512 KB, respectively) made each two-way set-associative. We did not increase the access times from the original baseline processor of [9] even though we increased the capacity and/or associativity (we actually decrease the L1 ICache access time while increasing its associativity). The access times are one cycle, two cycles, and 12 cycles for the L1 ICache, L1 DCache, and L2 cache, respectively.

5   Performance Results

In this section, we compare the performance of the SMT MCD microarchitecture with adaptive caches with that of the baseline fully synchronous design described in Section 4, for both dual-thread and single-thread SPEC2000 workloads. First, however, we demonstrate the variety of cache behavior observed in SMT machines, by comparing the best-performing cache configurations selected by the Accounting Cache algorithm for single and dual-thread workloads.

Figure 3 shows the percentage of time each application spends in a particular load/store domain cache configuration when run in isolation (non-SMT) on the adaptive MCD SMT processor, while Figure 4 shows the corresponding results for the dual-thread workloads. (We do not discuss the instruction caches since the control algorithm always selects the configuration with the smallest A partition. The reason is the front end is generally more sensitive to the clock frequency rather than L1 ICache capacity.) As the first figure shows, most applications exhibit a dominant behavior

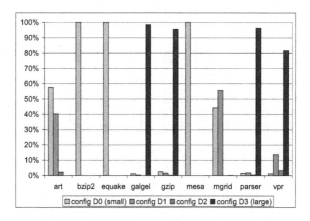

Fig. 3. Percentage of time individual SPEC2000 benchmarks spend in each load / store domain cache configuration

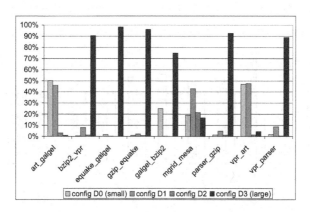

Fig. 4. Percentage of time dual-thread workloads spend in each load / store domain cache configuration

requiring a particular cache configuration. Exceptions are art, mgrid, and vpr which use multiple configurations a noticeable fraction of the time. While four of the benchmarks prefer the larger *A* partition configurations, five gravitate to the smaller *A* partition sizes.

In contrast, as shown in Figure 4, two-thirds of the dual-thread workloads highly favor the largest *A* partition cache configuration, due to the additional pressure on the caches with two threads. A noteworthy counter-example is the SMT pair art_galgel in which the preference of art for the smaller *A* partition configurations dominates the larger *A* partition preference of galgel. Even though galgel needs a large L1 *A* partition to avoid downstream accesses, the large fraction of memory accesses in art make it the bottleneck of the pair and the control algorithm adapts appropriately. The configuration changes of the SMT pair galgel_bzip2 are quite extreme. This pair runs for 75%

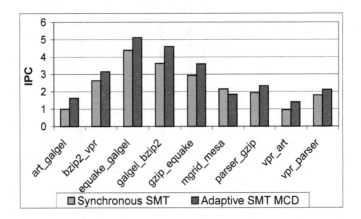

Fig. 5. IPC comparison of dual-thread workloads for the fully synchronous SMT baseline (left bars) and SMT MCD with adaptive caches (right bars)

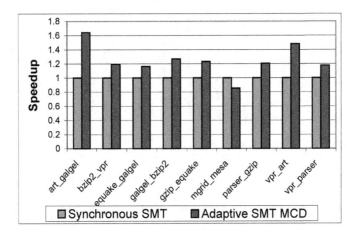

Fig. 6. Speedup of the adaptive design over the baseline with dual-thread workloads

of the time using the largest 256 KB *A* partition configuration (*D3*), but once `galgel` finishes, the algorithm selects the preferred configuration for `bzip2` (*D0*).

These results demonstrate the wide ranging cache behavior observed in a simple SMT processor design that supports either one or two threads (the behavior would vary even more widely for a four-thread machine). While single-thread workloads largely favor smaller, faster L1 *A* cache partitions (there are exceptions of course), the two-thread workloads more often select larger *A* partitions for best performance. Interestingly, for some dual-thread workloads containing an application that favors a large cache, the control algorithm gravitates towards the small fast *A* partition configurations. The performance sensitivity of both applications to memory latency is the deciding factor that

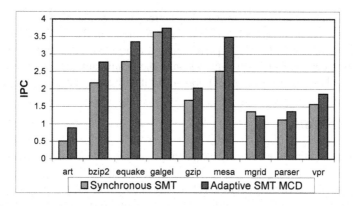

Fig. 7. IPC comparison of individual SPEC2000 applications for the fully synchronous SMT baseline (left bars) and SMT MCD with adaptive caches (right bars)

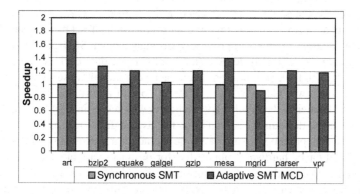

Fig. 8. Speedup of the adaptive design over the baseline with individual SPEC2000 applications

determines the chosen configuration. Finally, significant phase behavior is observed in several workloads that choose several different configurations during execution.

Figures 5, 6, 7, and 8 show how this phase varying cache behavior translates into a significant performance advantage for the adaptive SMT MCD configuration. The first figure compares the IPCs of the adaptive and fixed cache approaches for the dual-thread workloads, while the second figure graphs the corresponding speedup of the adaptive approach. Figures 7 and 8 show the same results for single-thread SPEC2000 applications. In all dual-thread cases, except mgrid_mesa, the adaptive organization outperforms the conventional approach, with art_galgel improving by 64%. The average dual-thread performance improvement is 24.7%. The overall improvement for the single SPEC2000 applications is almost as significant: an overall performance improvement of 19.2%.

The slight degradation seen in mgrid is due to an approximation made in the Accounting Cache cost estimation function. Significant temporal overlap in adjacent memory requests have a true delay cost that is lower than the heuristic estimates (the

Accounting Cache can only estimate the degree of parallelism between accesses). Including more accurate temporal overlap measurements in the cost estimation would improve the adaptive SMT MCD performance on `mgrid` and `mgrid_mesa`. Still, these performance losses pale in comparison to the significant gains observed with the other workloads using the SMT MCD organization with phase adaptive caches.

6   Related Work

Our work builds on prior efforts in both adaptive caches and GALS processor microarchitectures.

In terms of the former, Albonesi [1] first proposed the idea of trading off clock speed for hardware complexity within a single-threaded processor core, including the L1 DCache. Unlike our approach, the global clock within the synchronous processor is slowed down whenever the cache is upsized. Thus, only those applications whose performance is data-cache-bound show signficant benefit. Albonesi also proposed Selective Cache Ways in which energy is saved in single-threaded processors by disabling ways for application working sets that fit comfortably in a subset of the cache [2]. Our approach, by contrast, explores improving performance on an SMT processor.

Balasubramonian *et al.* [3] describe a reconfigurable data cache hierarchy whose latency adjusts with the configuration. Their cache organization uses a similar A/B organization as our own, but they use a different control algorithm. Powell *et al.* [13] devise a variable latency data cache. By predicting which way in a set associative cache holds the requested data, an access can be as fast as in a direct-mapped cache.

Both of these approaches assume a single threaded processor. In addition, they require additional cache hardware support for, for instance, variable cache latency. Our approach is to decouple the clock domains and adapt the frequencies within the cache clock domains along with the cache configurations. This approach maintains a constant latency (in terms of cycles), but adds the complexity of decoupled domains and asynchronous interfaces. If GALS designs are adopted for other reasons, such as lower clock overhead, energy efficiency, or increased tolerance to process variations, then our approach can be easily integrated. Our work also has the additional contribution of exploring the varying cache demands in an SMT processor, due in part to differences in the number of running threads.

Multiple clock domain architectures [4,11,16] permit the frequency of each domain to be set independently of the others. Semeraro *et al.* [14] adjust frequencies automatically at run time to reduce energy in domains that are not on the critical path of the instruction stream. These approaches attempt to downsize hardware structures in single-threaded workloads for energy efficiency. In contrast, we explore the integration of adaptive caches within MCD architectures built around SMT processors to improve performance.

Our work highly leverages the Accounting Cache research of [8] and the adaptive GALS processor design of [9]. The latter effort uses the Accounting Cache within an MCD processor design much like we do. We deviate from this work in that we investigate for the first time the use of adaptive caches within SMT processors, particularly, the benefits of adapting the caches to workloads that vary widely due in part to differences in the number of running threads.

In terms of adaptive SMT processors, [6] is perhaps the closest effort to our own. In this paper, the allocation of shared hardware resources to threads is dynamically managed at runtime by the hardware. While this effort focuses on the issue queues and register files, ours is concerned with the caches. In addition, [6] uses fixed size resources and allocates a certain number of entries to each thread. Our approach is to resize the hardware resources (caches in our case) to fit varying SMT cache behavior, and we add the ability to change the size/frequency tradeoff through the use of an MCD processor.

7 Conclusions

The advent of SMT processors creates significantly more variability in the cache behavior of workloads, due in part to the differing number of threads that may be running at any given time. We propose to integrate adaptive caches within an SMT MCD processor microarchitecture. Our approach is to decouple the execution core from the adaptive cache domains, to permit full speed operation of the execution core as the cache domain frequencies are dynamically altered to match the cache configurations.

We demonstrate significant differences in the configurations chosen by the cache algorithm under single and dual-thread workloads, and we also observe cases of strong phase behavior where multiple cache configurations are chosen for non-trivial periods of execution. Overall, a 24.7% improvement is realized for dual-thread workloads by implementing adaptive cache organizations and an MCD design style within an SMT processor. In addition, a 19.2% performance improvement is observed for single-threaded applications.

References

1. D. H. Albonesi. Dynamic IPC/Clock Rate Optimization. In *25th Intl. Symp. on Computer Architecture*, June 1998.
2. D. H. Albonesi. Selective Cache Ways: On-Demand Cache Resource Allocation. In *32nd Intl. Symp. on Microarchitecture*, Nov. 1999.
3. R. Balasubramonian, D. H. Albonesi, A. Buyuktosunoglu, and S. Dwarkadas. Memory Hierarchy Reconfiguration for Energy and Performance in General-Purpose Processor Architectures. In *33rd Intl. Symp. on Microarchitecture*, Dec. 2000.
4. L. Bengtsson and B. Svensson. A Globally Asynchronous, Locally Synchronous SIMD Processor. In *3rd Intl. Conf. on Massively Parallel Computing Systems*, Apr. 1998.
5. D. Burger and T. Austin. The Simplescalar Tool Set, Version 2.0. Technical Report CS-TR-97-1342, U. Wisc.–Madison, June 1997.
6. F. J. Cazorla, A. Ramirez, M. Valero, and E. Fernandez. Dynamically Controlled Resource Allocation in SMT Processors. In *37th Intl. Symp. on Microarchitecture*, Dec. 2004.
7. L. T. Clark. Circuit Design of XScale^{TM} Microprocessors. In *2001 Symposium on VLSI Circuits, Short Course on Physical Design for Low-Power and High-Performance Microprocessor Circuits*, June 2001.

8. S. Dropsho, A. Buyuktosunoglu, R. Balasubramonian, D. H. Albonesi, S. Dwarkadas, G. Se-meraro, G. Magklis, and M. Scott. Integrating Adaptive On-Chip Storage Structures for Reduced Dynamic Power. In *11th Intl. Conf. on Parallel Architectures and Compilation Techniques*, Sept. 2002.

9. S. Dropsho, G. Semeraro, D. H. Albonesi, G. Magklis, and M. L. Scott. Dynamically Trading Frequency for Complexity in a GALS Microprocessor. In *37th Intl. Symp. on Microarchitecture*, Dec. 2004.

10. M. Fleischmann. LongRun^{TM} Power Management. Technical report, Transmeta Corporation, Jan. 2001.

11. A. Iyer and D. Marculescu. Power and Performance Evaluation of Globally Asynchronous Locally Synchronous Processors. In *29th Intl. Symp. on Computer Architecture*, May 2002.

12. G. Magklis, M. L. Scott, G. Semeraro, D. H. Albonesi, and S. G. Dropsho. Profile-Based Dynamic Voltage and Frequency Scaling for a Multiple Clock Domain Microprocessor. In *30th Intl. Symp. on Computer Architecture*, June 2003.

13. M. Powell, A. Agrawal, T. N. Vijaykumar, B. Falsafi, and K. Roy. Reducing Set-Associative Cache Energy Via Selective Direct-Mapping and Way Prediction. In *34th Intl. Symp. on Microarchitecture*, Dec. 2001.

14. G. Semeraro, D. H. Albonesi, S. G. Dropsho, G. Magklis, S. Dwarkadas, and M. L. Scott. Dynamic Frequency and Voltage Control for a Multiple Clock Domain Microarchitecture. In *35th Intl. Symp. on Microarchitecture*, Nov. 2002.

15. G. Semeraro, D. H. Albonesi, G. Magklis, M. L. Scott, S. G. Dropsho, and S. Dwarkadas. Hiding Synchronization Delays in a GALS Processor Microarchitecture. In *10th Intl. Symp. on Asynchronous Circuits and Systems*, Apr. 2004.

16. G. Semeraro, G. Magklis, R. Balasubramonian, D. H. Albonesi, S. Dwarkadas, and M. L. Scott. Energy-Efficient Processor Design Using Multiple Clock Domains with Dynamic Voltage and Frequency Scaling. In *8th Intl. Symp. on High-Performance Computer Architecture*, Feb. 2002.

17. A. E. Sjogren and C. J. Myers. Interfacing Synchronous and Asynchronous Modules Within A High-Speed Pipeline. In *17th Conf. on Advanced Research in VLSI*, Sept. 1997.

18. D. Tullsen, S. Eggers, and H. Levy. Simultaneous Multithreading: Maximizing On-Chip Parallelism. In *22nd Intl. Symp. on Computer Architecture*, June 1995.

19. D. Tullsen, S. Eggers, H. Levy, J. Emer, J. Lo, and R. Stamm. Exploiting Choice: Instruction Fetch and Issue on an Implementable Simultaneous Multithreading Processor. In *23rd Intl. Symp. on Computer Architecture*, May 1996.

20. S. J. E. Wilton and N. P. Jouppi. CACTI: An Enhanced Cache Access and Cycle Time Model. *IEEE J. of Solid-State Circuits*, May 1996.

21. Y. Zhu, D. H. Albonesi, and A. Buyuktosunoglu. A High Performance, Energy Efficient, GALS Processor Microarchitecture with Reduced Implementation Complexity. In *Intl. Symp. on Performance Analysis of Systems and Software*, March 2005.

IV   Architecture Evaluation Techniques

Branch History Matching: Branch Predictor Warmup for Sampled Simulation

Simon Kluyskens and Lieven Eeckhout

ELIS Department, Ghent University
Sint-Pietersnieuwstraat 41, B-9000 Gent, Belgium
leeckhou@elis.UGent.be

Abstract. Computer architects and designers rely heavily on simulation. The downside of simulation is that it is very time-consuming — simulating an industry-standard benchmark on today's fastest machines and simulators takes several weeks. A practical solution to the simulation problem is sampling. Sampled simulation selects a number of sampling units out of a complete program execution and only simulates those sampling units in detail. An important problem with sampling however is the microarchitecture state at the beginning of each sampling unit. Large hardware structures such as caches and branch predictors suffer most from unknown hardware state. Although a great body of work exists on cache state warmup, very little work has been done on branch predictor warmup. This paper proposes Branch History Matching (BHM) for accurate branch predictor warmup during sampled simulation. The idea is to build a distribution for each sampling unit of how far one needs to go in the pre-sampling unit in order to find the same static branch with a similar global and local history as the branch instance appearing in the sampling unit. Those distributions are then used to determine where to start the warmup phase for each sampling unit for a given total warmup length budget. Using SPEC CPU2000 integer benchmarks, we show that BHM is substantially more efficient than fixed-length warmup in terms of warmup length for the same accuracy. Or reverse, BHM is substantially more accurate than fixed-length warmup for the same warmup budget.

1 Introduction

Architectural simulations are extensively used by computer architects and designers for evaluating various design tradeoffs. Unfortunately, architectural simulation is very time-consuming. Even on today's fastest machines and simulators, simulating an industry-standard benchmark easily takes several weeks to run to completion. As such, simulating entire benchmark executions is infeasible for exploring huge microarchitecture design spaces. Therefore, researchers have proposed sampled simulation [1,2,3,4]. Sampled simulation takes a number of so called sampling units that are simulated in detail. Statistics or appropriate weighting is then applied to the simulation results of the various sampling units for predicting the performance of the overall benchmark execution.

An important issue with sampled simulation is the microarchitecture state at the beginning of each sampling unit, *i.e.*, the microarchitecture state at the beginning of a

K. De Bosschere et al. (Eds.): HiPEAC 2007, LNCS 4367, pp. 153–167, 2007.

sampling unit is unknown during sampled simulation. This is well known in the literature as the cold-start problem. A solution to the cold-start problem is to warmup various
microarchitecture structures prior to each sampling unit. A large amount of work has
been done on cache structure warmup. However, the amount of work done on branch
predictor warmup is very limited.

This paper proposes *Branch History Matching (BHM)* as a novel branch predictor
warmup method. The basic idea is to inspect the pre-sampling unit, *i.e.*, the instructions
in the dynamic instruction stream prior to the sampling unit, for branch instances of the
same static branch with similar global and local histories as the branch instances in the
sampling unit. A BHM distribution is then built for all sampling units that quantifies
the locality in the branch execution stream taking into account both the global and
local histories of the branches. As a final step, the appropriate warmup length is then
determined for each sampling unit taking into account the BHM distributions as well as
the total warmup budget. In other words, the total warmup budget is distributed across
the various sampling units according to the BHM distribution. Sampling units that show
good locality are given a small warmup length; sampling units that show poor locality
are given a larger warmup length.

BHM is microarchitecture-independent, *i.e.*, the warmup lengths are computed once
and are then reused across branch predictors during design space exploration. An appealing way of using BHM in practice for sampled processor simulation is to use (i)
checkpointed sampling [5,6] maintaining reduced checkpoints of architecture state (registers and memory) along with (ii) checkpointed cache warmup [5,7,8,9] and (iii) compressed branch traces [10] that are reduced through BHM. In other words, instead of
having branch traces of full benchmark executions as proposed in [10], BHM limits the
length of the compressed branch traces. This would result in a reduction in required disk
space as well as a reduction in overall simulation time while pertaining the advantage
of compressed branch traces of being branch predictor independent.

This paper makes the following contributions:

- First, we show that branch predictor warmup is an issue when it comes to guar-
  anteeing an accurate hardware state at the beginning of a sampling unit. We show
  that for small sampling unit sizes, branch predictor warmup is required in order
  to achieve an accurate estimate of the hardware state at the beginning of the sampling unit. We provide results showing that even for (fairly large) 1M instruction
  sampling units branch predictor warmup is required.
- Second, we propose Branch History Matching (BHM) as a novel branch predictor warmup approach. Using the SPEC CPU2000 integer benchmarks and 10K-
  instruction sampling units, we show that BHM is 39% more accurate than fixed-
  length warmup for the same warmup length. Or reverse, BHM achieves the same
  accuracy as fixed-length warmup with a 1.6X shorter warmup length. Compared to
  MRRL, BHM is 87% more accurate.

This paper is organized as follows. We first revisit sampled simulation and cover the
main issues related to sampled simulation. We then present BHM as a branch predictor
warmup method. We subsequently evaluate BHM and compare it against fixed-length
warmup and MRRL. And finally, we conclude.

2   Sampled Simulation Background

In sampled simulation, a number of sampling units are chosen from a complete bench-mark execution. Those sampling units are then simulated in detail; the pre-sampling units, *i.e.*, the instructions prior to a given sampling unit, are skipped. The performance of the complete benchmark is then estimated by simply aggregating or weighting the performance numbers from the various sampling units.

There are basically three issues with sampled simulation. First, the sampling units need to be chosen in such a way that the sampling units are representative for the entire program execution. Various authors have proposed various approaches for achieving this, such as random sampling [1], periodic sampling as done in SMARTS [3] and targeted sampling based on program phase behavior as done in SimPoint [2].

The second issue is how to get to those sampling units. In other words, the archi-tecture state (register and memory state) needs to be reconstructed so that all sampling units can be functionally simulated in a correct way. This can be achieved through fast-forwarding or (reduced) checkpointing [5,9]. Checkpointing is especially beneficial for the parallel simulation of sampling units [11,12].

The third issue with sampled simulation is to estimate the microarchitecture state at the beginning of each sampling units. The microarchitecture structures that suffer the most from the cold-start problem are cache structures and branch predictors. We will discuss warmup approaches tailored towards these types of hardware structures in the following two subsections.

2.1   Cache Warmup

Given the fact that caches have the largest state in a microprocessor, they are likely to suffer the most from inaccurate microarchitecture warmup. In fact, most of the prior research on the cold-start problem has been done on cache warmup. Various ap-proaches have been proposed such as no warmup, stale state (also called stitch) [13], fixed warmup [1], cache miss rate estimators [14], no-state-loss [12,15], minimal sub-set evaluation (MSE) [16], memory reference reuse latency (MRRL) [17], boundary line reuse latency (BLRL) [8,18], self-monitored adaptive cache warmup (SMA) [19], memory hierarchy state (MHS) [5], memory timestamp record (MRT) [7], *etc.*

2.2   Branch Predictor Warmup

Compared to the amount of work done on cache warmup, very little work has been done on branch predictor warmup.

The first paper dealing with branch predictor warmup was by Conte *et al.* [1]. They proposed two approaches to branch predictor warmup, namely stale state and fixed-length warmup. Stale state (or stitch) means that the branch predictor state at the end of the previous sampling unit serves as an approximation for the branch predictor state at the beginning of the current sampling unit. An important disadvantage of stale state is that it serializes the simulation of the various sampling units, *i.e.*, it is impossible to simulate the current sampling unit without having finalized the simulation of the previous sampling unit. Fixed-length warmup is a simple-to-implement method that achieves good accuracy if sufficiently long warmup lengths are chosen.

The second paper mentioning branch predictor warmup is by Haskins and Conte [17,20] in which they propose memory reference reuse latency (MRRL). The idea of MRRL is to look in the pre-sampling unit how far one needs to go in order to encounter the same static branch as the one in the sampling unit. MRRL computes the reuse latency, *i.e.*, the number of instructions between the branch instance in the pre-sampling unit and the one in the sampling unit, for all branch instances in the pre-sampling unit and sampling unit. For a given target cumulative probability, for example 99.5%, it is then determined where warmup should start in the pre-sampling unit. During this warmup period, the branch predictor is warmed up but no misprediction rates are computed.

A number of papers have proposed checkpointed sampling techniques [5,7,9] in which the architecture state is stored on disk, as mentioned above. These techniques typically use checkpointed microarchitecture warming for warming cache state, such as memory timestamp record [7], live-points [9] and memory hierarchy state (MHS) [5]. They suggest to store the branch predictor state as part of the microarchitecture state for the various branch predictors one may be interested in during design space exploration. This can be space-inefficient in case multiple branch predictors need to be stored, and in addition, it prevents from simulating a branch predictor that is not contained in the microarchitecture warmup.

For addressing this problem, Barr and Asanovic [10] propose to employ branch trace compression. They store a compressed branch trace on disk and upon branch predictor warming they simply decompress the compressed branch trace and use the decompressed trace for branch predictor warming. This approach is branch predictor independent and can be used to warm any branch predictor during sampled simulation. The branch trace compression scheme by Barr and Asanovic [10] however does not address the issue of how far one needs to go back in the pre-sampling unit. They assume that the entire branch trace from the beginning of the benchmark execution up to the current sampling unit needs to be compressed and decompressed. This can be time-consuming in practice, especially for sampling units deep down the benchmark execution. BHM as proposed in this paper can be used to cut down the branch traces that need to be compressed. This saves both disk space and simulation time, while keeping the benefit of the warmup approach to be branch predictor independent.

3   The Need for Branch Predictor Warmup

Branch predictors need to be warmed up during sampled simulation. This is illustrated in Figure 1 where the number of branch mispredictions per thousand instructions (MPKI) is shown for gcc for four sampling unit sizes: 10K, 100K, 1M and 10M instruction sampling unit sizes. Note this is in the range of sampling units used in contemporary sampled simulation environments such as SMARTS [3,9] (sampling unit size of 10K instructions) and SimPoint [2,5,21] (sampling unit sizes from 1M to 100M instructions). Each graph shows the MPKI for four (fairly aggressive) branch predictors: a 128Kbit gshare predictor, a 256Kbit local predictor, a 128Kbit bimodal predictor and

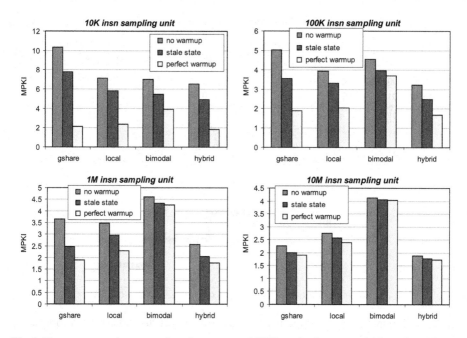

Fig. 1. No warmup, stale state and perfect warmup MPKI results for gcc and 4 branch predictors and 4 sampling unit sizes

a 192Kbit hybrid predictor — more details about the experimental setup and the branch predictors are given in section 5. The various bars correspond to various branch predictor warmup strategies: no warmup, stale state and perfect warmup. The no warmup approach assumes an initialized branch predictor at the beginning of a sampling unit, *i.e.*, the branch predictor content is flushed at the beginning of the sampling unit — two-bit saturating counters in adjacent entries are initialized in alternate '01' '10' states. The stale state approach assumes that the branch predictor at the beginning of the sampling unit equals the branch predictor state at the end of the previous sampling unit. Note that the stale state approach assumes that sampling units are simulated sequentially — this excludes parallel sampled simulation. The perfect warmup approach is an idealized warmup scenario where the branch predictor is perfectly warmed up, *i.e.*, the branch predictor state at the beginning of the sampling unit is the state as if all instructions prior to the sampling unit were simulated.

Figure 1 clearly shows that the no warmup and stale state approaches fail in being accurate, especially for small sampling unit sizes. For example for 10K instruction sampling units, the $\Delta MPKI$ can be very high for both no warmup and stale state. Even for 1M instruction sampling units, the error can be significant, more than 1.5 $\Delta MPKI$ for the no warmup strategy and the gshare predictor. Note that the error varies across branch predictors. The error is typically higher for the gshare predictor than for the bi-modal predictor, which is to be understood intuitively, the reason being the fact that the XOR hashing in the gshare predictor typically results in more entries being accessed in the branch predictor table than the bimodal predictor does.

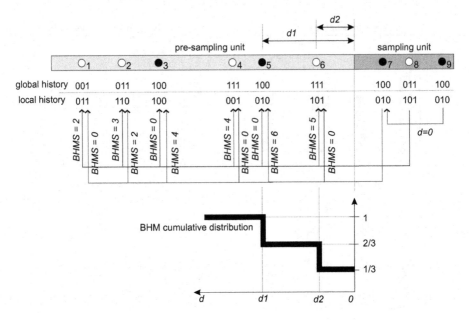

Fig. 2. An example illustrating how the cumulative Branch History Matching distribution is computed

As a result of the non-uniform warmup error across branch predictors, incorrect design decisions may be taken. For example, using the no warmup approach, a computer architect would conclude that the local predictor achieves a better accuracy (a lower MPKI) than the gshare predictor. This is the case for 10K, 100K and even 1M instruction sampling units. However, this conclusion is just an artifact of the inadequate warmup approach. Perfect warmup shows that the gshare predictor outperforms the local predictor. The stale state warmup approach only solves this problem for the 1M instruction sampling unit, however, it does not solve the problem for smaller sampling unit sizes and it cannot be used for parallel sampled simulation.

4   Branch History Matching

This paper proposes Branch History Matching (BHM) as a novel branch predictor warmup approach. Computing the branch predictor warmup length through Branch History Matching (BHM) is done in two steps. First, we compute the BHM distribution for all sampling units. In a second phase, we then determine the warmup length for each sampling unit for a given total warmup length budget using the BHM distributions for all sampling units.

4.1   Computing the BHM Distribution

Computing the BHM distribution for a given sampling unit is illustrated in Figure 2. At the top of Figure 2, a sampling unit along with its pre-sampling unit is shown. The bullets represent a single static branch being executed multiple times in the pre-sampling unit as well as in the sampling unit. Instructions with labels '1' thru '6' are part of the pre-sampling unit; instructions labeled '7', '8' and '9' are part of the sampling unit. A white bullet represents a non-taken branch; a black bullet shows a taken branch. Figure 2 also shows the global and local history for each dynamic instance of the given static branch; the example assumes three global history bits and three local history bits. Note that the most recent branch outcome is shifted in on the right hand side of the history register; for example, a non-taken branch changes the local history from '011' to '110'.

In order to compute the BHM distribution, we first compute the BHM histogram. The BHM histogram is computed by scanning all the branch instances in the sampling unit and proceeds as follows.

– *Searching the sampling unit.* We first determine whether there is a perfect match for the local and global history of the given branch instance in the sampling unit versus the local and global histories of all the preceding branch instances of the same static branch in the sampling unit. A perfect match means that both the local and global histories are identical for the two respective branch instances. For the example given in Figure 2, the local and global histories of branch instance '9' in the sampling unit show a perfect match with the local and global history of branch instance '7' in the sampling unit. This case increments the count for $d = 0$ in the BHM histogram.

– *Searching the pre-sampling unit.* In case there is no perfect match with a preceding branch instance in the sampling unit, we search the pre-sampling unit for the most recent branch instance that shows the highest match with the local and global history for the given branch instance. This is done by computing the Branch History Matching Score (BHMS) between the given branch instance in the sampling unit with all the branch instances of the same static branch in the pre-sampling unit. The BHMS between two branch instances is computed as the number of bit positions that are identical between the local and global histories of the respective branch instances. When computing the number of identical bit positions we count from the most recent bit to the least recent bit and we stop counting as soon as there is disagreement for a given bit, *i.e.*, we count the matching most recent history bits. This done for both the global and local histories; the overall BHMS then is the sum of the global and local BHMSs. Computed BHMSs are shown in Figure 2 for the first and second branch instances of the sampling unit. For example, the BHMS for branch instance '8' with relation to branch instance '4' equals 4, *i.e.*, 2 (compare global histories '0<u>11</u>' versus '1<u>11</u>') plus 2 (compare local histories '1<u>01</u>' versus '0<u>01</u>').

The first branch instance (with label '7') achieves a perfect match (BHMS equals 6) for the branch instance with label '5'. The idea is then to update the BHM histogram reflecting the fact that in order to have an accurate warmup for instruction '7' we need to go back to instruction '5' in the pre-sampling unit. For this purpose, the BHM histogram is incremented at distance $d1$ with '$d1$' being the number of instructions between the branch instance with label '5' and the beginning of the sampling unit — this is to say that branch predictor warmup should start at branch instruction '5'. For the second branch instance (with label '8') in the sampling unit,

```
/* this function computes the current warmup length */
int current_warmup_length (int* d) {
  for (i = 0; i < n; i++)
    sum += d[i];
  return sum;
}

/* main algorithm */

/* initialize warmup length for each sampling unit */
for (i = 0; i < n; i++)
  d[i] = 0;


/* iterate as long as the user defined total warmup length L_w is not reached */
while (current_warmup_length (d) < L_w) {

  /* find the sampling unit max_j that faces the maximum slope */
  max_prob = 0.0;
  max_i = -1;
  for (i = 0; i < n; i++) {
    if ((P[i][d[i] + b] - P[i][d[i]])/b > max_prob) {
      max_prob = (P[i][d[i] + b] - P[i][d[i]])/b;
      max_i = i;
    }
  }

  /* update warmup length for sampling unit facing the maximum slope */
  d[max_i] += d[max_i] + b;

}
```

Fig. 3. The algorithm in pseudocode for determining the warmup length per sampling unit using BHM distributions

the highest BHMS is obtained for the branch instance with label '6'; the number of instructions between that branch instance and the sampling unit starting point is denoted as $d2$ in Figure 2. We then increment the BHM histogram at distance $d2$.

Dividing the BHM histogram with the number of branch instances in the sampling unit, we then obtain the BHM distribution. Figure 2 shows the cumulative BHM distribution for the given sampling unit: since there are three branch instances in our example sampling unit, the cumulative distribution starts at $1/3$ for distance $d = 0$, reaches $2/3$ at distance $d = d2$ and finally reaches 1 at distance $d = d1$.

4.2 Determining Warmup Length

Once the BHM distribution is computed for each sampling unit we determine the warmup length per sampling unit for a given total warmup length budget. The goal is to partition a given warmup length budget over a number of sampling units so that accuracy is maximized. In other words, sampling units that do not require much warmup, are granted a small warmup length; sampling units that require much more warmup are given a much larger warmup length.

The algorithm for determining the appropriate warmup length per sampling unit works as follows, see also Figure 3 for the pseudocode of the algorithm. We start from n BHM distributions, with n being the number of sampling units. In each iteration,

Table 1. The branch predictors considered in this paper

predictor	configuration
gshare	16-bit history gshare predictor, 128Kbit total state
local	16-bit local predictor, 8K entries at first level, 64K entries at second level 256 Kbit total state
bimodal	64K-entry bimodal predictor, 128Kbit total state
hybrid	hybrid predictor consisting of a 32K-entry bimodal predictor, a 15-bit history gshare predictor and a 32K-entry PC-indexed meta predictor; 192Kbit total state

we determine the sampling unit i out of the n sampling units that faces the maximum slope in the BHM distribution. This means that the sampling unit i (called max_i in the pseudocode in Figure 3) is determined that maximizes the slope $\frac{P_i(d_i+b)-P_i(d_i)}{b}$, with $P_i(d)$ being the probability for distance d in the cumulative BHM distribution for sampling unit i, and d_i being the warmup length granted to sampling unit i in the current state of the algorithm. For the sampling unit i that maximizes the slope, we increase the granted warmup length d_i to $d_i + b$. This algorithm is iterated until the total warmup length over all sampling units equals a user-defined maximum warmup length L_w, i.e., $\sum_{i=1}^{n} d_i = L_w$. By doing so, we effectively budget warmup to samples that benefit the most from the granted warmup.

Note that this algorithm is only one possible design point in BHM warmup. More in particular, this algorithm heuristically determines to increase the warmup length for the sampling unit that faces the maximum slope in the BHM distribution. The algorithm does not take into account the distance over which this slope is observed; taking this distance into account for determining appropriate warmup lengths would be an interesting avenue for future work though.

4.3 Discussion

Most branch predictors in the literature as well as in today's commercial processors use a global and/or local branch history. Because BHM is also based on global and local branch history matching, it is to be expected that BHM will be an appropriate warmup technique for most branch predictors considered today. However, some branch predictors proposed in the literature are path-based and use a sequence of recent branch addresses as the branch history. In this paper though, we limit ourselves to branch predictors that are based on global and local branch histories. However, as part of our future work, we will further evaluate BHM for a broader range of branch predictors than the ones used in this paper.

5 Experimental Setup

We use SPEC CPU2000 integer benchmarks with reference inputs in our experimental setup. We include all integer benchmarks except for **perlbmk** because its branch misprediction rate is very low; in fact, no warmup is very accurate for **perlbmk**. The binaries which were compiled and optimized for the Alpha 21264 processor, were taken from the SimpleScalar website. All measurements presented in this paper are obtained using the binary instrumentation tool ATOM [22]. The branch predictors considered in this paper are shown in Table 1. We consider four fairly aggressive branch predictors: a gshare predictor, a local predictor, a bimodal predictor and a hybrid predictor [23,24].

Our primary metric for quantifying the accuracy of the branch predictor warmup approaches proposed in this paper is $\Delta MPKI$ which is defined as the absolute difference between the number of misses per thousand instructions under perfect warmup ($MPKI_{perfect}$) versus the number of misses per thousand instructions under the given branch predictor warmup approach ($MPKI_{warmup}$). In other words, $\Delta MPKI = \|MPKI_{warmup} - MPKI_{perfect}\|$ and thus the smaller $\Delta MPKI$, the better. Our second metric, next to accuracy, is warmup length which is defined as the number of instructions required by the given warmup technique. Likewise, the smaller the warmup length, the smaller the total simulation time, the better.

6   Evaluation

We now evaluate the accuracy and warmup length of BHM compared to fixed-length warmup; section 6.1 covers accuracy and section 6.2 covers warmup length. Throughout this evaluation we consider a sampling unit size of 10K instructions. The reason is that, as mentioned in section 3, small sampling unit sizes suffer most from the lack of warmup; small sampling unit sizes will stress our warmup approach the most. All the results presented in this paper are for 50 sampling units.

Further, we assume that the number of global and local history bits equals 16 for the BHM approach in sections 6.1 and 6.2. Section 6.3 then studies the impact of the BHM history length on accuracy and warmup length.

6.1   Accuracy

Comparison Against Fixed-Length Warmup. Figure 4 evaluates the accuracy of BHM compared to fixed-length warmup. Both warmup techniques are budgeted a 1M warmup length per sampling unit, *i.e.*, both warmup techniques use the same warmup length. The four graphs in Figure 4 represent four different branch predictors, namely the gshare, local, bimodal and hybrid branch predictors. The $\Delta MPKIs$ are shown for both warmup techniques. We observe that BHM substantially outperforms fixed-length warmup. Over all four branch predictors, the average $\Delta MPKI$ decreases from 0.48 (under fixed-length warmup) to 0.29 (under BHM) which is 39% more accurate.

Comparison Against MRRL. Figure 5 compares BHM against MRRL. As mentioned before, MRRL looks how far one needs to go back in the pre-sampling unit for encountering branch instances of the same static branch for all branch instances in the sampling unit. The results in Figure 5 show that BHM clearly outperforms MRRL. Over all four branch predictors, the average $\Delta MPKI$ decreases from 2.13 (under MRRL) to 0.29 (under BHM) which is 87% more accurate. The important difference between MRRL and BHM is that BHM, in contrast to MRRL, takes into account branch histories; this results in significantly more accurate branch predictor state warmup for BHM compared

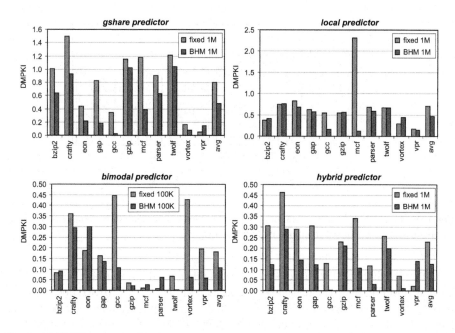

Fig. 4. $\Delta MPKI$ results for fixed 1M warmup and BHM for the gshare, local, bimodal and hybrid branch predictors

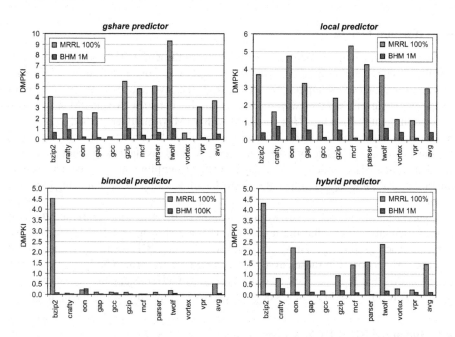

Fig. 5. $\Delta MPKI$ results for MRRL and BHM for the gshare, local, bimodal and hybrid branch predictors. For MRRL, we consider all branch instances in the sampling unit, hence the 'MRRL 100%' labels.

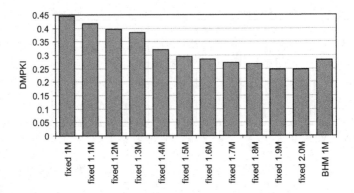

Fig. 6. Average $\Delta MPKI$ over the four branch predictors as a function of warmup length for the fixed-length warmup approach compared to BHM 1M

to MRRL. Note that MRRL also performs worse than fixed 1M warmup, compare Figure 4 against Figure 5. The reason is that, because of the fact that MRRL does not take into account branch history, MRRL is unable to come up with long enough warmup lengths for accurately warming up the branch predictors. The average warmup length through MRRL is only 200K instructions per sampling unit; according to our results, much larger warmup lengths are required to accurately warmup branch predictors.

6.2 Warmup Length

In order to quantify the reduction in warmup length through BHM compared to fixed-length warmup, we have measured the average $\Delta MPKI$ over the four branch predictors as a function of warmup length, see Figure 6. The average $\Delta MPKI$ is shown for fixed-length warmup with the warmup budget varying between 1M and 2M instructions per sampling unit. The $\Delta MPKI$ for BHM with a 1M warmup length budget per sampling unit is shown on the right. We observe that fixed-length warmup achieves about the same accuracy as BHM for a warmup length of 1.6M instructions per sampling unit. In other words, BHM with a 1M warmup budget per sampling unit results in a 1.6X reduction in warmup length compared to fixed-length warmup while achieving the same accuracy.

Figure 7 shows MPKI versus warmup length for the gcc benchmark and the four branch predictors. Note that the horizontal axes are shown on a log scale. The two curves in each graph represent fixed-length warmup and BHM warmup, respectively; and the various points in these curves represent different warmup budgets. This graph clearly shows that BHM achieves the same accuracy with substantially shorter warmup lengths, or reverse, BHM achieves better accuracy for the same warmup length.

6.3 Impact of BHM History Length

Note that the amount of branch history used by three of the four branch predictors, namely the gshare, local and hybrid predictors, equals 16 bits. The number of BHM

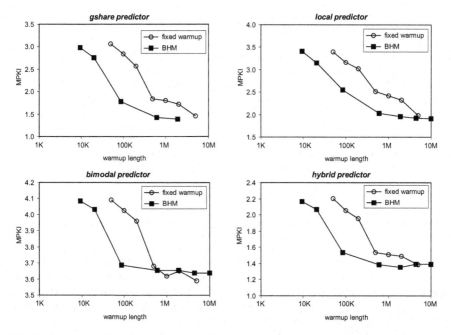

Fig. 7. Comparing BHM versus fixed warmup in terms of MPKI versus warmup length for gcc

history bits used for computing the warmup length also equals 16 bits. The question however is how sensitive BHM's accuracy is to the BHM history length.

Figure 8 explores the impact of the BHM history length. The average $\Delta MPKI$ over all benchmarks is shown on the vertical axis versus the warmup length on the horizontal axis. The five curves represent the five branch predictors. The different points on each curve represent different BHM history lengths. We varied the BHM history length from 0, 2, 4, 8 to 16; when varying the history length we simultaneously vary the global and local BHM history lengths. A zero BHM history length means that no global and local history is taken into account for building the BHM distribution. In other words, the BHM warmup method then simply looks for the last occurrence of the same static branch for updating the BHM distribution. In all of these experiments, we budgeted a warmup length to 1M instructions per sampling unit.

There are two interesting observations to be made from this graph. First, accuracy improves or $\Delta MPKI$ decreases with increasing BHM history lengths. This is to be expected because the more history is taken into account, the better BHM will be able to determine how far it needs to go back in the pre-sampling unit for appropriate warmup. Second, small BHM histories are unable to budget the warmup lengths so that the average warmup length per sampling unit effectively equals the 1M instruction warmup budget. For example, a zero BHM history only yields slightly more than 200K instructions of warmup per sampling unit. In other words, it is impossible for BHM with limited history to fully exploit the available warmup budget. By increasing the BHM history length, BHM is better able to approach the target 1M warmup length per sampling unit. (Note that the MRRL approach [17,20] corresponds to a zero BHM history

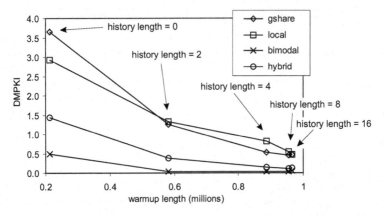

Fig. 8. Evaluating the impact of the BHM history length on accuracy and warmup length

length.) We further observe that an 8 bit and a 16 bit BHM history length yields approximately the same accuracy. From this experiment, we thus conclude that in order to achieve accurate warmup for branch predictors, the BHM history length needs to be set to an appropriate value, for example, to the maximum history length one would look at during the branch predictor design space exploration.

7   Conclusion

Sampled simulation is a well known approach to speed up architectural simulations that are heavily used by computer architects and designers. An important issue with sampled simulation however is the cold-start problem, *i.e.*, the microarchitecture state is unknown at the beginning of each sampling unit. Although a great deal of work has been done on cache structure warmup, very little research has been done on branch predictor warmup.

This paper proposed Branch History Matching (BHM) as a novel branch predictor warmup method. The idea is to analyze the sampling unit as well as the pre-sampling unit for recurring branch instances of the same static branch with similar global and local branch histories. By doing so, BHM builds a distribution for each sampling unit that characterizes the branch locality behavior. BHM then budgets its total warmup budget to the various sampling units. Sampling units that are warmup-sensitive are budgeted more warmup; sampling units that are warmup-insensitive are budgeted less warmup. Compared to fixed-length warmup, BHM achieves better accuracy for the same total warmup budget, or reverse, BHM achieves the same accuracy with a shorter total warmup budget.

Acknowledgements

The authors would like to thank the anonymous reviewers for their valuable feedback. Lieven Eeckhout is a Postdoctoral Fellow with the Fund for Scientific Research—Flanders (Belgium) (FWO—Vlaanderen). This research is also supported by Ghent University, IWT, HiPEAC and the European SARC project No. 27648.

References

1. Conte, T.M., Hirsch, M.A., Menezes, K.N.: Reducing state loss for effective trace sampling of superscalar processors. In: ICCD. (1996) 468–477
2. Sherwood, T., Perelman, E., Hamerly, G., Calder, B.: Automatically characterizing large scale program behavior. In: ASPLOS. (2002) 45–57
3. Wunderlich, R.E., Wenisch, T.F., Falsafi, B., Hoe, J.C.: SMARTS: Accelerating microarchitecture simulation via rigorous statistical sampling. In: ISCA. (2003) 84–95
4. Yi, J.J., Kodakara, S.V., Sendag, R., Lilja, D.J., Hawkins, D.M.: Characterizing and comparing prevailing simulation techniques. In: HPCA. (2005) 266–277
5. Van Biesbrouck, M., Eeckhout, L., Calder, B.: Efficient sampling startup for sampled processor simulation. In: HiPEAC. (2005) 47–67
6. Wenish, T., Wunderlich, R., Falsafi, B., Hoe, J.: TurboSMARTS: Accurate microarchitecture simulation in minutes. In: SIGMETRICS. (2005) 408–409
7. Barr, K.C., Pan, H., Zhang, M., Asanovic, K.: Accelerating multiprocessor simulation with a memory timestamp record. In: ISPASS. (2005) 66–77
8. Van Ertvelde, L., Hellebaut, F., Eeckhout, L., De Bosschere, K.: NSL-BLRL: Efficient cache warmup for sampled processor simulation. In: ANSS. (2006) 168–175
9. Wenisch, T.F., Wunderlich, R.E., Falsafi, B., Hoe, J.C.: Simulation sampling with live-points. In: ISPASS. (2006) 2–12
10. Barr, K.C., Asanovic, K.: Branch trace compression for snapshot-based simulation. In: ISPASS. (2006) 25–36
11. Girbal, S., Mouchard, G., Cohen, A., Temam, O.: DiST: A simple, reliable and scalable method to significantly reduce processor architecture simulation time. In: SIGMETRICS. (2003) 1–12
12. Lauterbach, G.: Accelerating architectural simulation by parallel execution of trace samples. Technical Report SMLI TR-93-22, Sun Microsystems Laboratories Inc. (1993)
13. Kessler, R.E., Hill, M.D., Wood, D.A.: A comparison of trace-sampling techniques for multi-megabyte caches. IEEE Transactions on Computers **43** (1994) 664–675
14. Wood, D.A., Hill, M.D., Kessler, R.E.: A model for estimating trace-sample miss ratios. In: SIGMETRICS. (1991) 79–89
15. Conte, T.M., Hirsch, M.A., Hwu, W.W.: Combining trace sampling with single pass methods for efficient cache simulation. IEEE Transactions on Computers **47** (1998) 714–720
16. Haskins Jr., J.W., Skadron, K.: Minimal subset evaluation: Rapid warm-up for simulated hardware state. In: ICCD-2001. (2001) 32–39
17. Haskins Jr., J.W., Skadron, K.: Memory Reference Reuse Latency: Accelerated warmup for sampled microarchitecture simulation. In: ISPASS. (2003) 195–203
18. Eeckhout, L., Luo, Y., De Bosschere, K., John, L.K.: BLRL: Accurate and efficient warmup for sampled processor simulation. The Computer Journal **48** (2005) 451–459
19. Luo, Y., John, L.K., Eeckhout, L.: Self-monitored adaptive cache warm-up for microprocessor simulation. In: SBAC-PAD. (2004) 10–17
20. Haskins, J.W., Skadron, K.: Accelerated warmup for sampled microarchitecture simulation. ACM Transactions on Architecture and Code Optimization (TACO) **2** (2005) 78–108
21. Perelman, E., Hamerly, G., Calder, B.: Picking statistically valid and early simulation points. In: PACT. (2003) 244–256
22. Srivastava, A., Eustace, A.: ATOM: A system for building customized program analysis tools. Technical Report 94/2, Western Research Lab, Compaq (1994)
23. McFarling, S.: Combining branch predictors. Technical Report WRL TN-36, Digital Western Research Laboratory (1993)
24. Yeh, T.Y., Patt, Y.N.: Alternative implementations of two-level adaptive branch prediction. In: ISCA. (1992) 124–134

Sunflower: Full-System, Embedded Microarchitecture Evaluation

Phillip Stanley-Marbell and Diana Marculescu

Department of Electrical and Computer Engineering
Carnegie Mellon University
Pittsburgh, PA 15217, USA

Abstract. This paper describes *Sunflower*, a full-system microarchitectural evaluation environment for embedded computing systems. The environment enables detailed microarchitectural simulation of multiple instances of complete embedded systems, their peripherals, and medium access control / physical layer communication between systems. The environment models the microarchitecture, computation and communication upset events under a variety of stochastic distributions, compute and communication power consumption, electrochemical battery systems, and power regulation circuitry, as well as analog signals external to the processing elements.

The simulation environment provides facilities for speeding up simulation performance, which tradeoff accuracy of simulated properties for simulation speed. Through the detailed simulation of benchmarks in which the effect of simulation speedup on correctness can be accurately quantified, it is demonstrated that traditional techniques proposed for simulation speedup can introduce significant error when simulating a combination of computation and analog physical phenomena external to a processor.

1   Introduction

The focus of computing systems has shifted over the years, from mainframes in the 1960's and minicomputers in the '70s, to workstations and personal computers (PCs) in the '80s. A majority of recent microarchitecture research has focused on architectures destined for PC, workstation and server-class systems. The last decade has however seen increasing use of computing systems that are *embedded* unobtrusively in our environments. Examples at the low end of the spectrum include low-power wired and wireless sensor networks, to home automation systems, and so-called "white goods" (e.g., microwaves, dishwashers). At the middle- to high-end, personal digital assistants (PDAs) and mobile telephones employ embedded processors for application execution and signal processing. Processors in embedded systems typically interact directly with analog signals in their environment, through analog-to-digital (A/D) and digital-to-analog (D/A) converters. For example, a processor in a home automation system might be connected through an on-chip or external A/D converter, to temperature and humidity sensors. These systems not only have power consumption

K. De Bosschere et al. (Eds.): HiPEAC 2007, LNCS 4367, pp. 168–182, 2007.

constraints, but are also often battery powered, necessitating the consideration of how the variation of power consumed over time affects the efficiency of energy sources such as electrochemical cells.

In order to accurately evaluate microarchitectures for embedded applications, it is desirable to model the *entire system* — from the detailed microarchitecture, to the typical integrated peripherals as well as the time-varying analog signals in the environment which often drive computation. It is desirable to be able to perform power and thermal estimation in these systems, and also to have a means of determining how the power consumption profile (variation in power dissipated over time) affects battery lifetime; this arises from the fact that two power consumption profiles with the same average, can result in different effective battery lifetimes, due to non-linearities in electrochemical cell characteristics. Since integrated circuits are usually connected to batteries through voltage regulators, which have variable efficiencies across different current loads, an ideal simulation environment would also provide capabilities for modeling the behavior of such regulators. Perhaps even more so than in PC-, workstation- and server-class systems, embedded computing systems are subject to failures. If investigating microarchitectural techniques for building reliable systems, it is desirable to be able to model intermittent processor and network failures, drawn from a variety of stochastic failure models.

This paper describes *Sunflower*, a full-system microarchitectural evaluation environment for embedded computing systems. The environment enables simulation of multiple instances of complete embedded systems, their peripherals (e.g., A/D converters, timers), as well as medium access control- (MAC) and physical-layer (PHY) communication between systems. For each system, the environment enables detailed microarchitectural simulation of instruction execution (pipelined instruction execution, caches, memory management hardware, on-chip buses), modeling of computation and communication faults, compute and communication power consumption, electrochemical battery systems and power regulation circuitry. The simulation environment enables the modeling of analog signals external to the processing elements, permitting realistic evaluation of a combination of computation, communication and their interaction with analog signals. The facilities provided by the environment include:

- Full-system simulation of multiple, networked embedded systems.
- Microarchitectural simulation of a choice of a 16-bit or 32-bit architecture.
- Integrated trace gathering capabilities harnessing debugging information in compiled binaries.
- Switching activity estimation and instruction-level power models.
- Voltage and frequency scaling across different values of process technology parameters (V_T, K, α).
- Electrochemical battery and voltage regulator models for several batteries and voltage regulators.
- Modeling propagation and spatial attenuation of analog signals.
- Medium Access Control (MAC) and physical-layer modeling of arbitrary communication topologies.

- Modeling of logic upsets in the microarchitecture, and whole-system failures in processor cores and network interfaces.
- Failure modeling supported by random variables generated from over 20 common probability distributions.

2 Related Research

Simulation forms the backbone of exploratory microarchitecture research. Through the use of appropriate tools, architects can gain insight into how design decisions affect metrics of interest, be they performance (throughput, latency), power consumption, thermal efficiency, reliability, or other domain-specific properties.

Tools that have been developed for use in microarchitecture simulation include the Wisconsin Wind tunnel simulators [1], SimpleScalar [2] and its derivatives, Trimaran's HPL-PD simulator [3], Microlib [4] and Liberty [5]. Each of these simulation environments have addressed specific needs of their developers, or have addressed trends in architecture research, such as multiprocessor systems and their coherence mechanisms, wide-issue, deeply pipelined superscalar out-of-order machines, EPIC/VLIW and embedded architectures, or modular simulator construction. It is sometimes the objective not to design a new microarchitecture, but rather, to design a *system architecture*, including the processor, complete memory hierarchy (caches, main memory, backing store), networking and other I/O. In such situations, architects typically use *full-system simulators*. These include tools like SimOS [6], M5 [7] and Simics [8].

Over the last decade, power consumption and thermal efficiency have emerged as leading design evaluation metrics, and this has led to the development of new tools and extensions of existing microarchitectural simulators, to enable power and thermal modeling. Examples include the HotSpot [9] thermal analysis framework, and the Wattch [10] extensions to the SimpleScalar toolset. New tools and techniques, such as the use of instruction-level power analysis in microarchitectural

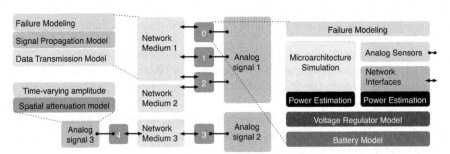

Fig. 1. Illustrative example of simulator organization. For any collection of nodes (processing element + memory + energy source), the separate instantiation of *network interfaces* and *network media* allows the creation of rich communication topologies. A collection of definitions of signal sources can similarly be used to create rich topologies of physical phenomena.

simulators [11,12,13] have also enabled faster power estimation, with adequate accuracy on embedded processor architectures.

3   Simulation Environment Architecture

The Sunflower simulator comprises components for modeling five primary entities: (1) processor microarchitecture, (2) networking between embedded systems and the attendant power dissipation, (3) battery systems (electrochemical cells and voltage regulators necessary to provide stable voltages to electronics as the battery terminal voltage declines with battery discharge), (4) failures in computation and communication, and (5) modeling the physics of signal propagation in the environment in which computation occurs. Each instantiated node has an associated location in three-dimensional space, which is used in the modeling of signal propagation and attenuation with distance, described in Section 3.6. Figure 1 illustrates these facilities with an example. In the Figure, five complete embedded systems, composed of processors and their peripherals, such as network interfaces, along with their energy sources, are shown. Each modeled embedded system (henceforth, *node*), is instantiated with one *network interface* (e.g., nodes 0, 1, 3 and 4) or more (e.g., two network interfaces for node 2). These network interfaces are attached to simulated *communication-* or *network media.* Three external *physical phenomena* (analog signals 1, 2 and 3) are instantiated, and these could be configured to model, e.g., an acoustic signal or a light source, by specifying signal propagation and attenuation models, as described in Section 3.6.

3.1   Instruction Execution

The simulator models two complementary instruction set architectures (ISAs): a 16-bit RISC ISA, the Texas Instruments MSP430, and a 32-bit RISC ISA, the Renesas SH; the Renesas SH ISA simulation core is adapted from our earlier work [13]. The default microarchitecture configurations for the two modeled ISAs are shown in Figure 2.

For each microarchitecture, the simulator models the movement of instructions through the pipeline latches, as well as signal transitions on the address/data buses and register file ports. The modeling of these structures facilitates two things. First, it enables the estimation of signal switching activity in these structures (Section 3.3), which account for a large fraction of the dynamic power consumption in embedded processors. Second, it enables the simulation of logic upsets, both single-event upsets (SEUs) and multi-bit upsets, as described in Section 3.5.

The default microarchitecture configuration for the 32-bit ISA model includes a shared instruction / data cache. The cache size, block size and associativity are simulation parameters, and an implementation of an LRU replacement algorithm is provided. The default 32-bit ISA model also includes a Translation Lookaside Buffer (TLB) implementation based on that in the Renesas SH3. Like the cache, it is configurable by number of entries, set size and associativity.

Asynchronous hardware *interrupts* and synchronous software *exceptions* constitute an important part of program execution in many embedded software

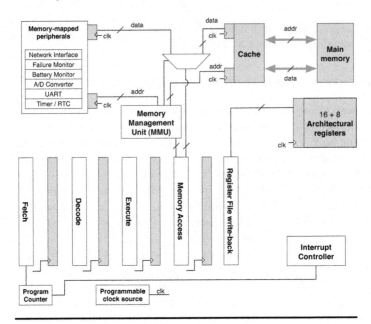

: Structures modeled at bit-level, enabling monitoring of signal transition activity and logic upset modeling

(a) Default configuration of the modeled, 32-bit architecture, employing the Renesas SH ISA.

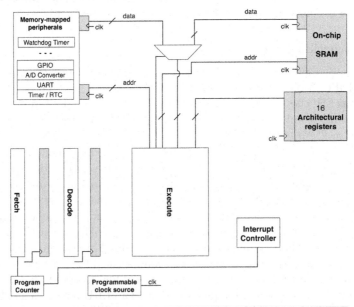

: Structures modeled at bit-level, enabling signal transition activity and logic upset modeling

(b) Default configuration of the modeled 16-bit architecture, employing the TI MSP430 ISA.

Fig. 2. Default configuration of the modeled microarchitectures

applications. In these systems, hardware interrupts are usually generated by peripherals within or external to the processor, such as communication interfaces, timers, and the like. Software exceptions on the other hand are also common as they are used to implement the boundary crossing between applications and an operating system kernel. Interrupts and exceptions are modeled for both architectures. In the case of the 32-bit architecture, the interrupt sources include timer interrupts (generated by the simulator at configurable intervals), low battery interrupts (described in Section 3.4) and several communication interface specific interrupts (described in Section 3.2). For the 16-bit ISA, the simulation environment models the signals at the I/O pins. The processor's I/O pins may be configured to generate interrupts on *level* or *edge* triggers, thus any analog signal configured outside the modeled processor (described in Section 3.6) may be used to trigger interrupts. Applications executing over the simulator which desire to interact with peripherals that generate interrupts, must therefore link in an assembly language low-level interrupt handler, to save machine state upon triggering the interrupt, and restore it after completion.

To enable the simulation of common benchmark suites, the applications within which often depend on executing above an operating system, the Sunflower simulation environment can intercept software exceptions corresponding to system calls. The exception value along with the machine state (according to the manufacturer and compiler defined application binary interface (ABI)) are then used to recreate the system call and pass it down to the simulation host's operating system; the results of the system call are similarly inserted into the machine state.

3.2 Communication Interconnect

There are a variety of communication protocols employed in embedded systems, ranging from serial protocols like RS-232, RS-485, SPI and I2C, to protocols like Ethernet (IEEE 802.3), 802.11a/b/g and the recent 802.15.3 short range low power MAC protocol. The approach taken for modeling networks in Sunflower attempts to accommodate the implementation, by the user, of any variety of protocols.

Communication between devices in the Sunflower framework may either be through a modeled MAC-layer communication interface, or by direct modulation of an analog signal as described in 3.6. This modeling of communication

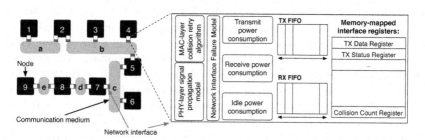

Fig. 3. Modeling of communication networks is separated into the modeling of *network interfaces*, connected to *communication media* to form communication topologies

comprises two parts. First, the interface to communication, as driven by computation, is a *network interface* peripheral. Each processor may be configured with multiple instances of such network interfaces. Each interface is parameterized by transmit and receive FIFO queue sizes, transmit, receive and idle power consumption, as well as a choice of collision back-off algorithms. Second, network interfaces must be explicitly connected to (at most one) *communication network medium*, at which point they inherit their remaining properties—communication speed, frame size and physical layer characteristics—from the medium to which they are attached.

A link failure probability can be selected for each communication medium, as well as the maximum number of simultaneous transmissions permitted on a medium. The latter permits the modeling of either a single access medium accessed via MAC layer protocols that perform, e.g., *Carrier-Sense Multiple Access with Collision Detection (CSMA/CD)*, or a multiplex medium. Network topologies are created by instantiating network media, and connecting to them network interfaces of nodes that must communicate over the same channel; this separation of network interfaces and network media enables the modeling of arbitrary sophisticated interconnection topologies. Figure 3 illustrates the organization of an example network. Applications being modeled within the microarchitecture simulation interact with the network interface through a set of memory-mapped registers and generated interrupts. The figure depicts an example network comprising nine nodes, connected in a topology consisting of 5 disjoint communication media. Some of the nodes, e.g., 2, 5, 7, and 8 have multiple network interfaces, and are attached to multiple media through these interfaces. Some media, e.g., **b** and **c** are "multi-drop" or shared links, while others (**a**, **d** and **e**), are point-to-point.

In addition to network traffic driven directly by computation being simulated within the framework, it is also possible to use real-world MAC-layer network traces in simulation studies (e.g., as gathered on networks using the open source Ethereal tool). Traces of the network communications obtained during simulation, resulting from the dynamic behavior of simulated benchmark execution, can also be dumped to disk.

3.3   Modeling Power Consumption

The simulator includes a set of complementary methods for power estimation. By modeling the movement of instructions through the microarchitecture, it is possible to obtain estimates of signal switching activity in many microarchitectural structures (Figure 2). These reports can be used in comparative analysis of dynamic power dominated systems; if the capacitances of the structures can be determined, they can be used to estimate actual dynamic power consumption.

The second, coarser-grain facility for power estimation is an instruction-level power model developed as part of our earlier research [13]. This model involved characterizing the average power for each instruction in the ISA through actual hardware measurements, and incorporating these measurements into the simulator as a lookup table. During instruction simulation, the lookup table is used

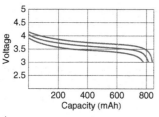

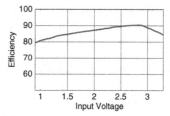

(a) Battery voltage versus charge, for the Panasonic CGR17500 (drain currents, top to bottom: 156mA, 780mA and 1560ma).

(b) Voltage regulator efficiency versus battery terminal voltage curve, for the TI TPS61070.

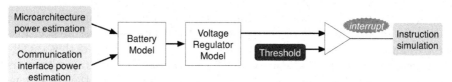

(c) Interaction between battery subsystem model and microarchitecture simulation.

Fig. 4. Examples of manufacturer supplied characterization data provided with the Sunflower simulator ((a) and (b)), and illustration of battery subsystem modeling organization (c)

to provide power estimates based on the cycle-by-cycle mix of instructions. It has been shown [11,12] that for embedded processors, which usually have simple in-order pipelines, such instruction-level power estimation provides acceptable accuracy in power estimation. The instruction-level power analysis characterization for the Renesas SH employed in Sunflower, has previously been verified against hardware measurements [13]; we are currently in the process of obtaining similar instruction-level power characterization for the TI MSP430.

In the third and coarsest grain power estimation facility, the average active and sleep power consumption for the CPU and network interface are provided by a user, obtained either from empirical measurements or from a manufacturer's data sheet. During simulation, as the simulated processor transitions between active and sleep modes, or engages in communication, the associated power consumption is fed into the power estimation and battery modeling framework. Unlike workstation and server class systems, many embedded systems spend most of their time idle. As a result, their overall energy consumption is largely dictated by the fraction of time they are active versus idle (in sleep mode). This coarse-grained power estimation, in conjunction with battery models, can therefore still provide a good indicator of system lifetime.

The net current drawn by the CPU and all its peripherals, based on the above power estimation methods, is fed to a model for a battery subsystem, made up of a voltage regulator (DC-DC converter) model, and a battery model.

Table 1. A list of some of the commercial electrochemical batteries and voltage regulators for which models are supplied with the Sunflower simulation framework. Parameters for additional models are easily supplied at simulation time.

Modeled Electrochemical Batteries	Modeled Voltage regulators
Panasonic CGP345010, CGP345010g CGR17500, CGR18650HM.	Dallas Semiconductor MAX1653, TI TPS6107x, TPS6110x, TPS6113x.

3.4   Battery Subsystem Modeling

Embedded systems are often powered by electrochemical batteries such as Lithium-ion (Li-ion), Li/MnO_2 or NiMh cells. The terminal voltage across these cells varies with their state of charge and discharge current (illustrated in Figure 4(a) for a Panasonic CGR17500 battery, at 20 °C), and they are thus usually connected to the circuits they drive through *voltage regulators*. Voltage regulators incur energy conversion losses, and their efficiency depends on their load current, as well as the battery terminal voltage; this is illustrated for a TI TPS61070 voltage regulator in Figure 4(b), for a load current of 5mA and output voltage of 3.3V. As a result, of these phenomena, two systems with identical average power consumption, but with different time-varying power consumption profiles, may witness different battery lifetimes.

In order to capture the effect of simulated system power consumption, and its variation over time, on battery lifetime, the Sunflower simulation environment enables the modeling of both batteries and the voltage regulators that are used to interface them to the systems they drive (Figure 4(c)). The simulator incorporates actual measured characteristics supplied by the manufacturers of batteries and regulators, into a discrete-time model adapted from [14]. The default set of such battery and regulator models supplied with the simulator are listed in Table 1. The curves shown in Figure 4 are plotted from this characterization data that is used by the simulation environment.

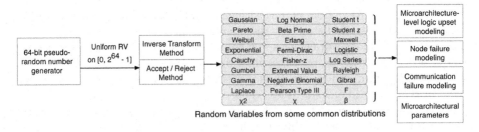

Fig. 5. A high periodicity 64-bit pseudo random number generator is used as the basis for generating random variables from a large set of distributions. In addition to the distributions listed here, a distribution having a "bathtub" shaped hazard function is also provided.

3.5   Modeling Processor and Interconnect Failures

Runtime faults in processing elements might be due to causes ranging from design errors, defects introduced during the manufacturing process and device aging, to external phenomena such as high energy particles (e.g., alpha particles). These faults, if not masked by fault-tolerance or fault-avoidance techniques, may manifest themselves as failures in the system.

The modeling of such faults in hardware may be performed using a variety of approaches. *Bit-level modeling of logic upsets* enables investigation of microarchitectural techniques for reliability-aware architectures. In most embedded systems, it is undesirable for a processor to get "wedged" or "stuck", as such systems often control critical infrastructure (e.g., the anti-lock braking system of a car). Many embedded processors therefore include a facility called a *watchdog timer* — a hardware peripheral that must be accessed by software at regular intervals, failure to do so causing a system reset. The modeling of *whole system-failures* is thus also of interest, due to the possible occurrence of such watchdog timer resets.

Underlying both the modeling of bit-level and whole-system failures is the generation of random events. For simulations which have long duration, it is desirable for any pseudo-random sequences they employ to not repeat. While useful for some simple applications, the standard C library pseudo-random number generation routines provided with most operating systems do not provide sufficiently high periodicity when simulating billions of random events. Fortunately, the research literature contains better solutions for generating pseudo-random numbers, and we have incorporated one of these [15] in the simulator.

Pseudo-random number generators typically generate values uniformly distributed on some support set. However, during systems evaluation, it is often desirable to use random numbers drawn from some other distribution, such as, e.g., a Gaussian, χ^2, or a heavy-tailed distribution like the Pareto distribution. Standard textbook methods [16] facilitate transforming random variables taken from one distribution (e.g., uniform) to obtain random variables drawn on a different distribution (e.g., exponential). The Sunflower simulation environment implements the generation of random variables from over twenty different distributions, shown in Figure 5. These distributions (with appropriate parameters,) can be used by a system architect to define the distribution of time between failures, duration of failures, or locations of logic upsets. When modeling bit-level logic upsets, the structures shaded grey in Figure 2 are treated as a single large bit vector. A bit in this vector is then forced to a logic 1 or logic zero, with probability across the bits determined by the chosen distribution.

Failures in communication can be induced either by directly configuring a communication link with a failure probability and duration distribution, or by defining time-varying external noise signals which interfere with the physical layer communication model (Section 3.6) associated with a communication link. During failures of the former kind, nodes that attempt to access the medium via a connected network interface will incur a *carrier-sense* error at the network interface. For the latter kind of failures, random bit errors are introduced into the transmitted data if the signal to noise ratio falls below the user-specified

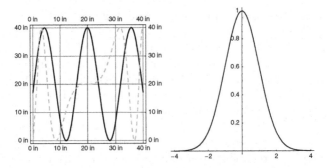

Fig. 6. Trajectories of two signal sources (solid black line and dashed gray line) across a 40"x40" area (left), and their attenuation with radial distance (right). The simulated target velocity was 10" per second.

Table 2. Relevant simulation configuration parameters

Network Parameter	Value	Other Parameters	Value
Bit rate	38.4 Kb/s	Voltage regulator	Maxim MAX1653
MAC layer frame size	128 bytes	Electrochemical cell	Panasonic CGR-18
Propagation model	Ricean	Battery capacity	0.1 mAh
TX power	89 mW	CPU active/sleep power	26.4 mW / 49μW
RX power	33 mW	Clock frequency	4 MHz

tolerable minimum. Such corrupted frames will lead to the generation of frame checksum errors (and the associated interrupt) at the MAC layer.

3.6 Modeling Analog Signals External to Processing Elements

The Sunflower framework enables the simulation of time-varying analog signals external to an embedded system, alongside microarchitecture, power and communication modeling. These real-valued analog signals are accessible to the modeled computation through the A/D converter peripherals. The modeling of analog signals consists of four components: (1) the modeling of the time-variation of signals; (2) signal location in three dimensional space; (3) signal attenuation with radial distance; (4) constructive and destructive interference between signals.

A signal propagation model may be associated with a communication medium, enabling the modeling of some aspects of a network's physical (PHY) layer. This can be used, for example, to model the signal propagation properties of a wireless channel. While it is widely understood that there is no single best model for capturing wireless network behavior in simulation, this approach lets the user of the simulation environment decide what signal propagation model to use.

4   Example

To illustrate the use of Sunflower in studying the behavior of an embedded application, this section presents an evaluation of a cluster formation and object tracking algorithm, *Distributed Aggregate Management (DAM)* and its extension, *Energy Based Activity Monitoring (EBAM)* [17]. Errors in the results of these algorithms can be exactly quantified, and we utilize this fact to demonstrate how traditional simulation speedup techniques, if applied naively, can introduce errors in the behavior of the simulated application. These errors result from the need, when simulating both instruction execution and analog signals external to the processor, to keep the passage of time synchronous across the two domains.

Figure 6 shows the two target (light source) trajectories, and the light intensity attenuation profile employed in subsequent simulations[1]. Since these trajectories may overlap, when a single location is reported by simulation, it may be due to two overlapping actual targets. The simulated network consisted of 25 nodes, located at the grid points in the figure. The nodes and their network interfaces were configured at simulation time to model the computation performance, network speed and power consumption properties listed in Table 2. The DAM and EBAM algorithms were implemented in C and Renesas SH assembly language (for parts of the interrupt handler), and compiled with the GCC toolsuite. The microarchitectural simulation of this code, on each simulated node, interacts with the modeled sensor and networking peripherals. The values read off sensors are driven by the simulator's analog signal modeling, and interaction with the network peripherals drives the simulator's communication network models. In the investigations that follow, each configuration of the algorithm was simulated until the modeled battery (sized to constrain simulation time) was fully depleted. Each data point in the following graphs thus corresponds to the simulation of over 150 million instructions.

4.1   Measuring Benchmark Error

The benchmark output from each architectural simulation includes a list of reported target locations with timestamps. Since the actual trajectory of the targets provided as input to simulation is known, the error in reported target locations can be computed. Three different error metrics were computed and are reported in what follows.

Optimistic Error (oerr). Whenever the simulation output, resulting from architectural simulation, indicates a reported target location, the true target locations *at that time instant* are determined. Then, for each *true* target location, the closest *reported* target location is determined. The Euclidean distance between this pair is computed, removing the reported target from further consideration. If there are more reported target locations than true target locations, such excess reports are discarded.

Optimistic Error with Uniform Sampling (o-uerr). When the error computation is performed as above, the error is only computed when the results of simulation report a target location. This does not capture the fact that during

---

[1] While the trajectories shown here are *regular*, the modeling of arbitrarily irregular trajectories is supported.

certain periods of the application, no target location is reported when one or more should be. In calculating the optimistic error with uniform sampling, a list of true target locations is generated for each sampling period of the application. For each such period, all reported locations falling within the period are grouped together. The error is then calculated as described above. If no reported target locations exist for a period, the optimistic error is set to zero.

Pessimistic Error with Uniform Sampling (p-uerr). In the pessimistic error computation, when the list of true target locations has been exhausted, the process is restarted for the remaining reported target locations. The pessimistic error will therefore be large when the application reports an excessive number of target locations compared to true locations (the optimistic error on the other hand ignores "over-reporting").

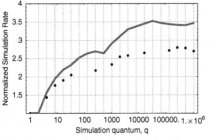

(a) Simulation speedup with increasing simulation quantum: DAM (solid), EBAM (points).

(b) Location error overestimation versus simulation quantum, for DAM (solid, dashed) and EBAM (points).

Fig. 7. Effect of simulation quantum size on simulation speed and accuracy of measured system parameters. The error plot in (b) shows oerr (light grey), o-uerr (black) and p-uerr (blue in color document, dark grey in greyscale). In (b), the data points for EBAM p-uerr are coincident with those for EBAM o-uerr (black points) and are thus not visible.

4.2   Effectiveness and Error of Simulation Speedup Techniques

A primary source of overhead in simulating systems comprising multiple processing elements, under the requirement of keeping their evolution in time synchronous, is the overhead of advancing each in time, in lock-step. In a simulator implementation, this implies that each processor is simulated for one clock cycle, and any relevant simulated state due for updating (e.g., external signal sources) are updated, before each processor is once more advanced for one clock cycle. An applicable simulation speedup method is to increase the number of cycles by which each modeled processor is advanced before returning to the main simulation loop. This number of cycles is referred to henceforth as the simulation *quantum*. Modeling analog signals external to the microarchitecture requires synchronization of the time-line of computation with these signals. Employing increasingly larger simulation quanta will therefore violate this synchronization, and possibly introduce errors in comparison to fine-grained interleaving. There is therefore a tradeoff between simulation speed and the degree of fine-grained interleaving (and hence, simulation accuracy).

Effect of Simulation Quantum Size on Simulation Error. Increasing the quantum from 1 to n causes n instructions to be simulated on one CPU before the next, round-robin. This leads to a simulation speedup since the time spent in the outer simulation loop is reduced. The trend in simulation speed as n is increased from 1 to 2^{20}, is shown in Figure 7(a), for the DAM and EBAM benchmarks; large quantum sizes can provide simulation speedups of up to 250%. The difference in speedup obtained for the two benchmarks is a result of their differing communication patterns.

Relaxing the synchronization of simulated time across simulated embedded systems in a network may however introduce errors in the simulation of an application. This phenomenon is illustrated in Figure 7(b). As can be seen in Figure 7(b), the error is also dependent on the application. The first source of error in using large fixed quantum sizes, is the disruption of the correct fine-grained interleaving of communication. For communication intensive benchmarks, employing large fixed quantum sizes is therefore undesirable. The second source of error arises from de-synchronization of the models for components external to the CPU (e.g., external modeled analog signals) during each quantum.

5   Summary and Future Work

This paper presented Sunflower, a simulation environment for networks of failure-prone, battery powered embedded systems. It models computation at the microarchitecture level, communication at the MAC and physical layers, failures in devices and communication media, and external analog signals, their location, and motion, in 3-dimensional space. Three complementary means of power estimation are provided, and instantaneous power estimates during simulation are fed into a model for a battery system consisting of a voltage regulator and an electrochemical cell. The simulation environment is implemented in ANSI C, and is available in source form, with pre-compiled binaries for several platforms including Linux, MacOS X, and Windows.

Based on the TI MSP430 architecture modeled in the simulation framework, we have developed a research hardware prototype, that we intend to make publicly available. We are currently in the process of performing detailed characterization of this prototype, and integrating our measurements into the simulation framework. It is our hope that this will enable future detailed investigations of microarchitectures for existent and emerging embedded platforms, that can be verified against cheaply available research hardware.

References

1. Reinhardt, S.K., Hill, M.D., Larus, J.R., Lebeck, A.R., Lewis, J.C., Wood, D.A.: The wisconsin wind tunnel: virtual prototyping of parallel computers. In: SIG-METRICS '93: Proceedings of the 1993 ACM SIGMETRICS conference on Measurement and modeling of computer systems, New York, NY, USA, ACM Press (1993) 48–60

2. Burger, D., Austin, T.M.: The simplescalar tool set, version 2.0. SIGARCH Comput. Archit. News **25**(3) (1997) 13–25
3. Hewlett-Packard Research Compiler and Architecture Research group: Trimaran HPL-PD simulator. (In: http://www.trimaran.org/ (accessed June 2006))
4. Perez, D.G., Mouchard, G., Temam, O.: Microlib: A case for the quantitative comparison of micro-architecture mechanisms. In: MICRO 37: Proceedings of the 37th annual IEEE/ACM International Symposium on Microarchitecture, Washington, DC, USA, IEEE Computer Society (2004) 43–54
5. Vachharajani, M., Vachharajani, N., Penry, D.A., Blome, J.A., August, D.I.: Microarchitectural exploration with liberty. In: MICRO 35: Proceedings of the 35th annual ACM/IEEE international symposium on Microarchitecture, Los Alamitos, CA, USA, IEEE Computer Society Press (2002) 271–282
6. Rosenblum, M., Herrod, S.A., Witchel, E., Gupta, A.: Complete computer system simulation: The simos approach. IEEE Parallel Distrib. Technol. **3**(4) (1995) 34–43
7. Reinhardt, S.K., Dreslinski, R.G., Hsu, L.R., Lim, K.T., Saidi, A.G.: Tutorial: Using the m5 simulator. In: ISCA '06: Proceedings of the 33rd annual international symposium on Computer architecture, New York, NY, USA, ACM Press (2006)
8. Magnusson, P.S., Christensson, M., Eskilson, J., Forsgren, D., Hållberg, G., Högberg, J., Larsson, F., Moestedt, A., Werner, B.: Simics: A full system simulation platform. Computer **35**(2) (2002) 50–58
9. Skadron, K., Stan, M.R., Sankaranarayanan, K., Huang, W., Velusamy, S., Tarjan, D.: Temperature-aware microarchitecture: Modeling and implementation. ACM Trans. Archit. Code Optim. **1**(1) (2004) 94–125
10. Brooks, D., Tiwari, V., Martonosi, M.: Wattch: a framework for architectural-level power analysis and optimizations. In: ISCA '00: Proceedings of the 27th annual international symposium on Computer architecture, New York, NY, USA, ACM Press (2000) 83–94
11. Tiwari, V., Malik, S., Wolfe, A.: Power analysis of embedded software: a first step towards software power minimization. IEEE Trans. Very Large Scale Integr. Syst. **2**(4) (1994) 437–445
12. Sinha, A., Chandrakasan, A.P.: Jouletrack: a web based tool for software energy profiling. In: DAC '01: Proceedings of the 38th conference on Design automation, New York, NY, USA, ACM Press (2001) 220–225
13. Stanley-Marbell, P., Hsiao, M.: Fast, flexible, cycle-accurate energy estimation. In: Proceedings of the 2001 international symposium on Low power electronics and design, ACM Press (2001) 141–146
14. Benini, L., Castelli, G., Macii, A., Macii, E., Poncino, M., Scarsi, R.: A discrete-time battery model for high-level power estimation. In: Proceedings of the conference on Design, automation and test in Europe, DATE'00. (2000) 35–39
15. Nishimura, T.: Tables of 64-bit mersenne twisters. ACM Trans. Model. Comput. Simul. **10**(4) (2000) 348–357
16. Ross, S.M.: Simulation. Academic Press, San Diego, CA (2001)
17. Fang, Q., Zhao, F., Guibas, L.: Lightweight sensing and communication protocols for target enumeration and aggregation. In: MobiHoc '03: Proceedings of the 4th ACM international symposium on Mobile ad hoc networking & computing, New York, NY, USA, ACM Press (2003) 165–176

Efficient Program Power Behavior Characterization

Chunling Hu, Daniel A. Jiménez, and Ulrich Kremer

Department of Computer Science
Rutgers University, Piscataway, NJ 08854
{chunling, djimenez, uli}@cs.rutgers.edu

Abstract. Fine-grained program power behavior is useful in both evaluating power optimizations and observing power optimization opportunities. Detailed power simulation is time consuming and often inaccurate. Physical power measurement is faster and objective. However, fine-grained measurement generates enormous amounts of data in which locating important features is difficult, while coarse-grained measurement sacrifices important detail.

We present a program power behavior characterization infrastructure that identifies program phases, selects a representative interval of execution for each phase, and instruments the program to enable precise power measurement of these intervals to get their time-dependent power behavior. We show that the representative intervals accurately model the fine-grained time-dependent behavior of the program. They also accurately estimate the total energy of a program. Our compiler infrastructure allows for easy mapping between a measurement result and its corresponding source code. We improve the accuracy of our technique over previous work by using *edge vectors*, i.e., counts of traversals of control-flow edges, instead of basic block vectors, as well as incorporating event counters into our phase classification.

We validate our infrastructure through the physical power measurement of 10 SPEC CPU 2000 integer benchmarks on an Intel Pentium 4 system. We show that using edge vectors reduces the error of estimating total program energy by 35% over using basic block vectors, and using edge vectors plus event counters reduces the error of estimating the fine-grained time-dependent power profile by 22% over using basic block vectors.

1 Introduction

Research in power and energy optimizations focuses not only on reducing overall program energy consumption, but also on improving time-dependent power behavior. Evaluating such optimizations requires both accurate total energy consumption estimation and precise detailed time-dependent power behavior. Simulators are often used for power and performance evaluation, but detailed power simulation is very time-consuming and often inaccurate. While physical measurement is much faster, fine-grained power measurement requires proper measurement equipment and a large amount of space to store measurement results.

An example optimization that requires fine-grained, time-dependent power behavior information for its experimental evaluation is instruction scheduling for peak power and step power (dI/dt problem) reduction, for instance in the context of VLIW architectures [20,19,18]. This previous work relies on simulation to evaluate the impact of

K. De Bosschere et al. (Eds.): HiPEAC 2007, LNCS 4367, pp. 183–197, 2007.

the proposed optimizations. The dI/dt problem is caused by large variations of current in a short time. Such variations in CPU current may cause undesired oscillation in CPU supply voltage, which may results in timing problems and incorrect calculations [5]. In this paper, we introduce a new strategy to enable time-dependent power behavior characterizations based on physical measurements.

1.1   Characterizing Phases with Representative Slices

Program phase behavior shows that many program execution slices have similar behavior in several metrics, such as instructions-per-cycle (IPC), cache miss rate, and branch misprediction rate. Phase classification makes it easier to measure the fine-grained program behavior. A representative slice from each phase instead of the whole program execution is measured and analyzed, and then the whole program behavior can be characterized based on the analysis result. Using this whole program behavior characterization method in power behavior analysis, we can obtain fine-grained power behavior with significant savings in both time and storage space.

1.2   Illustrating Time-Dependent Power Behavior

Figure 1 shows the measured CPU current of *256.bzip2* from SPEC CPU 2000 measured using an oscilloscope. Figure 1(a) shows that the program execution can be roughly partitioned into 4 phases based on its power behavior. One representative slice from each phase can be measured to characterize the detailed power behavior of the benchmark. Figure 1(b) is the measured power behavior of half of a second in the first phase with a resolution that is 100 times higher than the one used for Figure 1(a). There is a repeated power behavior period of 300 milliseconds. Figure 1(c) shows the detailed power behavior of a piece of 0.05 second, from 0.1 second to 0.15 second in Figure 1(b). It shows repeated power behavior periods of less than 5 milliseconds, indicating possible finer phase classification than Figure 1(b). Also, finer measurement gives more information of time-dependent CPU power due to the resolution of the oscilloscope that we use for power measurement. The oscilloscope reports the average power for a given time granularity. This is the reason why the difference between the observed peak power (peak current) in Figure 1(a) and (c) is almost 6 Watts (0.5 amperes).

1.3   An Infrastructure for Characterizing Time-Dependent Power Behavior

In this paper, we present our infrastructure for program time-dependent power behavior characterization and optimization evaluation. Our *Camino* compiler statically instruments the assembly code of a program for profiling and physical measurement. A SimPoint-like [16] method is used for phase classification. SimPoint identifies several intervals, or *simpoints*, of program execution that characterize the behavior of the entire program execution. It is often used to speed up simulation by simulating only the simpoints and estimating, for instance, IPC, by taking a weighted average of the IPCs of each simpoint.

SimPoint uses the Basic Block Vector (BBV), i.e., a vector of counts of basic block executions, as the feature for classification. We introduce the *edge vector* (EV), i.e., a

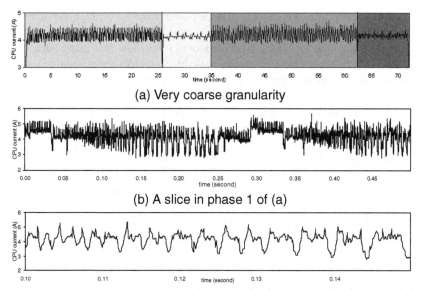

(a) Very coarse granularity

(b) A slice in phase 1 of (a)

(c) Detailed CPU power behavior of a small slice from 0.10 second to 0.15 second in (b)

Fig. 1. Measured power behavior of bzip2 with different granularity

vector of counts of control-flow-graph edge traversals, as the fingerprint of each interval of the program execution.

Instead of using a fixed number of instructions as interval length, we use infrequently executed basic blocks to demarcate intervals. This results in variable interval length, but much lower instrumentation overhead for physical power measurement of a representative interval. The selected simpoints are weighted based on the number of instructions executed in each phase, instead of number of intervals.

We show that our method enables us to do power measurement for simpoints with very low interference to program execution. To demonstrate the improved accuracy of using edge vectors for classification, we show that our infrastructure estimates the total energy of a program with an average error of 7.8%, compared with 12.0% using basic block vectors, an improvement of 35%. More importantly, we want to find representative intervals that represent the fine-grained time-dependent power profile of a phase. We develop a metric for measuring the accuracy of estimating a power profile and show that using edge vectors with event counter information improves accuracy by 22%.

Unlike simulation, physical measurement is sensitive to the overhead for identification of simpoints during program execution. So this low instrumentation overhead is very important. This infrastructure can be used to evaluate optimizations for energy consumption or time-dependent power behavior, for example, the impact on power behavior of pipeline gating [13] or dynamic voltage/frequency scaling [6].

We evaluate our infrastructure by measuring 10 SPEC CPU2000 integer benchmarks on a Pentium 4 machine, and we present the error rates in whole program energy consumption estimation as well as fine-grained power behavior estimation based on the measurement result of the selected simpoints.

This paper makes the following contributions: 1) We show that using edge vectors significantly improves accuracy over using basic block vectors for estimating total program energy as well as fine-grained power behavior. 2) We show that classification accuracy can further be improved by combining control-flow information such as edge vectors with event counter information. 3) We present our infrastructure that uses edge vectors and event counters to select representative intervals and to measure efficiently their power profiles with minimal perturbation of the running program.

The rest of this paper is organized as follows. Section 2 introduces some previous work related to this research. Section 3 presents our EV-based phase classification method, its implementation using our *Camino* compiler, and a finer phase classification using the combination of EV and IPC. Section 4 describes our physical measurement infrastructure for precise power measurement of selected intervals. and the experiments performed to evaluate our methodology. Section 5 shows the experimental results. Section 6 concludes the paper.

2   Related Work

Several techniques have been proposed to identify program phases. Some of them use control-flow information [15,16,14,11,12], such as counts of executed instructions, basic blocks, loops, or functions, as the fingerprint of program execution. This fingerprint depends on the executed source code. Some methods depend on run-time event counters or other metrics [2,3,17,9], such as IPC, power, cache misses rate and branch misprediction, to identify phases. Our infrastructure uses the edge vector of each interval, a vector that gives a count for each control-flow edge in the program, along with the measured IPC. This set of features allows for a precise characterization of power phases.

SimPoint [15,16] partitions a program execution into intervals with the same number of instructions and identifies the phases based on the BBV of each interval. One interval, called a *simpoint*, is selected as the representative of its phase. These simpoints are simulated or executed to estimate the behavior of the whole program execution. Sherwood *et al.* apply SimPoint to SPEC benchmarks to find simpoints and estimate the IPC, cache miss rate, and branch misprediction rate. The error rates are low and the simulation time saving is significant. A newer version of SimPoint supports variable length intervals [12]. That study shows a hierarchy of phase behavior in programs and the feasibility of variable length intervals in program phase classification. Procedure boundaries are used to separate variable length phases. We use infrequent basic blocks to break up intervals and at the same time use a pre-defined length to avoid intervals that are too long or too short, satisfying our requirements for low overhead and accuracy.

Shen *et al.* [14] propose a data locality phase identification method for run-time data locality phase prediction. A basic block that is always executed at the beginning of a phase is identified as the marker block of this phase, resulting in variable interval lengths. They introduce the notion of a phase hierarchy to identify composite phases.

PowerScope [4] maps energy consumption to program structure through runtime system power measurement and system activity sampling. System components responsible for the bulk of energy consumption are found and improved. The delay between power sampling and activity sampling results in possible imprecise attribution of energy consumption to program structure. Compared to the power measurement granularity used by PowerScope, which is 1.6ms, our infrastructure measures CPU current with much higher granularity. 1000 samples are collected for each 4ms. Precise mapping between power measurement and program structure is achieved through measuring the selected representative intervals.

Isci and Martonosi [1] show that program power behavior also falls into phases. Hu *et al.* propose using SimPoint to find representative program execution slices to simplify power behavior characterization, and validate the feasibility of SimPoint in power consumption estimation through power simulation of some Mediabench benchmarks [7]. Isci and Martonosi [10] compare two techniques of phase characterization for power and demonstrate that the event-counter-based technique offers a lower average power phase classification errors. Our goal is to characterize the time-dependent power behavior, instead of power consumption, of programs. Our method causes negligible overhead for identification of an interval during program execution, and the measurement result is very close to the real time-dependent power behavior of the interval. Furthermore, through the combination of edge vector and event counters, we get better phase characterization than using only control flow information as well as the mapping between observed power behavior and the source code. The latter is difficult for an event-counter-based technique by itself.

3 Phase Classification Based on Edge Vectors and Event Counters

This section describes our phase classification infrastructure. It is based on the ability to demarcate the start and end of a particular interval of execution with infrequently executed basic blocks. We instrument these infrequent basic blocks so that our instrumentation minimally perturbs the execution of the program.

Phase classification and power measurement of representative intervals for programs is implemented as an automatic process. The threshold for determining whether a basic block is infrequent, the minimum number of instructions in each interval, and the number of phases are the input to this process. The flowchart in Figure 2 illustrates its steps. The implementation of each step will be presented in the following sections.

3.1 Instrumentation Infrastructure for Profiling, Measurement, and Optimization

Camino [8] is a GCC post-processor developed in our lab. We use it to implement the static instrumentation for profiling and physical power measurement.

Camino reads the assembly code generated by GCC, parses it into a control-flow-graph (CFG) intermediate representation, performs transformations including instrumentation, and then writes the modified assembly language to a file to be assembled and linked.

Instrumentation using *Camino* is simple and minimally intrusive. Only two routines are required: an instrumentation routine that inserts a call to the analysis routine, and and an analysis routine that does profiling or generates special signals.

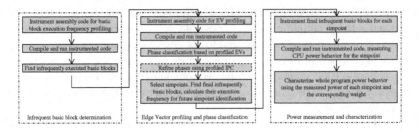

Fig. 2. Infrequent basic block-based phase classification and power measurement of simpoints

Note that our infrastructure does two kinds of instrumentations: 1) profiling for all basic blocks to identify infrequent basic blocks and gathering features used to do phase classification, and 2) infrequent basic block instrumentation for signaling the start and end of a representative interval to our measurement apparatus. The first kind of instrumentation results in a moderate slowdown, but the second kind results in no slowdown so that the measured program's behavior is as close as possible to that of the uninstrumented program.

3.2   Infrequent Basic Blocks Selection

Instrumentation is done through *Camino* to collect the execution frequency of each basic block. Each basic block makes a call to an execution frequency counting library function. The distinct reference value of the basic block is passed to the function that increments the frequency of this basic block. During the first profiling pass, we collect counts for each basic block.

A threshold is needed to determine which basic blocks are infrequently executed and can be used to demarcate intervals. An absolute value is infeasible, since different program/input pairs execute different number of basic blocks. Instead, we consider a basic block to be infrequent if it account for less than a certain percentage of all executed basic blocks. Intuitively, when a low threshold is used, the selected infrequent basic blocks will be distributed sparsely in program execution and there is more variance in interval size than when a higher threshold is used. We investigate 4 different threshold values, 0.05%, 0.1%, 1%, and 5%, to explore the trade-off between interval size variance and instrumentation overhead.

3.3   Program Execution Interval Partitioning and Edge Vector Profiling

We use the edge vector (EV) of all edges as the fingerprint of an interval used for the clustering phase of our SimPoint-like phase classification method. This vector is the absolute count for each control-flow edge traversed during the execution of an interval. Compared to basic block vectors (BBV), EVs give us more information about the control behavior of the program at run-time. BBVs contain information about what parts of a program were executed, but EVs tell us what decisions were made in arriving at these parts of the program. This extra information allows a classification of phases that more accurately reflects program behavior.

Partitioning program execution just based on the execution times of infrequent basic blocks will results in intervals with a variable number of instructions. Acquiring detailed information from very large intervals to characterize program behavior is inefficient. Moreover, a large variance in interval size affects the accuracy of the phase classification result. In order to make use of our physical measurement infrastructure to characterize the whole program behavior more correctly and efficiently, we use a pre-specified interval size to avoid largely variable intervals.

Instrumentation for EV profiling is similar to that for basic block execution frequency profiling. All basic blocks are instrumented so that we can get the complete fingerprint of an interval. An initial interval size of 30 million instructions is used to avoid too large or too small intervals. The library function remembers the last executed basic block and knows the taken edge based on the last and the current executed basic blocks. It counts each control flow edge originating in a basic block that ends in a conditional branch. It counts the total number of executed instructions for the current interval as well. When an infrequent basic block is encountered, if the count is larger than or equal to 30 million, this basic block indicates the end of the current interval and it is the first basic block of the next interval.

3.4 Phase Classification for Power Behavior Characterization

Intervals profiled in Section 3.3 are classified into phases based on their EVs. K-Means clustering is used to cluster the intervals with similar EVs and select a representative for each phase. The EV of each interval is projected to a vector with much smaller dimension. Then k initial cluster centers are selected. The distance between a vector and each center is calculated and each vector is classified into the cluster with the shortest distance. A cluster center is changed to the average of the current cluster members after each iteration. The iteration stops after the number of vectors in each cluster is stable. The simpoint of a phase is the one that is closest to the center of the cluster [16].

Since the intervals are demarcated by infrequently executed basic blocks and have variable number of instructions, weighting a simpoint with just the number of intervals in its phase cannot reflect the real proportion of this phase in whole program execution. In our method, each simpoint has two weights. One is based on the percentage of the number of executed instructions of the corresponding phase in that of the whole program, the other is based on the number of intervals in the corresponding phase as the one used in [16]. A recent version of the SimPoint tool also supports variable-length phases [12].

Given the number of phases, K-Means clustering is performed for different number of clusters and different cluster seeds. The BIC (Bayesian Information Criterion) score of each clustering is calculated and used to choose the clustering with the best trade-off between BIC score and number of phases. The BIC score calculation in our method is changed to use the number of executed instructions in each phase such that phases with longer intervals have larger influence.

To identify an interval during program execution, we need to find the beginning and end of the interval. We use the execution frequencies of one or two infrequent basic blocks that demarcate the interval. Infrequent basic blocks that mark the start or end of a desired representative interval are chosen as final infrequent basic blocks. Their execution frequencies in each interval are recorded, so that we know how many times a basic block has executed before the start of an interval. We instrument these final infrequent basic blocks with simple assembly code to increment a counter and trigger power measurement when the count indicates the beginning of the interval, or turn off measurement when the end of an interval is reached. The combination of infrequent basic blocks and static instrumentation enables us to identify the execution of an interval at run-time with negligible overhead.

3.5   Finer Phase Classification Using IPC

Two intervals that execute the same basic blocks may generate different time-dependent power behavior due to run-time events, such as cache misses and branch mispredictions. Phase classification only based on control flow information cannot precisely differentiate these intervals, so the resulting simpoints may not really be representative in terms of power behavior. Our infrastructure combines EV and instructions-per-cycle (IPC) as measured using performance counters provided by the architecture to take the run-time events into account.

IPC Profiling. Profiling IPC is easy to do in our infrastructure. After the program execution is partitioned into intervals, all of the infrequent basic blocks that demarcate the resulting intervals are instrumented to collect the number of clock cycles taken by each interval. By running the instrumented program once, we can get the IPC values of all intervals by dividing the number of instructions by the number of cycles. We already have the number of instructions executed from the edge vector profiling. Since we identify intervals based on infrequent basic block counts, the overhead is low and has a negligible impact on the accuracy of the profiling result.

Combining EV Clustering with IPC Clustering. For a program execution, we first perform the phase classification in Section 3.4 to group intervals with similar EVs together. Then we do another phase classification based on the profiled IPC values. K-Means clustering is also used in the second phase classification. Then we combine the results from the two classifications and get a refined phase classification for power behavior characterization through refining the classification result of the first one using that of the second one. Suppose the number of clusters from the two classifications are N_{ev} and N_{ipc} respectively. The initial number of final clusters is $N_{ev} \times N_{ipc}$. Let C_{ev} be the cluster ID of an interval in the first classification and C_{ipc} be the one in the second classification. The cluster of an interval C is determined by:

$$C = (C_{ev} - 1) \times N_{ipc} + (C_{ipc} - 1)) + 1$$

where C_{ev} ranges from 1 to N_{ev} and C_{ipc} ranges from 1 to N_{ipc}. It is unlikely that the IPC values of every cluster in classification 1 fall into N_{ipc} clusters in classification 2, so many clusters are empty. These clusters are pruned and cluster IDs are adjusted to get continuous IDs. The mechanism in the next section performs more control on the number of the resulting phases without a significant loss in accuracy. Our experiment result shows that after applying the controlling mechanism, if the given K value for IPC-based phase classification, that is, C_{ipc} in the above equation, is 10, the number of the resulting phases after the classification refinement is expanded to less than 3 times of the number after the first classification, instead of around 10 times.

Controlling Unnecessarily Fine Phase Classification. Using a constant K value for the IPC-based phase classification of all programs results in unnecessarily fine partitioning and more simpoints to simulate or measure when the IPC values of the intervals in the same phase are already very close to each other. We control the number of resulting phases based on IPC in two steps.

The first step controls the selection of the initial centers based on the maximum and minimum IPC of the program. A percentage of the minimum IPC value is used as the distance d between the initial centers. This ensures that intervals with very close IPCs need no further partitioning and the final number of simpoints does not explode with little benefit. This percentage is adjustable in our infrastructure. The maximum value is divided by d. The value of quotient plus 1 is then compared with the given k. The smaller one is used as number of clusters. This value may be 1, meaning that the IPC values of all of the intervals are very close and no finer partitioning is necessary.

The second step maintains the distance between centers during the initialization of the centers in case there is a IPC much higher than others, but there are only two different IPC values during program execution. The first step does not know this and the number of clusters will be k which results in unnecessarily more simpoints. This step is similar to the construction of a minimum spanning tree except that we use the largest values in each step to choose the next initial center. The first initial center is selected randomly. During the generation of the other initial centers, each time the value with largest distance to the existing centers is the candidate. If this distance value is less than half of d, no more initial centers are generated. This prevents intervals with the similar EVs and very close IPCs from being partitioned into different clusters.

4 Experimental Setup

We validate our infrastructure through physical power measurement of the CPU of a Pentium 4 machine. This machine runs Linux 2.6.9, GCC 3.4.2 and GCC 2.95.4. Benchmarks are from the members of SPEC CPU2000 INT that can be compiled by *Camino* successfully. The back-end compiler for *gzip, vpr, mcf, parser* and *twolf* is GCC 3.4.2. The back-end compiler for the other benchmarks is GCC 2.95.4 because the combination of *Camino* and GCC 3.4.2 fails to compile these programs correctly. We measure the current on the separate power cable to the CPU using a Tektronix TCP202 DC current probe, which is connected to a Tektronix TDS3014 oscilloscope. The data acquisition machine is a Pentium 4 Linux machine that reads data from the oscilloscope when a benchmark is running on the measured system. Simultaneous benchmark execution and power data acquisition on different machines eliminates interference with the measured benchmark.

4.1   Energy Consumption Estimation Based on Simpoints

The first step to verify that this infrastructure is useful in power behavior characterization is to calculate the error rate when the measurement result of the selected simpoints is used to estimate the power consumption of the whole program. Although we use EVs as the fingerprint of an interval in our infrastructure, we also measured the CPU power of the simpoints using BBVs for comparison.

The energy consumption of each simpoint is measured using the trigger mode of the oscilloscope. We generate an executable for each simpoint and measure the simpoints one by one so we can get very high resolution as well as the lowest possible instrumentation overhead. Program execution and data acquisition are on the same machine. Reading data from the oscilloscope is scheduled after the measurement of a simpoint is done. Data acquisition does not interfere with the running program. We implement an automatic measurement and data acquisition process to measure any number of simpoints as a single task.

4.2   Power Behavior Similarity Evaluation

Even though we can get low error rates in estimating whole program energy consumption, energy consumption is the average behavior of an interval. Intervals that are classified into the same phase may have different time-dependent power behavior. If intervals in the same phase have largely different power behavior, we cannot characterize the time-dependent power behavior of the whole program execution using the measurement result of the simpoints.

Comparing in the Frequency Domain. Our power measurements come in the form of discrete samples in the time domain. Power behavior is characterized by periodic activity, so a comparison in the frequency domain is more appropriate for determining whether two intervals are similar. For instance, two power curves might be slightly out of phase with one another, but have exactly the same impact on the system because they exhibit the same periodic behavior. Thus, we compare the power behavior similarity of two intervals by comparing their discrete Fourier transforms computed using Fast Fourier Transform (FFT).

A More Robust Sampling Approach for Verification. Measuring every interval in a long-running program is infeasible because of time and space constraints (indeed, this fact motivates our research). Thus, we use a more robust sampling methodology to verify that power behavior is consistent within a phase. We choose 20 intervals at random for each phase of each program to compare the FFT results of their curves. If the number of intervals in some phase is less than 20, all of the intervals are selected. The selected intervals for each phase are selected from a uniformly random distribution among all the intervals in the phase.

Instrumenting for Verification. Infrequent basic blocks demarcating the intervals from the same phase are instrumented to measure each interval in the same way we measure a simpoint. Each selected interval is measured separately. Then the FFT is performed on the measured power curve of each interval. The Root Mean Square (RMS) error of the FFT results is used to evaluate the variation of the power behavior of the intervals in this phase. For each phase, we calculate the arithmetic average of the FFT results of all measured intervals as the expected FFT of the phase. The distance between an interval i and the expected FFT is:

$$D_i = \sqrt{\frac{\sum_{j=1}^{N} (\sqrt{c_j^2 + d_j^2} - \sqrt{a_j^2 + b_j^2})}{N}}$$

c_j and d_j are the real and imaginary part of the jth frequency of interval i, respectively. a_j and b_j are the real and imaginary part of the jth frequency of the expected FFT respectively. N is the number of points used in Fast Fourier Transform. Then the FFT RMS of a phase is calculated as:

$$FFT_{RMS} = \sqrt{\frac{\sum_{i=1}^{M} D_i^2}{M}}$$

M is the number of measured intervals in the phase. The lower FFT_{RMS} is, the high the similarity among the time-dependent power behavior of the intervals in the phase.

The FFT_{RMS} for each phase is then weighted by the weight of the corresponding phase to get the RMS for the whole benchmark. We evaluated the weighted FFT_{RMS} for all of the 10 benchmarks in two cases: when phase classification is based on EV only, and when IPC is used to refine phase classification.

5   Experimental Results and Evaluation

Using the power measurement infrastructure described in Section 4, we measured the CPU power curves for the instrumented benchmarks, the ones with all final infrequent basic blocks instrumented, the simpoints, and the selected intervals from each phase.

5.1   Total Energy Consumption Estimation

We investigate both BBV and EV as the fingerprint of intervals in phase classification. A maximum number of clusters, 30, is used to find the best clustering in both cases. Simpoints are measured and the whole program energy consumption is estimated as

$$E_{est} = \sum_{i=1}^{k} E_i \times W_i$$

E_i is the measured energy consumption of the ith simpoint, W_i is its weight, and k is the number of phases. Although intervals have variable sizes, we estimate the total energy consumption using the weight based on the number of intervals in each phase.

For BBV-based phase classification, we use three percentage values 0.1%, 1%, and 5% to get the threshold for infrequent basic blocks. When the measured energy consumption of simpoints are used to estimate the whole program energy consumption. The error rate is the lowest when threshold is 1% due to the trade-off between uniform interval size and instrumentation overhead. Then we use 1%, 0.1% and 0.05% as threshold in EV-based phase classification. Energy consumption of a measured benchmark or simpoint is calculated as:

$$E = U \times \sum (I \times t)$$

where E is energy consumption, U is the voltage of the measured CPU power cable, I is the measured current on the CPU power cable, t is the time resolution of the power data points. The sum is over all of the data points for one benchmark or simpoint.

Energy estimation error rate is calculated as

$$error = \frac{|energy\_estimated - energy\_measured|}{energy\_measured}$$

Execution time estimation is similar to energy estimation.

Figure 3 shows the error rates of the infrequent basic block-based phase classification method using different program execution fingerprints. Error rate is calculated as in 5.1. The error reported is that of the estimate using the threshold that delivered the minimum overall error for each method: 1% for BBVs, and 0.1% for EVs. The figure shows that EV performs better than BBV for almost all of the benchmarks. EV improves the estimation accuracy by 35%. All of the following analysis and evaluation are for the experimental results of EV-based phase classification.

5.2   Time-Dependent Power Behavior Similarity

As mentioned in Section 4.2, we use the distance between the FFT results of their power curves to evaluate the similarity of two intervals in terms of power behavior. We use 4096 points in the Fast Fourier Transform. The maximum number of data points for a curve is 10,000 when the oscilloscope is in trigger mode. If the measured data points for the curve of an intervals is less than 4096, the curve is repeated to reach the number of frequencies. Figure 4 (a) shows the measured CPU current curves of two intervals from the same identified phase, while (b) shows that of two intervals from two different phases. Distance between the FFT values is included to show the relation between time-dependent power behavior similarity and FFT distance. In Figure 4 (a), the upper curve uses the left y axis, while the other one use the right y axis, to avoid overlapping curves. The second column of each group in Figure 5 is the weighted FFT_{RMS} for each benchmark when EV is used for phase classification.

We measure the IPC using performance counters for each interval and do phase classification based on IPC to refine the EV-based phase classification. The third column in each group in Figure 5 is the weighted FFT_{RMS} for each benchmark when EV+IPC is used for phase classification. The similarity among the intervals is improved by 22% over using BBVs. Compared to the FFT distance between an interval and another interval from a different phase, the distance inside a phase is much smaller. This shows that the combination of EV and IPC enables us to classify intervals into phases in which the

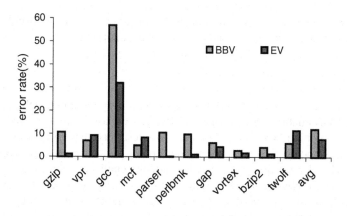

Fig. 3. Error rates of energy consumption estimation using different thresholds

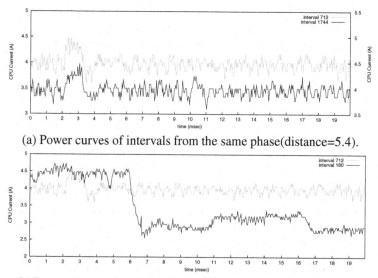

(a) Power curves of intervals from the same phase(distance=5.4).

(b) Power curves of intervals from different phases(distance=55.1).

Fig. 4. Similarity between measured CPU current of intervals

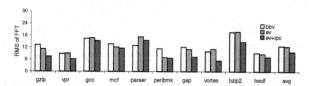

Fig. 5. Root Mean Squared error of the FFT calculated based on RMS of FFT and the weight of each phase

intervals have similar power behavior. Thus the power behavior of the whole program can be characterized by the measured behavior of the simpoints.

6   Conclusion

This paper introduced our infrastructure for efficient program power behavior characterization and evaluation. We presented a new phase classification method based on edge vectors combined with event counters. We described the physical measurement setup for precise power measurement. By demarcating intervals using infrequently executed basic blocks, we find intervals with variable lengths and negligible instrumentation overhead for physical measurement of simpoints. Through experiments on a real system, we demonstrated that our new phase classification method can find representative intervals for energy consumption with an accuracy superior to using basic block vectors. More importantly, we demonstrated the ability of our infrastructure to characterize the fine-grained time-dependent power behavior of each phase in the program using a single representative interval per phase. The ability of instrumenting programs on various levels, identifying phases, and obtaining detailed power behavior of program execution slices makes this infrastructure useful in power behavior characterization and optimization evaluation.

References

1. Canturk Isci, Margaret Martonosi.   Runtime power monitoring in high-end processors: Methodology and empirical data. *Proceedings of the 36th Annual IEEE/ACM International Symposium on Microarchitecture (MICRO'03)*, page 93, 2003.
2. E. Chi, A. M. Salem, and R. I. Bahar. Combining software and hardware monitoring for improved power and performance tuning. *Proceedings of the Seventh Annual Workshop on Interaction between Compilers and Computer Architectures (INTERACT'03)*, 2003.
3. E. Duesterwald, C. Cascaval, and S. Dwarkadas. Characterizing and predicting program behavior and its variability. *Proceedings of the 12th International Conference on Parallel Architectures and Compilation Techniques (PACT'03)*, page 220, 2003.
4. J. Flinn and M. Satyanarayanan. Powerscope: A tool for profiling the energy usage of mobile applications. *Proceedings of the Second IEEE Workshop on Mobile Computer Systems and Applications*, page 2, 1999.
5. K. Hazelwood and D. Brooks. Eliminating voltage emergencies via microarchitectural voltage control feedback and dynamic optimization. In *International Symposium on Low-Power Electronics and Design*, Newport Beach, CA, August 2004.
6. C.-H. Hsu and U. Kremer. The design, implementation, and evaluation of a compiler algorithm for cpu energy reduction. *Proceedings of the ACM SIGPLAN 2003 conference on Programming language design and implementation (PLDI'03)*, pages 38–48, 2003.
7. C. Hu, D. A. Jiménez, and U. Kremer. Toward an evaluation infrastructure for power and energy optimizations. In *19th International Parallel and Distributed Processing Symposium (IPDPS'05, Workshop 11), CD-ROM / Abstracts Proceedings*, April 2005.
8. C. Hu, J. McCabe, D. A. Jiménez, and U. Kremer. The camino compiler infrastructure. *SIGARCH Comput. Archit. News*, 33(5):3–8, 2005.
9. C. Isci and M. Martonosi. Identifying program power phase behavior using power vectors. *Proceedings of the IEEE International Workshop on Workload Characterization (WWC-6)*, 2003.

10. C. Isci and M. Martonosi. Phase characterization for power: Evaluating control-flow-based and event-counter-based techniques. *In 12th International Symposium on High-Performance Computer Architecture (HPCA-12)*, Febrary 2006.
11. A. Iyer and D. Marculescu. Power aware microarchitecture resource scaling. *Proceedings of the conference on Design, Automation and Test in Europe (DATE'01)*, pages 190–196, 2001.
12. J. Lau, E. Perelman, G. Hamerly, T. Sherwood, and B. Calder. Motivation for variable length intervals and hierarchical phase behavior. *In the Proceedings of the IEEE International Symposium on Performance Analysis of Systems and Software (ISPASS'05)*, pages 135–146, 2005.
13. S. Manne, A. Klauser, and D. Grunwald. Pipeline gating: speculation control for energy reduction. *Proceedings of the 25th Annual International Symposium on Computer Architecture (ISCA'98)*, pages 132–141, 1998.
14. X. Shen, Y. Zhong, and C. Ding. Locality phase prediction. *Proceedings of the 11th International Conference on Architectural Support for Programming Languages and Operating Systems (ASPLOS'04)*, pages 165–176, 2004.
15. T. Sherwood, E. Perelman, and B. Calder. Basic block distribution analysis to find periodic behavior and simulation points in applications. *Proceedings of the 2001 International Conference on Parallel Architectures and Compilation Techniques (PACT'01)*, pages 3–14, 2001.
16. T. Sherwood, E. Perelman, G. Hamerly, and B. Calder. Automatically characterizing large scale program behavior. In *Proceedings of the 10th International Conference on Architectural Support for Programming Languages and Operating Systems (ASPLOS'02)*, 2002.
17. R. Srinivasan, J. Cook, and S. Cooper. Fast, accurate microarchitecture simulation using statistical phase detection. *Proceedings of The 2005 IEEE International Symposium on Performance Analysis of Systems and Software (ISPASS'05)*, 2005.
18. C.-L. Su, C.-Y. Tsui, and A. Despain. Low power architecture and compilation techniques for high-performance processors. In *IEEE COMPCON*, pages 489–498, San Francisco, CA, February 1994.
19. M. Toburen, T. Conte, and M. Reilly. Instruction scheduling for low power dissipation in high performance microprocessors. In *Power Driven Microarchitecture Workshop*, Barcelona, Spain, June 1998.
20. H.-S. Yun and J. Kim. Power-aware modulo scheduling for high-performance VLIW. In *International Symposium on Low Power Electronics and Design (ISLPED'01)*, Huntington Beach, CA, August 2001.

V   Generation of Efficient Embedded Applications

Performance/Energy Optimization of DSP Transforms on the XScale Processor*

Paolo D'Alberto, Markus Püschel, and Franz Franchetti

Carnegie Mellon University
Department of Electric and Computer Engineering
Pittsburgh, PA, USA
{pdalbert,pueschel,franzf}@ece.cmu.edu

Abstract. The XScale processor family provides user-controllable independent configuration of CPU, bus, and memory frequencies. This feature introduces another handle for the code optimization with respect to energy consumption or runtime performance. We quantify the effect of frequency configurations on both performance and energy for three signal processing transforms: the discrete Fourier transform (DFT), finite impulse response (FIR) filters, and the Walsh-Hadamard Transform (WHT).

To do this, we use SPIRAL, a program generation and optimization system for signal processing transforms. For a given transform to be implemented, SPIRAL searches over different algorithms to find the best match to the given platform with respect to the chosen performance metric (usually runtime). In this paper we use SPIRAL to generate implementations for different frequency configurations and optimize for runtime and physically measured energy consumption. In doing so we show that first, each transform achieves best performance/energy consumption for a different system configuration; second, the best code depends on the chosen configuration, problem size and algorithm; third, the fastest implementation is not always the most energy efficient; fourth, we introduce dynamic (i.e., during execution) reconfiguration in order to further improve performance/energy. Finally, we benchmark SPIRAL generated code against Intel's vendor library routines. We show competitive results as well as 20% performance improvements or energy reduction for selected transforms and problem sizes.

1   Introduction

The rapidly increasing complexity of computing platforms keeps application developers under constant pressure to rewrite and re-optimize their software. A typical micro-architecture may feature one or multiple processors with several levels of memory hierarchy, special instruction sets, or software-controlled caches. One of the recent additions to this list of features is software-controlled scaling of the CPU core frequency. The idea is to enable the user (or the operating system) to scale up or down the CPU frequency and the supply voltage to save energy; this is especially important for devices operating on limited power sources such as batteries. Frequency scaling is available for

* This work was supported by DARPA through the Department of Interior grant NBCH1050009 and by NSF through awards 0234293 and 0325687.

K. De Bosschere et al. (Eds.): HiPEAC 2007, LNCS 4367, pp. 201–214, 2007.

different processors, such as AMD's Athlon 64, Intel's XScale (fixed-point processors targeted for embedded applications) and Core processor families.

XScale systems provide more reconfigurability options, namely the (to a certain degree) independent selection of CPU, bus, and memory frequency. Reconfigurability complicates the process of optimizing code because different configurations in essence correspond to different platforms. However, taking advantage of reconfigurability is crucial in the high-performance and power-aware signal processing domain.

Contribution of this paper. We consider three linear signal transforms: the discrete Fourier transform (DFT), finite impulse response (FIR) filters, and the Walsh-Hadamard transform (WHT). Our test platform is a SITSANG board with an XScale PXA255 fixed-point processor. The platform provides the above mentioned frequency scaling but no voltage scaling. To perform the experiments, we integrated frequency scaling in the automatic code generation and optimization framework SPIRAL [1]. Using SPIRAL, we generated code tuned for different frequency settings or to a dynamic frequency scaling strategy.

In this work, we show: First, code adaptation to one specific or the best setting can yield up to 20% higher performance or energy reduction than using an implementation optimized for a different setting (e.g., the fastest CPU vs. the fastest memory). Second, there are algorithms and configurations that achieve the same performance but have a 20% different energy consumption. For example, the fastest configuration can consume 5% more energy than the most energy efficient configuration. Third, we apply dynamic scaling (i.e., during execution) and are able to reduce energy consumption; however, this technique does not improve runtime performance. Finally, we show that SPIRAL generated code compares favorably with the hand-tuned Intel's vendor library IPP, which is oblivious to the frequency configuration.

Related work. Optimization for frequency and voltage scaling typically targets large-scale problems and more general codes. Recent work introduces compiler techniques [2], power modeling [3], and software/hardware monitoring of applications [4] to aid adaptation of frequency/voltage settings. [5] and [6] present a compile-time algorithm for the dynamic voltage scaling within an application, inserting switching points chosen by static analysis.

Different frequency settings yield memory hierarchies with different characteristics. Thus, a code generation tool that enables the tuning of codes to the architecture's characteristics is an ideal solution. Examples of such tools include for linear algebra kernels ATLAS [7] and Sparsity [8], for the DFT and related transforms FFTW [9], and for general linear signal transform SPIRAL, which is used in this paper.

Organization of the paper. In Section 2, we provide details on our platform and an overview of the program generator SPIRAL. In Section 3, we introduce the specific framework used to collect our results. In Section 4, we present experimental results for the DFT, FIR filters, and the WHT. We conclude in Section 5.

2   Background

In this section, we first describe the XScale architecture including its reconfigurability features and then the SPIRAL program generation framework.

2.1   Intel XScale PXA255

The Intel XScale architecture targets embedded devices. One crucial feature is the hardware support for energy conservation and high burst performance. Specifically, applications may control the frequency settings of the platforms's CPU, bus, and memory. In this paper, we consider the PXA255, a fixed-point processor in the XScale family [10] with no voltage scaling. We refer to this platform simply as XScale throughout the paper.

Frequency configuration. A frequency configuration is given by a memory frequency m (one of 99 MHz, 132 MHz, or 165 MHz), a bus multiplier α (one of 1, 2, or 4) and, a CPU multiplier β (one of 1, 1.5, 2, or 3). When we choose a configuration triple (m, α, β), the memory frequency is set to m, the bus frequency to $\alpha m/2$ and the CPU frequency to $\alpha\beta m$. Out of 36 possible choices for (m, α, β), not all are recommended or necessarily stable. In this paper, we consider a representative set of 13 configurations that are stable for the DSP transforms considered. The configurations are summarized in Table 1. The frequencies are given in MHz and each setting is assigned a mnemonic name that specifies the CPU frequency, and the ratio of memory and bus frequency to the CPU frequency, respectively. For example, 530-1/4-1/2 means that the memory runs at a quarter, and the bus at half of the 530 MHz CPU speed.

A change of configuration is not instantaneous and is done by writing appropriate configuration bits to a control register (called CCCR, [10]); we have measured an average penalty of 530 μs.

For a software developer the problem is at least two-fold. First, different configurations correspond in effect to different platforms and thus code optimized for one configuration may be suboptimal for another. Second, the choice of configuration is not straightforward. For example, if the highest performance is desired, there are three

Table 1. PXA255 Configurations: The frequencies are in MHz; 398-1/4-1/4 is the startup setting

CPU	Memory	Bus	Name
597	99	99	597-1/6-1/6
530	132	265	530-1/4-1/2
530	132	132	530-1/4-1/4
497	165	165	497-1/3-1/3
398	99	199	398-1/4-1/2
398	99	99	398-1/4-1/4
331	165	165	331-1/2-1/2
298	99	49	298-1/3-1/6
265	132	132	265-1/2-1/2
199	99	99	199-1/2-1/2
165	165	82	165-1-1/2
132	132	66	132-1-1/2
99	99	49	99-1-1/2

candidate settings: 597-1/6-1/6 (fastest CPU), 497-1/3-1/3 (fastest memory), and 530-1/4-1/2 (fastest bus). Energy constraints may further complicate the selection.

2.2 SPIRAL

SPIRAL is a program generator for linear signal transforms such as the DFT, the WHT, the discrete cosine and sine transforms, FIR filters, and the discrete wavelet transform. The input to SPIRAL is a formally specified transform (e.g., DFT of size 245), the output is a highly optimized C program implementing the transform. SPIRAL can generate fixed-point code for platforms such as XScale.

In the following, we first provide some details on transforms and their algorithms, then we explain the inner workings of SPIRAL.

Transforms and algorithms. We consider three transforms in this paper: the DFT, FIR filters, and the WHT. Each transform is a matrix-vector multiplication $y = Mx$, where M is the transform matrix. For example, for input size n, the DFT is defined by the matrix

$$\mathbf{DFT}_n = [\omega_n^{k\ell}]_{0 \le k, \ell < n}, \quad \omega_n = e^{-2\pi i/n}. \tag{1}$$

The output of the DFT is also of size n.

Algorithms for these transforms are sparse structure factorizations of the transform matrix. For example, the Cooley-Tukey fast Fourier transform (FFT) follows:

$$\mathbf{DFT}_{km} = (\mathbf{DFT}_k \otimes I_m) D (I_k \otimes \mathbf{DFT}_m) P, \quad n = km. \tag{2}$$

Here, I_m is the $m \times m$ identity matrix; D is a diagonal matrix, and P is a permutation matrix, both depending on k and m (see [11] for details). Most importantly, the Kronecker, or tensor product, is defined as

$$A \otimes B = [a_{k,\ell} B]_{k,\ell}, \quad \text{for } A = [a_{k,\ell}]_{k,\ell}. \tag{3}$$

If one of the tensor factors A, B is the identity matrix, as in (2), then $y = (A \otimes B)x$ can be implemented simply as a loop. For example, $y = (I_k \otimes B)x$ is a loop with k iterations. In each iteration, B is multiplied to a contiguous chunk of x to yield the corresponding chunk of y. $y = (A \otimes I_m)x$ is a loop with m iterations, but in this case, A is multiplied to subvectors of x extracted at stride m.

The WHT is a real transform defined recursively by $\mathbf{WHT}_2 = \mathbf{DFT}_2$, and

$$\mathbf{WHT}_{2^n} = (\mathbf{WHT}_{2^k} \otimes I_{2^m})(I_{2^k} \otimes \mathbf{WHT}_{2^m}), \quad n = k + m. \tag{4}$$

It only exists for two-power sizes. (4) also serves as algorithm for the WHT, similar to (2).

Algorithms for FIR filters can be described similarly; this includes different choices of blocking, Karatsuba, and frequency domain methods [12,13].

How SPIRAL works. In SPIRAL, a decomposition like (2) is called a *rule*. For a given transform, SPIRAL recursively applies these rules to generate one out of many possible algorithms represented as a *formula*. This formula is then structurally optimized using a rewriting system and finally translated into a C program (for computing the transform) using a special purpose compiler. The C program is further optimized and then a standard C compiler is used to generate an executable. Its runtime is measured and fed into a search engine, which decides how to modify the algorithm; that is, the engine changes the formula, and thus the code, by using a dynamic-programming search. Eventually, this feedback loop terminates and outputs the fastest program found in the search. The entire process is visualized in Fig. 1 (see [1,14] for a complete description).

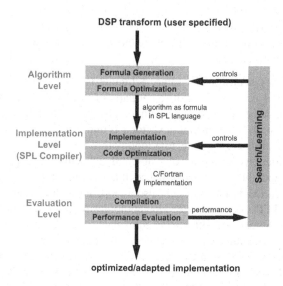

Fig. 1. The program generator SPIRAL

Note that there is a large degree of freedom in creating a formula, or algorithm, for a given transform due to the choices of decomposition in each step. For example, for computing a DFT of size 16 three different factorizations of 16 in (2) can be used: 2×8, 4×4, or 8×2. Similar choices apply recursively to the smaller transforms obtained after each decomposition.

3 Extension of SPIRAL

In this work, our goal is to automatically generate implementations of transforms for the XScale platform. These programs are optimized specifically for every frequency configuration (see Table 1). As optimization metric, we use both runtime performance and energy consumption. To achieve our goal, we extended SPIRAL in two directions. First, we included frequency scaling into SPIRAL's framework. Second, we enabled SPIRAL to run with physically measured energy consumption as performance measure in the feedback loop (see Fig. 1).

3.1 Frequency Scaling in SPIRAL

Static frequency scaling. We enable SPIRAL to generate code for different frequency configurations by a transform-transparent tagging framework that starts at the formula level. The basic idea is simple. Any formula F generated by SPIRAL can be tagged with a frequency configuration, for example 497-1/3-1/3, written as

$$[F]_{497-1/3-1/3}. \tag{5}$$

Next, we extended the SPL compiler (see Fig. 1) to understand these tags and translate them into the appropriate code. In the example (5), the entire formula would be executed at 497-1/3-1/3 with a potential[1] switch at the the beginning and at the end. We call this *static* frequency scaling.

Dynamic frequency scaling. The same technique is used to perform *dynamic* frequency scaling; that is, to perform different parts of the formula at different configurations. This is explained next, starting with a motivation. Consider the decomposition rule for the WHT in (4). First, the input vector x is multiplied by $(I_{2^k} \otimes \mathbf{WHT}_{2^m})$. As explained after (3), this corresponds to a loop with 2^k iterations. The loop body calls $\mathbf{WHT}_{2^m}$ on contiguous subvectors of x of length 2^m. This access pattern yields good cache utilization and, thus, high performance. It is *compute-bound*.

The second part, $(\mathbf{WHT}_{2^k} \otimes I_{2^m})$ is also a loop, but with 2^m iterations. Further, in the loop body $\mathbf{WHT}_{2^k}$ accesses a 2^k-element long subvector of x, but at stride 2^m. If 2^m is sufficiently large, this is effectively equivalent to reducing the cache size (unless the cache is fully associative), since the elements of x are mapped to the same cache set. The consequence is cache thrashing. The computation becomes *memory-bound*.

The basic idea is now to run both parts at different settings. Using tags and an example, this can be expressed as

$$[(\mathbf{WHT}_{2^k} \otimes I_{2^m})]_{497-1/3-1/3} \cdot [(I_{2^k} \otimes \mathbf{WHT}_{2^m})]_{530-1/4-1/2}. \tag{6}$$

The tag on the right has a higher CPU and bus speed and the tag on the left has a higher memory speed. SPIRAL will generate the corresponding code for easy evaluation. The question is how to distribute the tags in the formula. This is explained next.

Algorithm. We included an algorithm (see Table 2) for tagging a given formula into SPIRAL. The algorithm in principle applies to WHTs and DFTs but is shown only for WHT for simpler presentation. FIR filters are structured differently; they are compute-bound for all input sizes. The input to the tagging algorithm is the cache size N, two frequency configurations c and m to be assigned to memory and compute-bound formula parts respectively, and a formula F. The algorithm recursively descends the formula expression tree and assigns tags. The c tag is assigned once a subformula has an input that fits into the cache.

In the experiments, this algorithm is combined with search over the different formulas of the transform.

---

[1] We never perform unnecessary switches as it is very cheap to check whether the processor already runs at the desired configuration.

Table 2. Algorithm for assigning tags to a formula (example WHT). **Input:** Cache size N; tags c, m for compute-bound and memory-bound sub-formulas, respectively; a formula F for a $\mathbf{WHT}_{2^{k+\ell}}$ of the form $(\mathbf{WHT}_{2^k} \otimes I_{2^\ell})(I_{2^k} \otimes \mathbf{WHT}_{2^\ell})$ where $\mathbf{WHT}_{2^k}, \mathbf{WHT}_{2^\ell}$ are further expanded. **Output:** F tagged.

TagIt(F, N, c, m)
1: **if** $2^{k+\ell} \leq N$ **then**
2:    **return** F_c
3: **end if**
4: **if** $2^\ell \leq N$ **then**
5:    **return** $[(\mathbf{WHT}_{2^k} \otimes I_{2^\ell})]_m [(I_{2^k} \otimes \mathbf{WHT}_{2^\ell})]_c$
6: **else**
7:    **return** $[(\mathbf{WHT}_{2^k} \otimes I_{2^\ell})]_m (I_{2^k} \otimes \mathbf{TagIt}(\mathbf{WHT}_{2^\ell}))$
8: **end if**

3.2   Performance Measurement

We installed SPIRAL on a desktop computer (host machine) and connected the XS-cale board through the local network. On the host, SPIRAL generates tagged formulas, translates them into fixed-point code, cross-compiles for the XScale, and builds a load-able kernel module (LKM). We measure runtime or energy as explained next.

Runtime. We upload the LKM into the board. We first execute the code once (hence, we "warm up" the caches), and then measure a sufficient number of iterations. Finally, we return the runtime to the host and to SPIRAL's search engine to close the feedback loop.

Energy. The XScale board has a 3.5V battery as its power source. To measure energy, we unplug all external sources and we measure, sample, and collect the out-coming battery current through a digital multi meter (DMM).[2] The energy is measured using the following procedure: First, we measure the transform execution time t as explained above and determine the number of iterations sufficient to let the board run the transform for about 10 seconds. Second, we turn off all peripherals power supplies (e.g., LCD) and we take 512 samples 2 ms apart (a sampling period of about one second) of the battery current, then we compute the average current I. Third, we determine the energy by the formula $E = UIt$, where $U = 3.5V$. Notice that we assume that the battery voltage is anchored to its nominal value. This energy value is sent back to the host system and SPIRAL to close the feedback loop.

4   Experimental Results

We consider the following transforms: DFT, WHT, and 8-tap and 16-tap FIR filters. For each transform, we use SPIRAL in separate searches for each configuration to gener-ate the programs optimized for runtime or energy. Runtime and energy measurements are performed as explained in Section 3.2. We use gcc 3.4.2 to compile all generated

---

[2] We use an Agilent 34401A.

programs and and we used *crosstool* to build the cross compiler. In the following figures, we show performance for seven out of the thirteen configurations in Table 1.

The performance is reported in pseudo Mop/s (million operations per second). We exclude from the operations count the index computations and, for input size n, we assume $5n \log_2(n)$ for the DFT, $n \log_2(n)$ for the WHT, and $n(2d - 1)$ for a d-tap filter. The energy performance is reported in pseudo Mop/J (million operations per Joule). Both metrics (runtime performance and energy efficiency) preserve the runtime and energy relation, respectively.

We use the Intel vendor library IPP 4.1 as benchmark except for the WHT (not provided in IPP) and for DFTs of sizes larger than 2^{12} (outside the suggested range for IPP). IPP provides one implementation, which is oblivious of the configuration; in contrast, SPIRAL generates specific codes programs for each configuration.

4.1 Runtime Performance Results

General behavior. We achieve the best performance for the DFT (Fig. 2(a)) and WHT (Fig. 2(b)) for problems fitting in the cache. For larger sizes, ther performance drops. This is a property of these transforms as the structure of their algorithms produces strided memory access and hence cache thrashing (see also the discussion in Section 3.1).

For FIR filters (Figs. 2(c) and (d)), in contrast, the performance remains roughly constant across sizes due to the consecutive access of the input.

Best configuration. For the DFT and FIR filters, there is only one best configuration independently of the problem size, namely 530-1/4-1/2 (highest bus speed) for the DFT and 597-1/6-1/6 (highest CPU speed) for FIR filters. This again shows that FIR filters are compute-bound, whereas DFT and WHT are memory-bound. Note that the configuration 597-1/6-1/6 performs poorly with both DFT and WHT.

For the WHT, the best configuration depends on the problem size, namely, whether or not the problem fits into cache. For in-cache sizes, 530-1/4-1/2 is best, for out-of-cache sizes 497-1/3-1/3 is best. The difference, however, is less than 10%.

SPIRAL vs. IPP. In Fig. 4(a), we show the performance of IPP's DFT for different configurations. The relative speed of SPIRAL generated DFT over IPP is shown in Fig. 4(b). Here, IPP is the base line constant to zero and the performance improvement (in percent) of SPIRAL over IPP is shown. For problem sizes $n = 64$, 128, and 4096, SPIRAL generated code is faster; in contrast, it is slower for sizes $n = 256, \ldots, 2048$.

Further, the relative speed of SPIRAL over IPP may vary by more than 10% points for different configurations. For example, for $n = 128$, SPIRAL generated code is as fast as the IPP code in configuration 398-1/4-1/4, but almost 25% faster in configuration 497-1/3-1/3.

SPIRAL generated code for 8-tap FIR filters (Fig. 2(c)) outperforms the respective IPP routines (Fig. 3(a)) by a factor of two. In the case of 16-tap FIR filters, SPIRAL (Fig. 2(d)) and IPP (Fig. 3(b)) have roughly equal performance.

IPP does not provide a WHT library function.

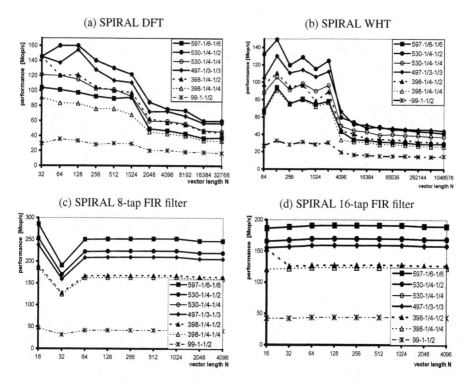

Fig. 2. Performance (in pseudo Mop/s) of SPIRAL generated code: (a) DFT, (b) WHT, (c) 8-tap FIR filter, and (d) 16-tap FIR filter

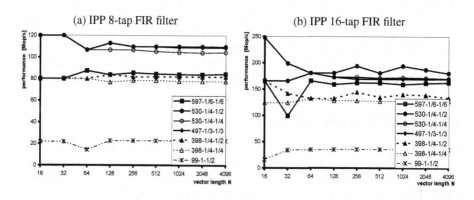

Fig. 3. Performance (in pseudo Mop/s) of IPP FIR filters: (a) 8-tap FIR filter, and (b) 16-tap FIR filter

4.2   Energy Results

General behavior. The energy efficiency of FIR filters (for both SPIRAL and IPP) does not depend on the problem size (see Figs. 5(c) and (d) and Fig. 6). In contrast, the

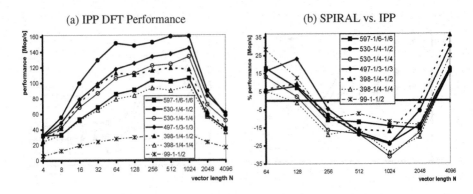

Fig. 4. (a) DFT performance of Intel's IPP (in pseudo Mop/s); (b) Relative performance of SPI-RAL generated DFT over IPP's DFT. The percentage is the performance improvement of SPI-RAL over IPP.

energy efficiency of the DFT (Fig. 5(a) and Fig. 7(b)) and of the WHT (Fig. 5(b)) is high for in-cache problem sizes and significantly lower for large problem sizes.

Best configuration. For SPIRAL generated DFT code, the configuration with the highest energy efficiency (Fig. 5(a)) depends on the problem size and it is a compromise among the speed of CPU, bus and memory. For example, 398-1/4-1/2 is clearly best for sizes 8, 16, and 32. For the SPIRAL generated WHT code (Fig. 5(b)) the best configuration in-cache is 530-1/4-1/4 and out-of-cache 398-1/4-1/2. Note that these configuration are different from the ones optimal for performance (see Section 4.1).

SPIRAL vs. IPP. In Fig. 7(a) we show the energy efficiency of IPP's DFT code for different configurations. The relative efficiency of SPIRAL generated code over IPP code is shown in Fig. 7(b). Qualitatively, the plot is similar to Fig. 4(b).

SPIRAL generated 8-tap FIR filter code Fig. 5(c) gains threefold over IPP (Fig. 6(a)) in energy efficiency. For 16-tap FIR filters, SPIRAL still gains about 20% (Fig. 5(d) versus Fig. 6(b)) even though the performance is roughly equal (Section 4.1).

4.3 Dynamic Frequency Scaling

Finally, we investigate the potential of dynamic frequency scaling; that is, the dynamic switching among configurations during the computation (see Section 3.1). For this technique to make sense, the best configuration for in-cache and out-of-cache sizes has to differ. This is the case only for the WHT. Both performance (Fig. 2(b)) and energy efficiency (Fig. 5(b)) are candidates for dynamic frequency scaling.

For both metrics we first choose two configurations. Then, for all problem sizes that do not fit into cache ($N \geq 2^{16}$) we apply the tagging algorithm given in Table 2 to the fastest formulae. This way, SPIRAL finds a WHT implementation that switches between the chosen configurations and automatically trades the switching overhead and

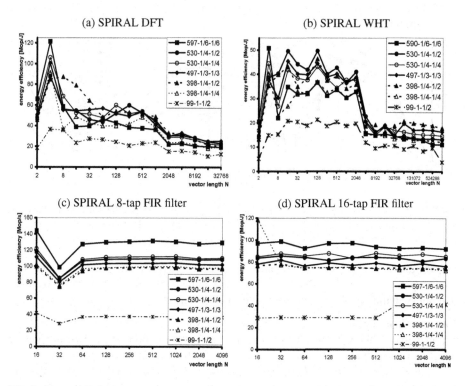

Fig. 5. Energy efficiency (in pseudo Mop/J) of SPIRAL generated code: (a) DFT, (b) WHT, (c) 8-tap FIR filter, and (d) 16-tap FIR filter

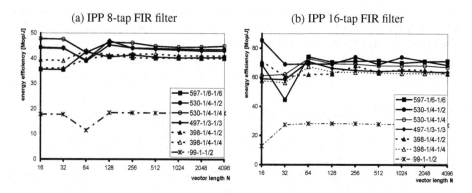

Fig. 6. Energy efficiency (in pseudo Mop/J) of IPP FIR filters: (a) 8-tap FIR filter, and (b) 16-tap FIR filter

the performance or energy efficiency gains obtained by switching, overall optimizing for the given metric.

Runtime performance. Based on Fig. 2(b) we find two configuration candidates to switch between: 1) 530-1/4-1/2 is the fastest configuration for small problem sizes and

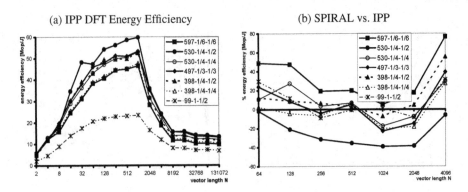

Fig. 7. (a) IPP's DFT energy efficiency (in pseudo Mop/J). (b) Energy efficiency gain or loss of SPIRAL generated DFT over IPP's DFT in percent. Higher means SPIRAL is more efficient.

thus the candidate for CPU bound parts, and 2) 497-1/3-1/3 for memory bound parts of the computation. However, due to the large switching overhead ($530\mu s$) SPIRAL finds that not switching at all leads to the highest performance.

Energy efficiency. Optimizing for energy efficiency leaves more room for the successful application of dynamic frequency scaling, as energy depends both on runtime and power, which in turn both depend nonlinearly on the CPU, bus, and memory frequencies.

Our experiments indicate that switching between 398-1/4-1/2 and 497-1/3-1/3 yields the most energy efficient implementations. Thus, we investigate switching between these configurations further detailing two approaches.

Starting from the statically most efficient configuration 398-1/4-1/2 (line "398-1/4-1/2 static" in Fig. 8) we can gain efficiency by switching to the faster configuration 497-1/3-1/3 for all sub-formulae of shape $\mathbf{WHT}_{2^3} \otimes I_{2^n}$ (line "dynamic 1" in Fig. 8). The efficiency gain is due to higher bandwidth requirements for $\mathbf{WHT}_{2^3} \otimes I_{2^n}$ as this formula trashes the mini cache and at the same time is able to fully utilize the CPU's 8 registers and thus the higher CPU frequency.

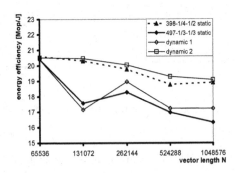

Fig. 8. Dynamic frequency scaling of SPIRAL generated WHT, switching between 497-1/3-1/3 and 398-1/4-1/4

Starting from the statically second most efficient configuration 497-1/3-1/3 (line "497-1/3-1/3 static" in Fig. 8) we can gain efficiency by switching to the slower configuration 398-1/4-1/2 for all sub-formulae of shape $\mathbf{WHT}_{2^2} \otimes I_{2^n}$ (line "dynamic 2" in Fig. 8). In the case of $\mathbf{WHT}_{2^2} \otimes I_{2^n}$ the CPU is not fully utilized and the mini cache is not trashed. Thus, we can slow down the CPU frequency without hurting runtime and can even slow down the memory and bus and still gain energy efficiency. However, this approach (line "dynamic 2" in Fig. 8) cannot compete with the first approach (line "dynamic 1" in Fig. 8).

Overall, dynamic frequency scaling between 398-1/4-1/2 and 497-1/3-1/3 yields a slight gain in energy efficiency with respect to *both* baseline configurations, however, due to different reasons.

5   Conclusions

We show how a program generation framework as SPIRAL can be used to produce efficient DSP kernels such as the DFT, the WHT, and FIR filters on the XScale embedded platform. We support frequency scaling and thus automatically generate and optimize programs tuned for different configurations. Our experiments show that the best configuration depends on the DSP kernel, the metric and sometimes even on the problem size.

References

1. Püschel, M., Moura, J.M.F., Johnson, J., Padua, D., Veloso, M., Singer, B.W., Xiong, J., Franchetti, F., Gačić, A., Voronenko, Y., Chen, K., Johnson, R.W., Rizzolo, N.: SPIRAL: Code generation for DSP transforms. Proc. of the IEEE **93**(2) (2005) 232–275 Special issue on *Program Generation, Optimization, and Adaptation*.
2. Halambi, A., Shrivastava, A., Dutt, N., Nicolau, A.: A customizable compiler framework for embedded systems. In: Proc. Workshop on Software and Compilers for Embedded Systems. (2001)
3. Contreras, G., Martonosi, M.: Power prediction for Intel XScale processors using performance monitoring unit events. In: Proc. International Symposium on Low Power Electronics and Design (ISLPED). (2005) 221–226
4. Singleton, L., Poellabauer, C., Schwan, K.: Monitoring of cache miss rates for accurate dynamic voltage and frequency scaling. In: Proc. Multimedia Computing and Networking Conference. (2005)
5. Hsu, C., Kremer, U.: The design, implementation, and evaluation of a compiler algorithm for CPU energy reduction. In: Proc. Conference on Programming Language Design and Implementation (PLDI). (2003) 38–48
6. Xie, F., Martonosi, M., Malik, S.: Compile-time dynamic voltage scaling settings: Opportunities and limits. In: Proc. Conference on Programming Language Design and Implementation (PLDI). (2003) 49–62
7. Whaley, R.C., Petitet, A., Dongarra, J.J.: Automated empirical optimization of software and the ATLAS project. Parallel Computing **27**(1–2) (2001) 3–35
8. Im, E.J., Yelick, K., Vuduc, R.: Sparsity: Optimization framework for sparse matrix kernels. Int'l J. High Performance Computing Applications **18**(1) (2004)

9. Frigo, M., Johnson, S.G.: The design and implementation of FFTW3. Proc. of the IEEE **93**(2) (2005) 216–231 Special issue on *Program Generation, Optimization, and Adaptation.*
10. Intel: Intel XScale Microarchitecture. (2001)
11. Van Loan, C.: Computational Framework of the Fast Fourier Transform. SIAM (1992)
12. Gačić, A., Püschel, M., Moura, J.M.F.: Fast automatic implementations of FIR filters. In: Proc. International Conference on Acoustics, Speech, and Signal Processing (ICASSP). Volume 2. (2003) 541–544
13. Gačić, A.: Automatic Implementation and Platform Adaptation of Discrete Filtering and Wavelet Algorithms. PhD thesis, Electrical and Computer Engineering, Carnegie Mellon University (2004)
14. Franchetti, F., Voronenko, Y., Püschel, M.: Loop merging for signal transforms. In: Proc. Programming Language Design and Implementation (PLDI). (2005) 315–326

Arx: A Toolset for the Efficient Simulation and Direct Synthesis of High-Performance Signal Processing Algorithms

Klaas L. Hofstra and Sabih H. Gerez

Department of Electrical Engineering, Signals and Systems Group
University of Twente, The Netherlands
k.l.hofstra@utwente.nl

Abstract. This paper addresses the efficient implementation of high-performance signal-processing algorithms. In early stages of such designs many computation-intensive simulations may be necessary. This calls for hardware description formalisms targeted for efficient simulation (such as the programming language C). In current practice, other formalisms (such as VHDL) will often be used to map the design on hardware by means of logic synthesis. A manual, error-prone, translation of a description is then necessary.

The line of thought of this paper is that the gap between simulation and synthesis should not be bridged by stretching the use of existing formalisms (e.g. defining a synthesizable subset of C), but by a language dedicated to an application domain. This resulted in Arx, which is meant for signal-processing hardware at the register-transfer level, either using floating-point or fixed-point data. Code generators with knowledge of the application domain then generate efficient simulation models and synthesizable VHDL.

Several designers have already completed complex signal-processing designs using Arx in a short time, proving in practice that Arx is easy to learn. Benchmarks presented in this paper show that the generated simulation code is significantly faster than SystemC.

1 Introduction

In the last four decades many hardware description languages (HDLs) have been proposed, each having their strengths and weaknesses. HDLs serve one or more of the following goals: specification, formal verification, simulation, and synthesis. Ideally, one would use one and the same description language for all goals. In practice, however, the different goals are difficult to satisfy: code written in synthesizable VHDL (see e.g. [1]) will be much slower to simulate than code written in C, while code written in e.g. *SystemC* [2] in a style to optimize simulation speed is not likely to be synthesizable.

In practice, multiple HDLs are used to overcome this problem. C is often used to create a first executable model of the system to be designed. Such a model is *untimed* [3] in general. It has the advantage of fast execution and allows extensive elaboration of the system's performance. Once the model has been

K. De Bosschere et al. (Eds.): HiPEAC 2007, LNCS 4367, pp. 215–226, 2007.

refined to the point that a hardware architecture can be specified, the design is manually recoded in a synthesizable HDL, such as VHDL. This is a cumbersome and error-prone process.

This paper addresses the problem of conflicting language requirements and proposes a solution for the domain of register-transfer level (RTL) descriptions of signal processing algorithms. The solution consists of a specification language called Arx in combination with tools. These tools can convert designs written in Arx to either C code for simulation or VHDL code for synthesis. The generated C code is optimized for simulation speed while the VHDL code is optimized for synthesis. The proposed approach has the advantage that a thorough design-space exploration can be performed due to high simulation speed, while it is not necessary to rewrite the simulation code by hand in order to synthesize hardware.

This paper is organized as follows. Section 2 describes our requirements for a language for simulation and synthesis and reviews some existing languages. In Section 3 the Arx tools and language are introduced. Section 4 describes the C and VHDL code generators. The results of the simulation speed benchmarks are discussed in Section 5. In Section 6, some implementation results are discussed.

2 Languages for Simulation and Synthesis

In this section we present a list of requirements that we feel should be met for languages (and tools) for fast simulation and synthesis of signal processing algorithms. Subsequently, we review some existing design languages.

2.1 Requirements

The design goal of the Arx toolset is to simplify the hardware design for fixed-point signal processing algorithms. The toolset has been designed with the following requirements in mind:

1. High performance simulation must be possible because the signal processing algorithms typically require computation-intensive simulations.
2. The designs should be made at the register-transfer level. Synthesis from behavioral descriptions has the advantage of higher design productivity but results in implementations with an area overhead as well as suboptimal speed and power. This is due to the fact that the design is mapped on some predefined hardware template which limits the design freedom.
3. The entire language should be synthesizable, making it unnecessary to isolate the synthesizable language subset.
4. Fixed-point data types and fixed-point arithmetic operators must be supported because they are extensively used in signal processing algorithms.
5. The toolset must be text based, giving full design freedom to designers. Graphical toolsets limit the design freedom to the available building blocks and become cumbersome when designs are control dominated or have complex data paths.
6. In order to take advantage of the available highly optimized C compilers, the toolset should emit C code for the simulator instead of machine code.

2.2 Language Overview

VHDL was originally designed as a powerful simulation language [4] meant to have an event-driven simulation engine. Such a simulation approach offers the possibility to model hardware at various levels of abstraction but is less suitable for computation-intensive simulations of signal-processing systems. The overhead involved with run-time scheduling of events can cause a considerable increase in the simulation time. Synthesis from VHDL was introduced later. It required the definition of a *synthesizable subset* [1] as not all language constructs could be associated with hardware in a direct way. In synthesizable VHDL, one is practically forced to use the standardized std_logic data type and types derived from it. This 9-valued data type is very useful to trace design errors as it contains special values for uninitialized and undefined signals. This nice property, however, also contributes to slowing down simulations.

General-purpose programming languages have been combined with libraries or extensions for hardware simulation and synthesis. A prominent example of this approach is SystemC. SystemC is a C++ class library that provides functionality for system-level design. Abstraction levels range from RTL to the system-level. A synthesizable subset has been defined to enable hardware design in SystemC. The definition of such a subset is required because of the great scope of SystemC, i.e. constructs required for high-level modeling do not map to the RTL domain. The great scope and flexibility of SystemC are its strenghts. However, when the scope of a design is limited to the domain of RTL, we feel that a simple domain-specific language is better suited for the task. Such an approach has the advantage of having a clean language of which all features can be used at wish. The effort to learn the SystemC library and the synthesizable subset is as high as or higher than the effort to learn a small dedicated language [5].

Synchronous languages [6] combine deterministic concurrency with synchrony (i.e. time advances in lockstep with one or more clocks). Lustre [7] and Esterel [8] are examples of such languages that have been successfully used for hardware simulation and synthesis [9]. Arx is also a synchronous language but differs from the ones mentioned because it combines concurrent statements and sequential statements in a way similar to VHDL. In Arx, unlike the other synchronous languages, registers are explicitly instantiated. Because Arx had been specifically designed for RTL design, the notion of synchrony is linked to the concept of registers.

3 The Arx Toolset

3.1 The Arx Language

Arx enforces a synchronous design style. The clock is implicit in the design and is only apparent through the registers. In order to guarantee correct behavior, systems written in Arx are not allowed to contain zero-delay loops. Arx has two types of data objects: *registers* and *variables*. When a register object is declared, its reset value must also be specified. Assignments to registers are concurrent while assignments to variables are sequential.

A design is implemented as a set of *components* and *functions*. Conceptually, components operate concurrently. Only components can contain registers. Functions are purely combinational. Both can be parameterized with *generic* types and constants. Generic types enable an efficient refinement methodology by allowing reuse of the same code in, for example, floating point and various fixed-point implementations. Functions can also be declared 'external', which means that the function is implemented in the target language (currently C or VHDL). This provides the designer with extensive library support at the algorithmic verification level. When the design is further refined into a synthesizable system, the external functions are replaced with synthesizable native Arx functions.

Table 1. Arx data types

type	description
bit	1 or 0
bitvector	vector of bits
boolean	*true* or *false*
integer	integer values
real	floating-point
signed	signed fixed-point
unsigned	unsigned fixed-point

The available data types include floating-point and fixed-point. Table 1 presents a list of all Arx data types. Additionally, users can define type aliases and enumerated types. For both `signed` and `unsigned` data types the number of bits is specified in the same way as the SystemC `sc_fixed` data type [10], i.e. `signed(wl,iwl)` and `unsigned(wl,iwl)`, where `wl` denotes the total word length and `iwl` denotes the number of integer bits. Arx supports all the *overflow* and *quantization* modes defined in SystemC [11].

Arx supports a large set of arithmetic operations. The conditional statements `if` and `case` and the loop statement `for` are also included in the language. Arrays can be constructed and individual bits or slices of vectors can be selected with special operators.

Figure 1 shows Arx code for an accumulator with generic types. The hardware block diagram is depicted in Fig. 2. This example also shows the difference between registers and variables. The value of r at line 19 refers to the current value of the register because it occurs on the right-hand-side of the assignment expression. When registers are referenced at the left-hand-side of an assignment, such as at line 18, they refer to the register value for the next clock cycle.

3.2   The Workflow

The Arx language and toolset enable a stepwise refinement design methodology that starts with a high-level description and iteratively reaches an optimized synthesizable description. At each stage of the design, the tools can generate C

```
01: component acc
02:      T_io        : generic type
03:      T_sum       : generic type
04:      clear       : in bit
05:      data_in     : in T_io
06:      data_out    : out T_io
07:
08: variable
09:      sum         : T_sum
10: register
11:      r           : T_sum = 0
12: begin
13:      if clear == 1
14:          sum = data_in
15:      else
16:          sum = r + data_in
17:      end
18:      r = sum
19:      data_out = r
20: end
```

Fig. 1. Arx code for an accumulator example

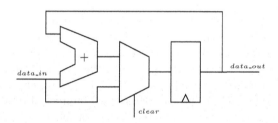

Fig. 2. Block diagram of the accumulator example

code for a simulator. This simulator can be used for high-speed verification and evaluation of the design and algorithms.

Figure 3 shows the typical Arx workflow. The high-level system description is used for algorithmic verification. At this level all data types, including floating point, are allowed. The generated simulator is neither bit-true nor clock-cycle-true. Subsequently, the design is further refined into a bit-true description that restricts the data types to fixed-point. At this step, the simulator is bit-true but not clock-cycle-true. The next refinement step transforms the design into RTL code. RTL in the context of Arx amounts to distinguishing between *registers* and *wires (or variables)* and assuming the presence of an implicit clock that controls the register updates. The refinement of the design leads to a careful placement of registers in the signal flow that eventually results in a clock-cycle true specification. Given this RTL description, the tools can generate both a fast bit-true and clock-cycle-true simulator as well as VHDL code for synthesis.

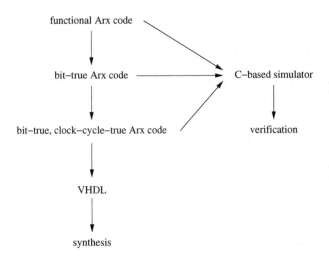

Fig. 3. Arx workflow

4   Code Generation

4.1   Fixed-Point Data Types for C Generation

For fast simulation of fixed-point arithmetic, the efficient mapping of fixed-point data-types on the host machine is crucial. SystemC offers two different fixed-point class implementations. The limited-precision implementation maps the fixed-point data-types on the 53 mantissa bits of the native C++ floating point type. This restricts the size of fixed-point to 53 bits. Another disadvantage of this approach is that fixed-point types with a small number of bits, are mapped on 64-bit floating-point numbers which require extra memory bandwidth. The other option offered by SystemC is the unlimited fixed-point implementation that is based on concatenated data containers.

We chose to implement the fixed-point mapping in a similar way as described in [12]. All fixed-point values are mapped on the native machine word-size, which is 32-bit or 64-bit for most general purpose processors. If a fixed-point type exceeds this word-size, the type is mapped on a number of concatenated words.

SystemC uses operator overloading to implement arithmetic operations on fixed-point data types. The Arx code generation tools generate speed optimized code for each individual operation. We do not use global optimization to reduce the number of shift operations as is proposed in [12] because the authors indicate that the gains are minimal.

4.2   Scheduling for the C Backend

A hardware design is conveniently modeled by a set of parallel communicating processes. Conceptually, an Arx component corresponds to such a process. For simulation, the Arx tools convert this concurrent process model to a sequential program by appropriately scheduling the processes. Process scheduling can be done dynamically by a run-time scheduler or statically by a compiler. Because of the synchronous nature of the Arx language, the C code generator tools can use static scheduling. Contrary to static scheduling, dynamic scheduling as used in SystemC incurs a run-time overhead. FastSysC [13] is a replacement for the SystemC simulation engine that uses acyclic scheduling instead of dynamic scheduling. This scheduling approach reduces the run-time overhead of the scheduler. FastSysC is designed for cycle-level simulators and only supports a subset of the SystemC syntax. We analyse the impact on the simulation performance of these three scheduling methods in Sect. 5.

The first step in the Arx C generator is to instantiate all components. Subsequently, the component hierarchy is flattened (i.e. component boundaries are removed). Next, constant values are propagated and loops are unrolled. After that, the scheduling phase begins. For each clock cycle the Arx simulator needs to compute the new value of each register and all top-level outputs, based on the current register values and all top-level inputs. Hence, the current value of all registers and all top-level inputs are at the start of the data-flow graph, and the next value for all registers and all top-level outputs are end points of the graph. Because the Arx language is synchronous and zero-delay cycles are not permitted, the graph will not have cycles. Therefore, the scheduling is straightforward. Currently, Arx only supports a single clock but static scheduling of synchronous programs with multiple clocks is possible (see e.g. [14]).

4.3 Generated C Code

The C code generator creates code for a C++ class with two member functions: **run** and **reset**. The **run** function has the same inputs and outputs as the top-level component of the design. This function should be called for every clock-cycle of the simulation. The **reset** function assigns to each register its reset value. A SystemC wrapper is automatically created to enable easy integration with the SystemC Verification Library.

There are a number of differences between SystemC code and the C code generated by Arx that have an impact on simulation performance. Contrary to Arx C code, SystemC code uses virtual methods which result in a run-time overhead. Another difference is the number of function calls. Because all the Arx simulation code is located in the **run** function, only a single function call is executed for the simulation of a single cycle. For the SystemC simulator the number of function calls is a lot higher and depends on the number of components. Because the Arx simulation code is not spread out across multiple functions in different files, the C compiler can use more aggressive optimizations.

4.4 VHDL Code Generation

The VHDL code generator maintains the component hierarchy of the original design. Fixed-point data types are mapped on the **signed** and **unsigned** data types defined in the **ieee.numeric_std** package. An optimized VHDL package has been developed for the implementation of the supported overflow and quantization modes. The testbench created for the verification of the C code can be reused for verification of the VHDL provided that the VHDL simulator has an interface for C/SystemC co-simulation.

5   Benchmark Results

Two FIR filter implementations have been implemented to compare the simulation performance of Arx, SystemC and FastSysC. The first design (FIR1) implements an unfolded version of a 16-tap FIR filter. This implementation is modeled as a single component and processes one sample per clock cycle. The code for the Arx and SystemC versions of the filter are shown in Fig. 4 and Fig. 5 respectively (notice the compactness of the Arx code). The FastSysC version of the code differs only slightly from the SystemC version and is therefore not shown.

```
component fir
    T_io          : generic type
    T_sum         : generic type
    T_coeff       : generic type
    data_in       : in T_io
    data_out      : out T_io
constant
    N             : integer = 16
    coeff         : array[N] of T_coeff = { ... }
register
    delay         : array[N] of T_io = 0.0
variable
    prod          : T_io
begin
    delay[0] = data_in * coeff[N-1]
    for i in 1:N-1
        prod = data_in * coeff[N-1-i]
        delay[i] = convert(T_sum, prod + delay[i-1])
    end
    data_out = delay[N-1]
end
```

Fig. 4. Arx code for the unfolded FIR filter

The second design (FIR2) is also a fully unfolded 16-tap FIR filter, However, in this design every adder, multiplier and register is modeled as a separate component. Therefore, instead of one filter component, this version has 47 components (16 multipliers, 15 adders and 16 registers) that all need to be scheduled. Both FIR1 and FIR2 implement exactly the same filter. Hence, any difference in simulation performance can be attributed to the scheduler.

```
SC_MODULE(fir) {
    sc_in<bool> clock;
    sc_in<bool> reset;
    sc_in<T_io> data_in;
    sc_out<T_io> data_out;

    T_coeff coeff[NR_TAPS];
    T_sum delay_reg[NR_TAPS];
    T_sum delay_nxt[NR_TAPS];

    SC_CTOR(fir)
    {
        SC_METHOD(update);
        sensitive_pos << clock;
        coeff[0] = ...
        ...
    };

    void update()
    {
        int i;
        T_io input, output, prod;

        if (reset.read()) {
            for (i=0; i<NR_TAPS; i++) {
                delay_reg[i] = 0;
            }
        }
        else {
            input = data_in.read();

            /* compute next values */
            delay_nxt[0] = (T_io)(input * coeff[NR_TAPS-1]);
            for (i=1; i<NR_TAPS; i++) {
                prod = (T_io)(input * coeff[NR_TAPS-1-i]);
                delay_nxt[i] = (T_sum)(prod + delay_reg[i-1]);
            }

            /* update registers */
            for (i=0; i<NR_TAPS; i++) {
                delay_reg[i] = delay_nxt[i];
            }
        }
        output = delay_reg[NR_TAPS-1];
        data_out.write(output);
    }
}
```

Fig. 5. SystemC code for the unfolded FIR filter

The FIR designs have been benchmarked with both fixed-point and floating-point data types. The floating-point version uses `float` for SystemC and Fast-SysC and `real` for Arx. All operations are floating-point and there are no type conversions. In case of the fixed-point version, all data types are signed 10-bit fixed-point. The result of the addition operation is saturated in order to stay within the 10-bit range. There is no FastSysC fixed-point version because we are only interested in the performance of the scheduler of FastSysC.

In order to benchmark the performance of the SystemC fixed-point data types separately from the SystemC scheduler, a special version of the fixed-point FIR1 benchmark was made that does not use the SystemC scheduler. Instead of using signals for input and output, this implementation uses function parameters.

The SystemC implementations use the synthesizable subset of SystemC, i.e. they use `SC_METHOD` and signals for communication between logic blocks. In order to reduce the simulation overhead, internal signals are declared as normal local variables and not as SystemC signals. Version 2.1 of the SystemC library and version 1.1 of the FastSysC simulator were used for the benchmarks.

The simulation times for the benchmarks are summarized in Table 2. The results have been scaled relative to the fastest simulation. The results show that the simulation times for the Arx versions of FIR1 and FIR2 are identical in the floating-point case and very close for the fixed-point data types. This shows that there is no extra scheduling overhead for the Arx simulator when the number of components is increased from 1 (FIR1) to 47 (FIR2).

Table 2. Simulation time results

simulator	data type	FIR1	FIR2
Arx	floating-point	1.00	1.00
SystemC	floating-point	23.5	201
FastSysC	floating-point	2.63	45.3
Arx	fixed-point	2.19	2.46
SystemC	fixed-point	467	1263
SystemC (without scheduler)	fixed-point	385	-

In case of the floating-point SystemC benchmarks, the simulation time for FIR2 is about 8 times longer than the simulation time for FIR1. This shows that the overhead of the dynamic scheduler increases when the number of components increases, which is to be expected. For the FastSysC benchmarks the increase in simulation time between FIR1 and FIR2 is roughly a factor of 17. This relative increase is larger than that for the SystemC benchmarks, but both FIR1 and FIR2 floating-point FastSysC simulation times are respectively 9 and 4 times faster than their SystemC counterparts. Compared to the results for the floating-point Arx benchmarks, the FastSysC benchmarks are 2.6 and 45.3 times slower while the SystemC benchmarks are 23.5 and 201 times slower. We can conclude that the FastSysC simulator is faster than the SystemC implementation but slower than the Arx simulator. The Arx simulator is one to two orders of magnitude faster than the SystemC versions, depending on the number of components in the simulation.

In order to compare the fixed-point data type implementations of SystemC and Arx, we compare the Arx fixed-point FIR1 benchmark with the SystemC FIR1 benchmark without scheduler. The simulation time results show that the Arx version is two orders of magnitude faster than the SystemC implementation without scheduler.

6 Implementation Results

Arx has successfully been applied to a number of designs, including an LDPC decoder, a CDMA equalizer [15] and a MIMO MMSE equalizer. The goal of efficient simulation has been met for these designs. The VHDL generated by Arx was successfully mapped on an experimental fast prototyping setup with an FPGA PCI board and also synthesized using modern ASIC standard-cell libraries. The simulation efficiency of Arx has made it possible to explore larger parts of the design space than usual.

7 Conclusions

In this paper we have briefly introduced the design language Arx and our workflow for simulation and synthesis. Arx has been created to enable synthesis and fast simulation of signal processing algorithms based on a single design description. For synthesis this description is transformed into VHDL, while C code is generated for fast simulation.

In order to benchmark the simulation speed of the generated C code, two FIR implementations have been realized using Arx, SystemC and FastSysC. The benchmark results show that the Arx simulator is faster than both the SystemC and FastSysC simulators. When we compare the fixed-point synthesizable implementations written in Arx and SystemC, the Arx simulators are two orders of magnitude faster than the SystemC versions. This speed advantage is achieved through a faster implementation of the fixed-point arithmetic and the use of static scheduling.

References

1. Rushton, A.: VHDL for Logic Synthesis, Second Editon. John Wiley and Sons (1998)
2. Groetker, T., S. Liao, G.M., Swan, S.: System Design with SystemC. Kluwer Academic Publishers (2002)
3. Jantsch, A.: Modeling Embedded Systems and SoCs, Concurrency and Time in Models of Computation. Morgan Kaufmann, San Francisco (2004)
4. Lipsett, R., Schaeffer, C., Ussery, C.: VHDL: Hardware Description and Design. Kluwer Academic Publishers, Boston (1989)

5. Edwards, S.A.: The challenges of hardware synthesis from C-like languages. In: Proceedings of the International Workshop on Logic and Synthesis (IWLS). (2004)
6. Benveniste, A., Caspi, P., Edwards, S., Halbwachs, N., Le Guernic, P., de Simone, R.: The synchronous languages 12 years later. In: Proceedings of the IEEE. Volume 91. (2003) 64–83
7. Caspi, P., Pilaud, D., Halbwachs, N., Plaice, J.A.: Lustre: a declarative language for real-time programming. In: POPL '87: Proceedings of the 14th ACM SIGACT-SIGPLAN symposium on Principles of programming languages, New York, NY, USA, ACM Press (1987) 178–188
8. Berry, G.: The Foundations of Esterel. MIT Press (2000)
9. Rocheteau, F., Halbwachs, N.: Pollux, a Lustre-based hardware design environment. In Quinton, P., Robert, Y., eds.: Conference on Algorithms and Parallel VLSI Architectures II, Chateau de Bonas (1991)
10. Black, D., Donovan, J.: SystemC: From the Ground Up. Kluwer Academic Publishers, Boston (2004)
11. OSCI: SystemC version 2.0 user's guide, update for SystemC 2.0.1. http://www.systemc.org (2002)
12. Keding, H., Coors, M., Lüthje, O., Meyr, H.: Fast bit-true simulation. In: DAC '01: Proceedings of the 38th conference on design automation, New York, NY, USA, ACM Press (2001) 708–713
13. Garcia Perez, D., Mouchard, G., Temam, O.: A new optimized implementation of the SystemC engine using acyclic scheduling. In: Design Automation and Test in Europe, DATE'04. (2004)
14. Lee, E.A., Messerschmitt, D.G.: Static scheduling of synchronous data flow programs for digital signal processing. IEEE Transactions on Computers **36**(1) (1987) 24–35
15. van Kampen, D., Hofstra, K.L., Potman, J., Gerez, S.H.: Implementation of a combined OFDM-demodulation and WCDMA-equalization module. In: Proceedings of the Workshop on Circuits, Systems and Signal Processing, ProRISC. (2006)

A Throughput-Driven Task Creation and Mapping for Network Processors

Lixia Liu[1], Xiao-Feng Li[1], Michael Chen[2], and Roy D.C. Ju[2]

[1] Intel China Research Center Ltd. Beijing, China
liulixia@purdue.edu, xiao.feng.li@intel.com
[2] Intel Corporation, Microprocessor Technology Lab Santa Clara, USA
mrchen@gmail.com, roy.ju@amd.com

Abstract. Network processors are programmable devices that can process packets at a high speed. A network processor is typified by multi-threading and heterogeneous multiprocessing, which usually requires programmers to manually create multiple tasks and map these tasks onto different processing elements. This paper addresses the problem of automating task creation and mapping of network applications onto the underlying hardware to maximize their throughput. We propose a throughput cost model to guide the task creation and mapping with the objective of both minimizing the number of stages in the processing pipeline and maximizing the average throughput of the slowest task simultaneously. The average throughput is modeled by taking communication cost, computation cost, memory access latency and synchronization cost into account. We envision that programmers write small functions for network applications, such that we use grouping and duplication to construct tasks from the functions. The optimal solution of creating tasks from m functions and mapping them to n processors is an NP-hard problem. Therefore, we present a practical and efficient heuristic algorithm with an $O((n + m)m)$ complexity and show that the obtained solutions produce excellent performance for typical network applications. The entire framework has been implemented in the Open Research Compiler (ORC) adapted to compile network applications written in a domain-specific dataflow language. Experimental results show that the code produced by our compiler can achieve the 100% throughput on the OC-48 input line rate. OC-48 is a fiber optic connection that can handle a 2.488Gbps connection speeds, which is what our targeted hardware was designed for. We also demonstrate the importance of good creation and mapping choices on achieving high throughput. Furthermore, we show that reducing communication cost and efficient resource management are the most important factors for maximizing throughput on the Intel IXP network processors.

Keywords: Network Processors, Throughput, Intel IXP, Dataflow Programming, Task Creation and Mapping.

K. De Bosschere et al. (Eds.): HiPEAC 2007, LNCS 4367, pp. 227–241, 2007.
© Springer-Verlag Berlin Heidelberg 2007

1   Introduction

While there are increasing demands for high throughput on network applications, network processors with their programmability and high processing rates have emerged to become important devices for packet processing applications in addition to ASICs (application-specific integrated circuits). Network processors typically incorporate multiple heterogeneous, multi-threaded cores, and programmers of network applications are often required to manually partition applications into tasks at design time and map the tasks onto different processing elements. However, most programmers find it challenging to produce efficient software for such a complex architecture. Because the type and number of processing elements that these tasks are mapped to greatly influence the overall performance, it is an important but tedious effort for programmers to carefully create and map tasks of applications to achieve a maximal throughput. It is also rather difficult to port these applications from one generation of an architecture to another while still achieving high performance.

The problem being addressed in this paper is the automatic task creation and mapping of packet processing applications on network processors while maximizing the throughput of these applications. We envision programmers writing small functions for modularity in our programming model, and focus on mapping coarse-grained task parallelism in this work. Hence, we apply grouping and duplication to construct tasks from functions as opposed to splitting functions to smaller tasks. Note that the cost model itself is applicable both for different task granularities and for function splitting. Our approach has been implemented in the Open Research Compiler (ORC)[4][6] and evaluated on Intel IXP2400 network processors. We also conjecture that our approach is applicable to other processor architectures that support multi-threading and chip multiprocessors (CMP).

The primary contributions of this paper are as follows. First, a throughput cost model is developed to model the critical factors that affect the throughput of a CMP system. Compared to other simpler models, we demonstrate our throughput cost model to be more accurate and effective. Second, we develop a practical and efficient heuristic algorithm guided by the throughput cost model to partition and map applications onto network processors automatically. This algorithm also manages hardware resources (e.g. processors and threads) and handles special hardware constraints (e.g. the limited size of control store allowed limits instructions for each task). Third, we have implemented and evaluated our partitioning and mapping approach on a real network processor system.

The rest of this paper is organized as follows. Section 2 introduces background on the Intel IXP network processors and the features of our domain-specific programming language, Baker. Section 3 states the problems of creation and mapping. Section 4 presents our throughput cost model and describes a practical heuristic algorithm for task creation and mapping. Section 5 evaluates the performance of three network applications using different heuristics in comparison to our proposed one. Section 6 covers the related work, and then we conclude this paper in Section 7.

2 Background[1]

The Intel IXP network processors are designed for high-speed packet processing [2][3][4]. We briefly introduce the architecture of a representative one from Intel IXP network processors, Intel IXP2400. IXP2400 is composed of an Intel XScale core (XSC) for control plane processing, such as route table maintenance and system-level management functions, and eight 32-bit multi-threaded MicroEngines (MEs) for data plane processing that can process critical packet processing tasks at a high rate.

There are eight hardware thread contexts available in each ME, and they share the same execution pipeline. Each ME has a limited control store(4K instructions) to hold the program instructions that the ME executes. Intel IXP2400 has a four-level memory hierarchy: Local Memory, Scratchpad, SRAM and DRAM, which have capacities that increase proportionally to access latencies. However, the MEs have no hardware caches because of little temporal and spatial locality in network applications and the desire to avoid non-deterministic performance behavior. Each of the four memory levels is designed for different purposes. In particular, DRAM is used to hold the large packet data because of its fast direct communication channel to network interfaces and also because it has the largest capacity.

```
wire {
    RX.eth0 ->l2_dsfr.input_chnl
    l3_fwdr_chnl -> l3_fwdr.input_chnl
    l2_bridge_chnl -> l2_bridge.input_chnl
    l3_fwdr_output_chnl -> TX.eth0
    l2_bridge_output_chnl -> TX.eth0
}
ppf l2_clsfr
{
    input_chnl passive process;

    process(packet_handle p) {
        if (p->type == IPV4_TYPE)
            channel_put(l3_fwdr_chnl, p);
        else
            channel_put(l2_bridge_chnl, p);
    }
}
ppf l2_bridge {
    input_chnl passive process;

    process(packet_handle p) {
        channel_put(l2_bridge_output_chnl, p);
    }
}
ppf l3_fwdr {
    input_chnl passive process;

    process(packet_handle p) {
        channel_put(l3_fwdr_output_chnl, p);
    }
}
```

Fig. 1. A simple example of Baker application

There have been much research recently on programming the Intel IXP network processors [2][10][11][19][21]. Various programming languages have been proposed, and most of the evaluations discussed performance issues[10][11], e.g. NP-Click, a programming model for the Intel IXP1200, shows a IPv4 router written in NP-Click performs within 7% of a hand-coded version of the same application. We use the Baker[21] programming language in our study. Baker is a dataflow language designed specifically for network application development. Applications written in Baker are organized as a dataflow graph starting from a receiver (Rx) and ending at a transmitter (Tx). Actors in the graph are packet processing functions (PPFs), which are wired with communication channels.

Figure 1 shows the dataflow graph and code snippets of a simple IPv4 forwarding application. A PPF contains C-like code that performs actual packet processing tasks. A PPF typically consists of a few

---

[1] We present the essential background information here. Interested readers may refer to [3][21] for more details.

functions and is a logical processing stage in a whole application. Packets enter and exit a PPF through the two respective communication channel endpoints. A channel can be implemented in a efficient way, and it only carries a packet handle instead. PPFs are programmed with the assumption that they could run in parallel with other PPFs or with same copies running as multiple threads.

Baker also imposes several language restrictions to simplify code generation, e.g. recursion within a PPF is not permitted. Baker does not support recursion for two reasons: our survey of network applications indicates recursion is not required; and recursion would complicate and add overhead to runtime stacks on processors with heterogeneous memories.

3   Problem Statement

A network application can be represented as a directed data-flow graph where vertexes are composed of all of the PPFs as Figure 1 shows. An edge of the graph is defined as a channel that a PPF transfers packet data to another PPF. An IXP network processor includes multiple MEs and one XScale core. As stated earlier, each ME has a limited, fixed size of available control store. After processing, the resulting application is a list of tasks represented as T: $t_1 \ldots t_p$. Each task is executed on one or multiple processors of IXP. If we want to map t_i to an ME, the number of instructions in a task t_i must be equal to or less than the size of ME's control store. Hence the mapping results are represented as (t_i, q_i) pairs, where t_i is a list of PPFs in the task and q_i is the set of processors on which t_i is executed. In our programming model, an ME can run only one task and a given task can be executed on one or multiple MEs. It is because much complexity of compiler backend is required to support multiple tasks on one ME, e.g. register allocation should split and allocate the registers of one ME according to different needs of those tasks. We can also extend our approach by considering threads in mapping strategy if multi-tasks are supported in the compiler backend.

We can apply various optimizations and actions to increase throughput. DRAM memory bandwidth is a precious resource on the IXP network processors due to the long latency in DRAM. We found that no more than two wide DRAM accesses (64B width) can be allocated to process each packet if we want to achieve the high throughput on IXP2400. Packets are stored in DRAM and the MEs have no cache, so we need to minimize the number of packet accesses for each processed packet. Unfortunately, we could incur additional DRAM accesses when communicating packets between pipelined tasks. For each task mapped to a processor, it must load packet header data from DRAM at its input channels and if the task modifies the packet header, it must write the changes back to DRAM before sending the packet to its output channels. The increased communication cost hinders the overall system throughput. Thus, we can reduce the communication cost by grouping two tasks into one and then running the new task on one processor.

As another fundamental property of pipelined tasks, if one task in a pipeline runs much more slowly than the others, the throughput of the pipelined tasks is determined by the progress of the slowest task. In this situation, this task can be duplicated to run on more MEs and hence different packets can be processed in parallel by different MEs to improve the throughput. Both grouping and duplication play important roles to achieve high throughput in our algorithm. Therefore, we apply both grouping and duplication to address the automatic task creation and mapping problem.

4   Our Approach: Throughput-Driven Partitioning and Mapping

We have developed a cost model to estimate system throughput and to guide the proposed partitioning and mapping algorithm. PPF acts as the smallest unit of application and the modularity of Baker provides an advantage for partitioning and mapping. As shown in Figure 2, the framework of our approach is composed of two major components: the Throughput Cost Model, and the Partitioning and Mapping Coordinator. The Partitioning and Mapping Coordinator iterates a number of times before settling on a final partition and mapping. The coordinator can choose to group or duplicate tasks. After selecting an action and updating the task list, the throughput cost model is queried to see whether the action benefits the throughput. If it is shown that the action does not benefit throughput, the coordinator will cancel the action, roll back all of the changes, and continue to the next iteration. We collectively call this a **Throughput-driven Partitioning and Mapping (TDPM)** approach.

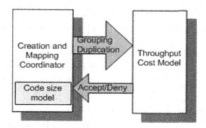

Fig. 2. The framework of our approach

The Partitioning and Mapping Coordinator also includes a code size model to estimate the number of instructions for each task to ensure that the fixed control store limit of the ME will not be exceeded. If the task has more instructions than the control store limit, it will abort when the task is loaded into the ME. The code size model estimates the number of static instructions from the intermediate representation of the application program. When two tasks are grouped together, the size of the newly created task must be recomputed. If the size of the newly created task is larger than the size of the ME's control store, the grouping action will be canceled and the changes will be rolled back.

In the rest of this section, we will illustrate how throughput will be affected by different actions using two examples and then describe our throughput cost model in detail. We then show that obtaining an optimal partitioning and mapping solution is an NP-hard problem. Finally, we will present our polynomial-time algorithm that is both practical and effective for the problem that we are addressing.

4.1   Illustrating Examples

f^{rsp} is the average response time of each task in processing one packet, including both the execution and communication costs[2]. λ is the average input packet rate for a task. Without loss of generality, we illustrate throughput using two examples of four tasks running on four MEs in Figure 3. The length of each bar stands for the relative response time of the corresponding task. The number on a bar identifies the packet, and the same number refers to the same packet. In the linear chain of tasks in Figure 3(a), task-D has the longest response time f_D^{rsp}. Thus, the total system throughput is determined by task-D since it processes fewer packets than other tasks during the same period. The overall throughput can be approximated as the reciprocal of the maximum f^{rsp} ($\frac{1}{\max_{t_i \in T} f_i^{rsp}}$). There are many prior works that use similar models to estimate throughput for linear chains of tasks [13][14].

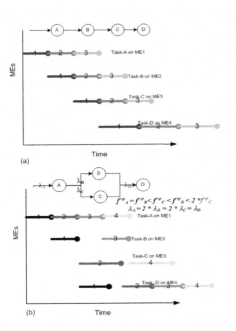

Fig. 3. Execution models for 4 tasks and 4 MEs on (a) linear chain of tasks and (b) non-linear chain of tasks

This framework does not hold for the applications that do not form a linear chain of tasks, like the one shown in Figure 3(b). In this dataflow graph of tasks, after completing task-A, half of packets go to task-B and the other half go to task-C. The input packet rates of different tasks are $\lambda_A = 2 \times \lambda_B = 2 \times \lambda_C = \lambda_D$. Let us assume that the response time of the four tasks has the relation of $f_A^{rsp} = f_B^{rsp} < f_D^{rsp} < f_C^{rsp} < 2 \times f_D^{rsp}$. Since task-C has the largest response time, the simple throughput model for the linear chain case will derive the overall throughput based on task-C. However, in this dataflow graph, the throughput should be determined by task-D, not task-C. This is because both ME2 and ME3 are partially idle during the interval between the arrivals of two successive packets, while ME4 is always busy. The utilization factor $f^{rsp} \times \lambda$ is introduced to

---

[2] We use the term response time to differentiate with the execution cost. However, we notice that it has a different meaning from that of prior works.

depict how busy each processor is [17][18]. When a task has the largest utilization factor, the processor allocated to the task is the busiest. Such a processor dominates the system throughput because packets are waiting in the processor's input queue. Therefore improving the overall throughput depends on minimizing the utilization factor instead of minimizing the response time of each task. This model also covers the cases of linear chain of tasks, because the utilization factor is proportional to response time when the input packet rates of all of the tasks are equal. In summary, we approximate the throughput of the dominant (or the slowest) task in our model as the reciprocal of the maximal utilization factor for all tasks on MEs, i.e. $\frac{1}{\max_{t_i \in T}(f_i^{rsp} \times \lambda_i)}$.

4.2   Throughput Cost Model

Suppose we have n available MEs in a given hardware configuration, with p the number of stages (normally the number of final tasks) in the processing pipeline. We approximate our system throughput ($\mathbf{H}$) with the formula below:

$$H = k \times \lfloor \frac{n}{p} \rfloor \quad \text{if } n \geq p$$

k is the average throughput of the dominant (or the slowest) task in a given partition of the application, and it is $\frac{1}{\max_{t_i \in T}(f_i^{rsp} \times \lambda_i)}$. If n is larger than or equal to p, we can create $\lfloor \frac{n}{p} \rfloor$ copies of the packet processing pipeline so the throughput can be improved by $\lfloor \frac{n}{p} \rfloor$ times. When n is less than p, some tasks will be assigned to the XScale core and it requires a different throughput model. Since the throughput of the XScale core is rather low, we then apply grouping to reduce the number of tasks continually until the condition is met. Thus, this is not the case that this paper is focusing on. From this model, it should be clear that p needs to be minimized and k needs to be maximized at the same time to maximize the overall throughput. However, these two factors often impose conflicting requirements. If we try to reduce p, the PPFs may be grouped into a smaller number of tasks. However, this tends to increase the number of executed instructions and consequently the response time, of the slowest task, which reduces k. On the other hand, if we try to increase k, we can duplicate the slowest task or avoid grouping many PPFs into a given task. In either case, more MEs must be made available to hold all of the tasks, thus increases p. Therefore, a balance must be achieved to get the minimal p and maximal k that can result in the best system throughput.

p can be easily computed by tracking the number of tasks created. k is more complicated to compute. It must account for the effect of multi-threading on each ME, task duplication, and various kinds of costs associated with the response time of the slowest task. Thus, k depends on multiple factors: duplication factor(d), number of threads(γ), input packet rate(λ), and f^{rsp_core} , where f^{rsp_core} is the average response time of the task for each packet without duplication and with single-threaded execution on one processor.

Duplication of the slowest task can reduce λ in k linearly because packets can be processed by multiple MEs independently. Hence, k is proportional to the duplication factor(d) in our model. Multiple hardware threads on a given processing element also affect f^{rsp} in k because multi-threading can hide memory latency, communication cost, synchronization cost, etc. A precise model will depend on the balance between computation and these costs. In our model, we approximate the benefit of multi-threading optimistically by scaling k with the value of γ.

After including the effect of duplication and multiple threads, k is modeled as: $k = \frac{\gamma}{\max_{t_i \in T}(f_i^{rsp\_core} \times \lambda_i \div d_i)}$. The input packet arrival rate λ is computed from the input packet trace of the Profiler phase. The Profiler also provides the frequency of executing each node. The four remaining critical components are computation cost, communication cost, memory access latency and synchronization cost. f^{rsp_core} is modeled as a combination of these four critical components. The computation cost depends on frequency of each computation node and the latency for executing the instructions of the computation node. The memory access latency is computed from the memory access frequency, the size of data accesses, and the latency for accessing a specific memory level. The communication cost is derived from the invocation frequency, the amount of data transferred on each channel, and the communication latency. We calculate the communication cost by modeling the number of DRAM accesses since we need load and store packets from DRAM, although we have a fast runtime implementation of a channel to transfer packet handles between different processors. When we group two tasks into one, we reduce the communication cost between the two tasks since packets can typically be cached in a much faster way within the same processor. For the synchronization cost, we found that it depends both on the acquire, release and critical section costs of each lock and the number of threads involved. When tasks are duplicated, the synchronization cost must be recomputed because the number of threads involved increases.

4.3   Optimal Partitioning and Mapping

Using our throughput cost model, an optimal algorithm compares throughput for all of the grouping and duplication possibilities and derives the partitioning and mapping configuration with the best throughput. A large scale network application can be composed of a large number of PPFs. Without considering grouping, we can get the optimal mapping in $O(nm)$ time for m PPFs on multiple processors, which include n MEs and one XScale core. Each processor is assigned to the slowest task which can be computed in $O(m)$ time by getting the largest utilization factor among m tasks. There are $n + 1$ processors, and if there is not enough MEs, we will assign the remaining tasks to the XScale core, so the optimal mapping without grouping is determined at $O(nm)$ time. Duplication is already considered in this case since one task can be assigned to multiple processors, which means that the task is duplicated multiple times. With grouping, the problem becomes more complicated and resembles a traditional clustering problem[22][23]. Just as a variation of a traditional bin packing problem, our problem attempts to maximize the throughput for each task and also packs maximal PPFs into each task to minimize the number of tasks. Thus, to find optimal partitioning and mapping is also an NP-hard problem because the traditional bin packing problem has been shown as NP-hard[24].

4.4   Heuristic Partitioning and Mapping Algorithm

Because finding an optimal partition and mapping of an application is NP-hard, we propose an iterative heuristic algorithm driven by our throughput cost model. This algorithm for the Partitioning and Mapping Coordinator is described in Figure 4.

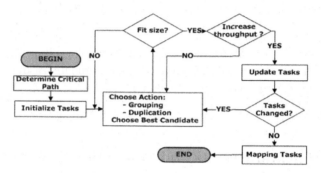

Fig. 4. The Framework of Practical Partitioning and Mapping Algorithm

This heuristic algorithm is primarily aimed at reducing communication cost. It first identifies the critical path of an application from statistics collected by a Profiler phase. Following that, we initialize new tasks with each PPF individually assigned to one task. Grouping and duplication for non-critical tasks is skipped because those tasks will simply be mapped to the XScale core. For all of the critical tasks, we then choose between duplication and grouping by analyzing the utilization factor of each task and the usage of hardware resources in the *Choose Action* step. We favor grouping except when task stages are imbalanced and there are available MEs for duplication. In the *Choose Best Candidate* step, we choose the best candidate according to the selected action. For grouping, the best candidate is chosen according to the benefit, e.g. the reduced communication cost between tasks. We build a candidate list prioritized by the reduced communication cost computed at initialization. The reduced communication cost can be estimated from channels that can be replaced by direct function calls. After partitioning, we are also required to ensure that there is no recursion within each task. Some channels replaced by calls may introduce recursion into the program, so we disallow those replacements in our algorithm. For duplication, the best processing candidate is the task with the largest utilization factor.

After choosing the action and a candidate, the candidate has to pass two additional checks before the action can be committed. The first check considers hardware constraints (e.g. whether the static instruction size of the task fits within the control store of an ME by the code size model). The second check evaluates the performance impact (i.e. whether the throughput increases or not).

If either of two checks fails, we will abort the action and look for another action and candidate. This algorithm iterates until all tasks are examined. The performance check in the algorithm simply uses the results of the throughput cost model. In the *Update Tasks* step, we update the task list and candidate list when the tasks are changed. In the end, we map the final partitioned tasks to the heterogeneous processors by running critical tasks on MEs and non-critical tasks on the XScale core. In this mapping step, tasks are sorted according to their computed utilization factors. We then map tasks to MEs and the XScale core in a descending order.

To partition and map m PPFs to n MEs and one XScale, the heuristic algorithm iterates at most $n + m$ times because the maximum possible groupings is m and the maximum times of duplications is n. We only spend $O(1)$ to choose the best candidate because the candidate list is ordered and the largest utilization factor is always tracked. The complexity of computing the candidate list during initialization is $O(m^2)$ since the candidate list can hold m^2 entries for every possible pair of tasks. We update the candidate list in $O(m)$ time because we change at most m entries. Hence, the total complexity for this algorithm is $O(m(n + m))$.

5   Experimental Results and Evaluations

We have implemented our proposed throughput-driven partitioning and mapping approach in ORC based on our language, Baker. The experiments were conducted on an IXP2400 network processor, which has eight MEs and one XScale core. Two of the MEs are reserved for the packet receiver and transmitter respectively. Thus six MEs are available for each application.

We use three typical packet processing applications for evaluation. They are kernel applications for high-end network processors often used in network routers: **L3-switch, MPLS, Firewall**.

We experiment under different configurations by partitioning and mapping these three applications using different heuristics to evaluate our approach. The baseline configuration is marked as *Base*, which shows the worst-case scenario when all of the tasks are mapped to the XScale core. Other configurations are evaluated by taking additional factors, such as resource constraints, communication cost, and critical paths differentiation, into consideration. Configuration *RES* considers the control store limitation, hardware resources, and other costs except for communication cost. In this configuration, we never group any pair of critical tasks to reduce communication cost, but we can duplicate tasks and map them to MEs. Configuration *COMM* uses a greedy algorithm to reduce communication cost and performs simple resource management, e.g. duplicating all tasks equally. It also handles the control store limitation, but it does not consider other costs. Configuration *TDPM-S* is a simplified version from our throughput-driven partitioning and mapping approach. This version does everything in our approach except for differentiating between non-critical and critical paths. Configuration *TDPM-all* is our full approach. We evaluate the benchmarks using the 3 Gbps packet line rate with the minimum packet size of

64B in Figure 5. The X-axis shows the number of available MEs, and the Y-axis shows the forwarding rate, which is the key performance metric.

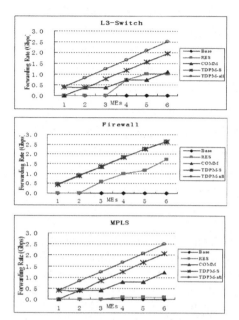

Fig. 5. Performance of three benchmarks under different configurations

In Figure 5, configuration *Base* receives a very low performance when all of the tasks are mapped to the XScale core. Configuration *RES* always performs better than the *Base* configuration. This is because configuration *RES* manages resource better than *Base* and can map the critical tasks to MEs. This shows the importance of resource management. For the *COMM* configuration, the curves for MPLS and L3-Switch are close to that of the *Base* configuration on a small number of MEs because critical tasks are mapped to the XScale core when the number of available MEs is smaller than what is needed. For MPLS, *COMM* typically has much better performance than *RES* because it reduces much of the communication cost that hinders the overall throughput. Certain compiler optimizations (e.g. packet caching and instruction scheduling) become more effective when the scope of a task increases (i.e.

includes more instructions). However, the greedy method of *COMM* consistently achieves worse performance than our proposed approach *TDPM-all* for MPLS and L3-Switch. There are several reasons for the poorer performance. One reason is that configuration *COMM* considers only communication cost and does not obtain good load balancing, which causes inefficient resource usage. As such, it duplicates the faster tasks instead of slower tasks. Another reason is that *COMM* may combine non-critical code together with critical tasks, which could have adverse effects on certain traditional optimizations, e.g. increasing the register pressure and leading to more spill code. The Firewall benchmark is an exception. On this application, *COMM* shows little difference on performance compared to configuration *TDPM-S* and *TDPM-all* because all of the tasks of Firewall are critical.

Configuration *TDPM-all* performs better than configuration *TDPM-S* for MPLS and L3-Switch on larger numbers of MEs. This result shows the importance of managing hardware resource effectively by differentiating between non-critical and critical tasks and making more MEs available for critical tasks. For these three benchmarks, configuration *TDPM-all* achieves the same optimal partitioning and mapping as the optimal solution. In general, configuration *TDPM-all* provides the best performance and scalability for all three applications. It demonstrates that our throughput cost model is effective in modeling key factors in throughput and that our partitioning and mapping algorithm produces efficient application tasks for the IXP network processors.

Table 1. Memory accesses for benchmarks

		Packet			Application		
		SCRATCH	SRAM	DRAM	SCRATCH	SRAM	Total
L3-Switch							
	TDPM-all	2	3	2	1	15	23
	TDPM-S	2	3	2	1	38	46
	COMM	2	3	2	5	299	311
	RES	8	3	6	1	19	37
Firewall							
	TDPM-all	2	10	1	3	17	33
	TDPM-S	2	10	1	3	17	33
	COMM	2	10	1	3	17	33
	RES	5	10	2	9	18	44
MPLS							
	TDPM-all	2	12	2	2	11	29
	TDPM-S	2	12	2	2	11	29
	COMM	3	12	2	2	11	30
	RES	4	12	8	2	13	39

To further understand where the performance benefit comes from, we measure the number of memory accesses for each packet in an application under major configurations in Table 1. We exclude configuration *Base* because the XScale core is not designed for fast packet processing, and hence memory accesses on the XScale core have much worse performance compared to MEs. From the results in Table 1, we can see that *COMM* can effectively reduce the number of DRAM accesses compared to *RES*, where most of the communication cost is attributed to the DRAM accesses mainly used to communicate packet information between tasks. *TDPM-S* and *TDPM-all* both reduce the number of SRAM accesses in application data, and the reduction is particularly effective on L3-Switch. However, in contrast to DRAM accesses, the reduction in SRAM accesses results in only a slight performance improvement.

We found that typically the best performing partition for our applications groups all of the critical code of an application into one task and leave as many MEs available for duplication as possible. The reason is that even with balanced pipelined tasks, the communication cost used to communicate among multiple tasks often has a large overhead from DRAM accesses, which degrades the overall throughput[3]. In Table 2, we show that we achieve the 100% forwarding rate for OC-48 with the minimum packet size of 64B on IXP2400 for all three benchmarks with our approach. OC-48 is the targeted best performance for all applications including hand-tuned code on IXP2400. We show the forwarding rates on different numbers of MEs used till the forwarding rate reaches 100%(only use four MEs among six available MEs). The performance is achieved by including not only the partitioning and mapping techniques presented here but also all other optimizations [1]. The good scalability (i.e. approximately a linear speedup) of

---

[3] It is a future work to investigate ways of using a less expensive communication mechanism than DRAM accesses, e.g. caching packet data in Next-Neighbor registers for an adjacent ME.

Table 2. Overall performances of benchmarks

MEs	L3-Switch	Firewall	MPLS
1	31.48%	30.79%	29.42%
2	62.66%	61.46%	58.82%
3	93.47%	91.87%	88.19%
4	100%	100%	100%

all applications shows that even in the presence of aggressive optimizations, our cost model and algorithm can effectively deliver high performance.

6 Related Work

There is a significant body of prior work in partitioning and mapping for high throughput [13][14][15][16][19][20][22]. Choudhary et al. [15] addressed the problem of optimal processor assignment, assuming that no communication cost or communication cost can be folded into computation cost. Our experiments show that an effective model of communication cost is an important factor in an actual throughput model. Subhlok and Vondran [13][14] introduced methods to perform optimal mapping of multiple tasks onto multiple processors while taking communication cost into consideration. However, these works focus only on how to partition simple applications composed of linear chains of tasks onto multi-processors. The SMP platforms studied in these work have dramatic differences from IXP network processor. For example, in IXP network processors, there is no cache for the four levels of memory hierarchies.

The IXP-C compiler [16][19] and the Pac-Lang project [20] have also been exploring solutions of partitioning applications for network processors. In contrast to the parallel program that we use in our system, the IXP-C compiler assumes that users develop large sequential programs. Thus, the IXP-C compiler is responsible for splitting sequential programs into small tasks and then duplicating them to maximize throughput. The compiler enumerates different partitions to find a solution that can achieve the performance goal specified by users, but does not attempt to get the best overall throughput. We demonstrate a different approach to achieve high throughput on network processors. The Pac-Lang project currently expects the user to specify in a script file how the compiler should split, group, and duplicate an application. The primary advantage of this approach is that the program logic is clearly separated from how it is compiled for a specific architecture. However, this approach is not fully automatic. Significant knowledge of the processor architecture is required to write and tune a script file.

7 Conclusions

This paper has presented a throughput cost model, which can effectively model those key factors affecting throughput, and a polynomial-time algorithm guided by the cost model to partition and map applications onto the Intel IXP network processors. The key idea in maximizing the overall throughput is to minimize the number of task stages in the application processing pipeline and maximize the average throughput of the slowest task at the same time. Our algorithm uses effective heuristics for grouping, duplication, and mapping to achieve superior performance while handling hardware constraints and managing hardware resources.

Compared to other simpler heuristics, the experimental results show that our approach is effective in achieving the best throughput. For all three applications, we were able to achieve the 100% packet forwarding rate for OC-48, which is the targeted performance for all applications including hand-tuned code on IXP2400. We also observe that reducing communication cost and conducting effective resource management are both important in achieving high throughput on the IXP network processors.

We conjecture that many of the partitioning and mapping techniques developed in this work are applicable to additional and more complex applications (such as streaming and multimedia applications) on other multi-core, multi-threaded processor architectures.

Acknowledgments

We would like to thank all people who were involved in the project, especially Jason H. Lin, Raghunath Arun, Vinod Balakrishnan, Stephen Goglin, Erik Johnson, Aaron Kunze, and Jamie Jason at Intel Corporation, and the collaborators in the Institute of Computing Technology (ICT), CAS and University of Texas at Austin. We also appreciate the reviewers for their helpful feedback.

References

1. Michael K. Chen, Xiao-Feng Li, Ruiqi Lian, Jason H. Lin, Lixia Liu, Tao Liu and Roy Ju. Shangri-la: Achieving high performance from compiled network applications while enabling ease of programming. In *Proceedings of the ACM SIGPLAN 2005 Conference on Programming Language Design and Implementation (PLDI'05)*, Chicago, IL, June 2005
2. Lal George and Matthias Blume. Taming the IXP Network Processor. In*Proceedings of the ACM SIGPLAN 2003 Conference on Programming Language Design and Implementation (PLDI'03)*, San Diego, CA, June 2003.
3. Intel Corporation. Intel IXP2400 Network Processors. *http://www. intel.com/design/network/products/npfamily/*.
4. Erik J. Johnson and Aaron Kunze. IXP2400/2800 Programming: The Complete Microengine Coding Guide. *Intel Press*, Hillsboro, OR, April 2003.
5. Roy Ju, Sun Chan, Chengyong Wu. Ruiqi Lian and Tony Tuo. Open Research Compiler for Itanium Processor Family. In *Proceedings of 34th Annual International Symposium on Microarchitecture (MICRO-34)*, Austin, TX, December 2001.
6. Roy Ju, Pen-Chung Yew, Ruiqi Lian, Lixia Liu, Tin-fook Ngai, Robert Cohn and Costin Iancu. Open Research Compiler (ORC): Proliferation of Technologies and Tools. In *Proceedings of 36th Annual International Symposium on Microarchitecture (MICRO-36)*, San Diego, CA, December 2003

7. Network Processing Forum. IP Forwarding Application Level Benchmark. *http://www.npforum.org/techinfo/ipforwarding_bm.pdf*.
8. Network Processing Forum. MPLS Forwarding Application Level Benchmark and Annex. *http://www.npforum.org/techinfo/MPLSBench mark.pdf*.
9. E. Rosen, A. Viswanathan and R. Callon. RFC 3031 - Multiprotocol Label Switching Architecture. *IETF*, January 2001.
10. Niraj Shah, William Plishker and Kurt Keutzer. NP-Click: A Programming Model for the Intel IXP1200. In *2nd Workshop on Network Processors (NP-2)*, Anaheim, CA, February 2003.
11. Niraj Shah, William Plishker and Kurt Keutzer. Comparing Network Processor Programming Environments: A Case Study. In *2004 Workshop on Productivity and Performance in High-End Computing (P-PHEC)*, HPCA-10, Madrid, Spain, February 2004.
12. Tammo Spalink, Scott Karlin, Larry Peterson and Yitzchak Gottlieb. Building a Robust Software-Based Router Using Network Processors. In *Proceedings of the 18th ACM symposium on Operation Systems Principles (SOSP'01)*, Banff, Canada, October 2001.
13. Jaspal Subholk and Gary Vondran. Optimal Latency-Throughput Tradeoffs for Data Parallel Pipelines. In *Proceedings of the 8th ACM symposium on Parallel Algorithms and Architectures (SPAA'96)*, Padua, Italy, 1996
14. Jaspal Subholk and Gary Vondran. Optimal Mapping of Sequences of Data Parallel Tasks. In *Proceedings of the 5th ACM SIGPLAN symposium on Principles and Practice of Parallel Programming (PPOPP'95)*, Santa Clara, USA, 1995
15. A.N. Choudhary, B. Narahari, D.M. Nicol, and R. Simha. Optimal Processor Assignment for a Class of Pipelined Computations. In *IEEE Transactions on Parallel and Distributed Systems*, April 1994
16. Long Li, Bo Huang, Jinquan Dai and Luddy Harrison. Automatic Multithreading and Multiprocessing of C Programs for IXP. In *Proceedings of the 10th ACM SIGPLAN symposium on Principles and Practice of Parallel Programming (PPOPP'05)*, June 2005
17. R.B. Copper. Introduction to Queueing Theory. Second Edition, New York: North Holland, 1981
18. Leonard Kleinrock, Queueing Systems Vol.1: Theory, *Wiley*, 1975
19. Jinquan Dai, Bo Huang, Long Li and Luddy Harrison. Automatically Partitioning Packet Processing Applications for Pipelined Architectures. In*Proceedings of the ACM SIGPLAN 2005 Conference on Programming Language Design and Implementation (PLDI'05)*, Chicago, IL, June 2005.
20. Robert Ennals, Richard Sharp and Alan Mycroft. Task Partitioning for Multi-Core Network Processors. In *Proceedings of International Conference on Compiler Construction (CC)*, 2005
21. Michael Chen, E.J. Johnson and Roy Ju. Tutorial: Compilation system for throughput-driven multi-core processors In *Proceedings of 37th Annual International Symposium on Microarchitecture (MICRO'37)*,Portland, OR, December 2004.
22. V. Sarkar. Partitioning and scheduling parallel programs for execution on multiprocessors. *MIT Press*, October 1989.
23. Apostolos Gerasoulis, Tao Yang. A Comparison of Clustering Heuristics for Scheduling DAGs on Multiprocessors. *J. Parallel Distrib. Comput.* 1992
24. Michael R. Garey and David S. Johnson. Computers and Intractability: A Guide to the Theory of NP-Completeness, *W.H. Freeman.* 1979

VI Optimizations and Architectural Tradeoffs for Embedded Systems

MiDataSets: Creating the Conditions for a More Realistic Evaluation of Iterative Optimization

Grigori Fursin[1], John Cavazos[2], Michael O'Boyle[2], and Olivier Temam[1]

[1] ALCHEMY Group, INRIA Futurs and LRI, Paris-Sud University, France
{grigori.fursin,olivier.temam}@inria.fr
[2] Institute for Computing Systems Architecture, University of Edinburgh, UK
{jcavazos,mob}@inf.ed.ac.uk

Abstract. Iterative optimization has become a popular technique to obtain improvements over the default settings in a compiler for performance-critical applications, such as embedded applications. An implicit assumption, however, is that the best configuration found for any arbitrary data set will work well with other data sets that a program uses.

In this article, we evaluate that assumption based on 20 data sets per benchmark of the MiBench suite. We find that, though a majority of programs exhibit stable performance across data sets, the variability can significantly increase with many optimizations. However, for the best optimization configurations, we find that this variability is in fact small. Furthermore, we show that it is possible to find a compromise optimization configuration across data sets which is often within 5% of the best possible configuration for most data sets, and that the iterative process can converge in less than 20 iterations (for a population of 200 optimization configurations). All these conclusions have significant and positive implications for the practical utilization of iterative optimization.

1   Introduction

Iterative optimization is an increasingly popular alternative to purely static compiler optimization [17,12,8,24,7,10,18,3,20,23]. This is due to the growing complexity of processor architectures and applications, its ability to adapt to new platforms and the fact it is a simple and systematic optimization process. However, with this approach comes new issues, e.g., the necessity to quickly explore a large optimization space [7,10,18,3,11], and the sensitivity to data sets.

Iterative optimization is based on the notion that the compiler will discover the best way to optimize a program through many evaluations of different optimization configurations. However, in reality, a user rarely executes the same data set twice. Therefore, iterative optimization is based on the implicit assumption that the best optimization configuration found will work *well* for *all data sets* of a program. To the best of our knowledge, this assumption has never been thoroughly investigated.

Most studies on iterative optimization repeatedly execute the same program/data set pair [7,12,10,18,3]. Therefore, they demonstrate the *potential* of iterative optimization, but not how it would behave in real conditions. Other studies [15] have used

K. De Bosschere et al. (Eds.): HiPEAC 2007, LNCS 4367, pp. 245–260, 2007.
© Springer-Verlag Berlin Heidelberg 2007

Table 1. Key questions about the impact of data sets on iterative program optimization

Questions
1. Do programs exhibit significant performance variations across data sets ?
2. More broadly, do data sets react similarly to most optimizations ?
3. Does it matter which data set you train on for iterative optimization ?
4. Can iterative optimization perform well when training is done over multiple data sets ?
5. How fast can iterative optimization converge across multiple data sets ?
6. In practice, is it possible to compare the effect of two optimizations on two data sets ?

the `test`/`train`/`ref` data sets provided by the SPEC benchmark suite. A few studies have gone further and collected several data sets for a small number of benchmarks [5,4], but these studies have only focussed on the effect of different data sets to one optimization.

In order to investigate whether a compiler can effectively discover optimizations that work well across data sets, we need to: (1) have a benchmark suite where each program comes with a significant number of data sets, (2) get a better statistical understanding of the impact of data sets on program performance and program optimization, and (3) evaluate iterative optimization under more "realistic" conditions where data sets change across executions.

We have assembled a collection of data sets, 20 per benchmark, for 26 benchmarks (560 data sets in total) of the free, commercially representative MiBench [14] benchmark suite, which especially (but not only) target embedded-like applications; we call this data set suite MiDataSets. Using this data set suite, we provide quantitative answers to 6 key questions listed in Table 1 about the impact of data sets on program performance and program optimization. Finally, we make a first attempt at emulating iterative compilation across different data sets, as it would happen in reality.

We find that, though a majority of programs exhibit stable performance across data sets, the variability can significantly increase with many optimizations. However, for the best optimization configurations, we find that this variability is in fact small. Furthermore, we show that it is possible to find a compromise configuration across data sets which is often within 5% of the best possible optimization configuration for most data sets, and that the iterative process can converge in less than 20 iterations (for a population of 200 optimization configurations).

Section 2 briefly explains how we evaluated the different data sets and varied program optimizations. Section 3 provides qualitative and quantitative answers to the questions listed in Table 1. Section 4 describe an attempt to emulate continuous optimization in a realistic setting, that is, across several data sets. Sections 5 and 6 describe related work and provide some initial conclusions.

2 Methodology

Platform, compiler and benchmarks. All our experiments are performed on a cluster with 16 AMD Athlon 64 3700+ processors running at 2.4GHz, each with 64KB of L1 cache, 1MB of L2 cache, and 3GB of memory. Each machine is running Mandriva

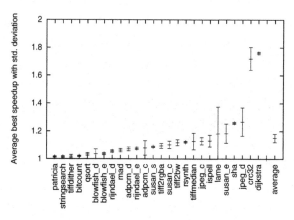

Fig. 1. Average best speedup and std. deviation across all data sets (baseline -Ofast optimization)

Linux 2006. To collect IPC, we use the PAPI 3.2.1 hardware counter library [1] and PAPIEx 0.99rc2 tool. We use the commercial PathScale EKOPath Compiler 2.3.1 [2] with the highest level of optimization, -Ofast, as the *baseline* optimization level. This compiler is specifically tuned to AMD processors, and on average performs the same or better than the Intel 9.0 compilers on the same platform. To perform iterative optimization on each program and data set, we use a tool called PathOpt that comes with the EKOPath compiler suite. This tool can run a program with a variety of global compiler flags to find a set of flags that obtains the best performance on the targeted platform. We use 121 compiler flags that are known to influence performance and we use PathOpt to iteratively select random configurations of flags. [1] We ran the same randomly generated 200 configurations for each of the MiBench benchmarks and data sets. The PathOpt tool uses CPU execution time to compare the effects of different transformations. Figure 1 shows the average speedups achieved for each benchmark and the standard deviation across all data sets (the benchmarks are sorted by decreasing speedup).

Data sets. Most of the data sets for MiBench benchmarks are based on standard file types, e.g., text, audio, image, etc. It is difficult to select a truly representative sample from the population of all possible data inputs. Instead we collected 18 different data sets per benchmark from a variety of sources including the internet, trying to vary size and nature as well as the data set properties as much as possible. For example, we collected images with various sizes, color depth, scenery, etc; texts and audio with various length and styles. Some benchmarks share the same data sets, and interestingly, the output of several benchmarks could be directly used as inputs to others. We largely decided against synthesizing data sets which would artificially exercise programs except for a few programs such as bitcount or quicksort which can readily accomodate synthetic data sets. Finally, we reused 2 data sets *small* and *large* from the original benchmarks, thus reaching 20 data sets per benchmark in total. Running all data sets usually did not require any modification of the benchmarks (except for stringsearch where

---

[1] For more information about EKOPath compiler flags and PathOpt tool refer to the EKOPath compiler manual [2].

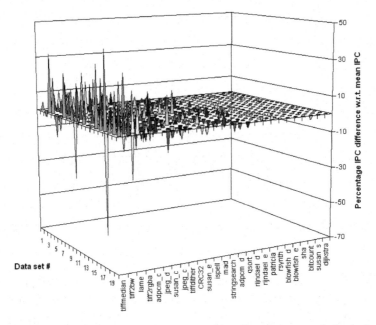

Fig. 2. Program IPC variation across data sets (baseline -Ofast optimization)

the data set is in fact embedded in the source code). It is our intention to make these data sets publically available for other researchers to use.

3 Impact of Data Sets on Program Performance and Optimization

In this section, we try to understand how varying data sets can affect program performance and iterative optimization by answering the key questions in Table 1. Beyond providing qualitative and quantitative answers to these questions, we observe a number of properties which are directly relevant to the practical implementation of iterative optimization.

3.1 Do Programs Exhibit Significant Performance Variations Across Data Sets ?

The purpose of this question is to understand whether program behavior is *stable* across data sets. One way of examining this is to observe the IPC of a program across different datasets. If the IPC varies considerably, it is likely that different parts of the program are exercised depending on data input. In such a case an optimization found by iterative compilation for a particular dataset may be inappropriate for another. It is important to note that higher IPC does *not* mean faster code. We are merely using IPC as a means of comparing the same program across different data sets,

We ran all data sets on the programs compiled with the -Ofast default optimization flag (our *baseline* performance). In Figure 2, we plot the percentage of IPC variation with respect to the average IPC over all data sets; the average is computed per

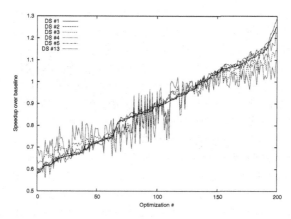

Fig. 3. Data sets reactions to optimizations (susan_e)

benchmark; the benchmarks are sorted by decreasing standard deviation of IPC across all their data sets.

Figure 2 shows that MiBench benchmarks vary in their level of stability. There are very stable benchmarks across data sets such as susan_s, partly stable ones such as adpcm_c and highly varying ones such as tiff2rgba. susan_s is an application that smoothes images and has a regular algorithm with little control flow dependencies. In this case, changing data set size or values does not influence the application's IPC. In contrast, adpcm_c, which is a convertor of Pulse Code Modulation (PCM) samples, and tiff2rgba, which is a convertor of TIFF images to RGBA color space, have most of their execution time spent in encoding/decoding subroutines. These procedures have many data and control flow dependencies and hence their behavior and IPC can vary considerably among different data sets. Still, only 6 out of 26 benchmarks can be considered unstable. The fact that the IPC of most benchmarks is fairly stable across data sets is good news for iterative optimization, as it potentially makes performance improvement across data sets possible in practice.

Yet, these experiments do not prove this trend will be consistent across all applications, or even across all data sets for a given application. For instance, crc32 is a simple application which performs a cyclic redundancy check. The core of the program is a loop which references a large pre-defined array with a complex access function (subscript). For some function and cache size parameters, this reference could potentially result in significant conflict misses, even though crc32 is only moderately unstable across all our data sets.

Even though there are few unstable programs, the performance variations, when they occur, are far from negligible. In 59 out of 560 experiments, a data set's IPC was more than ±10% away from the average, with a maximum of -64%.

3.2   Do Data Sets React Similarly to Optimizations ?

We now want to understand whether programs running different data sets react differently to program optimizations. This issue is even more closely related to iterative optimization.

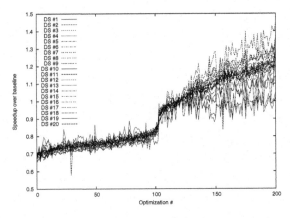

Fig. 4. Data sets reactions to optimizations (jpeg_d)

Experiments show that the conclusions of Section 3.1 can in fact be misleading. Programs can have fairly consistent behavior across data sets for a given optimization configuration, e.g., the baseline -Ofast as in Section 3.1, but can react quite differently when optimized in a different manner. Consider benchmark susan_e in Figure 3; for clarity, we only plotted 6 data sets, but they are representative of the different trends over the 20 data sets. The x-axis corresponds to the optimization configuration id. As explained in Section 2, an optimization configuration is a combination of optimization flags and parameters; recall we evaluated 200 configurations. The y-axis is the speedup over the baseline configuration. The configurations are sorted according to the speedup for data set #1; therefore, any non-monotonic behavior in one of the other data set curves means this data set reacts differently to one or several optimizations. In the rightmost 50 optimizations, the behavior of the benchmark across data sets varies wildly, with almost 30% difference for some optimizations. Similar variations are visible across the whole optimization spectrum. The behavior of susan_e as compared to the baseline results of Section 3.1 provides a striking contrast. When the program is compiled with -Ofast, its performance varies only moderately across all data sets. On the other hand, Figure 3 shows that for other optimizations this conclusion does not hold. Consequently, the results of Section 3.1 are misleading as they suggest iterative optimization can be easily applied because performance is stable. The stability properties across data sets can significantly vary with the program optimizations. As a result, iterative optimization across data sets may prove a more complicated task.

Moreover, other programs can naturally exhibit strong variations for many optimizations. Consider, for instance, jpeg_d in Figure 4; all 20 data sets are plotted. For some optimizations, the speedup difference across data sets can exceed 50%. Unfortunately, even though the rightmost 50 optimizations are consistently among the top performers across all data sets and benchmarks, the higher their potential speedup, the higher their variability as well.

Still, for some programs, the speedup variations across all optimizations can be strong, but very consistent across data sets, and thus confirm the stability observed in Section 3.1. Consider dijkstra in Figure 5; all 20 data sets have been plotted.

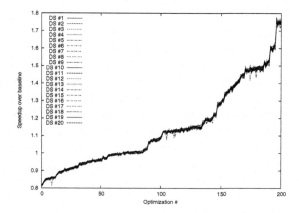

Fig. 5. Data sets reactions to optimizations (`dijkstra`)

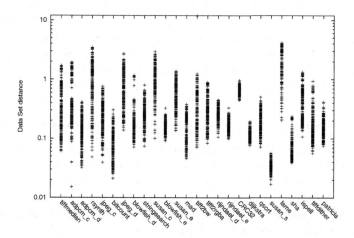

Fig. 6. Data set distances

Performance is obviously very stable across all data sets and optimizations, even though the speedups are far from negligible.

Overall, these three programs are fairly representative of the different possible behavior of the remaining benchmarks, and we roughly found the same number of benchmarks belong to each of the three aforementioned categories. Consequently, a significant number of benchmarks are not so stable across data sets when factoring in the optimizations, thereby complicating the iterative optimization task.

In order to summarize the stability of programs across data sets, we introduce a *data set distance* metric. We define the distance d between two data sets i, j as: $d = \sqrt{\sum_{1 \le opt \le 200}(s^i_{opt} - s^j_{opt})^2}$, where opt denotes an optimization configuration. This distance characterizes how differently two data sets react to optimizations. The repartition of distances of all possible pairs of data sets for a program is itself an indication of

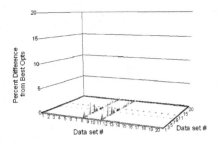

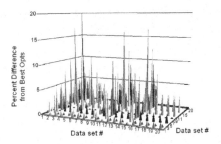

Fig. 7. Best optimizations across data sets (sha)

Fig. 8. Best optimizations across data sets (susan_c)

the program stability across data sets. On purpose, the metric is based on the *absolute* speedup difference rather than the relative speedup, in order to compare distances across programs. We compute the distances between all pairs of data sets for each program, and report them in Figure 6. Programs like dijkstra, which are very stable across data sets have small distances, no more than 0.1 to 0.5, while unstable programs like jpged_d have significant distances, more than 1; the maximum reported distance is greater than 10 (see tiff2bw). At least 8 programs have rather large data set distances, characteristic of their unstable behavior across optimizations.

3.3 Does It Matter Which Data Set You Train on for Iterative Optimization ?

Because iterative optimization techniques almost systematically experiment with single data sets, they both *train* and *test* on the same data set. With more data sets, it is possible to move closer to a more realistic implementation of iterative optimization where train and test sets are distinct.

In order to evaluate the impact of this more realistic situation, as well as the choice of the training data set, we implement a simple iterative optimization strategy where we train on a single data set and test on the 19 remaining data sets. For the training, we exhaustively search the 200 optimizations on the single data set. We then select the best configuration C for this data set, and run the remaining 19 data sets on the program optimized with C. We then measure the difference between the performance obtained with C and with the actual best possible optimization for each data set as shown in Figures 7 and 8, where the x-axis corresponds to the training data set, the z-axis corresponds to the testing data set.

While Section 3.2 shows that a significant fraction of the programs can react fairly differently across data sets for many optimizations, it turns out that, for the best optimization, programs have little or no variability with respect to data sets. Most programs show similar trends to Figure 7. Out of all the 26 benchmarks that we studied, 20 benchmarks show little variance when using the best optimization configuration of the different data sets, therefore any data set could be used for iterative optimization. The best optimization for that program will work well regardless of the data set used. This has positive implications for the practical application of iterative optimization. However, it should also be remebered that the sample number of configurations considered (200)

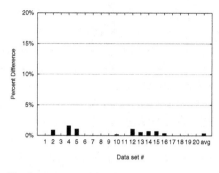

Fig. 9. Average best opt relative to best opt(dijkstra)

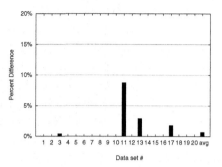

Fig. 10. Average best opt relative to best opt(tiff2rgba)

is small compared to the entire optimization space. It may be the case that for other non-sampled configurations, that variation is much greater.

However there is a small group of programs that show medium to high variability with regards to the best optimization among data sets. For this group of programs, a user cannot simply use any single data set for iterative optimization if they wish to obtain the best performance for the rest of that program's data sets. Using the best optimization configuration of iterative optimization for any particular data set can significantly degrade performance when used on other data sets of the same program over the compiler's baseline configuration. Fortunately, this occurs in only 6 of the 26 MiBench benchmarks we evaluated.

It is worth noting that programs that are related (i.e., encoders/decoders of the same audio/graphics formats or encryption/decryption algorithms for the same protocol) do not necessarily have similar sensitivity to data sets. For example, the encoding version of rijndael, has little variability with respect to the best performing optimization configuration across data sets. In contrast, its decoding version, has large variability in the performance of the best configuration across data sets.

3.4 Can Iterative Optimization Perform Well When Training Is Done over Multiple Data Sets ?

We now see if iterative optimization can perform well if we train over multiple data sets. It will also show whether it is possible to find an optimization configuration that is better on average over all the data sets of a program than the highest level of optimization available in the compiler.

For that purpose, we implement again a simple iterative optimization strategy which finds the "best average" optimization configuration across all data sets. For each data set, we compute the speedup achieved with each optimization, and determine which optimization performs best across all data sets on average. This strategy roughly emulates an iterative optimization process running for a long time, and finding the best optimization configuration compromise. We then compare this "best average" configuration against the actual best configuration for each data set.

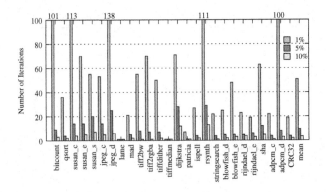

Fig. 11. Number of Iterations to get within 1%, 5%, and 10% for all benchmarks

Figures 9 and 10 depict the results of our analysis for two programs. Each graph shows the percent difference of the best optimization configuration found for each data set relative to the best average configuration across all data sets. Interestingly, the best average configuration across all data sets performs extremely well, typically within less than 5% of the best optimization configuration for each data set. This again has very positive implications for practitioners. We show in Section 3.3 that, for certain programs, it is important to not use one data set when performing iterative optimization. In that section, we showed that the best optimization configuration for any one data set can lead to potential degradation in performance when used with other data sets. Here we show that a possible answer is to collect various data sets for programs with high sensitivity to data sets and choose an optimization configuration that performs well on average over these data sets.

3.5   How Fast Can Iterative Optimization Converge Across Multiple Data Sets ?

In this section we evaluate the difficulty of quickly finding good optimization configurations using iterative optimization across multiple data sets, and more precisely of getting close to the "best average" optimization mentioned in Section 3.4. For that purpose, we iteratively pick random optimization configurations and apply them to all data sets until the performance of the configuration is within a certain target percentage threshold of the best average configuration found previously.

Figure 11 shows the average number of iterations needed to find optimizations that are within 1%, 5%, and 10% of the best optimizations we found from a large exploration of the space. The figure shows that with a relatively small number of evaluations (usually around 5 evaluations) we obtain an optimization configuration that is within 10% of the best configuration found. Interestingly, if we want to be within 5% of the best optimization configuration we found, for most programs, it requires on average less than 10 evaluations. For only one program, dijkstra, is it a bit harder to obtain a configuration within 5% of the best configuration we found. This program requires on average evaluating around 30 configurations. Still, overall, relatively very few evaluations of

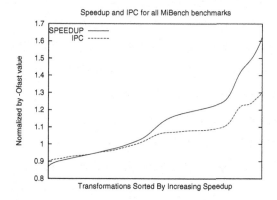

Fig. 12. Speedup and IPC for all MiBench benchmarks (normalized by -Ofast value)

optimization configurations are required to get much of the benefit of expensive iterative optimization. As one would expect on average it takes a much longer number of iterations to get within 1%.

3.6 In Practice, Is It Possible to Compare the Effect of Two Optimizations on Two Data Sets ?

Up to now, we have assumed that we can compare the impact of two optimizations and/or two data sets. However, in practice, we cannot compute the speedup due to an optimization because we would need two executions of the same data set: one to compute the execution time of the baseline optimization, and another run to compute the execution time of the optimization itself. As stated earlier, a user is unlikely to run the same program on the same data set twice. Instead we would like to consider IPC as a means of comparing the performance of two different optimization configurations on different runs and data sets. IPC is an absolute performance metric and thus potentially does not require a base line run to measure improvement in contrast to speedup. However, some optimizations, such as loop unrolling, can effect dynamic instruction count which, in turn, affects the IPC.

Our experiments show that for most of the MiBench benchmarks (except two) the best found option corresponds to the best found IPC. Figure 12 shows the average speedup and IPC for all benchmarks and data sets for the MiBench benchmark relative to using PathScale's -Ofast configuration. This result is good news for iterative optimization as it means that we can use IPC to evaluate the effect of two optimization configurations regardless of the data sets used.

However, we note that the observations in this section may not hold for some architectures and with other compiler optimizations not evaluated in this study. In future work, we plan to enhance the technique of comparing the effect of optimizations using additional metrics to IPC and without the knowledge of the baseline execution time and the data set.

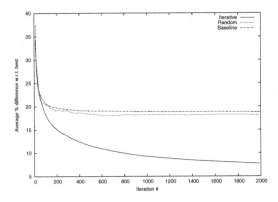

Fig. 13. Results of continuous optimization experiment

4   Emulating Continuous Optimization

If iterative compilation becomes mainstream, compilers will continuously optimize programs across executions with different data sets. After each execution, a program's performance results will be analyzed and a new optimization configuration to evaluate will be selected and the code will be optimized for the next execution. Some recent publications [19,16] describe run-time continuous optimization frameworks but do not evaluate the influence of various datasets on optimizations and performance.

We leverage the observations of previous sections and attempt to emulate continuous optimization under as real conditions as possible. In other words, we assume it is not possible to know the speedup brought by a given optimization over baseline for a data set, only IPC is available to understand the effect of an optimization, data sets are executed in any order, and for each data set a different optimization is applied.

In addition, we use a simple strategy for selecting optimization configurations continuously. Each time an optimization configuration is tried on a data set, the IPC is recorded, the average observed IPC for that configuration is updated, and the configurations ranking is then updated accordingly. Upon each iteration, configurations are randomly picked among the top N_{top} configurations (or we progressively bias the choice towards the current best known if not all optimizations have yet been tried; we use $N_{top} = 10$). In order to periodically revisit this ranking and adapt to new data sets, only 95% of the configurations are in fact picked among the N_{top} top, the remaining 5% are picked among all 200 configurations; the iterations where this occurs are themselves randomly picked according to the 95/5 uniform distribution.

Because continuous optimization is bound to occur over many iterations, our number of data sets is still too limited, so they have to be executed multiple times, but Section 3.2 suggests that there are not as many behavior as the number of data sets. Therefore, iterating over a collection of data sets is a much more reasonable approximation than iterating over a single data set.

Figure 13 shows the average difference with respect to the best possible configuration over the different iterations; this difference is itself averaged over all benchmarks, so the point at iteration i corresponds to the average difference over all benchmarks at that iteration. In addition to `iterative` compilation, the performance of a `random` strategy (configurations randomly picked according to a uniform distribution) and the `baseline` optimization are provided. The clear convergence of the iterative compilation process towards the best possible configuration shows that it is possible to learn the best optimizations, across data sets, and without any artificial means for evaluating the effect of optimizations.

In this section, no attempt was made to speed up the convergence, hence, our future work will take advantage of the existing literature on optimization search techniques [10,11].

5   Related Work

Berube *et al.* construct a system called *Aestimo* which allows experimentation of feedback-directed optimization using different inputs [5]. The authors collect a large set of additional inputs for 7 SPEC benchmarks and study the variability of different inputs on inlining. They use the Open Research Compiler (ORC) and use profile-directed input to control inlining. However, even though several data sets were collected for 7 benchmarks results and analysis in the paper are only presented for bzip2. The results show that the choice of inputs from which to generate profile information and control optimizations can have significant performance variability when used with different inputs. In contrast, we find that input variability largely depends on the benchmarks and/or the optimizations used, but for the most part most programs exhibit highly stable performance across data sets.

Bartolini *et al.* develop a software-based approach, called CAT, that repositions code chunks to improve cache performance [4]. The approach is profile-driven, that is, given an instrumented run of the program, a profile is collected which contains precise detection of possible interference between code chunks. The profile is then used to place code into memory in a way that reduces i-cache miss rates. Since the layout of the code is a function of the program input used during profiling, the authors evaluate different inputs and execution conditions to see the effect on input sensitivity. The authors evaluate different inputs on four multimedia application (jpeg encoder/decoder and mpeg encoder/decoder) and find that even though there is variability between inputs, their code placement technique is robust to this variability. These two papers are steps in the right direction to evaluating input sensitivity among programs, but they only present results for one optimization applied to a limited set of benchmarks and therefore general conclusions about data sets, applications, or optimizations cannot be drawn. In contrast, we look at the effects of many different optimizations applied to an entire benchmark suite using a larger number of data sets.

Haneda *et al.* attempt to investigate the sensitivity of data inputs to iterative optimization [15]. They perform iterative optimization using the `train` inputs on seven SPEC benchmarks. They perform iterative optimization using GCC 3.3.1 and control 42 of its options to find the best configuration for these benchmarks. They use a technique called Orthogonal Arrays to perform iterative optimization since it allows them to quickly find optimization flags that work well for a particular program. They obtain the best optimization flags using the train inputs for each benchmark and then apply this configuration to the benchmarks using the ref inputs. The authors find that the best optimization configuration found using train works well when applied to ref inputs.

Kulkarni *et al.* describe a partially user-assisted approach to select optimization sequences for embedded applications [18]. This approach combines user-guided and performance information with a genetic algorithm to select local and global optimization sequences. As is usually the case with iterative optimization papers, the authors do not consider input sensitivity and only show results for fixed benchmark/data set pairs. Other authors [13,6] have explored ways to search program- or domain-specific command line parameters to enable and disable specific options of various optimizing compilers. Again, these authors keep the benchmark/data set pairs fixed.

Machine learning predictive modelling has been recently used for non-search based optimization. Here the compiler attempts to learn a good optimization heuristic offline which is then used instead of the compiler writer's hand-tuned method. While this work is successful in speeding up the generation of compiler heuristics, the performance gains have been generally modest. Stephenson *et al.* used genetic programming to tune heuristic priority functions for three compiler optimizations: hyperblock selection, register allocation, and data prefetching within the Trimaran's IMPACT compiler [22]. The authors construct their heuristic on a training data set and report results on both a training data set and a test data set for the different optimizations. Using a data set different from the one used for training causes some degradation and in some cases dramatic reduction in performance. This may be due to the genetic algorithm "over-fitting" or specializing to the data set being trained on.

Eeckhout *et al.* attempt to find a minimal set of representative programs and inputs for architecture research [9]. They cluster program-input combinations using principal-component analysis (PCA) of dynamic program charateristics, such as cache misses and branch mispredictions. They find that while different inputs to the same program were often clustered together, in several cases different inputs to the same program result in data points in separate clusters.

MinneSPEC [21] is a set of reduced inputs for various SPEC CPU2000 benchmarks. They are derived from the reference inputs using a variety of techniques, such as modifying inputs (e.g., reducing number of iterations). They are often used to reduce simulation time for architecture research.

6   Conclusions and Future Work

In this article, we present a data set suite, called MiDataSets, for the MiBench benchmarks, which can be used for a more realistic evaluation of iterative optimization; this suite will be made publicly available. The scope of this suite extends beyond iterative optimization as many architecture research works are based on feedback mechanisms which are sensitive to data sets.

We use this data set suite to understand how iterative optimization behaves in a more realistic setting where the data set varies across executions. We find that, though programs can exhibit significant variability when transformed with several optimizations, it is often possible to find, in a few iterations, a compromise optimization which is within 5% of the best possible optimization, across all data sets. This observation, supported by a reasonable set of experiments (codes, optimizations, and data sets), has significant implications for the practical application and more widespread use of iterative optimization. Especially in embedded systems, but in general-purpose systems as well, the possibility that iterative optimization comes with great performance variability has slowed down its adoption up to now.

In future work, we plan on implementing a practical continuous optimization framework and enhance techniques of comparing the effect of optimizations without the knowledge about the data set or base line execution. This will help both validating the results of this article on a larger scale and in making iterative optimization more practical. We also plan to investigate the many different possible continuous optimization strategies on a fine-grain level, including for codes with high variability. We plan to enhance our MiDataSets based on program behaviour and code coverage. We also plan to evalute the influence of datasets on power and memory consumption which is critical for embedded systems.

References

1. PAPI: A Portable Interface to Hardware Performance Counters. http://icl.cs.utk.edu/papi, 2005.
2. PathScale EKOPath Compilers. http://www.pathscale.com, 2005.
3. F. Agakov, E. Bonilla, J. Cavazos, B. Franke, G. Fursin, M. O'Boyle, J. Thomson, M. Toussaint, and C. Williams. Using machine learning to focus iterative optimization. In *CGO-4: The Fourth Annual International Symposium on Code Generation and Optimization*, 2006.
4. S. Bartolini and C. A. Prete. Optimizing instruction cache performance of embedded systems. *ACM Trans. Embedded Comput. Syst.*, 4(4):934–965, 2005.
5. P. Berube and J. Amaral. Aestimo: a feedback-directed optimization evaluation tool. In *Proceedings of the International Symposium on Performance Analysis of Systems and Software (ISPASS)*, 2006.
6. K. Chow and Y. Wu. Feedback-directed selection and characterization of compiler optimizations. In *Proceedings of the Workshop on Feedback-Directed and Dynamic Optimization (FDDO)*, 2001.
7. K. D. Cooper, A. Grosul, T. J. Harvey, S. Reeves, D. Subramanian, L. Torczon, and T. Waterman. Acme: adaptive compilation made efficient. In *Proceedings of the Conference on Languages, Compilers, and Tools for Embedded Systems (LCTES)*, pages 69–77, 2005.
8. K. D. Cooper, P. J. Schielke, and D. Subramanian. Optimizing for reduced code space using genetic algorithms. In *Proceedings of the Conference on Languages, Compilers, and Tools for Embedded Systems (LCTES)*, pages 1–9, 1999.
9. L. Eeckhout, H. Vandierendonck, and K. D. Bosschere. Quantifying the impact of input data sets on program behavior and its applications. *Journal of Instruction-level Parallelism*, 2003.
10. B. Franke, M. O'Boyle, J. Thomson, and G. Fursin. Probabilistic source-level optimisation of embedded programs. In *Proceedings of the Conference on Languages, Compilers, and Tools for Embedded Systems (LCTES)*, 2005.
11. G. Fursin, A. Cohen, M. O'Boyle, and O. Temam. A practical method for quickly evaluating program optimizations. In *Proceedings of the International Conference on High Performance Embedded Architectures & Compilers (HiPEAC 2005)*, pages 29–46, November 2005.
12. G. Fursin, M. O'Boyle, and P. Knijnenburg. Evaluating iterative compilation. In *Proc. Languages and Compilers for Parallel Computers (LCPC)*, pages 305–315, 2002.

13. E. Granston and A. Holler. Automatic recommendation of compiler options. In *Proceedings of the Workshop on Feedback-Directed and Dynamic Optimization (FDDO)*, 2001.

14. M. R. Guthaus, J. S. Ringenberg, D. Ernst, T. M. Austin, T. Mudge, and R. B. Brown. Mibench: A free, commercially representative embedded benchmark suite. In *IEEE 4th Annual Workshop on Workload Characterization*, Austin, TX, December 2001.

15. M. Haneda, P. Knijnenburg, and H. Wijshoff. On the impact of data input sets on statistical compiler tuning. In *Workshop on Performance Optimization for High-Level Languages and Libraries (POHLL)*, 2006.

16. T. Kistler and M. Franz. Continuous program optimization: A case study. *ACM Trans. Program. Lang. Syst.*, 25(4):500–548, 2003.

17. T. Kisuki, P. M. W. Knijnenburg, and M. F. P. O'Boyle. Combined selection of tile sizes and unroll factors using iterative compilation. In *The International Conference on Parallel Architectures and Compilation Techniques*, pages 237–248, 2000.

18. P. Kulkarni, S. Hines, J. Hiser, D. Whalley, J. Davidson, and D. Jones. Fast searches for effective optimization phase sequences. In *Proceedings of the ACM SIGPLAN Conference on Programming Language Design and Implementation (PLDI)*, pages 171–182, 2004.

19. C. Lattner and V. Adve. Llvm: a compilation framework for lifelong program analysis & transformation. In *Proceedings of the International Symposium on Code Generation and Optimization (CGO)*, 2004.

20. A. Nisbet. GAPS: Genetic algorithm optimised parallelization. In *Proc. Workshop on Profile and Feedback Directed Compilation*, 1998.

21. A. J. K. Osowski and D. J. Lilja. MinneSPEC: A new SPEC benchmark workload for simulation-based computer architecture research. *Computer Architecture Letters*, 1(2):10–13, June 2002.

22. M. Stephenson, M. Martin, and U. O'Reilly. Meta optimization: Improving compiler heuristics with machine learning. In *Proceedings of the ACM SIGPLAN Conference on Programming Language Design and Implementation (PLDI)*, pages 77–90, 2003.

23. S. Triantafyllis, M. Vachharajani, and D. I. August. Compiler optimization-space exploration. In *Journal of Instruction-level Parallelism*, 2005.

24. R. C. Whaley, A. Petitet, and J. J. Dongarra. Automated empirical optimization of software and the ATLAS project. *Parallel Computing*, 27(1–2):3–35, 2001.

Evaluation of Offset Assignment Heuristics

Johnny Huynh[1,*], José Nelson Amaral[1], Paul Berube[1],
and Sid-Ahmed-Ali Touati[2]

[1] University of Alberta, Canada
[2] Université de Versailles, France

Abstract. In digital signal processors (DSPs) variables are accessed using k address registers. The problem of finding a memory layout, for a set of variables, that minimizes the address-computation overhead is known as the *General Offset Assignment* (GOA) Problem. The most common approach to this problem is to partition the set of variables into k partitions and to assign each partition to an address register. Thus effectively decomposing the GOA problem into several *Simple Offset Assignment* (SOA) problems. Many heuristic-based algorithms are proposed in the literature to approximate solutions to the partitioning and SOA problems. However, the address-computation overhead of the resulting memory layouts are not accurately evaluated. In this paper we use Gebotys' optimal address-code generation technique to evaluate memory layouts. Using this evaluation method introduces a new problem which we call the Memory Layout Permutation (MLP) problem. We then use the Gebotys' technique and an exhaustive solution to the MLP problem to evaluate heuristic-based offset-assignment algorithms. The memory layouts produced by each algorithm are compared against each other and against the optimal layouts. Our results show that even in small access sequences with 12 variables or less, current heuristics may produce memory layouts with address-computation overheads up to two times higher than the overhead of an optimal layout.

1 Introduction

The extensive use of data in digital-signal-processing applications requires frequent memory accesses. Many digital signal processors (DSPs) provide dedicated address registers (ARs) to facilitate the access of variables stored in memory through indirect addressing modes. Post-increment and post-decrementing addressing modes are often supported, allowing the processor to update the AR in the same cycle a memory location is accessed. When two consecutive memory accesses, indexed by the same AR, are not adjacent in the memory, an extra address-computation instruction is required. Thus, the placement of data in memory affects how effectively the post-increment or post-decrement addressing

---

* This research is supported by fellowships and grants from the Natural Sciences and Engineering Research Council of Canada (NSERC), the Informatics Circle of Research Excellence (iCORE), and the Canadian Foundation for Innovation (CFI).

modes can be used. This placement is called a memory layout; and the problem of finding a memory layout that minimizes address-computation overhead is called the General Offset Assignment (GOA) problem.

Given a memory layout and an instruction sequence, Gebotys' network-flow solution finds the optimal usage of ARs to access the data [1]. While this technique works well for a fixed memory layout, we discovered that the initial memory layout greatly affects the final code performance. Even in small test cases that access 12 variables, some memory layouts require twice as many cycles for address computations as other memory layouts.

Several heuristic algorithms have been proposed to generate a memory layout that minimizes address-computation overhead [2,3,4,5]. The algorithms simplify the GOA problem by assuming that every access to a variable uses the same AR. With this simplification, the GOA problem can be addressed as follows. First, variables accessed in an instruction sequence are partitioned, and each partition is assigned to an AR. We call this partitioning problem the Address Register Assignment (ARA) problem. Next, individual sub-layouts for each partition are generated by approximating a solution to the Simple Offset Assignment (SOA) problem [3]. Last, the sub-layouts can be ordered to form a single, contiguous memory layout. We call this ordering problem the Memory Layout Permutation (MLP) problem, and it arises because the overhead of solutions found by the network-flow technique is sensitive to the ordering of sub-layouts.

Although many algorithms have been proposed to address the GOA problem, only heuristics for the SOA problem have been comprehensively compared [6]. Furthermore, the address-computation overhead of the produced memory layouts has only been measured using the cost models of the heuristic algorithms, and not by an optimal technique such as Gebotys' network-flow formulation. The experiments reported in this paper show that different orderings of sub-layouts have a significant impact on the optimal address-computation overhead, producing layouts with overheads that span the entire solution space. Specifically, the worst layouts have a minimum overhead of twice as many cycles as the optimal layouts. Additionally, using different algorithms for the ARA and SOA problems does not significantly impact the overhead of the resulting memory layouts.

The main contributions of this paper are:

- a demonstration that existing heuristic solutions to the GOA problem poorly approximate the minimization of address-computation overhead;
- the formulation of a new optimization problem, the memory-layout permutation problem, that must be solved in order to use a minimum-cost circulation (MCC) technique to evaluate the minimum address-computation overhead incurred in memory layouts produced by heuristic solutions to GOA;
- an experimental evaluation, based on the MCC technique, of heuristic-based ARA and SOA algorithms.

This paper is organized as follows. Section 2 presents the background to the offset assignment problem and discusses how the address-computation overhead of a memory layout can be computed. Current algorithms used to find memory layouts are presented in Section 3. The experimental evaluation of offset assignment algorithms is presented in Section 4. Finally, related work and conclusions are presented in Section 5 and 6.

2   Background

Many DSPs have a set of ARs used to access variables stored in memory. Post-incrementing and post-decrementing addressing modes allow an AR r to access a variable v and modify the content of r by one word in the same instruction. Thus, if the next access using r is to location v, or to the locations immediately adjacent to v in memory, r can be updated without any additional cost. However, if r accesses a location that is non-adjacent to v, an explicit address computation is necessary. The computational overhead required to initialize or update ARs is architecture-dependent.

All experiments in this paper model the Texas Instruments TMS320C54X family of processors. These DSPs have eight 16-bit ARs. Most instructions are one word in length and have one cycle of overhead. Initializing an AR requires a two-word instruction and two cycles of overhead. Similarly, auto-incrementing (or auto-decrementing) an AR by more than one word requires one extra word to encode the instruction and one extra cycle to execute. Thus, inefficiently using address registers results in an increase in both code size and run-time overheads.

Similar to many other DSP architectures, the address registers in the C54X processors can also be used to store values other than addresses; however, the values stored in the address registers are subject to two limitations:

1. Address registers can only hold 16-bit values, while data in memory and the accumulator are typically 32-bit values.
2. Address registers can only be manipulated by the address-generation unit, which is limited to addition and subtraction of 16-bit values.

Thus, it may be infeasible to use ARs as general purpose registers, and the offset assignment problem must be solved to effectively place variables in memory.

2.1   The Offset Assignment Problem

Given a set of variables stored contiguously in memory, a *memory layout* is an ordering of these variables in memory. A basic block in a program accesses n variables. The order of variable accesses by the instructions in the basic block defines an *access sequence*. The *Offset-Assignment Problem* is defined as:

> Given k address registers and a basic block accessing n variables, find a *memory layout* that minimizes address-computation overhead.

Memory layouts with minimum address-computation overhead are called optimal memory layouts. This problem is called "offset assignment" because the address of each variable can be obtained by adding an *offset* to a common base address.

If $k = 1$, then the problem is know as the *Simple Offset Assignment* (SOA). If $k > 1$ the problem is referred to as the *General Offset Assignment* (GOA).

In the Simple Offset-Assignment (SOA) problem, a single AR is available to access all the variables in the memory. Liao *et al.* [3] convert the access sequence to an undirected *access graph*. Variables are vertices in the graph, and edge weights indicate the number of times two variables are adjacent in the access sequence. Liao *et al.* [3] reduce the SOA problem for an access graph to the NP-Complete maximum-weight path cover problem, and propose a heuristic to solve SOA in polynomial time (see Section 3.1).

In the General Offset-Assignment (GOA) problem, each *access* to one of the n variables in an access sequence must be assigned to one of k ARs. This assignment creates multiple access *sub-sequences* — one for each AR. A memory *sub-layout* can be found for each sub-sequence. Sub-layouts cannot be computed independently because a variable may appear in multiple address registers, but the union of all sub-layouts must still form a contiguous layout. Liao *et al.* [3] simplify the GOA problem by assigning *variables*, instead of *variable accesses*, to address registers. This simplification produces sub-sequences that access disjoint sets of variables. A memory layout can be obtained by solving the SOA problem for each sub-sequence. We call the problem of assigning *variables* to address registers the Address-Register Assignment (ARA) problem (see Section 3.2).

Figure 1 illustrates the traditional approach to produce a memory layout from a basic block. First, the instruction scheduler emits the sequence of memory accesses. Then, the ARA problem is solved to produce sub-sequences. Offsets are assigned in each sub-sequences by solving several instances of the SOAproblem. All the heuristic-based algorithms for the ARA and SOA problems examined in this paper generate approximate solutions. Alternative techniques to reduce address-computation overhead are discussed in Section 5.

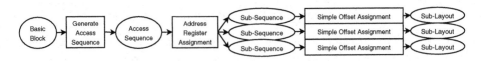

Fig. 1. The traditional approach to generate a memory layout for the access sequence of a basic block. The sub-sequences generated by address register assignment access disjoint sets of variables. The resulting set of sub-layouts can then be placed independently in memory to form the final memory layout.

2.2   Computing Address-Computation Overhead

The traditional approach to finding a memory layout assumes that each variable is accessed exclusively by one AR. Thus, the resulting addressing-code and address-computation overhead are based on assigning *variables* to ARs. However, an *optimal* addressing code for a memory layout, M, is an assignment of *accesses* to ARs such that the access sequence, S, can be accessed with the minimum overhead. In order to accurately evaluate the overhead of memory layouts, optimal addressing code is required.

Gebotys proposes an algorithm to find optimal addressing code [1]. The assignment of *accesses* to ARs can be found by transforming M and S into a directed cyclic network-flow graph. The minimum cost circulation (MCC) of the graph represents the optimal addressing code, and the cost of the circulation represents the minimum overhead for the memory layout. The MCC for these network-flow graphs can be solved in polynomial time. In this paper, the MCC technique is used to evaluate the quality of all memory layouts.

3   Offset Assignment Algorithms

Existing heuristic-based algorithms solve the GOA problem as described in Section 2.1. Given an access sequence S, and k ARs, a memory layout is found by:

1. ARA assigns each variable $v \in S$ to a single AR $A_i, 1 \le i \le k$.
2. SOA finds a sub-layout m_i for the variables assigned to each AR A_i.
3. The *memory-layout permutation* (MLP) problem combines all sub-layouts $m_1 \ldots m_k$ into a contiguous memory layout. MLP is absent from the literature because previous solutions to GOA assigned *variables*, rather than *accesses*, to ARs. The MLP problem only appears when using traditional algorithms in conjunction with the MCC technique.

We use MCC to evaluate the performance of several ARA and SOA algorithms.

3.1   Simple Offset Assignment

The SOA problem was introduced by Bartley and solved as a *maximum-weight Hamiltonian-path* problem [7]. Given an access sequence S, a weighted access graph G, can be constructed. A path in G represents an ordering of variables in memory. Liao *et al.* refine the SOA problem formulation to a *maximum-weight path cover* problem [3], which is NP-complete. Thus, all subsequently proposed algorithms approximate a solution to the SOA problem by finding a path cover on G.

We implement and evaluate five solutions to the SOA problem:

1. Liao *et al.* propose an algorithm that builds the path cover, one edge at a time, by using a greedy heuristic to select edges in G [3].
2. Leupers extends the algorithm by Liao *et al.* by proposing a tie-break function to decide between edges of equal weights [2] [6].
3. Sugino *et al.* propose an algorithm that uses a greedy heuristic to remove one edge at a time from G until a valid path cover is formed [4].
4. Liao and Leupers present a naive algorithm which builds a memory layout based on the declaration order of variables in the access sequence. The algorithm is also known as Order First Use (OFU).

5. Liao also presents a branch-and-bound algorithm that finds the maximum-weight path cover. The algorithm has exponential time-complexity, but for small graphs, our implementation runs in a reasonable amount of time.

3.2   Address Register Assignment

In the GOA problem, $k > 1$ ARs are used to access variables in memory. Liao *et al.* decompose the GOA problem into multiple instances of SOA by assigning each variable to an AR A_i. Let $C(A_i)$ be the address-computation overhead for an optimal SOA solution to variables assigned to A_i. Liao *et al.* define the GOA problem as follows:

> Given an access sequence S, the set of variables V, and k ARs, assign each $v \in V$ to an AR $A_i, 1 \leq i \leq k$, such that $\sum_{i=1}^{k} C(A_i)$ is minimum.

Solving this problem does not produce a memory layout — it is only an assignment of variables to ARs. Thus, this problem should not be considered the *real* GOA problem. We call this problem the Address-Register Assignment (ARA) problem. We conjecture that ARA is NP-hard because SOA is NP-complete and is an instance of ARA.

This paper examines several heuristic-based algorithms for ARA. In each case, an approximation of $C(A_i)$ is required to estimate the overhead of assigning a variable to an AR. Any of the SOA algorithms in Section 3.1 can be used as a sub-routine to approximate $C(A_i)$ for the following ARA algorithms:

1. Leupers and David propose a greedy algorithm that assigns variables to ARs by selecting one edge at a time from the access graph [2].
2. Sugino *et al.* use a heuristic-based algorithm that iteratively partitions the variables and selects the partitioning with the lowest estimated overhead [4].
3. Zhuang *et al.*'s variable coalescing algorithm for offset-assignment problems includes assigning variables to ARs [5]. The assignment portion of the algorithm greedily assigns one variable to an AR until all variables are assigned.

3.3   Memory Layout Permutations

As illustrated in Figure 2, the traditional approach to offset assignment produces a set of disjoint sub-layouts. ARA produces a set of disjoint access sub-sequences that are solved as independent SOA problems. Each SOA instance is solved to produce a memory layout called an ARA sub-layout. However, each ARA sub-layout is formed by the combination of disjoint paths from the SOA path cover. Each disjoint path in the path cover is called an SOA sub-layout and defines an ordering of variables in memory. Unless otherwise stated, the term *sub-layout* refers to an SOA sub-layout. In the traditional approach to offset assignment, each sub-layout is independent, and can be placed in memory arbitrarily.

However, sub-layouts are only considered independent because of the traditional assumption that variables are accessed exclusively by one AR. Since the

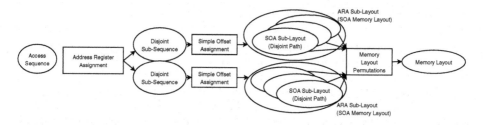

Fig. 2. Performing address register assignment followed by simple offset assignment generates memory sub-layouts that must be placed in memory. The problem of finding a placement that minimizes overhead is called the memory-layout permutation problem.

MCC technique allows variables to be accessed by multiple ARs, it is possible to reduce address-computation overhead by placing sub-layouts contiguously in memory. Let M_i be a sub-layout and M_i^r be a sub-layout with the variables of M_i in reverse order in memory. Let $(M_i|M_i^r)$ stand for an instance of either M_i or M_i^r. We introduce the *memory-layout permutation* (MLP) problem as follows:

> Given an access sequence S and a set of m disjoint memory sub-layouts, find an ordering of the sub-layouts $\{(M_1|M_1^r), \ldots, (M_m|M_m^r)\}$ such that address-computation overhead is minimum when the sub-layouts are placed contiguously in memory.

The MLP solution space is extremely large: m sub-layouts can form $m!$ permutations. For each permutation, each sub-layout can be placed in memory as either M_i or M_i^r. Thus, m sub-layouts originate $(m!)(2^m)$ layouts. However, an ordering of layouts $M_1, \ldots, M_m$ is equivalent to its reciprocal layout, $M_m^r, \ldots, M_1^r$, since all variables have the same relative offset to each other. Thus, the MLP solution space is $\frac{(m!)(2^m)}{2}$ memory layouts. Figure 3 shows how 2 sub-layouts can form 8 possible layouts, half of which are reciprocals of another.

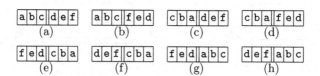

Fig. 3. Permutations of two sub-layouts

When reciprocals are considered, an offset assignment problem with n variables has a solution space of $\frac{n!}{2}$ memory layouts. If we let each variable be a sub-layout, then $m = n$ and the MLP problem is reduced to the offset assignment problem. This implies that if an algorithm solves the MLP problem, the same algorithm solves the offset assignment problem.

4   Evaluating Offset Assignment Algorithms

An extensive empirical evaluation of the available heuristic offset-assignment algorithms supports the following conclusions:

- Contrary to the conjectures of other authors [1], the selection of memory layout has a significant impact on address-computation overhead. Less than 0.1% of all memory layouts for the examined access sequences result in minimum overhead. Using optimal address-code generation alone (using the MCC technique) is not sufficient to minimize overhead.
- The algorithms seldom produce memory sub-layouts that admit MLP solutions with the minimum possible overhead. For some access sequences, none of the algorithms produce sub-layouts that can form an optimal solution.
- Using different ARA algorithms greatly impacts the quantity and quality of memory layout permutations. Conversely, using different SOA algorithms has little impact.

4.1   Experimental Methodology

Figure 4 outlines the experimental methodology. For each access sequence, heuristic solutions to the offset assignment problem are found by using all combinations of three ARA and five SOA algorithms. Each combination produces a set of memory sub-layouts (see Figure 1). If m sub-layouts are produced, then there are $p = \frac{(m!)(2^m)}{2}$ possible memory layouts. The address-computation overhead of each memory layout is computed using the MCC method. The results of this empirical evaluation are examined in terms of the *distribution* of overhead values for the layouts produced by each combination of ARA and SOA algorithms.

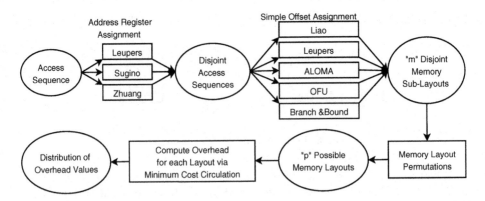

Fig. 4. Procedure for evaluating offset assignment algorithms. There are 15 paths in the chart, for the 15 combinations of ARA and SOA algorithms.

4.2   Test Environment

This evaluation uses a processor model based on the TI C54X family of DSPs. This architecture requires two cycles of overhead to initialize an address registers (INIT) and one extra cycle to access non-adjacent memory locations (JUMP).

Access sequences are obtained from kernels in the UTDSP benchmark suite. Each kernel is compiled using -O2 optimization by gcc version 3.3.2. Unfortunately, the gcc compiler does not generate code for the C54X family of DSPs. Instead, we modified gcc to output access sequences from inner-most loops prior to register allocation. Then the overhead of access sequences and memory layouts are evaluated statically, using the MCC technique described in Section 2.2.

Given an access sequence with n variables, we compute the optimal memory layout by evaluating the MCC of all possible $\frac{n!}{2}$ layouts (see Section 3.3). Due to the exponential growth of the solution space, experiments are restricted to sequences with up to 12 variables. The five access sequences used in this study are from five kernels in the UTDSP benchmark suite which produced access sequences with $n \leq 12$.

4.3   The Efficiency of Offset Assignment Heuristics

Table 1 shows a summary of the address-computation overhead for all memory layouts evaluated in this study. The *Exhaustive* column shows the number of memory layouts with a particular overhead in the solution space for each GOA problem. The average overhead of all layouts in each GOA problem ranges from 49% to 75% higher than minimum. Additionally, at least 98% of all layouts have an overhead 33% to 100% higher than minimum. Thus, even when the MCC technique is used to find optimal addressing code, the selection of memory layout has a significant impact on address-computation overhead.

The *Algorithmic* column of Table 1 shows the *combined* distribution and average address-computation overhead for memory layouts produced by *all 15 combinations* of the ARA and SOA algorithms. The distribution of the overheads obtained using the heuristic-based algorithms presented in Section 3.2 and 3.1 indicate that, in general, the algorithms are not very effective at minimizing overhead. The average overhead of layouts produced by the algorithms for each access sequence ranges from 40% to 60% higher than minimum and is only slightly lower than average overhead of all layouts in the solution space. The importance of selecting a suitable way to combine sub-layouts cannot be overstated. For instance, a surprising finding is that the heuristically generated sub-layouts for a given instance of the problem can be combined in one way to generate the best possible overhead for that instance, and the same sub-layouts can be combined in another way to generate the worst possible overhead.

4.4   The Efficiency of ARA Heuristics

Each of the three ARA algorithms — Leupers, Sugino, and Zhuang — can be combined with five SOA algorithms (Figure 4) to produces a memory layout.

Table 1. Number of layouts with a specific address-computation overhead, for the entire solution space. The *Exhaustive* column shows distribution of memory layouts in the solution space. The *Algorithmic* column shows the combined distribution of layouts produced by the 15 different ARA and SOA combinations.

Access Sequence	overhead (cycles)	Exhaustive Number of Layouts	% of Layouts	Algorithmic Number of Layouts	% of Layouts
	4	5	0.02%	0	0.00%
	5	281	1.39%	125	34.72%
iir_arr	6	5707	28.31%	235	65.28%
	7	10526	52.21%	0	0.00%
	8	3641	18.06%	0	0.00%
Average overhead		6.87		5.65	
	6	144	0.00%	0	0.00%
	7	19557	0.01%	72	0.33%
	8	1514917	0.63%	2240	10.23%
iir_arr_swp	9	21757157	9.08%	6515	29.77%
	10	90478895	37.78%	10496	47.95%
	11	104101226	43.47%	2565	11.72%
	12	21628904	9.03%	0	0.00%
Average overhead		10.51		9.60	
	6	323	0.02%	117	0.60%
	7	10785	0.59%	303	1.55%
latnrm_arr_swp	8	253379	13.96%	7067	36.26%
	9	918134	50.60%	8198	42.07%
	10	631779	34.82%	3803	19.51%
Average overhead		9.20		8.78	
	6	1449	0.08%	28	0.21%
	7	29682	1.64%	481	3.68%
latnrm_ptr	8	456647	25.17%	6093	46.58%
	9	929244	51.21%	6268	47.92%
	10	397378	21.90%	210	1.61%
Average overhead		8.93		8.47	
	6	323	0.02%	5	0.04%
	7	7706	0.42%	138	1.04%
latnrm_ptr_swp	8	225109	12.41%	3734	28.19%
	9	905303	49.90%	5881	44.39%
	10	675959	37.26%	3490	26.34%
Average overhead		9.24		8.96	

All of the layouts produced by an ARA algorithm are combined into a set. The distribution of overhead values for the possible layouts produced by each ARA algorithm are shown in Figure 5. For instance, Figure 5(a) shows that Leupers' ARA algorithm can admit over 100 layouts with 6 cycles of overhead and 5 layouts with 5 cycles of overhead. Each of these layouts are obtained by using different SOA and MLP solutions, but all use Leupers' ARA algorithm.

For each access sequence, the total number of layouts varies between each ARA algorithm because each algorithm may use a different number of ARs, yielding a different number of permutations (see Section 3.3). Figure 5 indicates that ARA algorithms producing fewer layouts, such as Sugino's, tend to produce better layouts. This result indicates that it is frequently disadvantageous to use all available ARs. For instance, in Figure 5(b), Leupers and Marwedel's ARA algorithm yields a total of 9600 possible layouts, two of which have a 7-cycle overhead. Alternatively, the ARA algorithm proposed by Sugino *et al.* generates a total of 2688 possible layouts, with 61 7-cycle-overhead layouts. Similar distributions occur for the other access sequences.

The results also suggest that locally optimal sub-layouts do not lead to globally optimal memory layouts. An ARA algorithm using more ARs assigns fewer variables to each register. In the case of Leupers and Marwedel's algorithm, and occasionally Zhuang's algorithm, as few as two variables may be assigned to an AR. Two variables can be trivially accessed without incurring JUMP overhead and are locally optimal. However, if the two variables are not adjacent in the optimal memory layouts, then the MLP solution space will never contain an optimal layout.

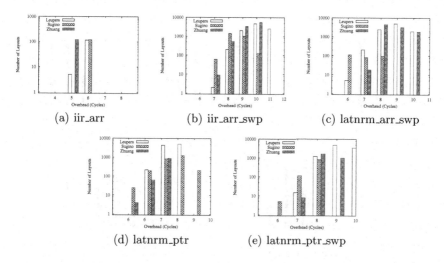

Fig. 5. Distribution of overhead values produced by each ARA algorithm on different test cases. The number of layouts shown for each algorithm is the union of 5 sets of layouts, each produced with one of the 5 different SOA algorithms, but using the same ARA algorithm.

4.5 The Efficiency of SOA Heuristics

The distributions in Figure 6 are complementary to those in Figure 5, but focused on the layouts produced by each of the five SOA algorithms. For instance, Figure 6(b) shows that the SOA algorithm designed by Sugino *et al.* can admit over 1000 layouts with 9 cycles of overhead. Each of these layouts are obtained by combining Sugino *et al.*'s ARA algorithm with one of the three SOA algorithms.

SOA algorithms are used to estimate increases in overhead when variables are assigned to ARs; which, in turn, affects the number of sub-layouts produced by the ARA algorithms. Consequently, the total number of layouts varies between each SOA algorithm for each access sequence in Figure 6. Low variability between the algorithms can be partly attributed to the problem sizes. The access sequences only access 8 to 12 variables, and the ARA algorithms assign at most 6 variables to each address register. Because the SOA sub-problems are small the algorithms produce similar, and possibly optimal, sub-layouts. Specifically, no SOA algorithm consistently produces sub-layouts that admit the greatest number of optimal or near-optimal layouts. In two access sequences, OFU admits the most number of low-overhead layouts, while in one other sequence, Sugino *et al.*'s SOA algorithm admits the most number of optimal layouts.

Figure 6 also further supports previous suggestions that combining optimal sub-layouts does not result in optimal layouts. For instance, in Figure 6(e), the OFU algorithm generates sub-layouts that combined to form optimal memory layouts, while the Branch-and-Bound algorithm, which finds optimal sub-layouts, does not admit any optimal memory layouts.

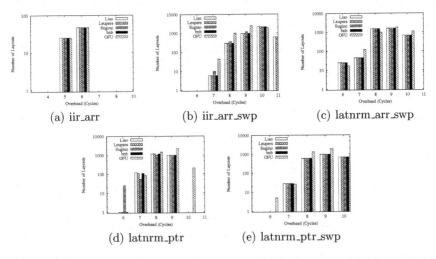

Fig. 6. Distribution of overhead values produced by each SOA algorithm on different test cases. The number of layouts shown for each algorithm is the union of 3 sets of layouts, each produced with one of the 3 different ARA algorithms, but using the same SOA algorithm.

5   Related Work

In 2003, Leupers presented a comprehensive experimental evaluation of algorithms for the SOA [6]. This is the first comparative evaluation of algorithms for the GOA problem. It has three distinguishing features:

- The GOA problem is evaluated as three problems: address register assignment, simple offset assignment, and memory-layout permutation.
- All known *heuristic-based* algorithms that generate a *single* approximate solution to the ARA or SOA problems are compared against each other, and against the optimal solutions.
- The minimum address-computation overhead of each memory layout generated is computed using a minimum cost circulation technique.

Some algorithms for generating a memory layout were not included in our study. Atri *et al.* and Wess and Zeitlhofer, propose algorithms that attempt to iteratively improve a memory layout [8,9]. Leupers and David, and Wess and Gotschlich, propose simulation-based algorithms to generate memory layouts. These algorithms were omitted because they are computationally expensive. The algorithms must compute the overhead of many memory layouts before a final memory layout is produced.

This study only focused on evaluating offset assignment for *scalar* variables in straight line code. Reducing address-computation overhead in loops is more difficult because the problem of finding optimal addressing code for a loop is NP-complete [1]. Many researchers have proposed alternative methods to reduce overhead for array accesses in loops. Leupers and David, Cheng and Lin, and Chen and Kandemir, all propose algorithms to reduce address-computation overhead in loops through improved address register allocation and data and instruction re-ordering [10,11,12].

Although our study investigates algorithms that directly generate a memory layout, overhead can also be reduced by manipulating the access sequence. Rao and Pande, Lim *et al.*, and Kandemir *et al.* each propose an algorithm that re-orders the access sequence so that an offset assignment algorithm can produce a lower-overhead layout [13,14,15]. Choi and Kim propose a unified algorithm to simultaneously find an instruction schedule and a low-overhead offset assignment [16]. The access sequence can also be manipulated by reducing the number of unique variables accessed. Ottoni *et al.*, and Zhuang *et al.*, propose algorithms to coalesce variables [17,5]. Although some of the scheduling and coalescing algorithms simultaneously find memory layouts, it is still possible to perform an additional offset assignment pass to further reduce overhead.

6   Conclusion

The minimum cost circulation technique produces the optimal addressing code for a *fixed* memory layout and access sequence by allowing variables to be accessed by multiple address registers. This paper shows that the memory layout has a significant impact on the address-computation overhead, even when using optimal address-code generation. Furthermore, current offset assignment algorithms produce sub-layouts that can span the full range of values in the solution space. In order for current algorithms to generate only low-overhead layouts, a new combinatorial problem, the memory-layout permutation problem, must be solved.

Layouts generated by different ARA algorithms have different distributions of overhead values. Distributions with fewer memory layouts (due to ARA using fewer ARs) consistently produce more low-overhead layouts. Thus, the average overhead of memory layouts produced by Sugino's ARA algorithm is usually the lowest. When an ARA algorithm uses more address registers, optimal sub-layouts are more easily found. However, locally optimal sub-layouts do not necessarily produce globally optimal memory layouts. We observe instances where the naive OFU algorithm produces sub-layouts that can be combined to form optimal layouts, while the branch-and-bound algorithm produces optimal sub-layouts that cannot be combined into optimal layouts.

Conversely, heuristic-based SOA algorithms have very little impact on either layout quantity or quality. However, the minimal differences between the SOA algorithms may be attributed to the small problem sizes. The SOA algorithms are given problem instances with 6 variables or less, and the same path cover is usually found regardless of the algorithm. Thus, for GOA problems with 12 or fewer variables, an ARA algorithm that generates fewer sub-layouts combined with any SOA algorithm has the greatest chance of producing sub-layouts that combine to form memory layouts with low or minimum overhead.

This paper shows that regardless of the ARA and SOA algorithms used, placing the resulting sub-layouts contiguously in memory is a necessary optimization problem that must be solved in order to minimize address-computation overhead in a basic block. We call this new problem the memory-layout permutation (MLP) problem. The order of sub-layouts in memory has a significant impact on overhead, especially when the number of sub-layouts is high. Additionally, as more variables are assigned to individual sub-layouts, the MLP problem is reduced to the GOA problem itself. Thus, if we can find an algorithm to address the MLP problem, the algorithm can be used to solve GOA.

Our study suggests two new directions for improving GOA solutions. One direction is to propose a solution to the MLP problem. An alternative direction is to replace the individual solutions of the ARA, SOA, and MLP problems with a combined method that generates memory layouts that minimizes overhead, as computed by the minimum-cost circulation technique.

References

1. Gebotys, C.: DSP address optimization using a minimum cost circulation technique. In: ICCAD '97: Proceedings of the 1997 IEEE/ACM International Conference on Computer-Aided Design, Washington, DC, USA, IEEE Computer Society (1997) 100–103
2. Leupers, R., Marwedel, P.: Algorithms for address assignment in DSP code generation. In: Proceedings of the 1996 IEEE/ACM International Conference on Computer-Aided Design. (1996) 109–112
3. Liao, S., Devadas, S., Keutzer, K., Tjiang, S., Wang, A.: Storage assignment to decrease code size. ACM Transactions on Programming Languages and Systems 18(3) (1996) 235–253
4. Sugino, N., Iimuro, S., Nishihara, A., Jujii, N.: DSP code optimization utilizing memory addressing operation. IEICE Trans Fundamentals (8) (1996) 1217–1223

5. Zhuang, X., Lau, C., Pande, S.: Storage assignment optimizations through variable coalescence for embedded processors. In: LCTES '03: Proceedings of the 2003 ACM SIGPLAN Conference on Language, Compiler, and Tools for Embedded Systems, New York, NY, USA, ACM Press (2003) 220–231
6. Leupers, R.: Offset assignment showdown: Evaluation of dsp address code optimization algorithms. In: CC '03: Proceedings of the 12th International Conference on Compiler Construction. (2003) 290–302
7. Bartley, D.H.: Optimizing stack frame accesses for processors with restricted addressing modes. Software – Practice & Experience 22(2) (1992) 101–110
8. Atri, S., Ramanujam, J., Kandemir, M.: Improving offset assignment for embedded processors. Lecture Notes in Computer Science 2017 (2001) 158–172
9. Wess, B., Zeitlhofer, T.: On the phase coupling problem between data memory layout generation and address pointer assignment. In: SCOPES. (2004) 152–166
10. Leupers, R., Basu, A., Marwedel, P.: Optimized array index computation in DSP programs. In: Asia and South Pacific Design Automation Conference. (1998) 87–92
11. Cheng, W.K., Lin, Y.L.: Addressing optimization for loop execution targeting dsp with auto-increment/decrement architecture. In: ISSS '98: Proceedings of the 11th International Symposium on System Synthesis, Washington, DC, USA, IEEE Computer Society (1998) 15–20
12. Chen, G., Kandemir, M.: Optimizing address code generation for array-intensive dsp applications. In: CGO '05: Proceedings of the International Symposium on Code Generation and Optimization, Washington, DC, USA, IEEE Computer Society (2005) 141–152
13. Rao, A., Pande, S.: Storage assignment optimizations to generate compact and efficient code on embedded DSPs. In: PLDI '99: Proceedings of the ACM SIGPLAN 1999 Conference on Programming Language Design and Implementation, New York, NY, USA, ACM Press (1999) 128–138
14. Lim, S., Kim, J., Choi, K.: Scheduling-based code size reduction in processors with indirect addressing mode. In: CODES '01: Proceedings of the 9th International Symposium on Hardware/Software Codesign, New York, NY, USA, ACM Press (2001) 165–169
15. Kandemir, M.T., Irwin, M.J., Chen, G., Ramanujam, J.: Address register assignment for reducing code size. In: CC '03: Proceedings of the 12th International Conference on Compiler Construction. (2003) 273–289
16. Choi, Y., Kim, T.: Address assignment combined with scheduling in DSP code generation. In: DAC '02: Proceedings of the 39th Conference on Design Automation, New York, NY, USA, ACM Press (2002) 225–230
17. Ottoni, D., Ottoni, G., Araujo, G., Leupers, R.: Improving offset assignment through simultaneous variable coalescing. In: 7th International Workshop on Software and Compilers for Embedded Systems. (2003) 285–297

Customizing the Datapath and ISA of Soft VLIW Processors

Mazen A.R. Saghir, Mohamad El-Majzoub, and Patrick Akl

Department of Electrical and Computer Engineering
American University of Beirut
P.O. Box 11-0236 Riad El-Solh, Beirut, Lebanon
{mazen,mte01,pea02}@aub.edu.lb

Abstract. In this paper, we examine the trade-offs in performance and area due to customizing the datapath and instruction set architecture of a soft VLIW processor implemented in a high-density FPGA. In addition to describing our processor, we describe a number of microarchitectural optimizations we used to reduce the area of the datapath. We also describe the tools we developed to customize, generate, and program our processor. Our experimental results show that datapath and instruction set customization achieve high levels of performance, and that using on-chip resources and implementing microarchitectural optimizations like selective data forwarding help keep FPGA resource utilization in check.

1 Introduction

The proliferation of fast, high-density, and feature-rich FPGAs has transformed these versatile devices into powerful embedded computational platforms. In addition to embedding hard microprocessor cores in FPGAs, vendors are providing *soft* processor cores that can be implemented in the logic fabrics of their FPGAs [1,2]. Soft processors enable designers to configure their datapaths to meet the needs of target applications. In most cases, designers can also create new custom instructions to accelerate performance-critical operations. So far, commercial soft processors have remained simple, featuring datapaths and instruction set architectures that resemble early RISC processors. However, as the speeds and logic densities of FPGAs increase, and as more on-chip resources (e.g. hardware multipliers and block memories) become available, it is becoming possible to implement more complex processor datapaths and instruction set architectures.

In this paper we present the results of a study we conducted to assess the impact of datapath and ISA customization on the performance and area of soft VLIW processors. In Sect. 2 we discuss related work and compare it with our own. In Sect. 3 we describe the datapath organization and instruction set architecture of our soft VLIW processor. Next, in Sect. 4, we describe a number of microarchitectural optimizations we used to reduce the area of our processors. In Sect. 5 we describe our development tools and work flow, and in Sect. 6 we present and discuss our results. Finally, in Sect. 7, we present our conclusions and describe future work.

K. De Bosschere et al. (Eds.): HiPEAC 2007, LNCS 4367, pp. 276–290, 2007.

2   Related Work

VLIW processors have long been used to implement application-specific instruction processors (ASIPs) for embedded applications [3]. In addition to their simple hardware implementations, VLIW processors achieve high levels of performance by exploiting ILP and supporting datapath and ISA customization [4,5]. However, since most ASIPs are custom processors implemented as standalone components or embedded within ASICs they are difficult and expensive to reconfigure or re-customize after they have been designed and manufactured.

To address this shortcoming, there has been increased commercial and academic interest in configurable, customizable, and reconfigurable processor architectures over the past few years. Companies like ARC and Tensilica have long been offering configurable and customizable processors along with supporting tool chains [6,7]. Academic researchers have also been embedding FPGA-like reconfigurable functional units (RFUs) in processor datapaths to implement custom instructions [8,9], and customizable co-processors to offload performance-critical computations from their host processors [10]. However, most customizable processors are also aimed at the ASIC market, making them difficult to re-customize once they have been manufactured; and RFUs are often constrained by fixed architectures that limit the range of custom operations they can support. Although soft-core versions of these processors are commonly used for functional validation, they are not designed to be implemented in FPGAs.

Soft processors are an alternative to ASIPs and customizable processors since they can easily and quickly be reconfigured and implemented in FPGAs. They can also leverage available FPGA resources to provide very efficient implementations. In [11,12], the authors describe the Soft Processor Rapid Exploration Environment (SPREE), which they used to create and evaluate the area, execution performance, and energy consumption of various soft processor implementations. The results of this study provide several insights into the trade-offs involved in designing soft processors that issue and execute *single* instructions. Our work builds upon these results and examines the effects of datapath and ISA customization on the performance and area of soft VLIW datapaths.

Our VLIW processor is not the first to be implemented in an FPGA. In [13,14], the authors describe a soft VLIW processor consisting of four, identical, 32-bit ALUs and a customizable hardware block for accelerating performance-critical loop kernels. The ALUs and the hardware block operate in parallel and are interconnected through a single, multi-ported, 32×32-bit register file. Our processor differs from this processor in several ways, and in Sect. 3 we describe its organization and architecture in more detail.

3   Processor Architecture

In this section we describe the datapath, instruction set architecture, and pipeline organization of our processor.

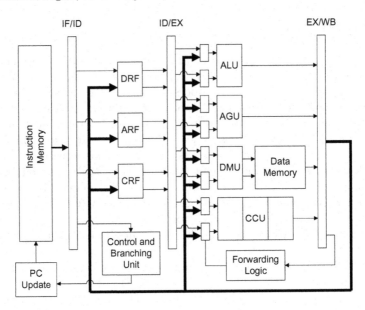

Fig. 1. Datapath of our soft VLIW processor

3.1 Datapath Organization

Figure 1 shows the datapath of our soft VLIW processor. The datapath can be configured to include any number of 16, 32, or 64-bit general-purpose functional units. These include arithmetic and logic units (ALUs), multiply-accumulate units (MACs), address generation units (AGUs), and data memory units (DMUs). AGUs compute data memory addresses and DMUs execute memory-access operations. Every DMU is connected to a single-ported data memory bank that is implemented using an on-chip RAM block. The datapath may also include a number of custom computational units (CCUs), which execute user-defined machine operations that are used to customize and extend the basic ISA. Finally, the datapath includes a single control and branching unit (CTL) that performs data movement, branching, and other control-flow operations.

The datapath also includes up to three distributed register files, each with a configurable number of registers and access ports. Distributed register files use fewer read and write ports, and are smaller and faster than a unified, multi-ported register file of the same aggregate size. The distributed register files include a data register file (DRF), an address register file (ARF), and an optional custom register file (CRF). Data can be transferred between the different register files using special data movement operations executed by the CTL unit.

Finally, to provide basic functionality, each processor must be configured with a minimal mix of functional units that includes one ALU, one AGU, and one DMU. These, in turn, require the use of the DRF and ARF. By default, each functional unit is 32 bits wide and each register file consists of 32 registers with

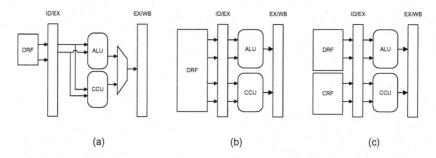

Fig. 2. Different ways for adding CCUs to the datapath

two read ports and one write port. For the remainder of this paper, we will refer to this configuration as our *base processor* (BP).

3.2 Instruction Set Architecture

Our processor executes a basic set of integer machine operations that resemble MIPS R2000 instructions [15]. Most operations, including data memory access operations, have a latency of one processor clock cycle. On the other hand, custom machine operations extend the basic instruction set and may have, depending on their complexities, multi-clock-cycle latencies.

The length of an instruction depends on the underlying datapath configuration since every functional unit in the datapath has a corresponding operation field in the instruction word. Although such instruction formats result in poor code density, several techniques are available to tackle this problem [3]. Since we are only interested in studying the effect of customization on the performance and area of the datapath, we do not address the issue of code density in this paper. Accordingly, we do not account for the area or latency of instruction memory in our results.

3.3 Custom Computational Units

Custom computational units (CCUs) are user-designed combinational logic blocks that realize custom machine operations in hardware. CCUs may be pipelined but do not have to be. Figure 2 shows three different ways for adding CCUs to the datapath. The first (Fig. 2(a)) extends the functionality of a regular functional unit by augmenting it with custom logic. Custom operations executing on such CCUs are constrained to only operate on a pair of operands, produce a single result, and have a latency of one processor clock cycle. Another way to add a CCU to the datapath is to cluster the CCU with other functional units that share a register file (Fig. 2(b)). This provides a tight coupling between the CCU and the other functional units, which enables the units to share and exchange data efficiently. However, this also requires additional register ports, which increase the size and latency of the register file. Finally, a CCU can be added to the datapath by connecting it to a dedicated CRF (Fig. 2(c)). This approach provides a looser coupling between the CCU and other functional units in the datapath, and requires explicit machine operations to move data between the CRF and other register files.

3.4 Pipeline Structure

Our base processor is designed around a classical, four-stage pipeline that includes instruction fetch (IF), instruction decode (ID), execute (EX), and write-back (WB) stages [15]. During the ID stage, long instructions fetched from instruction memory are decoded and their corresponding machine operations are dispatched for execution on the appropriate functional units. During the EX stage, these operations are executed in parallel on available functional units. Although most operations complete execution in a single clock cycle, some custome machine operations may require several clock cycles to complete. During this time, other operations, from later instructions, can continue executing on other functional units. Although this leads to out-of-order operation completion, which may lead to contention for register write ports and WAW hazards, both can easily be avoided through careful instruction scheduling. Contention for register write ports can also be eliminated by increasing the number of register write ports. Finally, the results of various operations are written back to the corresponding register files during the WB stage. To minimize the effect of RAW data hazards, data forwarding is used to bypass results between the WB and EX stages.

4 Microarchitecture Optimizations

In this section we describe the various microarchitectural optimizations we used to reduce the area of the datapath.

4.1 Hardware Multipliers

Contemporary FPGAs provide on-chip hardware multipliers that are faster and smaller alternatives to implementing multipliers using the logic resources of the FPGA. We used hardware multipliers to implement the MAC functional units in our datapath. To support 32×32 multiplications, each MAC unit uses four, 18×18, hardware multipliers.

Hardware multipliers can also be used to implement fast and area-efficient shifters since shifting a value by one bit position to the left is equivalent to multiplying it by two [16]. That is why we also used the hardware multipliers to implement arithmetic and logical shifters for the ALU functional unit. To support 32-bit shift operations, each shifter uses two, 18×18, hardware multipliers.

4.2 RAM Blocks

RAM blocks are memory cells embedded within the FPGA fabric and used to implement a wide range of storage devices [17]. Memory banks and register files

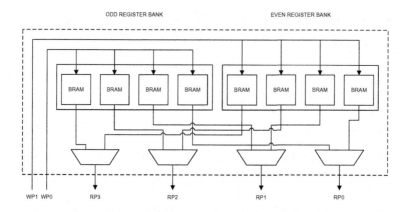

Fig. 3. Multiported register file with 4 read and 2 write ports

implemented using RAM blocks are faster and smaller than those implemented using the flips-flops found in FPGA logic blocks. The dual-ported RAM blocks embedded within the Xilinx Virtex-II FPGA we used for this study can each be configured to store 32- or 64-bit words. The two ports on each RAM block can also be configured to serve as read, write, or read/write ports.

We used RAM blocks in our processor to implement a distributed data memory bank. Every DMU in the datapath is connected to a dedicated RAM block, which enables multiple data words to be accessed simultaneously. Distributed data memory banks are commonly used in programmable DSPs and provide a fast, low-cost, and high-bandwidth alternative to a large, unified, multiported data memory bank.

We also used RAM blocks to implement multi-ported register files. Figure 3 shows how eight, dual-ported RAM blocks can be used to implement a register file with four read and two write ports. In general, a register file with M read ports and N write ports requires $M \times N$ RAM blocks distributed across N banks. Each bank stores duplicate copies of a *subset* of the registers and provides parallel access to this subset.

4.3   Selective Data Forwarding

Data forwarding is a well known technique for eliminating RAW data hazards in pipelined processors. In a VLIW datapath, the number of forwarding paths and the complexity of the forwarding logic grow in proportion to the number of functional units used in the datapath. When implemented in FPGAs, the area occupied by forwarding paths, multiplexers, and control logic can grow significantly. To reduce this area, we use *selective* data forwarding where only the forwarding paths actually needed to support performance-critical code blocks are maintained. Although this makes forwarding difficult in code blocks that have other bypassing needs, dependent operations in these blocks can be scheduled in a way that eliminates RAW hazards. If dependencies cannot be eliminated through code scheduling, NOPs can be inserted between dependent operations,

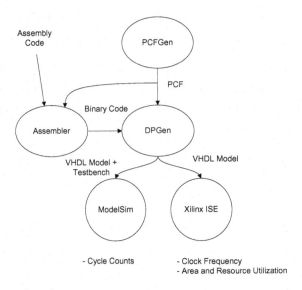

Fig. 4. Development tools and work flow

which, of course, degrades performance. Another solution exploits the field programmability of FPGAs to load processor configurations on a per-application basis to benefit from selective data forwarding without affecting execution performance. In this case, the only overhead is that involved in reprogramming the FPGA.

5   Development Tools

Configurable processors require a flexible tool chain that enables designers to quickly configure, generate, implement, and program new processor designs. Figure 4 shows the various tools we developed for our VLIW processor and the way they interact with each other. A key component in our tool chain is the processor configuration file (PCF), which captures the architectural and organizational parameters of a processor and is used to retarget both the datapath generator and the assembler. The PCF also describes the CCUs in the datapath and includes the VHDL implementations of their custom operations. PCFs are automatically generated by our processor configuration file generator (PCFGen), which provides a graphical user interface for specifying the architectural parameters of a target processor. The datapath generator (DPGen) extracts relevant information from the PCF and generates VHDL code and a testbench for the corresponding processor datapath. The retargettable assembler also extracts relevant information about the processor's ISA from the PCF and uses the information to generate long machine instructions in a binary format that matches the architecture of the target processor. To validate the functional behavior and measure the execution cycle counts of our processor, we used Mentor Graphics

Table 1. Kernel benchmarks

Benchmark	Description
FIB100	Computes the first 100 terms of the Fibonacci Series.
FACT100	Computes 100 factorial.
FIR256	Implements a 256-tap finite impulse response filter.
REV32	Implements 32-bit reverse.
SCB	Implements a bit scrambling function [18].
PUNC	Implements a bit puncturing function [18].
SAD16	Implements the 16×1 sum of absolute differences function [19].

ModelSim 6.0a. We also used Xilinx ISE 7.1 to synthesize and implement the corresponding datapaths in a 190 MHz Xilinx XCV2000-F896 Virtex-II FPGA. Finally, we used the various reports generated by the Xilinx tools to measure processor clock frequencies and FPGA resource utilization.

6   Results

In this section we present the outcomes of different experiments that illustrate the performance and area trade-offs due to datapath and ISA customization of various soft VLIW datapaths. Since we still do not have a working high-level C compiler, we developed short assembly-language routines to assess the impact of specific architectural configurations on performance and area. To ensure our results reflect typical design trade-offs, we chose our kernel benchmarks from a range of embedded application domains. Table 1 shows the different kernel benchmarks we developed for this study.

In our results, we report the execution performance of a given benchmark as its wall clock execution time. This is computed as the product of the dynamic cycle count for the benchmark, obtained from the ModelSim behavioral simulation, and the processor clock cycle time, obtained from the Xilinx XST synthesis report. We also report the area for a given datapath implementation in terms of the number of FPGA slices, RAM blocks, and hardware multipliers used. These numbers are also obtained from the Xilinx XST synthesis report.

6.1   Base Processor vs. Xilinx MicroBlaze

In our first experiment, we compared the performance and area of our base processor with the Xilinx MicroBlaze soft processor. Tables 2 and 3 summarize the performance and area of different implementations of our base processor (BP and BP+MAC) with those of the MicroBlaze (MB and MB+MUL) when executing two general-purpose computational kernels. To avoid giving our VLIW processor an unfair performance advantage, we made sure both kernels did not exploit any parallelism.

Our results show that our base processor is 1.42 to 2.23 times faster than the MicroBlaze when executing the FIB100 benchmark and 2.11 to 3.23 times faster when executing the FACT100 benchmark. The higher performance of our

Table 2. Base processor vs. MicroBlaze

FIB100	BP			MB
	FULL	SEL	NO	
INSTR LENGTH	114	114	114	32
INSTR COUNT	5	5	8	8
CYCLE COUNT	305	305	605	707
CLOCK (MHz)	100.3	126.5	126.5	104.4
EXEC TIME (μs)	3.04	2.41	4.78	6.77
SLICES	1,520	931	907	1,032
BRAMS	11	11	11	4
MULT18×18	2	2	2	0

Table 3. Base processor + MAC vs. MicroBlaze + multiplier

FACT100	BP+MAC			MB+MUL
	FULL	SEL	NO	
INSTR LENGTH	132	132	132	32
INSTR COUNT	4	4	6	5
CYCLE COUNT	205	205	405	706
CLOCK (MHz)	98.0	126.5	126.5	104.4
EXEC TIME (μs)	2.09	1.62	3.20	6.76
SLICES	2,086	1,098	1,040	1,069
BRAMS	14	14	14	4
MULT18×18	6	6	6	3

processor is mainly due to lower cycle counts, which are achieved because of low-overhead looping operations. These operations are part of the base instruction set and are used to eliminate test-and-branch operations in conditional loops. The higher performance is also due to faster processor clock frequencies, particularly when selective and no data forwarding are used (cf. columns labeled SEL and NO, respectively), which are due to the deeper pipeline of our processor. When full forwarding is used (cf. columns labeled FULL), longer delays in the datapath cause our processor to achieve clock frequencies that are comparable to the MicroBlaze. When no data forwarding is used, the cycle counts in our processors increase significantly due to additional NOP operations that must be inserted in the code to eliminate RAW data hazards.

Our results also show that our base processor uses 0.88 to 1.47 times the slices used by the MicroBlaze. When we add a multiplier unit to both processors, our processor uses 0.97 to 1.95 times the slices used by the MicroBlaze. When full forwarding is used, our processors use more slices due to additional forwarding logic and data paths. On the other hand, when selective or no data forwarding are used, our processors use fewer slices. However, since the MicroBlaze uses additional logic to implement bus interfaces and support interrupts, these results are slightly skewed in our favor. Finally, since our processors use distributed register files with a large number of read ports they use significantly more RAM blocks than the MicroBlaze.

Table 4. Impact of customizing the datapath to exploit ILP

FIR256	BP+MAC			BP+MAC+DRF2W			FIR+DRF3W+ARF2W		
	FULL	SEL	NO	FULL	SEL	NO	FULL	SEL	NO
INSTR LENGTH	132	132	132	131	131	131	187	187	187
INSTR COUNT	9	9	14	8	8	13	5	5	11
CYCLE COUNT	774	774	1,287	519	519	1,032	262	262	776
CLOCK (MHz)	98.0	126.5	126.5	97.6	129.8	129.8	84.5	97.6	97.6
EXEC TIME (μs)	7.90	6.12	10.17	5.32	4.00	7.95	3.10	2.68	7.95
SLICES	2,086	1,050	1,040	2,327	1,393	1,359	3,019	3,012	3,000
BRAMS	14	14	14	22	22	22	45	45	45
MULT18×18	6	6	6	6	6	6	6	6	6

6.2   Customizing the Datapath to Exploit ILP

In our second experiment, we studied the effects of customizing the datapath to support instruction-level parallelism. For this experiment, we used the FIR256 kernel because it exhibits high levels of parallelism, and we examined three processor implementations with progressively increasing support for parallelism: the base processor augmented with a MAC unit (BP+MAC); BP+MAC with a two-write-port DRF (BP+MAC+DRF2W); and a custom datapath that includes 1 ALU, 1 MAC, 2 AGUs, 2 DMUs, a three-write-port DRF, and a two-write-port ARF (FIR+DRF3W+ARF2W). Table 4 summaries our results.

Our result show that as support for parallelism increases in the datapath, performance increases accordingly. For example, with full forwarding, BP+MAC+DRF2W and FIR+DRF3W+ARF2W are 1.49 and 2.55 times faster than BP+MAC, respectively. This is mainly due to lower cycle counts, which are a direct consequence of exploiting higher levels of parallelism. On the other hand, supporting higher levels of parallelism increases datapath complexity, which reduces processor clock frequency. Still, the result is a net improvement in performance. Performance can be further improved by using selective forwarding. For example, using selective forwarding, BP+MAC, BP+MAC+DRF2W, and FIR+DRF3W+ARF2W are 1.29, 1.98, and 2.94 times faster, respectively, than BP+MAC with full forwarding. This is mainly due to the faster processor clock frequencies that can be derived by reducing the complexity of the datapath. Finally, when no data forwarding is used, and despite higher clock frequencies, performance is consistently poorer than BP+MAC with full forwarding. This is mainly due to the excessive overhead introduced by NOP operations used to eliminate RAW data hazards.

Our results also show that supporting parallelism increases the number of FPGA resources used to implement the datapath. For example, when full forwarding is used, BP+MAC+DRF2W and FIR+DRF3W+ARF2W use 1.12 and 2.16 times as many slices as BP+MAC, respectively. Although the number of slices can be reduced significantly by using selective or no data forwarding, the savings must be weighed against the resulting levels of performance. When no data forwarding is used, the savings are achieved at the expense of degraded performance. Finally, the

Table 5. Impact of customizing a functional unit

REV32	BP		BP+REVAGU	
	FULL	NO	FULL	NO
INSTR LENGTH	114	114	114	114
INSTR COUNT	11	14	1	1
CYCLE COUNT	200	296	4	4
CLOCK (MHz)	100.3	126.5	100.3	130.9
EXEC TIME (μs)	1.99	2.34	0.04	0.03
SLICES	1,520	907	1,527	929
BRAMS	11	11	11	11
MULT18×18	2	2	2	2

number of RAM blocks used in BP+MAC+DRF2W and FIR+DRF3W+ARF2W is 1.57 and 3.21 times the number used in BP+MAC, respectively, due to the increased number of read and write ports in both register files.

6.3   Adding a Custom Operation to the AGU

In our third experiment, we studied the effect of adding a bit-reverse operation to the base instruction set by augmenting the AGU with custom logic. We used the REV32 benchmark to compare the performance and area of our base processor (BP) with another implementation of BP that uses an augmented AGU (BP+REVAGU). Table 5 summarizes our results, which show that the custom operation in BP+REVAGU is 50.00 to 76.57 times faster than a software implementation executing on BP when full and no data forwarding are used, respectively. The higher performance is due to the significantly lower cycle count achieved by using the custom operation, and, in the case of no data forwarding, the higher processor clock frequency. Our results also show that the impact of adding the custom operation on FPGA resources is negligible. This is due to the simple implementation of the bit-reverse operation, which requires a few additional slices only. It is also due to the microarchitectural constraints on adding custom logic to a functional unit, which do not affect the number of register ports and keep the number of RAM blocks in the datapath constant.

6.4   Adding Multi-cycle CCUs to the Datapath

In our fourth experiment, we studied the effects of customizing the instruction set by adding three, different, non-pipelined CCUs to the datapath. The SCB CCU implements a bit scrambling function used in WLAN OFDM modems [18]. It uses two 32-bit inputs, produces a single 32-bit output, and has a latency of eight clock cycles. The PUNC CCU implements a bit puncturing function, which is also used in the convolutional encoders and interleavers of WLAN OFDM modems [18]. It uses four 32-bit inputs, produces one 32-bit output, and has a latency of 16 clock cycles. Finally, the SAD16 CCU implements the 16 × 1 sum-of-absolute-differences function, which is used for motion estimation

Table 6. Impact of adding multi-cycle CCUs to the datapath

SCB	BP		BP+DRFSCB		BP+CRFSCB	
	FULL	NO	FULL	NO	FULL	NO
INSTR LENGTH	114	114	152	152	153	153
INSTR COUNT	9	12	1	1	4	4
CYCLE COUNT	162	255	11	11	14	14
CLOCK (MHz)	100.3	126.5	76.8	133.0	73.8	114.0
EXEC TIME (μs)	1.62	2.02	0.14	0.08	0.19	0.12
SLICES	1,520	907	2,077	1,188	2,103	1,314
BRAMS	11	11	13	13	16	16
MULT18×18	2	2	2	2	2	2
PUNC	BP		BP+DRFPUNC		BP+CRFPUNC	
	FULL	NO	FULL	NO	FULL	NO
INSTR LENGTH	114	114	155	155	157	157
INSTR COUNT	37	49	1	1	6	6
CYCLE COUNT	366	503	19	19	24	24
CLOCK (MHz)	100.3	126.5	43.1	82.9	71.6	82.9
EXEC TIME (μs)	3.65	3.98	0.44	0.23	0.34	0.29
SLICES	1,520	907	5,112	4,036	5,027	4,158
BRAMS	11	11	16	16	19	19
MULT18×18	2	2	2	2	2	2
SAD16	BP		BP+DRFSAD16		BP+CRFSAD16	
	FULL	NO	FULL	NO	FULL	NO
INSTR LENGTH	114	114	200	200	202	202
INSTR COUNT	42	62	1	1	10	10
CYCLE COUNT	153	233	4	4	16	16
CLOCK (MHz)	100.3	126.5	61.9	112.9	62.7	114.0
EXEC TIME (μs)	1.53	1.84	0.06	0.04	0.26	0.14
SLICES	1,520	907	2,785	1,419	2,303	1,559
BRAMS	11	11	19	19	22	22
MULT18×18	2	2	2	2	2	2

in MPEG4 video encoders [19]. It uses eight 32-bit inputs, produces one 32-bit output, and has a latency of four clock cycles. For each of these CCUs we created two processor implementations: one that connects the CCU to the DRF (BP+DRFSCB, BP+DRFPUNC, and BP+DRFSAD16) and another that connects the CCU to a dedicated 32 × 32-bit CRF (BP+CRFSCB, BP+CRFPUNC, and BP+CRFSAD16). Moreover, for each implementation, we considered the cases where full and no data forwarding were used, respectively. We then compared these processors to our base processor when executing the SCB, PUNC, and SAD16 kernels, which are software implementations of the corresponding CCU functions. Table 6 summarizes our results.

Our results show that, when connected to the DRF, the CCUs increase the performance of the BP by factors of 8.28 to 23.61 when full forwarding is used, and 15.92 to 43.06 when no forwarding is used. This is mainly due to the significantly lower cycle counts achieved when implementing the CCU functions in hardware. However, it is worth noting that in most cases the additional complexity resulting from introducing CCUs to the datapath also decreases the processor clock frequency. Still, the net effect is an improvement in performance. Our results also show that when full forwarding is used, the number of FPGA slices used by the CCU-enhanced datapaths is 1.37 to 3.38 times greater than those used by the BP, and that they use more RAM blocks. This is due to the additional logic required to implement the CCUs, additional forwarding paths and logic, and support for more DRF read ports. When no data forwarding is used, the CCU-enhanced datapaths use significantly less FPGA slices. However, these still correspond to 1.31 to 4.45 times the number of slices used by the BP. On the other hand, the number of RAM blocks used by each processor remains the same.

Our results also show that, when connected to a dedicated CRF, the CCUs increase the performance of the BP by factors of 5.98 to 10.89 when full forwarding is used, and 10.87 to 13.15 when no forwarding is used. This, again, is due to the significantly lower cycle counts achieved by implementing the CCU functions in hardware. However, these generally lower levels of performance are due to the overhead of transferring data and results between the DRF and the CRF, and the lower processor clock frequencies resulting from introducing the CCUs to the datapath. Our results also show that the number of FPGA slices used by the CCU-enhanced datapaths are 1.38 to 3.31 times greater than those used by the BP, and that they also use more RAM blocks. Again, this is due to the additional logic required to implement the CCUs, additional forwarding paths and logic, and the new CRF. When no data forwarding is used, the CCU-enhanced datapaths use significantly less FPGA slices, but still amount to 1.45 and 4.58 times the number of slices used by the BP. However, the number of RAM blocks used by each processor remains the same.

7   Conclusions and Future Work

In this paper, we described the architecture and microarchitecture of a customizable soft VLIW processor. We also described the tools we developed to customize, generate, and program this processor. We also examined the performance and area trade-offs achieved by customizing the processor's datapath and instruction set architecture. The following points summarize our main results and conclusions.

1. As with hard processors, careful design of the instruction-set architecture and the pipeline has a significant impact on performance. Without exploiting ILP, our soft processor ran 1.42 to 3.23 times faster than the Xilinx MicroBlaze processor due to a low-overhead looping operation and a faster clock frequency achieved by using a deeper pipeline. Using available FPGA resources, such as hardware multipliers and block memories, and implementing microarchitectural optimizations such as selective data forwarding also reduce the complexity and area of the datapath and contribute to increasing the processor clock frequency.

2. Duplicating functional units and increasing the number of register ports to exploit instruction-level parallelism improves execution performance, particularly when coupled with selective data forwarding. However, the increased performance is achieved at the cost of increased FPGA resource utilization. Although selective or no data forwarding can be used to reduce resource utilization, the savings must be weighed against the achievable levels of performance.

3. Augmenting a functional unit with custom logic can achieve significant improvements in performance while having little impact on FPGA resource utilization. While the resulting improvement in performance is due to implementing the logic function in hardware, the limited impact on resource utilization is due to the microarchitectural constraints on adding custom logic to a functional unit.

4. Adding a CCU to the datapath can achieve high levels of performance while using up significant FPGA resources. The higher performance is due to implementing custom operations in hardware, while the increased resource utilization is due to implementing CCU logic, forwarding paths, and additional registers or register ports. Our results show that connecting the CCU to the data register file achieves better performance than connecting it to a dedicated custom register file due to the lower overhead of transferring data between different register files.

Having demonstrated the value of datapath and ISA customization, we will next be focusing on developing an optimizing compiler for our processor and an architectural exploration framework for automating the customization tasks.

References

1. MicroBlaze Processor Reference Guide. http://www.xilinx.com.
2. NIOS-II Processor Reference Handbook. http://www.altera.com.
3. J. A. Fisher, P. Faraboschi, and C. Young, *Embedded Computing: A VLIW Approach to Architecture, Compilers, and Tools*, Morgan Kaufmann Publishers/Elsevier, 2005.
4. P. Faraboschi, G. Brown, and J. A. Fisher, "Lx: A Technology Platform for Customizable VLIW Embedded Processing", *Proceedings of the 27th International Symposium on Computer Architecture (ISCA 2000)*, pp. 203–213, ACM/IEEE, May, 2000.
5. D. Jain et al. "Automatically Customizing VLIW Architectures with Coarse-Grained Application-Specific Functional Units", *Proceedings of the Eighth International Workshop on Software and Compilers for Embedded Systems (SCOPES 2004)*, pp. 17–32, Springer Berlin/Heidelberg, Sept. 2-3, 2004.
6. http://www.arc.com.
7. T. Halfhill, "Tensilica Tackles Bottlenecks: New Xtensa LX Configurable Processor Shatters Industry Benchmarks", *Microprocessor Report*, In-Stat/MDR, May 31, 2004.
8. A. Lodi et al., "A VLIW Processor With Reconfigurable Instruction Set for Embedded Applications", *IEEE Journal of Solid-State Circuits*, pp. 1876–1886, Vol. 38, No. 11, November, 2003.

9. N. Vassiliadis et al., "A RISC Architecture Extended by an Efficient Tightly Coupled Reconfigurable Unit", *Proceedings of the 2005 International Workshop on Applied Reconfigurable Computing (ARC 2005)*, pp. 41–49, Feb. 22-23, 2005.
10. S. Vassiliadis et al., "The MOLEN Ploymorphic Processor", *IEEE Transactions on Computers*, pp. 1363–1375, Vol. 53, No. 11, November, 2004.
11. P. Yiannacouras, J. Rose, and J. G. Steffan, "The Microarchitecture of FPGA-Based Soft Processors", *Proceedings of the 2005 International Conference on Compilers, Architectures, and Synthesis for Embedded Systems, (CASES 2005)*, pp. 202–212, ACM, Sept. 24-27, 2005.
12. P. Yiannacouras, J. G. Steffan, and J. Rose, "Application-Specific Customization of Soft Processor Microarchitecture", *Proceedings of the 14th ACM/SIGDA International Symposium on Field-Programmable Gate Arrays (FPGA 2006)*, pp. 201–210, ACM, Feb. 22-24, 2006.
13. A. Jones et al., "A 64-way VLIW/SIMD FPGA Architecture and Design Flow", *Proceedings of the 11th IEEE International Conference on Electronics, Circuits, and Systems (ICECS 2004)*, pp. 499–502, IEEE, Dec. 13-15, 2004.
14. A. Jones et al., "An FPGA-based VLIW Processor with Custom Hardware Execution", *Proceedings of the 13th ACM/SIGDA International Symposium on Field-Programmable Gate Arrays (FPGA 2005)*, pp. 107–117, ACM, Feb. 20-22, 2005.
15. D. A. Patterson and J. L. Hennessey, *Computer Organization and Design: The Hardware/Software Interface*, Third Edition, Morgan Kaufmann Publishers, 2004.
16. Xilinx Corportaion, "Using Embedded Multipliers in Spartan-3 FPGAs", *Xilinx Application Note XAPP467 (v1.1)*, May 13, 2003.
17. Xilinx Corportaion, "Using Block RAM in Spartan-3 Generation FPGAs", *Xilinx Application Note XAPP463 (v2.0)*, March 1, 2005.
18. S. H. Jeong, M. H. Sunwoo, and S. K. Oh, "Bit Manipulation Accelerator for Communication Systems Digital Signal Processor", *EURASIP Journal on Applied Signal Processing*, Vol. 2005:16, pp. 2655–2663, 2005.
19. S. Wong, S. Vassiliadis, and S. Cotofana, "A Sum of Absoulte Differences Implementation in FPGA Hardware", *Proceedings of the 28th EUROMICRO Conference*, pp. 183–188, Sept. 4-6, 2002.

Instruction Set Extension Generation with Considering Physical Constraints

I-Wei Wu, Shih-Chia Huang, Chung-Ping Chung, and Jyh-Jiun Shann

Dept. of Computer Science, National Chiao Tung University, Hsinchu, Taiwan
gis93808@csie.nctu.edu.tw, shihchia@csie.nctu.edu.tw,
cpchung@cs.nctu.edu.tw

Abstract. In this paper, we propose new algorithms for both ISE exploration and selection with considering important physical constraints such as pipestage timing and instruction set architecture (ISA) format, silicon area and register file. To handle these considerations, an ISE exploration algorithm is proposed. It not only explores ISE candidates but also their implementation option to minimize the execution time meanwhile using less silicon area. In ISE selection, many researches only take silicon area into account, but it is not comprehensive. In this paper, we formulate ISE selection as a multiconstrained 0-1 knapsack problem so that it can consider multiple constraints. Results with MiBench indicate that under same number of ISE, our approach achieves 69.43%, 1.26% and 33.8% (max., min. and avg., respectively) of further reduction in silicon area and also has maximally 1.6% performance improvement compared with the previous one.

Keywords: Instruction set extension, ASIP, Extensible Processors, Pipestage Timing Constraint.

1 Introduction

Instruction set extension (ISE) is an effective means of meeting the growing efficiency demands for both circuit and speed in many applications. Because most applications frequently execute the same several instruction patterns, grouping these instruction patterns into instructions in ISE is an effective way to enhance the performance. For simplicity, instruction(s) in ISE are called ISE(s) hereinafter. ISEs are realized by application specific functional units (ASFU) within the execution stage of the pipeline. Notably, since this work adopts a load-store architecture, the ASFU cannot access data directly from main memory.

The ISE design flow, as illustrated in Figure 1, comprises application profiling, basic block (BB) selection and ISE generation which consists of ISE exploration and selection phases. After profiling, BBs are selected as the input of ISE exploration based on their execution time. ISE exploration explores frequently executed instruction patterns as ISE candidates, which have to conform to predefined physical constraints, including ISA format, pipestage timing and instruction/operation types. In other words, ISE exploration determines which operation in BB should be implemented in hardware (i.e. ASFU) or software (i.e. executed in CPU core). Apart from exploring ISE candidate(s),

K. De Bosschere et al. (Eds.): HiPEAC 2007, LNCS 4367, pp. 291–305, 2007.

the proposed algorithm also explores the hardware implementation option for each ISE candidate. After generating ISE candidates, ISE selection chooses as many ISEs as possible to attain the highest performance improvement under predefined physical constraints, such as silicon area and ISA format.

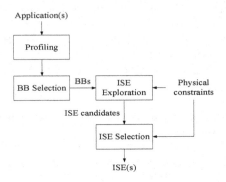

Fig. 1. ISE design flow

In ISE generation, many investigations overlook several important physical constraints, e.g., pipestage timing, instruction set architecture (ISA) format, silicon area and register file, or only consider them in part. These physical constraints are described as follows:

Pipestage Timing
The pipestage timing constraint refers to a situation in which the execution time of ASFU should fit in the original pipestage, i.e. be an integral number of original pipeline cycles. In ISE exploration, to achieve the highest speed-up ratio, most works [3, 4, 5, 6, 7, 8 and 9] may deploy the fastest implementation option for each operation in ASFU. Nevertheless, the fastest implementation option may not be the best choice unless it can make the execution time of ASFU to fit in the original pipestage. Most operations in ASFU often have multiple hardware implementation options owing to different area requirements and speed limitations. Under pipestage timing constraint, we believe that an ASFU using miser hardware implementation option, i.e. less silicon area, has a manufacturing cost benefit.

Instruction Set Architecture (ISA) Format
The ISA format represents two constraints. The first constraint limits the number of input/output operands employed by an ISE. The second constraint is the number of ISEs. That is, the number of ISEs generally cannot exceed the number of unused opcodes.

Silicon Area
The silicon area constraint restricts the total silicon area utilized by the ASFU.

Register File
The Register file constraint resembles the first constraint of the ISA format. Under the register file constraint, the number of input/output operands adopted by an ISE cannot exceed the number of read/write ports of the register file.

To handle these constraints, new algorithms are proposed for both ISE exploration and selection. The ISE exploration algorithm is derived from the ant colony optimization (ACO) algorithm [1, 2]. In contrast with previous studies [3, 4, 5, 6, 7, 8 and 9], the proposed ISE exploration algorithm not only explores ISE candidates, but also their hardware implementation option, thus minimizing the execution time and reducing the silicon area. In ISE selection, many studies [10, 11] only address the silicon area. We believe that ISE selection should at least consider the silicon area, ISA format and register file constraints. To comply with multiple constraints, ISE selection is formulated as a multiconstrained 0-1 knapsack problem, which is polynomial time solvable using a greedy or genetic algorithm. Results with MiBench reveal that under same number of ISE, the proposed approach achieves 69.43%, 1.26% and 33.8% (max., min. and avg., respectively) of further reduction in silicon area, and also has maximally 1.6% performance improvement over the previous one [3]. Conversely, under the same silicon area constraint, the proposed approach reaches up to 3.85%, 0.97% and 2.17% (max., min. and avg., respectively) more speedup than the previous one [3].

This study has the following contributions:

1.   An ISE exploration algorithm is proposed, which explores not only ISE candidates, but also their hardware implementation options, thus increasing the silicon area that can be reserved.
2.   The proposed ISE exploration algorithm not only significantly lowers silicon area cost, but also enhances performance over the previous algorithm.
3.   The proposed ISE exploration algorithm can explore a search space comprising hundreds of instructions in a few minutes, and has a near-optimal solution.
4.   ISE selection is formulated as a multiconstrained 0-1 knapsack problem, such that it can conform to multiple constraints.

The rest of this work is structured as follows. Section 2 studies the previous related work. Section 3 and 4 then presents the proposed approach. Next, Section 5 presents the simulation results and discussion. Conclusions are finally drawn in Section 6.

2   Relative Work

2.1   Relative Works

Instruction Set Extension (ISE) generation in most works [3, 4, 5, 6, 7, 8, 9, 10 and 11] can be divided into two phases: ISE exploration and ISE selection.

ISE exploration
Pozzi [3] proposed an algorithm, called the exact algorithm, to examine all possible ISE candidates such that it can obtain an optimal solution. The exact algorithm maps the ISE search space, such as a basic block, to a binary tree, and then discards some portion of the tree that violates predefined constraints. Nevertheless, this algorithm is highly computing-intensive, so does not process a larger search space. For instance, if a BB has N operations, and each operation has only one hardware implementation option, then it has 2N possible ISE patterns (legal or illegal). Notably, one ISE candidate may represent one or multiple legal ISE pattern(s). When N = 100 (the

standard case), then the number of possible ISE patterns is 2100. Obviously, this number of patterns cannot be computed in a reasonable time. To decrease the computing complexity, heuristic algorithms derived from genetic [3], Kernighan-Lin (KL) [4] and greedy algorithms [5] have been developed.

Yu [6] investigated the effect of various constraints, such as ISA format, hardware area and control flow, for ISE generation. Such constraints restrict the performance improvement of the ISEs. The ISA format limits the number of read and write ports to the register file. The limitation of the control flow is whether the search space can cross basic block boundaries. To meet real-time constraints, the search spaces are identified based on whether they locate on the worst-case execution path rather than the execution time, as in [7]. This is because the most frequently executed basic block or instruction may not contribute to the worst-case execution path. The granularity of each vertex within the search space can be varied from one instruction to multiple subroutine calls [8]. Borin also claim that one search space can consist of multiple basic blocks in their proposed algorithm. From a different perspective, Peymandoust [9] characterized each basic block as a polynomial representation. First, the multiple-input single-output (MISO) algorithm extracts symbolic algebraic patterns from the search spaces, and represents them as polynomials on behalf of ISE candidates. These ISE candidates are then mapped to the polynomial representations of program segments using symbolic algebraic manipulations. Nevertheless, some algorithms [3, 4, 5, 6, 7, 8 and 9] do not consider the pipestage timing constraint, and therefore waste silicon area unnecessarily.

ISE selection

Cong [10] transformed ISE selection into an area minimization problem. The area minimization problem has been widely studied in the logic synthesis domain. Das [11] presented another algorithm, using divide-and-conquer searching to solve ISE selection. However, Cong [10] and Das [11], only addressed silicon area constraint in ISE selection, but it is not comprehensive. We believe that ISE selection should at least consider the silicon area, ISA format and register file constraints.

Additionally, to lower the hardware cost, Clark [5] added a new phase, called ISE combination, between ISE exploration and ISE selection, to merge multiple similar ISE candidates.

3 ISE Exploration

ISE exploration in this paper not only identifies frequently executed instruction patterns as ISE candidates, but also evaluates hardware implementation options of each operation in ISE candidates to minimize the execution time while using less silicon area. The input and output of ISE exploration algorithm are BBs and ISE candidates, respectively, as well as their hardware implementation options. The implementation option(s) of an operation denote(s) its implementation method(s), and can be roughly divided into two categories, namely hardware and software.

The flow of ISE exploration is briefly described as follows. Each input BB is first transformed to a data flow graph (DFG). Then, an implementation option (IO) table representing all implementation options for an operation is appended to each operation in a DFG. After appending IO table in DFG, ISE exploration algorithm is repeatedly executed until no ISE candidate can be discovered. Significantly, the ISE exploration algorithm identifies one or multiple ISE candidate(s) at each round. A round usually consists of multiple iterations.

At each iteration, the ISE exploration algorithm initially selects one implementation option in each operation according to a probability value (p), which is a function of trail and merit values. The meaning of trail is the same with the pheromone in the ACO algorithm, i.e. how many times an implementation option is chosen in previous iterations. The merit value is the benefit of one implementation option being chosen. The trail value is updated after making a choice. The algorithm then evaluates all implementation options of each operation in DFG, i.e. it computes their merit value using merit function. This process is iteratively performed until the probability values (p) of all operations in DFG have exceeded a predefined threshold value, P_END.

3.1 Implementation Option

According to the profiling results, a BB with longer execution time is transformed to a DFG, which is represented by a directed acyclic graph $G(V,E)$ where V denotes a set

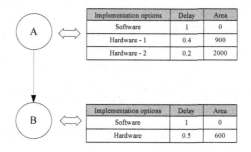

Fig. 2. An example of G^+

of vertices, and E represents a set of directed edges. Every vertex $v \in V$ is an assembly instruction, called an "operation" or "node" hereafter in BB. Each edge $(u,v) \in E$ from operation u to operation v signifies that the execution of operation v needs the data generated by operation u.

To represent all implementation options for an operation, a table, called implementation option (IO) table, is added to every operation. Each entry in the IO table comprises three fields, namely implementation option, delay and area. The name of implementation option is shown in implementation option field. Obviously, using software implementation option for an operation requires at least one execution cycle, but does not introduce any extra silicon cost. Conversely, using the hardware implementation option can reduce the number of execution cycle, but increases the silicon area consumed. The delay and area denote the execution time and the extra silicon area cost of one implementation option, respectively. A new graph G^+ is generated after the IO table is added to G. Figure 2 shows an example of G^+, consisting of two operations, A and B.

3.2 ISE Exploration Algorithm

The ISE exploration algorithm is derived from the ACO algorithm. As with the ACO algorithm, the implementation option would be chosen according to its probability value (p). The probability value (p) of each implementation option in an operation is its probability of being selected at each iteration of the ISE exploration algorithm. Notably, selecting the implementation option based on the probability value (p) is to avoid local optimal solutions as much as possible. The probability value ($p_{x,j}$) of implementation option j in operation x is a function of the trail and the merit values, as revealed in Equation (1). The significance of the trail value is identical to that of the pheromone in the ACO algorithm, and reveals the number of times that an implementation option is selected in previous iterations. Here, the trail value of implementation option j in operation x is denoted by $trail_{x,j}$, and $trail_{x,0}$ is designated as the trail value of software implementation option. The trail value, like the pheromone, must be updated after each iteration. The merit value is defined as the benefit of one implementation option being selected, and it is obtained using the merit function, which is described in detail later. The merit value of implementation option j in operation x is represented by $merit_{x,j}$, and $merit_{x,0}$ is designated as the merit value of the software implementation option. The probability of implementation option j in operation x being chosen ($p_{x,j}$) is derived with:

$$p_{x,j} = \frac{\alpha \cdot trail_{x,j} + (1-\alpha) \cdot merit_{x,j}}{\sum_{j=0}^{k} (\alpha \cdot trail_{x,j} + (1-\alpha) \cdot merit_{x,j})} \quad , \ 0 \leq j \leq k \text{ and } 0 \leq \alpha \leq 1 \tag{1}$$

where k is the number of hardware implementation options in operation x, and α is utilized to determine the relative influence of trail and merit, and

$$\sum_{j=0}^{k} p_{x,j} = 1 \tag{2}$$

Figure 3 shows the proposed ISE exploration algorithm. Here, a DFG is assumed to have m ($m > 0$) operations, each with n ($n > 0$) implementation options. Initially, i.e. in step 1, the algorithm sets initial values for the trail and merit values of each implementation option of all operations. Notably, the hardware implementation options have higher initial merit values than software one, because the algorithm is designed to preferentially choose the hardware implementation option at the start of execution. In step 2, the algorithm verifies all operations to determine whether they have hardware implementation options. If yes, then the algorithm selects one implementation option in each operation based on the probability value; if no, then it selects the software implementation option.

In Step 3, the ISE exploration algorithm updates the trail value of each implementation option in all operations according to the implementation option that is chosen.

The trail value of the chosen implementation option is raised ρ, a positive constant value, while those of others are reduced. The ISE exploration algorithm in Step 4 derives the merit value of each implementation option in all operations. As in Step 2, the algorithm first checks each operation to determine whether it has a hardware implementation option. If yes, then the ISE exploration algorithm executes the Hardware Grouping function, which determines whether an operation can be grouped with its reachable operations as a virtual ISE candidate. If it can be grouped, then the Hardware-Grouping function adopts this virtual ISE candidate to obtain the execution time and silicon area for every hardware implementation option in this operation. The Hardware-Grouping function is described in detail later. The ISE exploration algorithm then computes the merit value with the merit function. Finally, the ISE exploration algorithm checks the end condition in Step 5. If the end condition is not fulfilled, then the ISE exploration algorithm returns to step 2 and enters the next iteration; otherwise, it terminates.

The end condition is that for all operations in DFG, the probability value (p) of one of implementation options exceeds P_END, which is a predefined threshold value and is very close to 100%. A larger P_END has a higher opportunity of obtaining a better result, but typically takes a longer time to converge. An implementation option with the probability value (p) above P_END is called a taken implementation option. An ISE candidate is a set of reachable nodes (i.e. operations) all of which have taken hardware implementation option in the DFG.

---

1.   (Initialization)
    For implementation option j ($j=0$ to n) of operation x ($x=1$ to m) in DFG
        $trail_{x,j} = 0$;
        If ($j=0$)
                $merit_{x,0}$ = initial value of software implementation option;
        Else
                $merit_{x,j}$ = initial value of hardware implementation option;
2.   (Calculating probability value (p) and choosing implementation option)
    For operation x ($x=1$ to m)
        If (x has hardware implementation option)
            For implementation option j ($j=0$ to n) in operation x
                Calculate $p_{x,j}$;
            Choose one implementation option according to its probability value (p);
        Else
            Choose software implementation option;
3.   (Trail update)
    For implementation option j ($j=0$ to n) of operation x ($x=1$ to m) in DFG
    If the implementation option is selected
        $trail_{x,j} = trail_{x,j} + \rho$;
    Else
        $trail_{x,j} = trail_{x,j} - \rho$;
4.   (Calculating merit)
    For operation x ($x=1$ to m)
        If (x has hardware implementation option)
            For implementation option j ($j=1$ to n) in operation x
                Execute Hardware_Grouping;
                Calculate $merit_{x,j}$;
5.   (Terminating condition)
    If not (end_condition) **goto** step 2;

Fig. 3. ISE Exploration Algorithm

Hardware-Grouping

If operation x has a hardware implementation option, then a function, called Hardware-Grouping, must be performed before computing the merit value. Hardware-Grouping checks whether the operation x can be grouped with its reachable nodes (i.e. operations) as a virtual ISE candidate; if yes, it recursively groups operation x with its reachable nodes, which have chosen hardware implementation option in the previous iteration, as a virtual ISE candidate, i.e. a virtual subgraph vS_x. The result of Hardware-Grouping of operation x using implementation option j is denoted as $vS_{x,j}$. Significantly, $vS_{x,0}$ is meaningless, since implementation option 0 is the software option. Using $vS_{x,j}$, Hardware-Grouping measures the execution time and silicon area of $vS_{x,j}$. Notably, the execution time of $vS_{x,j}$ is the critical path time in $vS_{x,j}$, and the silicon area of $vS_{x,j}$ is the sum of silicon areas used by all operations in $vS_{x,j}$.

Merit Function

The merit function determines the benefit, i.e. merit value, of different implementation options in an operation. Briefly, the merit function consists of three cases, size checking (case 1), constraints violation determination (case 2) and benefit calculating (case 3). Figure 4 shows the merit function algorithm. Notably, the merit of software implementation option ($merit_{x,0}$) is always set as a constant to be a baseline. Initially, in case 1, the algorithm checks whether $size(vS_{x,j})$, which is the number of operation in $vS_{x,j}$, is equal to 1. Notably, this work assumes that every operation is one-cycle delay in original processor specification. If a multiple-cycle delay is assumed, then case 1 should be tailored to fit this situation. If $size(vS_{x,j}) = 1$, then $vS_{x,j}$ only has one operation x, and therefore the performance cannot be improved. Therefore, the algorithm multiplies the merit value of the hardware implementation option by a constant β_1 ($0 < \beta_1 < 1$) to lower the chance of it being chosen. The calculation of the merit function is then terminated. If no, then goto case 2.

Case 2 verifies whether vS_x violates input/output port and/or convex constraints. If yes, then the merit value of each hardware implementation option is multiplied by constant β_2 and/or β_3 ($0 < \beta_2 < 1$ and $0 < \beta_3 < 1$), reducing the opportunity for selecting the hardware implementation option, as in case 1. The calculation of the merit function is then terminated. The reason for only dividing the merit value of each hardware implementation option in operation x by a constant, rather than excluding the possibility of operation x becoming an operation in an ISE candidate, is to give operation x an opportunity to be grouped as an ISE candidate in the following iterations. If no, then enter case 3.

In case 3, the merit value of implementation option j ($merit_{x,j}$, $j > 0$) in operation x is obtained according to (1) the speedup that can be achieved by $vS_{x,j}$, and (2) the extra area utilized by $vS_{x,j}$. The execution cycle reduction and silicon area of the virtual subgraph $vS_{x,j}$ is represented by $cycle\_saving_{x,j}$ and $area_{x,j}$, respectively. The basic concept of case 3 is: (1) if $vS_{x,j}$ can improve the performance, then implementation option j should have a larger merit value than the software implementation option; (2) a hardware implementation option in operation x with a higher execution time reduction should have a larger merit value, and (3) if several hardware implementation options in the operation x have the highest execution time reduction, then the option that employs the smaller silicon area should have the higher merit value. In case 3, the algorithm first sets the merit value of implementation option j as the product of $(cycle\_saving_{MAX,x} + 1)$ and $merit_{x,0}$, where $cycle\_saving_{MAX,x}$ is the maximal execution cycle reduction that can be achieved for vS_x. The algorithm then checks whether the execution time reduction of implementation option j is equal to the $cycle\_saving_{MAX,x}$. If yes, then the algorithm scales its merit value based on the silicon area of implementation option j. $Area_{MAX,x}$ represents the largest silicon area used by the implementation option(s) in operation x. If no, then the merit of implementation option j is divided by the difference between its execution time reduction ($cycle\_saving_{x,j}$) and ($cycle\_saving_{MAX,x} + 1$).

Case 1. (The size of vS_x is equal to 1)
If ($size(vS_x) = 1$)
    For each hardware implementation option (j=1 to k) in operation x
$$merit_{x,j} = merit_{x,j} \times \beta_1;$$
Case 2. (Violate constraints and the size of $vS_{x,j}$ is larger than 1)
If (vS_x violates in/out constraint)
    For each hardware implementation option (j=1 to k) in operation x
$$merit_{x,j} = merit_{x,j} \times \beta_2;$$
If (vS_x violates convex constraint)
    For each hardware implementation option (j=1 to k) in operation x
$$merit_{x,j} = merit_{x,j} \times \beta_3;$$
Case 3. (Conform with constraints and the size of $vS_{x,j}$ is larger than 1)
If (vS_x observes in/out and convex constraint)
    For each hardware implementation option (j=1 to k) in operation x
$$merit_{x,j} = (1 + cycle\_saving_{MAX,x}) \times merit_{x,0}$$
    If ($cycle\_saving_{x,j} = cycle\_saving_{MAX,x}$)
$$merit_{x,j} = merit_{x,j} \times \frac{Area_{MAX,x}}{Area_{x,j}};$$
    Else
$$merit_{x,j} = \frac{merit_{x,j}}{(1 + cycle\_saving_{MAX,x}) - cycle\_saving_{x,j}};$$

Fig. 4. Algorithm of merit function

4   ISE Selection

Because of the constraints of silicon area and original ISA format, the subset of ISE candidates that can achieve highest performance under the constraints should be chosen. This problem is formulated as the multi-constrained 0/1 Knapsack problem as follows:

ISE selection: Considering n ISE candidates, where the area of ISE i is a_i, and its performance improvement is w_i, then the area of selected ISEs should not exceed the total area A. The maximum number of ISEs is given by E, and then gets the maximum of

$$f(x_1,...,x_n) = \sum_{i=1}^{n} w_i x_i \text{ and } x_i \in \{0,1\}, \quad 1 \le i \le n \tag{3}$$

where $x_i = 1$ if ISE i is selected, and subject to

$$\sum_{i=1}^{n} x_i \le E, \quad \sum_{i=1}^{n} a_i x_i \le A \text{ and } x_i \in \{0,1\}, \quad 1 \le i \le n \tag{4}$$

Notably, the constraints on ISE selection in this work are the silicon area and origi nal ISA format. However, if new constraints are added to the ISE selection, then only Eq. (4) needs to be modified as follows:

$$C_j : \sum_{i=1}^{n} ct_{i,j} x_i \le b_j \text{ and } x_i \in \{0,1\}, \quad 1 \le i \le n \tag{5}$$

where C_j is the constraint that is applied; $ct_{i,j}$ represents resource consumption values of ISE I, and b_j denotes the resource limit.

5   Experimental Results

5.1   Experimental Setup

The Portable Instruction Set Architecture (PISA) [12], which is a MIPS-like ISA, and MiBench [13] was employed to evaluate the proposed ISE exploration algorithm and genetic algorithm [3]. Each benchmark was compiled by gcc 2.7.2.3 for PISA with -O0 and -O3 optimizations. Owing to the limitation in the corresponding glibc and compiler, 6 benchmarks, namely mad, typeset, ghostscript, rsynth, sphinx and pgp, could not be compiled successfully. For both algorithms, 6 cases were evaluated, includes.2/1, 4/2 and 6/3 register file read/write ports as well as using -O0 and -O3 optimization.

In this simulation, we assume that: (1) the CPU core is synthesized in 0.13 μm CMOS technology and executes in 100MHz; (2) the CPU core area is 1.5 mm²; (3) the read/write ports of register file are 2/1, 4/2 and 6/3, respectively; and (4) the execution cycle of all instructions in PISA is one cycle, i.e. 10 (ns).The hardware implementation option settings (delay and area) of instructions in PISA were either obtained from Lindstrom [14], or modeled by Verilog and synthesized with Synopsys Design Compiler. Since increasing the number of read/write ports in the register file increases the required silicon area, different read/write ports of register file were also synthesized. Therefore, the silicon areas of the CPU cores with 4/2 and 6/3 (register file read/write ports) were 1574138.80μm² and 1631359.54μm², respectively.

Because of the heuristic nature of the ISE exploration algorithm, the exploration was repeated 5 times within each basic block, and the result among the 5 iterations having minimal execution cycle count and using the smallest silicon area was chosen.

The parameters adopted in this work and their meanings are listed below.

♦ α : The weight of merit and pheromone in $p_{x,j}$. A large α obtains a solution slowly. A small α obtains a poor solution, but quickly.

♦ β_1 : The tendency to choose hardware implementation option in a operation.

♦ β_2 : The decay speed when the input/output constraint is violated.

♦ β_3 : The decay speed when the convex constraint is violated.

In our experiments, the initial merit value of the software and hardware implementation option was 100 and 200, respectively; P_END was 99%. The probability value adopted $\alpha = 0.25$, and the merit function had $\beta_1 = 0.9$, $\beta_2 = 0.9$ and $\beta_3 = 0.5$.

Additionally, since Pozzi [3] does not consider pipestage timing constraint, it does not explore the implementation option for each operation in ASFU either during or after the exploration of ISE candidates. Therefore, in this paper, Pozzi's approach [3] is assumed to always deploy the fastest implementation option for each operation in ASFU.

5.2 Experimental Results

Figure 5 and 6 depict the average execution time reduction and average extra silicon area cost of Mibench with different numbers of ISE, respectively. Each bar in Figs. 5 and 6, comprises several segments, which indicate the execution time reduction with 1, 2, 4, 8, 16 and 32 ISEs. The first word of each label on X axis in both Figs. 7 and 8 indicates which ISE exploration algorithm is adopted. "Proposed" and "genetic" denote the proposed ISE exploration algorithm and that of Pozzi [3], respectively. The first and second symbols in parentheses of each label on the X-axis are the number of register file read/write ports in use, and which optimization method (-O0 or -O3) is used. For instance, (4/2, O3) means that the register file has 4 read ports and 2 write ports, and that the -O3 optimization method is employed.

For both algorithms, -O3 exhibits better execution time reduction than -O0 under same read/write port constraint, possibly because -O3 generally makes program execution faster with various compiler optimization techniques. Some of these techniques (like loop unrolling, function inlining, etc.) remove branch instructions, and increase the size of basic blocks. The bigger basic block usually has a larger search space, such that it has a greater opportunity to obtain the ISEs, which have more execution time reduction. Notably, most of execution time reduction is dominated by several ISEs within hot basic blocks, since most execution time is spent in a small portion (hot basic blocks) of a program. In most cases, 8 ISEs can perform over half of execution time reduction achieved by 32 ISEs, and only utilize less than quarter of silicon area used by 32 ISEs. For instance, while using 4/2 (register file read/write ports) register file, 8 ISEs can save average 14.95% execution time and cost $81467.5\mu m^2$ silicon area, which is 5.43% of the original core area. Conversely, if 32 ISEs are adopted, then the average execution time reduction can rise to 20.62%, but extra area cost also increases to $345135.45\mu m^2$, which is 23.01% of the original core area.

Except for several cases in 6/3 (register file read/write ports), the proposed ISE exploration algorithm achieved a better execution time reduction than Pozzi [3]. The proposed approach has lower improvement in some cases, because one set of parameters (α, β_1, β_2 and β_3) does not work well in all cases. This problem can be mitigated by dynamically adjusting these parameters according to different basic block sizes. This issue is currently being studied. Theoretically, ISE candidates always adopting the fastest hardware implementation option would have the best performance. However, as revealed in Fig. 5, the proposed ISE exploration algorithm has better execution time reduction in most cases, since even in the same BB, the operations grouped into an ISE candidate and the number of ISE candidate explored by both algorithms may be not identical.

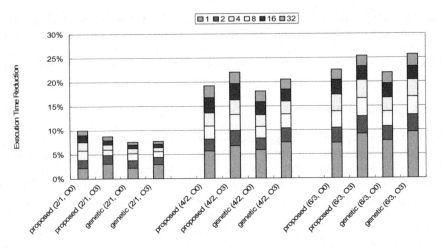

Fig. 5. Execution time reduction

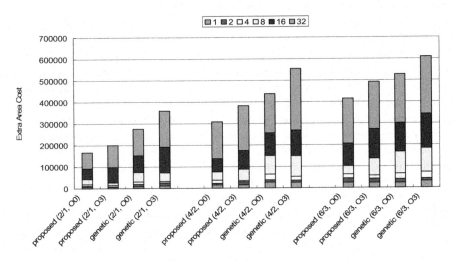

Fig. 6. Extra silicon area cost

Because the proposed ISE exploration algorithm explores not only ISE candidate but also their implementation options, less extra silicon area is used in all cases. Figure 7 displays the silicon area saving for all cases. Obviously, the proposed ISE algorithm can significantly reduce the extra silicon area cost. Figure 7 reveals that relaxing the constraint of register file read/write ports tends to decrease the silicon area saving. Relaxing the constraint of register file read/write ports can increase the number of operations grouped into ISE. However, the operations grouped into ISE due to relaxing the constraint of register file read/write ports do not usually locate on the critical path of ISE and generally have only one hardware implementation option. That is, the operations not located on the critical path of ISE usually have only one

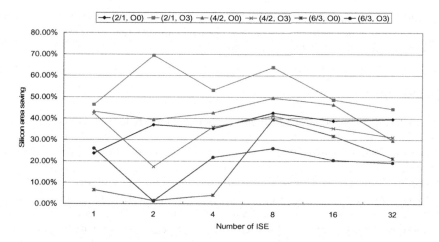

Fig. 7. Silicon area saving

hardware implementation option. If the operations not located on the critical path are given more hardware implementation options, then this problem can be alleviated significantly.

From another perspective, under the same silicon area constraints, adopting the miser implementation option increases the number of ISEs that can be utilized in processor core, significantly increasing the level of performance improvement. Figure 8 shows this perspective. In Fig. 8, each bar consists of several segments, which indicate the execution time reduction under different silicon area constraints, namely 5%, 10%, 15%, 20%, 25% and 30% of the original CPU core. In all cases, the proposed ISE exploration algorithm has better improvement in the execution time

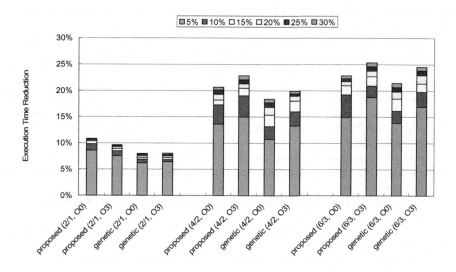

Fig. 8. Execution time reduction under different silicon area constraint

reduction than genetic algorithm [3]. Significantly, the improvement in execution time reduction is not in proportion to the available silicon area, since most execution time reduction is dominated by several ISEs.

6 Conclusion

The proposed ISE generation algorithm can significantly reduce the silicon area cost with almost no performance loss. Previous studies in ISE exploration deploy the fastest implementation option for each operation in ASFU to achieve the highest speed-up ratio. Nevertheless, the fastest implementation option is not always the best choice in terms of performance and silicon area cost. This work considers the pipestage timing constraint, such that the proposed ISE exploration algorithm explores not only ISE candidates, but also their implementation option. To comply with various micro-architectural constraints, ISE selection is formulated as the multi-constrained 0/1 Knapsack problem. The advantages of the proposed approach are as follows: (1) both the ISE exploration and selection algorithms conform to various important physical constraints; (2) ISE exploration algorithms can significantly lower the extra silicon area cost with almost no performance loss; (3) ISE selection is formulated as a multiconstrained 0-1 knapsack problem, such that it complies with multiple constraints, and (4) both ISE exploration and selection are polynomial time solvable. Experiment results demonstrate that the proposed design can further decrease the extra silicon area by up to 69.43%, 1.26% and 33.8% (max., min. and avg., respectively), and also has a maximum performance improvement of 1.6%.

References

1. Gang Wang, Wenrui Gong and Ryan Kastner, "Application Partitioning on Programmable Platforms Using the Ant Colony Optimization", *Journal of Embedded Computing*, 2006.
2. Mouloud Koudil, Karima Benatchba, Said Gharout and Nacer Hamani, "Solving Partitioning Problem in Codesign with Ant Colonies," *IWINAC*, 2005.
3. Laura Pozzi, Kubilay Atasu, and Paolo Ienne, "Exact and Approximate Algorithms for the Extension of Embedded Processor Instruction Sets," *IEEE Transactions on Computer Aided Design*, July, 2006.
4. Partha Biswas, Sudarshan Banerjee, Nikil Dutt, Laura Pozzi, and Paolo Ienne, "Fast automated generation of high-quality instruction set extensions for processor customization," *In Proceedings of the 3rd Workshop on Application Specific Processors*, September 2004.
5. Nathan T. Clark, Hongtao Zhong and Scott A. Mahlke, "Automated Custom Instruction Generation for Domain-Specific Processor Acceleration," *IEEE Transactions on Computers*, October, 2005.
6. Pan Yu and Tulika Mitra, "Characterizing embedded applications for instruction-set extensible processors," *DAC*, 2004.
7. Pan Yu and Tulika Mitra "Satisfying real-time constraints with custom instructions," *CODES+ISSS*, 2005.
8. Edson Borin, Felipe Klein, Nahri Moreano, Rodolfo Azevedo, and Guido Araujo. "Fast Instruction Set Customization", *ESTIMedia*, September 2004.

9. Armita Peymandoust, Laura Pozzi, Paolo Ienne, and Giovanni De Micheli, "Automatic Instruction-Set Extension and Utilization for Embedded Processors," *In Proceedings of the 14th International Conference on Application-specific Systems, Architectures and Processors*, June 2003.

10. Jason Cong, Yiping Fan, Guoling Han and Zhiru Zhang, "Application-Specific Instruction Generation for Configurable Processor Architectures," *Twelfth International Symposium on Field Programmable Gate Arrays*, 2004.

11. Samik Das, P. P. Chakrabarti, Pallab Dasgupta, "Instruction-Set-Extension Exploration Using Decomposable Heuristic Search," *VLSI Design*, 2006.

12. T. Austin, E. Larson, and D. Ernst, "SimpleScalar: An infrastructure for computer system modeling," *IEEE Computer*, 2002.

13. M. R. Guthaus, J. S. Ringenberg, D. Ernst, T. M. Austin, T. Mudge and R. B. Brown, "Mibench: A free, commercially representative embedded benchmark suite," *IEEE Annual Workshop on Workload Characterization*, 2001.

14. A Lindstrom and M. Nordseth. Arithmetic Database. Available:
http:// www.ce.chalmers.se/arithdb/

Author Index

Lecture Notes in Computer Science

For information about Vols. 1–4265

please contact your bookseller or Springer